The Beauty
and Splendor of
North America

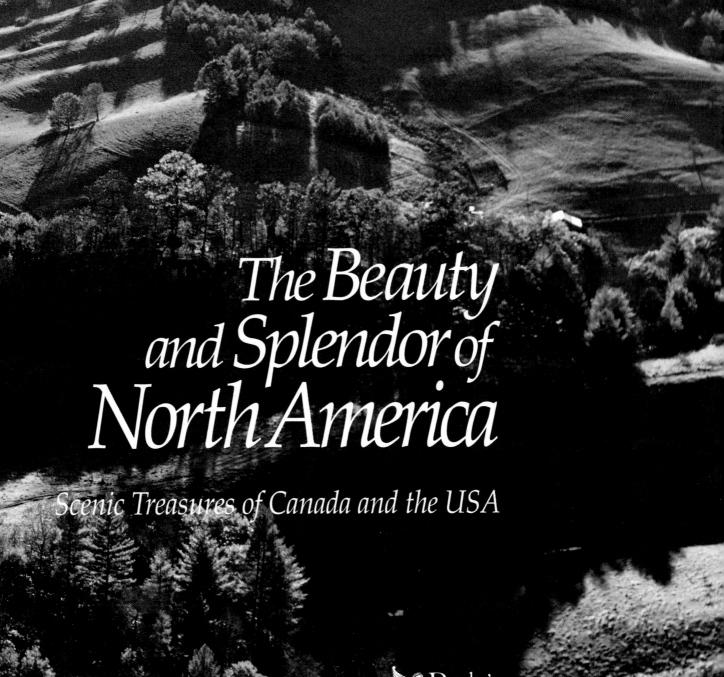

The Beauty
and Splendor of
North America

Scenic Treasures of Canada and the USA

Reader's Digest

The Reader's Digest Association Canada Ltd. Montreal

The Beauty and Splendor of North America

CANADIAN STAFF

Project Editor
Alice Philomena Rutherford

Project Art Director
John McGuffie

Project Designer
Andrée Payette

Picture Editor
Rachel Irwin

Research Editor
Wadad Bashour

Designer (Maps)
Cécile Germain

Copy Editor
Joseph Marchetti

Editorial Assistant
Elizabeth Eastman

Production Manager
Holger Lorenzen

Production Coordinator
Susan Wong

The credits on pages 479-480 are hereby made a part of this copyright page

Printed in Canada
95 96 97 98 99 / 5 4 3 2 1

CANADIAN CONTRIBUTORS

Writers
Shawn Apel
Aleli Balagtas
Vincenza Micheletti
Mike McGarry
Ken Ramstead
Robert B. Ronald

Map Artist
Ronald Du Repos

Animal Artist
Olena Kassian

Indexer
Jane Broderick

Canadian Cataloguing in Publication Data

Main entry under title:
The Beauty and Splendor of North America: Scenic Treasures of Canada and the USA

1st Canadian ed.
Includes index.
ISBN 0–88850-244-3

1. United States—Pictorial works. 2. Canada—Pictorial works. 3. United States—Description and travel. 4. Canada—Description and travel. I. Reader's Digest Association (Canada).

E169.04B43 1995 973'.022'2
C94–900634-3

The editors thank the following for their assistance
Adobe Systems Incorporated
Hammond Incorporated
The Flag Research Center.
   Provincial and territorial flags and flowers, the national flag, the governor general's flag, and the national coat of arms are reproduced from *Symbols of Nationhood* with permission of the Minister of Supply and Services Canada, 1995

U.S. STAFF

Project Editor
Inge N. Dobelis

Project Art Editor
Joel Musler

Editors
Fred DuBose
David Palmer

Associate Editor
David Diefendorf

Art Associate
Susan Desser

Project Research Editor
Eileen Einfrank

Research Editors
Kathryn Bonomi
Sandra Streepy Burgheim

Associate Librarian
Nettie Seaberry

Editorial Assistant
Vita Gardner

With special assistance from Senior Staff Editor
Richard L. Scheffel

U.S. CONTRIBUTORS

General Consultant
Robert H. Mohlenbrock, Ph.D

Art Production Associate
Bruce R. McKillip

Research Associate
Mary Hart

Researchers
Tim Guzley
Mary Lyn Maiscott
Eleanor Schwartz

Writers
Craig Canine
Jared Carter
Ben Cate
Rita Christopher
Cort Conley
Richard Comerford
Jack Connor
David A. DeVoss
Sharon Fitzgerald
Jean Freeman

Jill Goetz
Alice Gordon
Lea Gordon
Martha Hailey
Kenn Kaufman
B. Cory Kilvert, Jr.
Scott M. Kraft
Mary Lyn Maiscott
Howard Millard
Frazier Moore
Richard Nelson
Karla Powell
Ronn Ronck
Rollene Saal
Kathy Sagan
Mitchell J. Shields
Susan Spano Wells
Henry Wiencek
Suzanne Winckler
Mel White

Map Artist
Lazlo Kubinyi

Flower Artist
Susan Desser

Bird Artists
John Dawson
Walter Ferguson
Albert Earl Gilbert
Pedro Julio Gonzalez
Cynthia J. House
Lawrence B. McQueen
Hans Peeters
Douglas Pratt
Chuck Ripper
John Cameron Yrizarry

Picture Researchers
Romy Charlesworth
Penne Franklin
Paula Gillen

Copy Editor
Marianne Emmet

Opening photographs
P. 1: Wheat fields, Washington
Pp. 2–3: New River, Virginia
Pp. 4–5: Ontario State Park, Oregon
Pp. 6–7: Pacific Rim National Park, British Columbia
Pp. 8–9: Grande Ronde Canyon, Washington

Contents

Preface

Travelers from around the world are enthralled by North America's magnificent scenery. But even the most avid traveler cannot hope to see every province and state firsthand.

You, however, can take a visual tour of that vast continent simply by opening the covers of THE BEAUTY AND SPLENDOR OF NORTH AMERICA — SCENIC TREASURES OF CANADA AND THE USA. It contains hundreds of the awe-inspiring sights that make this continent a traveler's delight. And you will see them through the eyes of some of today's finest and most imaginative photographers.

The photographs are as varied as the landscapes of the 19 million square kilometres (10 million of them Canadian) covered. Consider the alpine splendors of the Rocky Mountains alone. In their stretch from Alaska to Mexico, the Rockies encompass icy peaks and glacial lakes (in Alberta and Montana), glistening streams (in the San Juan Mountains of Colorado), and flower-filled meadows (in New Mexico's Sangre de Cristo range). The rugged Canadian Shield that covers much of Canada is edged by the flat wheat fields and prairie pastures of Western Canada and the farms and small towns of Ontario and Quebec. Hawaii's blue waters and green-ridged volcanic slopes are in sharp contrast with the languid lagoons and coconut palms of Florida's southern tip. Individual states and provinces possess not only their own kind of beauty, but often surprisingly diverse scenery. Tennesseans claim theirs could better be called three states: East Tennessee, where the Great Smoky Mountains predominate; pastoral Middle Tennessee, with its elegant horse farms; and, on the bluffs of the mighty Mississippi, West Tennessee and its fertile farmland. Ontario has even more diversity — stretches of flat farmland, belts of rolling hills, the Niagara Escarpment, great forested chunks of Canadian Shield, and a vast moss-covered swamp.

In addition to the broad panoramas of mountain and plain, THE BEAUTY AND SPLENDOR OF NORTH AMERICA also seeks out the simple beauty of shaded lanes and old millponds, mysterious bayous and sunlit gardens, natural bridges and secluded glades. Revealing portraits of each province, territory, and state — 62 essays in all — complement the breathtaking photographs. These essays are arranged alphabetically opening with Canada (Alberta to Yukon) and followed by the United States (Alabama to Wyoming). Each essay conveys the flavors and textures of the particular province or state, touching on its history, people, culture, and terrain. Special features highlight the outstanding and the unusual — British Columbia's remarkable totems, for example, and Frank Lloyd Wright's architectural embodiment of the Illinois prairie, the bashful lizards and play-dead snakes of Manitoba's Spirit Sands and Florida's unlikely "mermaids."

Rounding out these portraits is an illustrated fact-filled two-page almanac that captures the essence of each province and state at a glance. Here are vital statistics for each one, its flag, official bird, and motto, historical highlights, notable people who were born there or are otherwise associated with it, oddities and specialties, places to visit and things to do. The centerpiece of this information-in-a-nutshell is a specially commissioned pictorial map showing major cities and rivers, with colorful drawings of places, products, natural wonders, and other regional attractions.

Every corner of North America is filled with beautiful places both familiar and little known, and all of us would like to get to know them better. This gallery of portraits shows you these beautiful places — and evokes the singular qualities of each of the 10 provinces, two territories, and 50 states in a way that readers will find both fascinating and informative.

— THE EDITORS

Canada's landscape is often described in terms of six regions, the largest being the *Canadian* (sometimes called Precambrian) *Shield*, which covers almost one half of the total land area. The others are the Western Cordillera, the Interior Plains, the Arctic and Appalachian regions, and the Great Lakes–St. Lawrence Lowlands.

Dense forests, granite outcrops, thin soil, and muskeg swamps characterize the rugged, mineral-rich *Canadian Shield* which covers most of Ontario and Quebec, northern Manitoba and Saskatchewan, and some two-thirds of the Northwest Territories. The *Shield's* countless lakes and rivers contain one quarter of the world's fresh water. White pine, spruce, and fir spread an evergreen arch over the southern portion, and mosses and short grasses sprout on the treeless northern sections. Marshy mud flats predominate around Hudson Bay.

The *Western Cordillera* consists of four more or less parallel mountain ranges — the Coast, Rocky, Columbia, and St. Elias mountains — straddling an 800-kilometre-wide band to the west of the country. Mostly found in British Columbia and Yukon, the *Western Cordillera's* great rocky spine also extends into Alberta and the Northwest Territories.

The *Cordillera* encompasses a great variety of climates, soils, and vegetation, and has more species of animals and plants than any other part of the country. Its snowcapped, conifer-skirted slopes overlook such fertile districts as the Fraser River delta and the orchard- and vineyard-rich Kootenay and Okanagan valleys.

In terms of mineral wealth — particularly copper, lead, zinc, and silver, which are found in abundance in its igneous rocks

to the west — the *Western Cordillera* is a close second to the *Canadian Shield*. In addition, the sedimentary rocks on the *Cordillera's* eastern flanks have extensive deposits of coal and petroleum.

Tundra — the undulating, lichen-covered, spongy landscape north of the treeline — typifies the *Arctic Region*. Hunks of rock, hummocks of sedge, and mats of dwarf trees dot the plain, an area often called "the barrens." During a brief growing period, sometimes no more than a six weeks a year, the thawed tundra topsoil springs to colorful life, as numerous dwarf flowering plants burst into bloom. Below the shallow layer of muck that nurtures them, however, the subsoil remains permanently frozen, in places to a 500-metre depth. Much of the *Arctic Region* consists of a triangle of islands north of the mainland.

A patchwork of ranchlands and golden grainfields dominates the *Interior Plains*, which encompass large chunks of Alberta, Saskatchewan, and Manitoba. Early explorers named the region for the French word *prairie* (meadow). Short grasses predominate in the southernmost prairies, where drought is often a problem, but taller grasses flourish to the north. Higher rainfall over the northerly section gathers in sloughs, or small ponds, that are breeding grounds for one half of North America's ducks and geese. A transitional "park belt" of grasslands and trees separates the *Interior Plains* from the *Canadian Shield*.

Fertile valleys and smooth-topped uplands cloaked in mixed forests — mostly spruce and sugar maple — characterize the *Appalachian Region*, which encompasses southern Quebec and the provinces of New Brunswick, Nova Scotia,

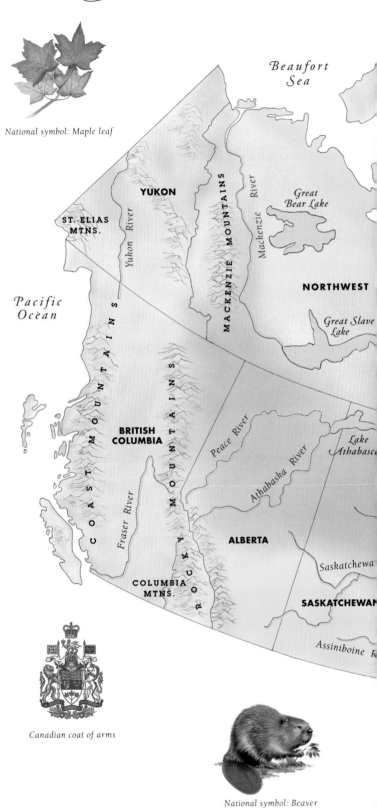

National symbol: Maple leaf

Canadian coat of arms

National symbol: Beaver

Prince Edward Island, and Newfoundland. The Canadian Appalachians are at their highest in the Chic-Chocs of Gaspé. Over the past 300 million years, the original peaks have been ground flat or gently rounded by glaciers, wind, and water.

Diversified farming and industry both thrive in the *Great Lakes–St. Lawrence Lowlands*, a trough of land enriched by glacial deposits from the *Shield* to its north and the Appalachians to its south. Even though the *Great Lakes–St. Lawrence Lowlands* region is the most populous and most industrialized part of the country, it is also the most productive agriculturally.

Canadian flag

Governor general's flag

Arctic Ocean

TERRITORIES

Thelon River

Nettilling Lake

Ungava Bay

Atlantic Ocean

Hudson Bay

Churchill River

Nelson River

MANITOBA

Lake Winnipeg

Severn River

La Grande Rivière

Smallwood Reservoir

James Bay

Lake Winnipegosis

Manicouagan Reservoir

NEWFOUNDLAND

Lake Manitoba

Albany River

QUEBEC

Lake of the Woods

ONTARIO

PRINCE EDWARD ISLAND

Lake Nipigon

NEW BRUNSWICK

Lake Superior

St. Lawrence River

NOVA SCOTIA

Ottawa River

Lake Huron

Lake Ontario

Lake Erie

Alberta

Beside majestic peaks, golden grain-fields and "black gold" gushers

A godsend wind called the chinook, big prairie skies, oceans of wheat, oil rigs, one of the world's finest fossil sites, badlands laced with labyrinthine canyons, and the rugged Rockies towering along its western boundary are part and parcel of the Alberta landscape.

Mineral-rich hot springs, white strips of glaciers, and luminous lakes dot its Rocky Mountain ranges, which screen the province from the moderating influence of the Pacific Ocean. Alberta summers are hot and its winters cold, except when the chinook — warm dry Pacific air — arrives. Then temperatures can rise by 25°C in one hour. Chinooks are most frequent in southern Alberta where places such as Calgary and Fort Macleod may get 30 to 40 chinook days a winter.

Oil has brought prosperity and a down-to-earth sophistication to Alberta's cities. Edmonton, a modern city of skyscrapers and shopping centers, flourished when oil was discovered near Leduc in 1947, but relives its frontier past each year during Klondike Days. With some 74 square kilometres of green space, Edmontonians have more parkland per capita than city dwellers anywhere else in North America.

Cowboy hats and boots are not unknown at performances by the city's philharmonic orchestra in Calgary, a city fueled by oil and ranching. Chuck wagon races — an Alberta invention — bronco busting, buffalo riding, and calf wrestling have made the annual Calgary Stampede world famous.

Crowfoot Mountain overlooks Crowfoot Glacier and fireweed-filled meadows along the Icefields Parkway.

AN ICE AGE REMNANT

The Columbia Icefield, part of the greater shroud of ice that once clothed most of Canada, covers 325 square kilometres of Alberta and British Columbia, in places to a depth of 900 metres. It straddles the Great Divide, the high point in the Rockies where meltwaters flow in different directions, and ultimately to three different oceans: the Pacific, the Atlantic, and the Arctic.

The icefield is home to more than 30 glaciers, literally rivers of ice. Glaciers are created when winter's snowfalls fail to melt the following spring and summer. If the pattern is repeated year after year, the snow is compressed and turned into ice. Eventually, the weight of the ice forces the glacier to move.

Depending on the severity of cold and snowfall in the winter, and the intensity of heat in summer, a glacier can either continue to grow and crawl forward, or melt and recede. Since about 1840, the glaciers of the Columbia Icefield have been receding. The Athabasca, for example, one of the largest glaciers, has been receding about 14 metres each year.

That particular glacier is visible, and easily accessible, from the Icefields Parkway, a picturesque drive that runs through Jasper National Park. Visitors can tour the glacier itself in what could be best described as snowmobile buses. These vehicles provide a close-up look at mill holes (deep, circular depressions) and crevasses (long, vertical fissures) — reminders of an age when ice covered the land.

FIRST SETTLERS

During the last great ice age, the area east of the Rocky Mountains was the only place in Canada not completely covered in ice. The open plain, stretching southeast from the Bering Strait, provided migrant peoples with an open door to the heart of the continent.

Before Europeans arrived, southern Alberta was occupied by Blackfoot Indians and the great western plains teemed with herds of buffalo, a staple of their diet. Their hunting forays can be relived at Head-Smashed-In Buffalo Jump Interpretive Center, a United Nations World Heritage Site near Fort Macleod. There, descendants of the ancient hunters show how the herds were corralled down narrowing paths, then driven over cliffs to their deaths.

Another Blackfoot stronghold is now the majestic Waterton-Glacier International Peace Park, a combination of Glacier (Montana) and Waterton Lakes national parks. This bridge between countries also links — often within a short hike — prairie and mountain habitats. In places, the road separates grasslands alive with antelope from spruce- and pine-cloaked slopes, where black bears and grizzlies, moose and mule deer forage for buffalo berries. Relics of glaciation remain in sparkling blue lakes and crashing waterfalls hugging the high elevations. At these levels, even the mountain goat and bighorn sheep tread carefully.

Spectacular wildlife and vestiges of ancient hunters continue into Kananaskis Country, a 5,200-square-kilometre blend of prairie and mountain set aside by the province for outdoor recreation and nature conservation. Although primarily a winter playground, the region offers a superb range of year-round activities and hotels, lodges, and restaurants, a legacy of Calgary's 1988 Winter Olympics. Kananaskis' inheritance includes thousands of kilometres of groomed and backcountry trails from the ski events it hosted.

MOUNTAIN GRANDEUR

Some of Canada's most breathtaking mountain scenery is found to the west and north in Banff and Jasper national parks. Each year, millions from around the world visit Banff, where snowcapped peaks flanked by Douglas firs and flower-strewn meadows extend 240 kilometres along the Continental Divide.

Canada's oldest national park, Banff was set aside in 1885 to ensure perpetual public access to its sulphur hot springs. They were discovered in 1883 when Canadian Pacific Railway workers saw wisps of steam rising

from the ground and discovered a cavern of steaming water. Banff's outdoor spring pools have a year-round temperature of 47°C.

Today the park also has a townsite, youth hostels, campgrounds, and the world famous Banff Springs Hotel and Chateau Lake Louise. Hiking trails wind through steep valleys and along swift moving rivers spawned by one of several glaciers in the park. Always present are the sights and sounds of wildlife — grazing elk, deer, and bighorn sheep, chattering squirrels and, occasionally, a coyote's haunting howl. At high elevations the ferocious wolverine competes for space with grizzly bears. Travelers should be especially wary after dark, as animals regularly wander onto the roadways.

One of the park's roads, the picturesque Bow Valley Parkway, follows the Bow River north to Johnston Canyon, where two spectacular waterfalls tumble down the deep gorge gouged by rushing water. Not far away are the seven cold water springs known as the Ink Pots because of the suspended sediment that gives a blue-green sheen to the waters.

The parkway continues north to what may be one of the world's most photographed vistas, Lake Louise with Chateau Lake Louise and Victoria Glacier as a backdrop. Fed by the mineral-laden meltwaters of Victoria Glacier, silt gives Lake Louise its incredible turquoise color. Small wonder that Tom Wilson, the CPR employee who was led there

Cattail-rimmed wetlands lie at the edge of straggly mats of rough northern fescue, oat grass, and other prairie vegetation in the eastern sections of Waterton Lakes National Park. The park conserves plants and wildflowers peculiar to the transitional habitat between mountain and prairie.

The setting sun adds a momentary softness to the great expanse of badlands that form a wide band along vast stretches of the Red Deer River.

by Stoney Indians in 1882, named it Emerald Lake. (Its present-day name was adopted to honor Queen Victoria's daughter, Princess Louise Alberta, for whom the province also was named.)

Hiking trails abound around Lake Louise, where higher elevations offer ever more striking views. Long-tailed weasels scurry in the bush, and bushy-tailed marten dwell high in the Engelmann spruce. Black-billed magpies commonly soar overhead and, on occasion, a bald eagle may be seen in flight.

The Icefields Parkway runs 230 kilometres northwest from Lake Louise to Jasper National Park. Enroute, it plunges through the wide valleys of the Bow, North Saskatchewan, Sunwapta, and Athabasca rivers. It passes within a few kilometres of

kilometres compared to Banff's 6,641 square kilometres), Jasper has a wealth of glacially fed lakes, chief of which is aquamarine Maligne Lake. The Miette Hot Springs and 3,747-metre Mount Columbia, Alberta's highest peak, are other Jasper attractions. The town of Jasper began life as the base camp for explorer David Thompson's 1811 trek through the Athabasca Pass into what is now British Columbia. But the park is named for Jasper Hawse, who built a North West Company supply post here in 1813.

THE RED DEER BADLANDS

"The most paintable valley in western Canada" is how artist A. Y. Jackson described Alberta's Badlands, the 300-kilometre, barren, windswept, rain-eroded gash in the prairies of southern Alberta. Dinosaurs stomped and swooped through marshy forests there some 65 million years ago and their skeletal remains have made the area a paleontologist's heaven.

Dinosaur Trail, a 50-kilometre circular drive from Drumheller, passes the steep gullies and hoodoos — mushroom-shaped columns of rock and clay — that characterize the area. Some of the best-preserved badlands are in Dinosaur Provincial Park (see page 18). Remnants of clams, crocodiles, snails, and turtles dot this prehistoric graveyard. Scattered in the dry earth are plants unique to the region: sagebrush, saskatoon, and chokecherry. The multilayered canyon walls are clearly seen from Horsethief Canyon Viewpoint. The name dates from frontier days when many horses entered the badlands bearing one brand, only to emerge sporting another.

The surrounding prairies are home to a diverse collection of flora and fauna — cottonwoods, poplars, silverberries, and willows; Richardson's ground squirrels, meadowlarks, and coyotes; and visiting Canada geese, pelicans, and marsh hawks. The region's fertile black soil is excellent for growing grains. Fields yield waist-high crops of barley, canola, flax, oats, rye, and wheat. Dairy, poultry, cattle, hog, and sheep farms are found around Calgary and Edmonton.

It would be hard to find more contrasting species than this Nutall's cottontail photographed recently in Dinosaur Provincial Park and the giant creatures that once inhabited that region.

the Athabasca Glacier, one of six major glaciers creeping from the icefield. Just off the parkway is the torrential cascade of Athabasca Falls, where a rainbow's glow is always present in daylight hours. Every twist and turn of the road reveals more elk, mule deer, and bighorn sheep.

Less developed and less crowded, but considerably larger than Banff (10,878 square

WHERE DINOSAURS ROAMED

Dinosaur Provincial Park, which stretches for some 27 kilometres along the Red Deer River, is one of the world's richest sources of dinosaur bones. Several complete skeletons are among hundreds of fossils of 35 species of dinosaur unearthed in the 90-square-kilometre park, a United Nations World Heritage Site. During the Mesozoic era — 66 to 245 million years ago — the prehistoric beasts populated lush, tropical swamplands beside the Mowry Sea, which once covered the great plains of North America. Some 63 million years ago, for reasons not yet known, they disappeared. Over the years, layers of sediments containing the bones of dinosaurs, fish, crocodiles, and turtles built up and hardened into rock. The fossilized remains were exposed as wind and water eroded the region's hoodoos and sandstone buttes.

Hadrosaurs — duck-billed, plant-eating creatures weighing up to 3,600 kilograms — were the most common dinosaurs in what is now the park. The shallow water at the sea's edge suited their partially webbed feet and provided vegetation for their diet. The water also served as a refuge from the giant meat-eating gorgosauruses that preyed on them. Long-necked plesiosaurs with 12-metre wingspans also roamed this area.

When the first fossils were discovered in 1884, scavengers began scouring the area. By the time the park was created in 1955, souvenir hunters had already removed many bones. Today's visitors can learn about ongoing research into dinosaurs from exhibits and audiovisual presentations at a field station of the Royal Tyrrell Museum of Palaeontology in the park.

Visitors can hike or join a packtrain through this picturesque Tonquin Valley on the eastern flank of the Ramparts, a craggy rock wall on the Continental Divide in Jasper National Park.

LAND OF THE MIGHTY PEACE

A patchwork of spruce and poplar forests and field after golden field of grain cover the Peace River Country, Canada's most northerly farmland. Canola helped bring prosperity to this river plain where warring Cree and Beaver Indians made their peace long ago. The oil-yielding crop was introduced to the region in the 1940's when there was dire need of lubricants for World War II ships.

This is a region of abundant wildlife, spectacular scenery, and mighty lakes and rivers. One breathtaking panorama marks the confluence of the Peace, Smoky, and Heart rivers. The view was a favorite of one of the Peace River's beloved characters — Vermont-born trader and prospector Henry Fuller "Twelve-Foot" Davis (1820-93), whose statue overlooks the town of Peace River (pop. 6,717). Davis used the $15,000 he took from his 12-foot claim in the Cariboo goldfields to establish trading posts at Dunvegan, Fort Vermilion (the province's oldest settled community), and Lesser Slave Lake, where his honesty, his generosity, and his pumpkin pies were legendary. The epitaph on the wooden

Oil and Alberta have been synonymous since 1947, when oil gushed from the Leduc No.1 well through this pump sunk where Devon now stands.

statue marking his final resting place reads: "He was every man's friend and never locked his cabin door."

Clover grows in profusion around the small town of Falher, the Honey Capital of Canada on the eastern edge of Peace River Country. Some 25,000 beehives in this area produce 2 million kilograms of honey a year. Neighboring McLennan, a small town on Kimiwan Lake, is known as the Bird Capital of Canada. Located on a major flyway, it is a yearly stopover point for some 27,000 ducks, geese, and other aquatic birds, plus 250,000 land birds.

A LAST HAVEN

Despite the prosperity of the Peace River area and the abundant natural resources, including oil and coal, of adjoining regions, northern Alberta for the most part remains sparsely populated. Its remoteness has been a blessing for endangered wildlife such as the bison and the whooping crane, which find refuge in vast Wood Buffalo National Park. Encompassing some 44,840 square kilometres of Alberta and the Northwest Territories, it is Canada's largest park. The bison it was set up to protect numbered 500 when the park was established in 1922. Today, the herd numbers well over 5,000.

The park contains the Peace-Athabasca delta, an immense expanse of poorly drained bogs and silty channels. The delta's lakes are frequented by beaver and muskrat. The park is also home to wolves, moose, and caribou.

A GARDEN OF EDEN

The Cypress Hills, some 2,500 square kilometres of flat-topped uplands, jut 600 metres above the arid plains of southeastern Alberta and Saskatchewan. They were named by French explorers, who often incorrectly referred to pine trees as *cyprès* (cypress).

Fossils of early mammals found in the hills date back 40 million years. There is evidence, too, that an aboriginal culture flourished in the area more than 7,000 years ago.

Today, forests of white spruce and lodgepole pine clothe the hillsides, which are a paradise of flora and fauna. Temperatures in

Brightly painted grain elevators, such as this one at Strome, southeast of Edmonton, are used for storing, cleaning, and weighing grain, and loading it onto railway cars and trucks. These distinctive prairie symbols follow railway tracks through the Canadian west.

A tree trunk provides the perfect nesting site for the northern flicker, a species of woodpecker often seen in fall flocking loosely around farmland and open forest.

THE BEAUTY AND SPLENDOR OF NORTH AMERICA

the hills are 6° to 8°C lower than the surrounding prairies.

In Cypress Hills Provincial Park, the forest gives way to rolling meadows dotted with wildflowers — daisies, harebells, and crocus. Red-tailed hawks, mourning doves, red-breasted nuthatches, and endangered trumpeter swans are just some of the 200 bird species in the park. Small red foxes and coyotes share park meadows with massive moose and wapiti.

In September 1877, the Cypress Hills were the site of Treaty No. 7, when leaders of the Blackfoot Confederacy, the last Plains Indians to surrender their lands, ceded 50,000 square miles of what is now southern Alberta. A cairn on the Bow River near Cluny identifies the signing site, Blackfoot Crossing.

Hiking trails in Cypress Hills Provincial Park follow the flow of Battle Creek to Lake Reesor, home to fine northern pike and river trout. The park is a miniature mirror of Alberta's diverse plant and animal life.

THE PEOPLE AND THE LAND

Population: 2,546,553

Area: 661,190 sq km

Population per sq km: 3.8

Capital: Edmonton (pop. 616,700)

Largest city: Calgary (pop. 710,700)

Major rivers: Peace, Bow, North Saskatchewan, South Saskatchewan, Red Deer, Athabasca

Elevation: 183 m (Salt River) to 3,747 m (Mt. Columbia)

Leading industries: Manufacturing (petrochemicals, plastics, electronics), agriculture (wheat, sugar beets, potatoes), livestock, tourism, natural resources (oil, coal)

Bird: Great horned owl

Flower: Wild rose

Tree: Lodgepole pine

Motto: *Foris et liber* (Strong and Free)

Origin of name: After Princess Louise Alberta, daughter of Queen Victoria and Prince Albert

Nicknames: None

HISTORICAL HIGHLIGHTS

1754-55 Explorer Anthony Henday travels up the Red Deer River just short of the Rocky Mountains.

1869 Canada buys the territory known as Rupert's Land from the Hudson's Bay Company.

1874 The North West Mounted Police establish Fort Macleod.

1905 Alberta becomes a province.

1932 National parks in Alberta and Montana are combined to form Waterton-Glacier International Peace Park.

1947 Oil is discovered at Leduc.

Great horned owl

Wild rose

Provincial flag

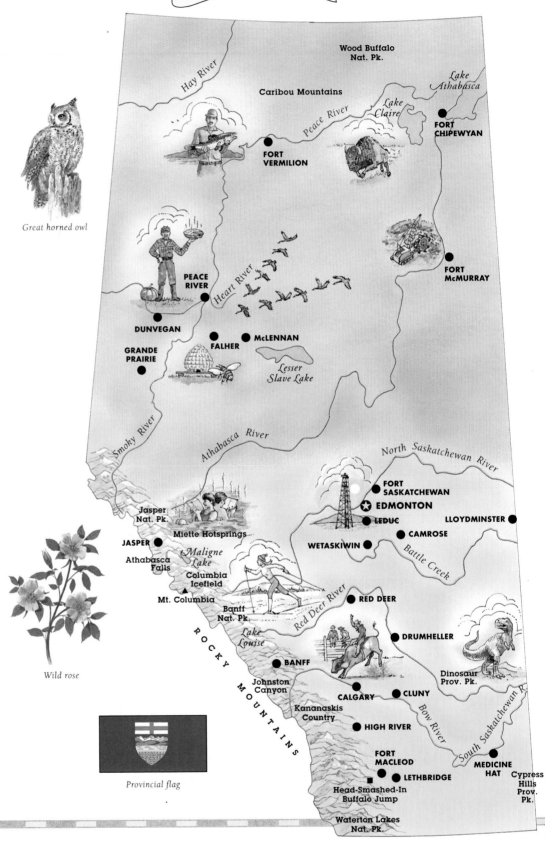

Travel Alberta
Economic Development &
Tourism
Box 2500
Edmonton, Alta. T5J 2Z4
1-403-427-4321
1-800-661-8888

FAMOUS SONS AND DAUGHTERS

William "Bible Bill" Aberhart (1878 – 1943). Premier from 1935 until his death, he never fulfilled his preelection promise to pay each Albertan $25 a month for basic needs.

Alfred Earle Birney (1904 –). An outstanding poet, Calgary-born Birney is also a successful novelist and playwright.

John George Brown (1839 – 1916). This army officer, whisky trader, and prospector is best remembered for his work as a forest ranger in the Kootenay Forest Reserve, present-day Waterton Lakes National Park.

Rod Cameron (1910 – 83). Beginning as a stuntman, this Calgary-born actor starred in scores of westerns.

Charles J. "Joe" Clark (1939 –).

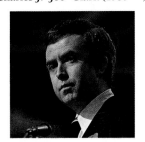

In 1979, Clark, then leader of the Progressive Conservative Party, became the 16th Prime Minister of Canada.

Crowfoot (1830 – 90). This Blackfoot chief, an intimidating warrior and a skilled diplomat, survived battle 19 times and welcomed the arrival of the North West Mounted Police to deal with whisky traders.

W. P. Kinsella (1935 –). His writings focus either on Indian life or on the world of baseball. The film *Field of Dreams* was based on his novel *Shoeless Joe.*

Albert Lacombe (1827 – 1916). The Cree and Blackfoot nations called this missionary "The Man of Good Heart."

k. d. Lang (1962 –). *Crying* is one of many hits that contributed to the popularity of this country singer whose first album was released in 1983.

Peter Lougheed (1928 –). Premier of Alberta from 1971 to 1985, he became a strong voice for Western Canada.

George Millward McDougall (1821 – 76). This Scottish missionary and his son John established numerous schools.

Joni Mitchell (1943 –).

This popular singer-songwriter was born in Fort Macleod.

Emily Murphy (1868 – 1933). A popular writer (under the pen name Janey Canuck), she was the British Commonwealth's first woman magistrate (1916). When her appointment was challenged, she launched a decade-long campaign to have women declared legal "persons."

Robert Terrill Rundle (1811 – 96). Mount Rundle is named for this Methodist missionary to the Cree of northern Alberta.

Arthur Lewis Sifton (1858 – 1921). This first chief justice of Alberta served as Premier of the province. As a federal member of Parliament, he was a delegate to the Paris Peace Conference of 1919.

David Thompson (1770 – 1857). A fur trader and explorer, Thompson mapped much of the western plains and Rockies.

Fay Wray (1907 –). She starred in many films, but is most closely identified with her 1933 role in *King Kong.*

ODDITIES AND SPECIALTIES

The lodgepole pine, Alberta's official tree, only releases seeds when the temperature is at, or higher than, 40°C. Due to the climate of its home, the foothills, its seeds can only be released during a forest fire.

Many lakes in the parkland belt of central Alberta are so alkaline that plants and marine life cannot survive. One exception is the plant family halophytes, which includes sea blite, salt grass, and samphire.

A large pile of bones is all that remains of the thousands of buffalo that were stampeded over the edge of a cliff in Dry Island Buffalo Jump Provincial Park.

The city of Medicine Hat derives its name from a Cree medicine man who lost his headdress while fleeing battle with Blackfoot warriors.

PLACES TO VISIT, THINGS TO DO

Canada Olympic Park (Calgary). Skiing and skating facilities as well as luge and bobsled runs where the brave can reach speeds of 100 km an hour are included in this park, site of the 1988 Winter Olympics.

Calgary Stampede. This 10-day, world-famous July event features chuck wagon races, bronco busting, wild cow milking, calf roping, thoroughbred horse racing, and livestock exhibits.

Fort Edmonton Historical Park. This park takes visitors back in time — along three streets re-created to 1885, 1905, and 1920.

Fort McMurray Oil Sands Interpretive Centre. Presentations focus on the history, technology, and future of the Athabasca oil sands.

Glenbow Museum (Calgary). You can try on cowboy chaps or a suit of armor, or research your family tree, at one of western Canada's largest museums.

Royal Tyrrell Museum of Palaeontology (Drumheller). This museum contains the most extensive display of dinosaur specimens in the world.

West Edmonton Mall. One of the world's largest shopping centers, the mall includes 800 stores, 11 being major department stores, 19 movie theaters, 110 eateries, and a full-size hockey rink.

British Columbia

A paradise of rain forest, mountains, and lush valleys

A perfect Eden." So declared James Douglas in 1843 when he first sighted the splendid coast of southern Vancouver Island. The man who would later become British Columbia's first governor was entranced by the marriage of contrasts — a shoreline where roaring Pacific surf embraced the silent, temperate rain forest. Clad now, as then, in green forests and blue-tinged, snow-tipped mountains, British Columbia stands before its Pacific consort with a bountiful dowry of giant cedars, firs, and pines, hot springs, fjords, steep-walled canyons, cold lakes, and more than 27,000 kilometres of marine coastline.

MOSTLY CROWN LAND

British Columbia encompasses 948,600 square kilometres, an area comparable to Germany, France, Austria, and Switzerland combined. Ninety-one percent of this is Crown land, a provincially owned unpeopled wilderness. More than 1.6 million people, half the population, live in or near Vancouver, a financial, industrial, commercial, and transportation center splendidly set between the sea and the Coast Mountains. Vancouver's crown jewel is 400-hectare Stanley Park with its picturesque lake, forest trails, and a 10-kilometre walk along a seawall promenade.

Fertile farmlands of the Fraser Valley and Fraser delta lie east and south of the city. The delta area, Vancouver, and its suburbs (Rich-

Towering pine-clad slopes enclose turquoise Lake O' Hara, one of many glacial lakes in Yoho National Park.

Evergreen clumps, hard-packed sand, and algae-capped boulders separate the rain forest from the ocean's fury at Long Beach in Pacific Rim National Park.

A LIFESAVING TRAIL ALONG THE PACIFIC'S GRAVEYARD

In the 19th century, it was not unusual for ships to be swept to destruction on the rocky, reef-strewn shores of Vancouver Island's west coast. More than 50 shipwrecks were recorded from 1854 to 1923 alone. Small wonder that the Juan de Fuca Strait became known as the graveyard of the Pacific, its wind-tossed seas and unpredictable tides feared by the most seasoned of sailors.

In 1906, 126 passengers aboard the SS *Valencia* died when the ship sank. Some had survived the wreck only to perish from exposure on shore as they desperately tried to penetrate the dense rain forest.

In response to the public outcry, the federal government cut a trail through the thick undergrowth. Cabins, positioned at 10-kilometre intervals, were designed as havens for shipwreck victims. In time the trail became known as the West Coast Trail. It runs 77 kilometres along the coast from Bamfield to Port Renfrew.

The trail's original purpose disappeared as 20th-century technology sharpened naval visibility. In 1970, the West Coast Trail became part of Pacific Rim National Park. Today only the most adventurous hikers attempt the rugged six-day trek. At some points, they must still scale steep, 30-metre gullies using vertical ladders.

Even so, the trail is extremely popular, and reservations must be made with Tourism British Columbia (see Information, p.35).

THE BEAUTY AND SPLENDOR OF NORTH AMERICA

mond, Burnaby, Delta, Surrey, North and West Vancouver, New Westminster, and Coquitlam) are collectively known as the Lower Mainland.

Turreted Parliament buildings and the sprawling, ivy-covered Empress Hotel dominate Victoria, the province's elegant capital sitting across the Strait of Georgia on Vancouver Island. Trim gardens, cricket pitches, double-decker buses, and antique, china, and linen shops proclaim its quintessential English character.

AN UNTOUCHED LAND

British Columbia remained largely unexplored into the late 18th century. When Capt. James Cook steered *Resolution* and *Discovery* into Nootka Sound in 1778, he made no attempts to colonize the land. Capt. George Vancouver arrived in 1792, spent three summers mapping the coast up to Alaska, and produced maps that navigators would use for the next 100 years.

Both men centered their activities around Vancouver Island — the largest island off North America's Pacific Coast. "Desolate" and "forbidding" was how they characterized its 32,134 square kilometres of emerald forest and the conifer-rimmed inlets slashing its western coast.

Pacific Rim National Park and its Broken Group Islands — a cluster of 100-odd isles scattered in Barkley Sound — are typical of the scenery they encountered. Today, the park's rocky northern shore tapers into Long Beach, an 11-kilometre stretch of sand inhabited by offshore colonies of sea lions, and by nesting Brandt's cormorants, auklets, and storm-petrels. In the waters near Tofino, harbor seals share their space each summer with some of the 14-metre-long Pacific gray whales found off the island's west coast. A pod of perhaps 50 whales rest here before migrating south in the fall to their calving grounds off Mexico.

Johnstone Strait on the island's northeastern coast is one of the best places in the world to spot orcas (commonly known as killer whales). About 16 pods, close to 200 whales, inhabit these waters year-round.

Orcas (killer whales) are often seen from ferries linking the mainland and Vancouver Island.

A ready supply of fish and crustaceans support colonies of cormorants, one of myriad bird species that frequent the estuaries and rocky headlands of Vancouver Island's western coast.

THE HAIDA TOTEMS —- A LEGACY IN CEDAR

At the southern tip of the Queen Charlottes' Moresby Island, a sheltered bay guards the Haida village of Ninstints from the open sweep of the Pacific Ocean. The shore there contains the remains of longhouses and mortuary and memorial poles dating back more than 2,000 years. The buildings and sculptures are among British Columbia's most important cultural monuments — remains of the best preserved ancient Haida village.

During the 19th century, Haidas would gather each winter at this village they called *Sqan Gwaii Lnaga'i,* "Red Cod Island Town." They built 17 longhouses, and five memorial, 12 frontal, and 26 mortuary poles. The wood they used, western redcedar, was slow to decay but fine grained enough to carve.

The people abandoned the village in the late 1800's, leaving a legacy of Haida art behind. In the late 1950's, some of the best poles were moved to the University of British Columbia's Museum of Anthropology in Vancouver and to the Royal B.C. Museum in Victoria and, later, to the Queen Charlotte Islands Museum in Skidegate. Conservation efforts have slowed the natural decay process of those at the original site.

The United Nations declared Ninstints a World Heritage Site in 1981. Today, it resembles a natural cathedral under the open sky. Many of the cedar logs lie on the ground. Others lean out, waiting for the cedar forest to reclaim them. Watchmen (site guardians) stand guard, interpreting the village for visitors and instructing young Haida people on their culture and history.

Three pods of "southern resident" orcas are found in Victoria, Georgia, and Juan de Fuca straits. Day-long whale-watching excursions depart regularly from Victoria and the near-by communities of Alert Bay, Port McNeill, and Sointula. The orcas rid themselves of barnacles and flaking skin by rubbing their sides against the pebbly areas of an ecological reserve at Robson Bight.

LEGACY OF THE FORESTS

Vancouver Island's moderate rainy climate nurtures giant stands of western redcedar, western hemlock, Sitka spruce, and Douglas fir. Some of North America's tallest, broadest trees are found in its coastal regions.

One of the world's largest lowland temperate rain forests is found at Clayoquot Sound, north of Tofino, its undergrowth thick with decayed nurse logs and a carpet of oxalis, foamflower, trillium, vanilla leaf, and sword fern. Some western redcedars here are 1,800 years old, taller than 20-storey buildings, and their bases measure up to five metres around. Beards of club moss, fern, and epiphytic lichen cling to their branches. A Carmanah Valley Sitka spruce, 10 metres around and 95 metres tall, is said to be the largest in the world.

These forests are sacred to the native tribes of the Pacific Northwest, particularly the Kwakiutl, Coast Salish, Nootka, and Haida. Their ancestors used the western redcedar's pliable, lightweight wood for their long-houses and canoes, wove its thin rootlets into baskets and conical hats, and recycled its bark into long waterproof capes.

From the giant cedar trunks they carved totem poles and ceremonial masks embel–lished with motifs of legendary trickster ravens, "grandfather" bears, killer whales, and mighty eagles. Today, British Columbia's largest concentration of totem poles is found in the heart of the Coast Mountains — around Hazelton and the villages of Kitwan-cool, Kitwanga, Kispiox, and 'Ksan.

There are totems, too, across the Hecate Strait, on the Queen Charlotte Islands, ancestral home of the Haida. Experts consider Ninstints, an abandoned Haida village at the

About once every four years, the Adams River, linking Adams and Shuswap lakes, runs red as millions of sockeye salmon return from the ocean to spawn and die in the cold waters where they were hatched and grew to fingerlings.

Silt from melting glaciers gives an incomparable blue-green hue to Emerald Lake (above), an everergreen-encircled jewel set amid the craggy, snowcapped peaks of Yoho National Park.

In summer, some 400 glaciers creep along the Selkirk and Purcell mountainsides in Glacier National Park (right). In winter, avalanches roar down at speeds of up to 320 km an hour.

islands' southern tip and a United Nations World Heritage Site, to be the best preserved remains of a Northwest Coast Indian village in the world.

MOUNTAIN GRANDEUR

Three-quarters of British Columbia's countryside is mountainous: the only major flatland is the Peace River valley in the northeast. North to south for 1,300 kilometres, the Coast Mountains form a 130-kilometre-wide swath to the west; the Rockies thrust skyward in an 80-kilometre-wide band to the east.

Stunning mountain scenery dominates what is known as "The Interior," the land east of the Coast Mountains. In the north, this includes the Hazelton, Skeena, Omineca, and Cassiar Mountains. The Stewart-Cassiar Highway pierces some of this remote country, cutting through boreal forest inhabited by Stone's sheep, wolves, grizzly bears, and the last remaining herd of Osborne caribou.

The southern section of this highway touches the Terrace-Kitimat territory of the elusive white Kermode bear (*Ursus americanus kermodei*), a rare, white-coated species of black bear, found exclusively in this coastal region.

Mount Robson (at 3,954 metres, the tallest peak in the Rockies) and Mount Assiniboine are among peaks towering more than 3,000 metres where the Rockies straddle the province's eastern border. Spring arrives late in this alpine zone. By July, the valley meadows are alive with yellow avalanche lilies, white mountain heather, bog laurel, and dwarf willow.

Some of Canada's highest waterfalls are found there, many in Yoho National Park, which is renowned worldwide for its Burgess Shale — fossil beds containing 500-million-year-old remains of marine invertebrates. Neighboring Kootenay National Park is remarkable for its twisting glaciers and steaming, 35°C Radium Hot Springs.

Another highlight of this area is the Rocky Mountain Trench, a great valley separating the Rockies from the Purcell, Selkirk, Monashee, Cariboo, Cassiar, and Omenica ranges of the Columbia Mountain system to the west. The longest valley in North America, it stretches the full length of the province, extending more than 1,500 kilometres from Montana to Yukon and containing headwaters of the Fraser, Columbia, Peace, Kootenay, Parsnip, Finlay, Kechika, and Liard rivers.

Alexander Mackenzie traversed some of these rivers when he made his way through the Rockies in 1793. Two other North West Company traders, David Thompson and Simon Fraser, followed in the early 1800's, founding fur posts that became British Columbia's first permanent settlements. Thompson explored the Kootenay and Columbia rivers, and in 1808 Fraser navigated the 1,368-kilometre-long river which now bears his name.

The scenic Columbia flows north past the easternmost flank of the Purcell Mountains, then south between the Monashee and Selkirk mountains, to form the elongated basins of Upper and Lower Arrow lakes.

Nearby are Mount Revelstoke and Glacier national parks, where the Selkirk mountain peaks challenge even the most experienced nordic skiers. Their frozen peaks support snow, perpetual glaciers, and sometimes, small tufts of alpine tundra. Avalanches, frequent here from November to May, have been clocked at speeds of more than 320 kilometres an hour. Ravens, hawk owls, and gray jays inhabit the subalpine region. Sightings of mountain caribou and black bears are also common.

The alpine meadows of Mount Revelstoke National Park are blanketed in deep snow from October to late June. Within weeks of the snow's disappearance, these clearings become a kaleidoscope of color, as wild anemones, arnicas, asters, glacier lilies, heathers, Indian paintbrushes, lupines, and mountain valerians burst into bloom.

Dramatic landscapes of snow-capped peaks and silent patches of forest suggest that Yoho National Park is aptly named: Yoho is Cree for "inspiring awe."

THE BEAUTY AND SPLENDOR OF NORTH AMERICA

EGG-SIZED GOLD NUGGETS

The Cariboo gold rush began in 1858 when news leaked out that gold could be panned from the streambeds and sandbars of the Fraser River and its tributaries. By 1862, the trail into the Cariboo was alive with packers, merchants, and prospectors, among them a 38-year-old Cornish seaman named Billy Barker. Billy was broke that August when he dug a crude shaft beside Williams Creek and saw gold nuggets as big as eggs. His find triggered a rush of prospectors eager to stake nearby claims and the town of tents, shacks, and stores that sprouted along the creek was known as Barkerville.

At its peak, it swarmed with 10,000 inhabitants and boasted it was the largest settlement "west of Chicago and north of San Francisco." Billy squandered his fortune in its saloons and dance halls. When he died in 1892, he was buried in a pauper's grave. The town named for him ended its glory days with an 1868 fire that leveled the community. By then the gold had petered out and the gold seekers had moved on to other prospects to the north and east.

Today, staff in period costume and 127 restored and reconstructed buildings bring the past alive in this 65-hectare 1860's historic town.

FRUIT BASKET TO NORTH AMERICA

Some 7 percent of British Columbians live in cities such as Kelowna, Penticton, and Vernon in the Okanagan Valley, a major tourist area and one of the great fruit baskets of North America. Cradled between the Cascade and the Monashee mountains, this year-round sunny oasis enjoys some 2,000 hours of sunlight and no more than 35 centimetres of precipitation a year. Summers are so hot and arid that desert species, such as native cacti and rattlesnakes, flourish there.

Nowhere else is British Columbia's bounty as apparent as there amid the Okanagan's luscious crops and mild weather. The valley produces Canada's sweetest apples, cherries, apricots, peaches, and plums.

Fruit trees bud in orchards near Kelowna, center of the fruit and vegetable farms and vineyards that characterize the sunny Okanagan Valley. One-third of Canada's apples are harvested in the area. Some of its local vineyards have produced notable, award-winning wines.

Manitoba

Evergreens, wheat fields, and a town where polar bears are king

L ake after quiet lake laces the giant swath of forested, ore-rich Canadian Shield that forms much of Manitoba. In the south, grainfields and open grasslands begin where the shield's evergreens and woodlands end and, in the north, polar bears plod pigeon-toed across arctic tundra beside a bay where summering pods of white belugas trill their high-pitched songs. Such is the diversity of Manitoba, at 650,000 square kilometres the smallest prairie province.

LAND OF 100,000 LAKES

Almost one sixth of Manitoba, some 102,000 square kilometres, is covered by 100,000 or more lakes — among them giants such as 24,340-square-kilometre Lake Winnipeg, 5,446-square-kilometre Lake Winnipegosis, and 4,700-square-kilometre Lake Manitoba, all remnants of Lake Agassiz, which covered the province 12,000 years ago — and scores of rivers. Not surprisingly, the province's name is linked to water. Early Indians ascribed the sound of waves swishing through a narrow channel on present-day Lake Manitoba to spirit voices and gave the narrows the name *Manitobau* or Channel of the Great Spirit Manitou.

Rivers that are now used for hydro development, fishing, white-water rafting, canoeing, and pleasure boating were once the all-important highways of exploration and fur-trading days. For centuries Indians of many tribes had plied those waterways. European interest in the area came with the search

Stream-fed valleys cut through coniferous forests and deciduous woods in Riding Mountain National Park.

Luxuriant undergrowth nourishes and shelters a wide variety of birds and game animals in the parklands and woodlands predominating in southwestern Manitoba.

for a trade route around North America to the spice-rich Orient. In 1610, explorer Henry Hudson discovered the huge bay that bears his name. The fur traders followed, first the Hudson's Bay Company (HBC) men, later their North West Company rivals. As the fur trade developed, Métis — mostly offspring of European fathers and Indian women — became the trade's guides.

In 1811, the first permanent European settlers, a group of mostly Highland Scots, sailed into Hudson Bay. They were sponsored by Thomas Douglas, earl of Selkirk, an HBC shareholder who had obtained a tract of HBC land covering parts of present-day Manitoba, Saskatchewan, North Dakota, Minnesota, and Ontario. After wintering near York Factory, an HBC post on Hudson Bay, the new arrivals sailed up the Hayes River, then down Lake Winnipeg to the Red River. They settled north of the junction of the Red and Assiniboine rivers and named the place Point Douglas. "The Forks," a national historic site in downtown Winnipeg, marks the settlement site.

The North West Company and the HBC feared the new colony would disrupt the fur trade and the Métis resented settlers occupying land that was traditionally theirs. Spring floods, harsh winters, sweltering summers, crop-devouring grasshoppers, and disease also plagued the settlers' early years. But by 1822, the settlement, augmented by Irish, French, German, and Swiss immigrants, had begun to prosper from the wheat crops that built Winnipeg.

By 1869, the federal government had purchased most of the HBC holdings in North America. This opened the way for Manitoba to become Canada's fifth province the following year. Settlers of many nationalities and religions poured in creating the mosaic that is Manitoba today. Cultural and ethnic diversity is richer here than anywhere else in Canada, where many of the province's 40 nationalities, and religious groups such as Hutterites, live side by side in their own communities.

Settlement began in the south, and although present-day Manitoba is 18 times

Dense evergreens surround Manitoba's highest accessible waterfall, Pisew Falls, on the Grass River near Thompson. A 500-metre boardwalk cuts through the dense bush separating the falls from the nearest highway, leading visitors to platforms overlooking the unharnessed falls.

greater than the "postage-stamp" size province that joined Confederation, 95 percent of the 1,116,000 inhabitants still live in southern towns and farm communities. More than half live in or near Winnipeg, the provincial melting pot. The city thrives on its inner culture, producing scores of actors, artists, dancers, and musicians, who hone their skills on myriad festivals of art, dance, music, and theater. Members of the various groups come together at least once a year at festivals such as Folklorama, Winnipeg's Festival of Nations.

Just about every Manitoba community of any size hosts some cultural event with strong ethnic seasoning: the Icelandic Festival at Gimli, the town on Lake Winnipeg that is the largest Icelandic settlement outside Iceland; Mennonite Pioneer Days at Steinbach; Festival du Voyageur in the largely French city of St. Boniface; and the National Ukrainian Festival at Dauphin. Crops such as barley, flax, sunflowers, canola, and especially wheat are harvested each fall from the fertile land around these communities. Many of the landmark grain elevators have disappeared, however, due to the centralization of grain storage and the closure of some family farms.

More than 1,200 oil pump jacks nod busily among the low hills north of Virden, the main oil producing area in the province. Oil was discovered there in 1951.

BASHFUL LIZARDS AND PLAY-DEAD SNAKES

The section of Spruce Woods Provincial Heritage Park known as the Manitoba Desert (known also as the Spirit Sands, the Carbery Sand Hills, and the Bald Head Hills) has a remarkably rich plant and animal life. One creature, a profusely streaked lizard known as the northern prairie skink, is found nowhere else. These Manitoba skinks are believed to be a colony that separated from a species of horned lizards found from Minnesota to Texas.

Northern prairie skinks can be as long as 20 centimetres. A female lays up to a dozen eggs in late spring or early summer, depositing them in holes dug out under stones or logs. The young hatch in 40 to 52 days.

Skinks hibernate in burrows dug in sandy soil to a depth of almost 1.5 metres. Even in summer they are seldom seen in the open, preferring to dig into sand or soft loose soil.

Metre-long hognose snakes are other desert dwellers. If provoked or frightened suddenly, the hognose snake (see below) will puff up, hiss, and lunge. But it is mostly bluff, for the snake will eventually roll over and play dead.

The relatively smooth skinned, fat plains spadefoot toad is another fascinating desert creature. This toad uses the hard "spades" of its hind feet to burrow backward in sand or loose dirt. As it progresses backward into the excavation, it shuffles rapidly out of sight. A spadefoot's development from egg to tadpole to adult may take as little as two weeks, the shortest for any North American frog or toad. Spadefoots breed in pools of rainwater that disappear quickly, so this accelerated development means they spend little time in environments that require water for survival.

Painted turtles can also be seen basking on sunny rocks in another section of the park known as the Devils' Punchbowl, a blue-green pond fed by an underground stream. As with all painted turtles, they slide quickly into the water when approached.

Huge quartzite, glacier-rounded boulders litter Churchill's ice-clogged coastline.

The Spirit Sands, five square kilometres of blowing sand dunes amid the rolling hills of Spruce Woods Provincial Heritage Park, were formed by a melting glacier some 12,000 years ago.

CANADA'S ONLY DESERT

Spruce Woods Provincial Heritage Park lies west of Brandon (pop. 40,000), Manitoba's second largest city. The park encompasses oxbow lakes, marshes, quicksand, and Canada's only desert, Spirit Sands, which was formed when retreating glaciers dumped sand in their wake. When summer rains fall, the 25-square-kilometre desert's shifting dunes come alive with yellow prickly pear blossoms and blushing pincushion cacti.

North of Brandon, Riding Mountain rises sharply above the surrounding sea of wheat, oats, flax, barley, and rapeseed. The mountain, part of the Manitoba escarpment, is the centerpiece of a national park that preserves habitats characteristic of Canada's north (boreal forest), west (grasslands), and east (deciduous woodland). For a few brief days each spring, pale lavender prairie crocuses splash the park's grasslands.

A portion of the park is speckled with potholes that are rich breeding grounds for waterfowl. Pelicans, black bears, cougars, and timber wolves are also found in this park. An enclosure near Lake Audy protects a herd of bison, descendants of the mighty herds that once roamed the Manitoba plains. The cabin where conservationist Archibald Stansfeld Belaney (alias Grey Owl) wrote about his beavers can be seen in the park.

Farther north, where the prairies give way to thick forests, Manitoba's highest peak, Baldy Mountain, stands 831 metres high in Duck Mountain Provincial Park. Only a handful of Manitobans — loggers, miners, prospectors, hunters, and trappers — live farther north. Those who do are scattered in isolated communities and Indian reserves.

Thompson, 740 kilometres north of Winnipeg and by far the largest of the northern communities, was built when significant nickel deposits were found in the area in 1956. Five years later the world's first integrated nickel-mining, -smelting, -concentrating, and -refining center opened there.

Gold-mining Lynn Lake, 1,060 kilometres northwest of Winnipeg, is known as "The Town That Moved." In the 1950's, some 150 of its houses, churches, and a school were hauled hundreds of kilometres from communities where mines had closed down.

POLAR BEARS AND WHITE BELUGAS

The port of Churchill has a somewhat longer history than Lynn Lake. Although the present town dates from 1931 when the Hudson Bay Railway terminal and harbor facilities were built, the HBC had a post there as far back as 1689. Home year-round to 1,000 persons, and accessible only by plane or train, Churchill nevertheless attracts thousands of visitors annually, most drawn by the certainty of seeing 300- to 600-kilogram polar bears up close in their natural habitat.

From October to November as many as 150 of these lords of the arctic migrate north from their summer ranges below Churchill to begin their annual seal hunt wherever ice is thick enough to support their weight. Special "tundra vehicles" take visitors to where these skilled hunters — a polar bear can detect a scent at 32 kilometres and sense seals under a metre of snow and ice — forage for supper among the crowberry, dwarf cranberry, and lichens. Often a bear will approach one of the vehicles and attempt to look inside.

Polar bears may be Churchill's star attraction but they are far from being the only one. This is the best place in the world to see beluga whales, thousands of which congregate in the Churchill River estuary each summer, blowing and "singing" their high-pitched notes, molting their flaking, yellowed outer skin, and nursing their young. Birders are drawn by bird populations that include up to 250 species — ducks, shorebirds, Canada geese and snow geese, and boreal forest species. Arctic loons, jaegers, Ross's gulls, gyrfalcons, and golden plovers all nest here.

And of course there is the aurora borealis extravaganza, dancing bands of green, red, yellow, and white that are at their grandest from August through April.

Despite their placid mien — easy since they have no natural enemies — polar bears are no teddy bears, but rather wild, unpredictable creatures that can run down a caribou. After a winter hunting on frozen Hudson Bay, they migrate inland for the summer, returning in fall when the bay refreezes.

New Brunswick

A picture-postcard province, washed by the world's highest tides

During the crisp autumn months, the brilliant birch and maple foliage and the solid green of balsam fir create a rainbow of colors across New Brunswick. Forests cover more than 80 percent of this province, which is also blessed with 2,000 kilometres of Atlantic-washed shorelines, and rivers that are world-renowned for their grandeur and their trout and salmon harvests.

As winter steals away, spring thaws send water cascading down the province's wooded slopes — the northeastern arm of the Appalachian Mountains — to swell its many rivers. Its principal waterway, the Saint John River, often called the Rhine of North America, offers one of the most picturesque drives in Canada. The world's longest covered bridge spans the Saint John at Hartland. The 391-metre structure is among 70 covered bridges in New Brunswick.

"THE GOODLY RIVER"

Indians of old called the Saint John River *Woolastook*, "the goodly river." It has enriched the scenic valley through which it flows and today that fertile soil yields abundant apple and potato crops.

As New Brunswick's western boundary with Maine, the river provided a ready escape route for United Empire Loyalists, who, in 1783, found themselves outcasts in the fledgling United States. Their arrival played a vital role in the province's development. Their

Fields of lupins border a stretch of the Saint John River on its 700-km run from north Maine to the Bay of Fundy.

White-tailed deer, moose, snowshoe hares, raccoons, and porcupines are frequently seen from trails in Fundy National Park, one of the best places in the province to see wildlife.

Spectacular views of lonely grandeur and bird-rich forested uplands reward those who follow the park trail to the top of 800-m Mount Carleton, the highest peak in the Maritimes.

off Bermuda and wriggle upstream to ponds where they will spend most of their adult life. As many as 10 years later, they return to the Sargasso sea, where they mate, lay eggs, and die.

Each summer, salmon too can be seen fighting their way upriver to resting pools and shallow spawning beds. The salmon have been reintroduced in recent years, having been depleted by logging and overfishing before the park was created in 1948. As yet, they are nowhere near their original numbers, either in the park or along the Miramichi River, nor even the Magaguadavic.

Near St. George, stretches of the latter river glisten silver when salmon swim upriver to spawn. In the early 1900's, this fishing village was nicknamed "Granite Town" for the rich red granite quarried locally and used in many structures, including the Parliament Buildings in Ottawa.

Blacks Harbour, south of St. George, is the departure point for ferries to Grand Manan, an island full of geological curiosities that seems moored in the 19th century. Naturalist James Audubon, who visited it in 1833, was awed by the island's bird life. Birds in the thousands still stop over every year — as many as 275 species have been sighted.

A short walk from driftwood-strewn pebble beaches, hiking trails offer spectacular views of the Bay of Fundy. Legend has it that Captain Kidd's gold lies buried at Dark Harbour. The humpback, minke, and finback are among whale species that pass offshore. A ferry ride north of Grand Manan takes you to Campobello Island, where U.S. President Franklin D. Roosevelt spent his childhood summers.

DISPUTED LAND

The first Europeans to reach New Brunswick were Portuguese and Spanish fishermen. Nevertheless, Samuel de Champlain claimed it for France, when he and Pierre du Goa sailed into the Bay of Fundy in 1604. The territory remained in French hands until the Treaty of Utrecht ceded Acadia (most of today's Maritime provinces and part of Maine) to England in 1713.

THE BEAUTY AND SPLENDOR OF NORTH AMERICA

One of the darkest periods of the colony's history came in 1755 when Britain deported thousands of Acadians to Louisiana and other British possessions. Lamèque Island was one of the first places resettled when the Acadians straggled back in the 1760's. Island descendants of the five families — 26 people — who returned now number 10,000.

Loyalists who arrived after the American Revolution pressed for a colony of their own and New Brunswick was officially established in 1784. Saint John, one of the most active seaports on the Atlantic Coast, was incorporated the following year. Loyalist Days, a week-long series of parades and celebrations in July, reenacts the arrival of those first Loyalists whose vision and hard work built the bustling city.

By the 19th century a booming lumbering industry had brought prosperity to the province. Logs floated down rivers to ocean ports, where they were used to construct great wooden sailing vessels. Once built, the ships were filled with more lumber, and fish. Upon arrival in England, the United States, or the West Indies, the vessels and their contents would be sold.

Eventually, the advent of steam-driven, iron-hulled vessels dealt a deathblow to the builders of wooden ships and, in turn, to the lumbering industry. Faced with a faltering economy, New Brunswickers saw the need to build on manufacturing, and wanted access to the markets John A. Macdonald's transcontinental railway would provide.

There were other concerns, too. After the American Civil War, some New Brunswickers and the British government feared the victors might attempt to annex British North America in retaliation for British support of the South during the war. A united colony, independent of Britain, seemed like the best deterrent, and on July 1, 1867, New Brunswick joined with Nova Scotia and Canada (present-day Ontario and Quebec) to form the Dominion of Canada.

Iron foundries, textile mills, and sugar refineries built a profitable manufacturing base after 1867, but the province's small size and population were no match for the stronger manufacturing centers in central Canada. Present-day New Brunswick still relies on its original resources, lumber and fisheries, for its economic well-being.

Swallowtail lighthouse, named for the flocks of swallows that converge on this northern terminal of the Atlantic flyway, stands guard on tranquil Grand Manan, an island of awesome cliffs, pirate coves, and craggy trails framed by woods and wildflowers, and a mecca for artists, bird-watchers, photographers, rock hounds, and whale-watchers.

THE PEOPLE AND THE LAND

Population: 723,900

Area: 73,437 sq km

Population per sq km: 9.9

Capital: Fredericton (pop. 46,466)

Largest city: Saint John (pop. 74,969)

Major rivers: Saint John, Miramichi, Tobique, Restigouche

Elevation: Sea level to 820 m (Mt. Carleton)

Leading industries: Manufacturing, fishing, mining, forestry, pulp and paper, agriculture

Bird: Black-capped chickadee

Flower: Purple violet

Tree: Balsam fir

Motto: *Spem reduxit* (Hope restored)

Origin of Name: In honor of the House of Brunswick, which ruled England in 1784 when the colony adopted its name.

Nickname: The Picture Province

INFORMATION

Department of Economic Development and Tourism
P.O. Box 6000
Fredericton, N.B. E3B 5H1
1-800 561-0123

HISTORICAL HIGHLIGHTS

1604 Samuel de Champlain and Pierre du Goa sail into the Bay of Fundy and claim the land for France.

1713 Under the Treaty of Utrecht, France cedes the New Brunswick area to Britain.

1755 The British deport thousands of French settlers.

1783 Upward of 7,000 Loyalists settle in New Brunswick.

1784 New Brunswickers withdraw from the greater colony of Nova Scotia and form the separate colony of New Brunswick.

1785 Saint John becomes Canada's first incorporated city.

1825 The great Miramichi forest fire kills 160 people.

1854 New Brunswick is given responsible government.

1867 New Brunswick, along with Nova Scotia, Ontario, and Quebec, becomes a province within the Dominion of Canada.

1876 Intercolonial Railway links New Brunswick to Montreal.

1910 The chocolate bar is invented by Ganong Brothers.

1965 New Brunswick adopts its provincial flag.

1984 The province celebrates its centennial, and is visited by Pope John Paul II.

1994 Le Congrès mondial acadien, the first world congress of Acadians, convenes in New Brunswick.

FAMOUS SONS AND DAUGHTERS

William Maxwell Aitken, Lord Beaverbrook (1879 – 1964). This newspaper magnate was raised in Newcastle. (See p. 47.)

Richard Bedford Bennett (1870 – 1947). A successful businessman and lawyer, Bennett was Prime Minister of Canada from 1930 to 1935.

Joseph Cunard (1799 – 1865). Nova Scotia-born Cunard managed his father's businesses in New Brunswick, where he built a lumber and shipbuilding empire.

Nicolas Denys (1598 – 1688). A French merchant, Denys founded Bathurst in 1652.

Gilbert White Ganong (1851 – 1917). The grocery store he opened in St. Stephen in 1873 became the huge confectionery company Ganong Brothers Ltd.

Kenneth Colin Irving (1899 – 1992). This industrialist built an empire of service stations, and construction and transport companies.

Andrew Bonar Law (1858 – 1923). This Kingston-born iron merchant became Prime Minister of Britain.

Roméo LeBlanc (1927 –). The former professor, journalist, federal cabinet minister, and Senate speaker became governor general in 1995.

Antonine Maillet (1929 –).

This Acadian novelist's books have captured the spirit and hardships of the Acadian settlers. Her *Pelagie-la-Charrette* (1979) won a French literary award that helped bring her fame in Europe.

Donald Sutherland (1935 –). The Saint John-born actor began his career on the London stage before going on to star in films such as *M.A.S.H.* and *Bethune.*

Samuel Leonard Tilley (1818 – 96). He led New Brunswick into Confederation, held federal cabinet posts, and was lieutenant governor from 1873 to 1878.

ODDITIES AND SPECIALTIES

Magnetic Hill, just outside Moncton, creates the illusion that one's car, parked in neutral, is coasting uphill. Locals attribute the phenomenon to the power of the underlying ore.

The steps of the circular staircase in the Carleton Martello Tower, an early 19th-century stone fortress near Saint John, were purposely built uneven. The intent was to slow down, even trip, potential invaders.

The force of Fundy tides meets the Saint John River in a gorge, forcing it to reverse upstream, creating what is known as the Reversing Falls.

The Republic of Madawaska is an area around Edmundston that figured in boundary disputes with Maine in the early 1800's. The conflict was resolved in 1842 but, in 1949, locals jokingly decided to create their own republic, including their own flag and language. Edmundston mayors have the title of president of the republic.

PLACES TO VISIT, THINGS TO DO

Beaverbrook Art Gallery (Fredericton). Dali's *Santiago el Grande* is among its outstanding collection.

Fort Beauséjour National Historic Park (Sackville). Earthen ramparts and stone foundations recall the turbulent past of this fort built by the French in 1751 and captured by New England forces in 1755.

Huntsman Marine Laboratory Aquarium (St. Andrews). Sea urchins and starfish are among marine oddities on display.

Lamèque International Baroque Music Festival. Each July, Sainte-Cécile Church on Lamèque Island becomes a concert stage for musicians from around the world.

New Brunswick Craft Centre (Fredericton). Works of the province's artisans are displayed in a gallery and boutique.

New Brunswick

The Rocks Provincial Park (Alma). At high tide this park at the mouth of the Petitcodiac River is a series of small islands covered with balsam firs and black spruces. At low tide the islands become mushroom-shaped pillars sprouting from the beach. The tides have tunneled through the pillars (see photo, right) and sculpted caves and crevices in the red shoreline cliffs. At low tide visitors can take a staircase from the park parking lot (where tide schedules are posted) to the beach.

Rockwood Park (Saint John). Woodlands, freshwater lakes, campgrounds, hiking trails, a golf course, and a zoo are among attractions in this 8,903-square-kilometre park in the city center.

Trinity Royal Preservation Area (Saint John). This restored 10-block area of the downtown features antique and craft shops, restaurants, and art galleries.

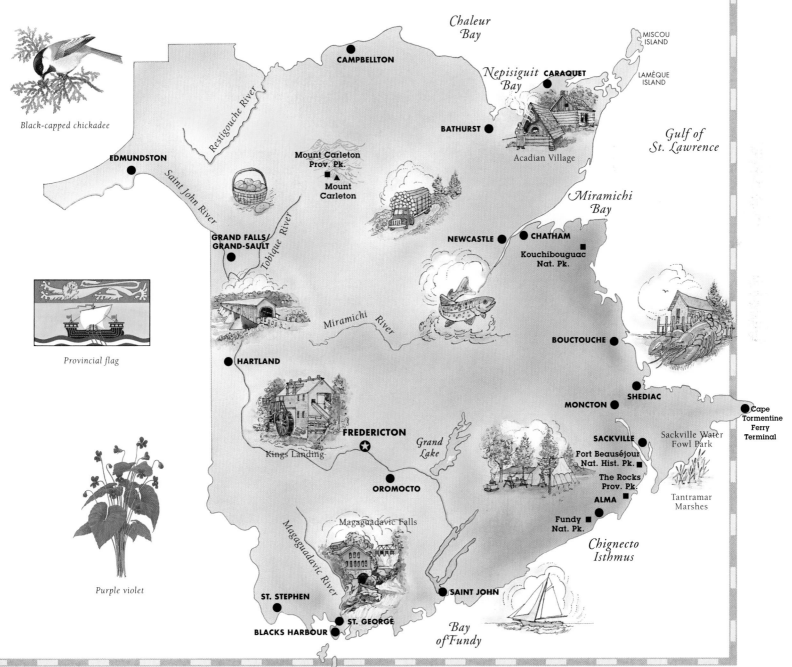

Black-capped chickadee

Provincial flag

Purple violet

Chaleur Bay

MISCOU ISLAND

CAMPBELLTON

Nepisiguit Bay **CARAQUET**

LAMÈQUE ISLAND

BATHURST

Gulf of St. Lawrence

Acadian Village

Restigouche River

EDMUNDSTON

Mount Carleton Prov. Pk.

Mount Carleton

Miramichi Bay

Saint John River

Tobique River

GRAND FALLS/ GRAND-SAULT

NEWCASTLE   **CHATHAM**

Kouchibouguac Nat. Pk.

HARTLAND

Miramichi River

BOUCTOUCHE

SHEDIAC

MONCTON

Cape Tormentine Ferry Terminal

Sackville Water Fowl Park

FREDERICTON

Kings Landing

Grand Lake

SACKVILLE

Fort Beauséjour Nat. Hist. Pk.

The Rocks Prov. Pk.

Tantramar Marshes

OROMOCTO

ALMA

Fundy Nat. Pk.

Chignecto Isthmus

Magaguadavic Falls

Magaguadavic River

ST. STEPHEN

ST. GEORGE

BLACKS HARBOUR

SAINT JOHN

Bay of Fundy

CAMPOBELLO ISLAND

GRAND MANAN ISLAND

Newfoundland

Storied outports and indomitable fisherfolk in our oldest settlement

The first recorded visit to the New World occurred when Vikings sailed through the fog into Newfoundland's craggy coves a thousand years ago. People have been slogging ashore ever since, enduring rainy summers and blustery winters to forge a way of life all their own on the magnificent island they've named the Rock.

Communities ringing the coastline trace their roots to hardy seafarers of old — a connection reflected in their outlook, customs, and the Elizabethan idiom of everyday speech. On occasion, they celebrate the ancestral link at festivals replete with fiddle music and a hardy local rum called *screech*.

Newfoundlanders share their home with countless wild creatures: moose, black and polar bears, beaver, fox, lynx, rabbit, otter, muskrat, herds of caribou, and seabirds by the millions. Whales and seals cavort in offshore waters. This mix of land and water is at its best in Terra Nova National Park. There, white beaches sprawl next to towering headlands. Firs and junipers push inland to murky bogs and ponds and, out to sea, in early summer, high-rise icebergs sail by.

DEFINED BY FISH

All its wild creatures and natural wonders notwithstanding, Newfoundland is best known for fish. When John Cabot returned to England after his 1497 "discovery" of the island, he described a sea "swarming with fish" that could be taken "in baskets let down

The pretty village of Back Harbour north of Twillingate is accessible via the "Tickles and Runs" — the Notre Dame Bay causeways linking islands and mainland.

The house snugly sheltered from the sea and the boat riding peacefully at anchor in Tor Bay give no sense of the hardships fisherfolk have always endured in these parts. Many who settled these picture-perfect shores relied on the danger and inaccessibility of the harbors to keep prying ships and overzealous administrators away: for centuries, British law forbade permanent settlement on Newfoundland.

IT'S FOR THE BIRDS

Millions of birds nest in the steep, jagged cliffs of protected coastal reserves and islands along Newfoundland's shores. Witless Bay, an easy drive south of St. John's, has the biggest puffin colony in North America. The black-winged birds with multicolored beaks fly in from the open ocean each spring and summer to breed on three small islands in the bay.

The puffins are not alone at Witless Bay or any of the provincial reserves. There are more than 300 species in all, including storm petrels, razorbills, hawks, falcons, and ospreys. Nesting at different levels on the cliff walls, they swoop down simultaneously to compete for the same fish. Boat tours are the best way to get a close-up of the birds diving for a meal — often trying to beat a hungry humpback or minke whale to the prey.

There are dozens of sites to choose from. Bird Rock on Cape St. Mary's, southwest of St. John's, is probably the most accessible spot anywhere to gaze at the gannet's great wingspan. However, do not be misled by Labrador's Gannet Island. There is not a single gannet on it — it was named for a 19th-century British ship. However, it is home to thousands of puffins, murres, and kittiwakes. Placentia Bay has North America's largest colony of bald eagles.

with a stone." British merchants promptly financed fishing expeditions, and when one such fleet sailed into St. John's in 1583, its commander, Sir Humphrey Gilbert, claimed the region for England. For years to come, the merchants dominated the fishery. Not wishing to have settlers compete for the bonanza, the merchants used floggings and hangings to discourage settlement.

But settlers came anyway. In sheltered bays and inlets along the jagged eastern coast, they established remote villages, called outports, with fanciful names like Farewell, Heart's Content, Come by Chance, Eastern Tickle, and Joe Batt's Arm. Conception, Placentia, St. Mary's, and Trinity bays were among the earliest fishing sites. The first settlements were on the Avalon Peninsula, an H-shaped chunk of land joined to the rest of the island by a narrow isthmus. The first permanent British colony was founded in 1610 at Cuper's Cove, the site of present-day Cupids. About 40 percent of Newfoundlanders still live on the Avalon Peninsula. The region has weathered more than its share of battles — between English and French, settlers and buccaneers — and other tumultuous events, and the memories are enshrined in numerous historic sites.

St. John's, the provincial capital, is soaked in history and old-world charm. Water Street, now a tourist mecca, was a port of call for European fishermen long before Sir Humphrey Gilbert arrived. St. John's received the first transatlantic wireless message in 1901, and Alcock and Brown set out from there in 1919 on the first nonstop transatlantic flight. (The more northerly and relatively fog-free Gander got the nod, however, when the province's first international airport and strategic transatlantic refueling hub was built in 1938.)

Nearby Harbour Grace revels in its own colorful past. From his 1600's fort there, pirate Peter Easton raided vessels at sea, and there, in 1932, Amelia Earhart began the first transatlantic solo flight by a woman. The lighthouse at Cape Spear marks the easternmost point in North America. The nearest landfall east is Ireland or the Azores.

THE FRENCH SHORE

While the British were busy with the east coast, the French established fishing stations on the west. This is the part of Newfoundland first seen by those arriving at the main ferry terminal of Channel-Port aux Basques.

Many fishing villages on the southern coast are accessible only by boat. Roads and towns are also rare in the interior, a world of birch, pine, spruce, and salmon- and trout-filled streams. The region is home to far more caribou and moose than people.

Tourists get an upclose look at one of the menacing but sparkling blue- and jade-tinged mountains of Arctic ice that drift down Newfoundland's eastern coastline in May and June.

Quilts of epiphytes, plants that absorb water and nutrients from the air, cover the forest floor at Ochre Hill in Terra Nova National Park. Some moss species there are found nowhere else.

Grand Falls–Windsor in the interior and west coast Corner Brook, the province's second-largest city, are pulp-and-paper centers. Corner Brook also showcases Newfoundland's best traditional performers at its annual Hangashore Folk Art Festival. Some of the island's finest scenery is found in the valley of the Humber River, one of the world's great salmon rivers.

The Long Range Mountains run the length of the "French Shore," and in the middle of the ancient range sits perhaps the finest of all Newfoundland's unrefined treasures, Gros Morne National Park, a United Nations World Heritage Site. The name translates as "Big Gloomy," and from time to time this mountainous wonderland of bogs, treeless plateaus, dramatic canyons, and deep lakes is battered by the same winds that used to topple railcars, but those who climb flat-topped, 806-metre Gros Morne Mountain will find the view positively exhilarating. Down below, boats ply Western Brook Pond — a glacier-gouged, ice-blue lake surrounded by towering cliffs — and seabirds glide over rocks heaved from the sea floor by ancient seismic collisions.

Archaeological excavations along this coastline have yielded a treasure trove. Tools, weapons, and jewelry of the Maritime Archaic Indians, who inhabited the area some 4,000 years ago, have been unearthed in burial sites at Port au Choix. Traces of a Viking settlement dating from about A.D. 1000 have been discovered at L'Anse aux Meadows, a settlement many scholars believe to be the Vinland of the Norse sagas.

A FOOTHOLD ON THE MAINLAND

Three times the size of the Island of Newfoundland, Labrador lies across the Strait of Belle Isle from L'Anse aux Meadows. Many of its 30,000 inhabitants are Innu. The world's largest herd of barren ground caribou, the George River herd, roams Labrador's dense interior forests, which are broken only by rushing rivers and huge, frigid lakes. Mount Caubvick (1,652 metres) in the Torngat Mountains is the highest peak east of the Rockies.

Caribou abound in Labrador's Torngat Mountains. The vegetation-sparse Torngats ("home of spirits" in Inuktitut) are part of the Precambrian Shield.

Labrador had the first industrial site in the New World. Between 1540 and 1610, about 1,000 Basque fishermen encamped each summer at Red Bay, rendering whale blubber into oil. In 1771, Moravian missionaries started settlements consisting of a church, school, and trading post. Nain, Hopedale, and Happy Valley began in this way. Wilfred Grenfell launched his hospital/nursing station network at Battle Harbour in 1893. By then Europeans were settling along the Labrador coast.

In 1965, work began at Happy Valley–Goose Bay on the Trans-Labrador Highway to Churchill Falls, site of the western hemisphere's largest hydroelectric plant. The unpaved highway linked up with iron-ore mining Wabush and Labrador City, and northern Quebec in 1992. Today, a passenger boat from Lewisporte serves outposts on Labrador's rugged eastern shore, and there is a ferry link from St. Barbe to Blanc-Sablon, a Quebec community bordering Labrador.

DIFFICULT TIMES

Broadcaster Rex Murphy has described affection for Newfoundland as "stronger than a chemical dependency." That affection embodies the spirit of the outports — the courage, decency, fortitude, and friendliness

of a centuries-old way of life. Sadly, the outports are threatened. Dwindling cod stocks have led to the fishery's collapse, and without the fish, the outports have no longer a reason to be. As Murphy sees it, once the outports are gone, "something privileged . . . utterly unrepeatable" has vanished. Those affected are looking for new answers and new sources of income, such as cod farms and offshore oil. These may become means of survival in a rugged and beautiful part of the world.

Excavations at L'Anse aux Meadows National Historic Site have uncovered traces of seven sod houses, two cook pits, an iron smithy, and a kiln built by Norse who settled at the tip of the Great Northern Peninsula late in the 10th century. The place is now a United Nations World Heritage Site.

The Northwest Territories

Northern lights in a "north of summer" land

They comprise one-third of Canada's land mass, yet are home to only 63,000 people, mostly Dene and Inuit. Much of the area is all but cloaked in darkness for months on end, then bathed in increasing hours of sunlight from March to June 21 when the sun dips below the horizon only briefly. Summers there can be as ephemeral as the greens, purples, and reds of the northern lights playing eerily above an icy landscape, or the brief explosion of wildflowers on the tundra.

"A SCALE OUTSIDE THAT OF HUMANITY"

On visiting the Great Slave Lake area in 1937, John Buchan (Lord Tweedsmuir) wrote: "It is impossible to describe the country, for it is built on a scale outside that of humanity." Yet the land that overwhelmed him is merely the "near north," the southwest subarctic region that has most of the population and the territory's few highways.

The Slave River was once the main freight route into the north and Fort Smith was a service depot for those portaging freight around the river's treacherous 22-kilometre Rapids of the Drowned. Today, the town is at the entrance to Wood Buffalo National Park, nesting grounds of the endangered whooping crane and home to one of the largest wood bison herds in the world.

Prehistoric seas left thick layers of pure gypsum in the area. Rain and groundwater,

Magnificent mountains, deep canyons, and spectacular waterways define Nahanni National Park.

Just 1,500 kilometres from the North Pole, gulls circle sunny cliffs at Ellesmere Island's Grise Fjord, a wildlife paradise reputed to be the most beautiful spot in the Northwest Territories.

eating into this carbonate rock, have formed the world's largest concentration of karst lands — landforms characterized by caves, tunnels, valleys, and sinkholes.

Almost a quarter of the Territories' population (15,200) lives in Yellowknife, the capital city on the northern shore of Great Slave Lake, 515 kilometres south of the Arctic Circle. The city dates from the 1934 discovery of gold, which is still mined there.

Communities such as Hay River, Fort Simpson, Wrigley, and Fort Norman began life as fur-trade posts on the Mackenzie River, which winds north from Great Slave Lake to the Beaufort Sea. Crowded forests of spruce and birch along its banks eventually give way to rolling tundra as the river reaches its delta and feeds into a myriad network of channels, lakes, and muskeg swamps.

Inuvik ("the place of man" in Inuvialuktun, the language of the Mackenzie Delta people) was built in the Mackenzie's east channel in 1954 as an administrative center for the western Arctic. There was concern at the time that Aklavik, the former center, in the west channel, would be flooded out. Inuvik was built on pilings embedded in the permafrost, with public utilities delivered through aboveground conduits called utilidors. Inuvik thus became the first place north of the Arctic Circle to have the basic services more southerly communities take for granted. A giant reindeer grazing reserve stretches north from the city to Tuktoyaktuk and the Beaufort Sea.

"THE RIVER OF FEAR"

Although it has softer aspects, such as fields of arctic cotton, Nahanni National Park, a United Nations World Heritage site in the heart of the Mackenzie Mountains, is best known for its rugged waterways, especially the wild South Nahanni River — "the river of fear." Even in the myth-filled north, this river holds a special place. There are countless tales of giants, lost gold mines, tropical edens, mysterious deaths, and prospectors who vanished without trace.

The real Nahanni is scarcely less romantic — a formidable but breathtakingly beau-

tiful world of limestone cliffs and pinnacles, warm crystal-clear pools fringed with wild mint, goldenrods, yellow monkey flowers, and asters, and spectacular waterfalls. A great rock pinnacle divides the 1.6-hectare face of magnificent Virginia Falls. At 90 metres, it is twice as high as Niagara's torrent.

Elsewhere in the 4,662-square-kilometre park, golden eagles soar in canyon updrafts and northern moose browse through alder and poplar thickets. Flocks of white Dall sheep race across tundra pastures, black bears prowl dense forests, and grizzlies saunter through the open country above highland timberlines. The highest mountain walls are the domain of the mountain goat.

ARCTIC PRAIRIE AND ARCHIPELAGO

An arctic prairie dotted with glacier-carved lakes and ponds graces the barren lands north of the treeline. Caribou trails — age-old migration routes of herds that summer on the tundra, then head south for the winter — meander through the lichens, mosses, and grasses that cover much of the region.

Only a few arctic islands will remain in the Northwest Territories after April 1, 1999. Most others will become part of Nunavut, a separate territory, which will extend from Manitoba north to Ellesmere Island.

Inukshuks, rock piles that resemble people and serve as landmarks, dot these islands.

Although, quite properly, one imagines the arctic islands blanketed in snow, Ellesmere Island National Park Reserve is a polar desert. With only two to three centimetres of precipitation annually, it is counted among the world's driest places. The reserve also encompasses Lake Hazen, the largest lake north of the Arctic Circle.

Iqaluit ("the place of fish" in Inuktitut, the language of the Inuit) on Baffin Island is the largest eastern Arctic community (pop. 3,600). Originally a whalers' trading post, it is now an administrative center for the region. The vast tracts of vertical rock and precipitous fjords of Baffin's Auyuittuq National Park typify the eastern Arctic coastline. "North of summer" was how poet Al Purdy described Pangnirtung, the tiny settlement at the southern entrance to Auyuittuq (pronounced "Ah-you-we-took" and translated from Inuktitut as "the land that never melts"). The Penny Ice Cap, a holdout from the last Ice Age, covers 5,700 square kilometres of this park off which ringed, harp, and bearded seals, walruses, narwhal (the spiral-tusked whale of sea-unicorn lore), white, killer, bowhead, and humpbacked whales play in deep blue Arctic waters.

Perpetual ice and snow are a fact on life on Ellesmere Island, where glaciers up to 40 kilometres long reach into fjords and valleys. From the island's northern coast, "ice shelves" extend into the Arctic Ocean.

Banks Island northwest of the Coppermine estuary is renowned for its herds of musk-oxen, shaggy relatives of wild sheep and goats that occur naturally only in the Canadian Arctic and Greenland.

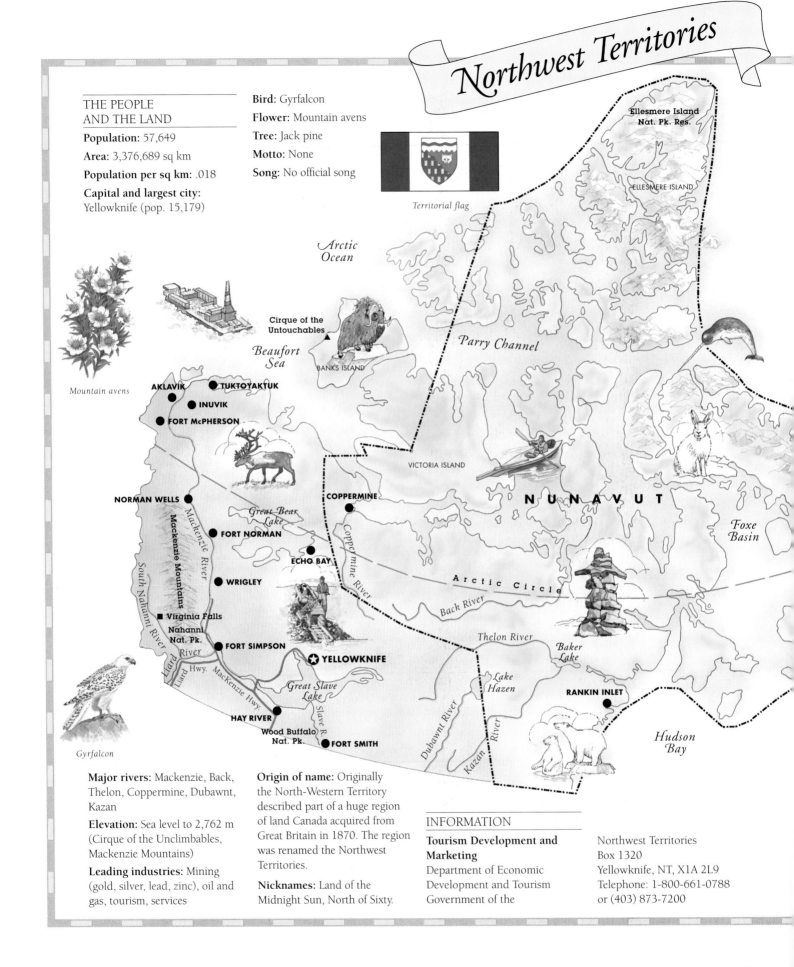

THE PEOPLE AND THE LAND

Population: 57,649

Area: 3,376,689 sq km

Population per sq km: .018

Capital and largest city:
Yellowknife (pop. 15,179)

Bird: Gyrfalcon

Flower: Mountain avens

Tree: Jack pine

Motto: None

Song: No official song

Territorial flag

Mountain avens

Gyrfalcon

Arctic Ocean

Beaufort Sea

Cirque of the Untouchables

BANKS ISLAND

Parry Channel

Ellesmere Island Nat. Pk. Res.

ELLESMERE ISLAND

VICTORIA ISLAND

N U N A V U T

Foxe Basin

AKLAVIK
TUKTOYAKTUK
INUVIK
FORT McPHERSON

NORMAN WELLS

Great Bear Lake

COPPERMINE

FORT NORMAN

ECHO BAY

WRIGLEY

Mackenzie Mountains

Mackenzie River

South Nahanni River

Virginia Falls

Nahanni Nat. Pk.

FORT SIMPSON

Liard River

Liard Hwy.

Mackenzie Hwy.

YELLOWKNIFE

Great Slave Lake

Coppermine River

Arctic Circle

Back River

Thelon River

Lake Hazen

Baker Lake

RANKIN INLET

Dubawnt River

Kazan River

Slave R.

HAY RIVER

Wood Buffalo Nat. Pk.

FORT SMITH

Hudson Bay

Major rivers: Mackenzie, Back, Thelon, Coppermine, Dubawnt, Kazan

Elevation: Sea level to 2,762 m (Cirque of the Unclimbables, Mackenzie Mountains)

Leading industries: Mining (gold, silver, lead, zinc), oil and gas, tourism, services

Origin of name: Originally the North-Western Territory described part of a huge region of land Canada acquired from Great Britain in 1870. The region was renamed the Northwest Territories.

Nicknames: Land of the Midnight Sun, North of Sixty.

INFORMATION

Tourism Development and Marketing
Department of Economic Development and Tourism
Government of the

Northwest Territories
Box 1320
Yellowknife, NT, X1A 2L9
Telephone: 1-800-661-0788
or (403) 873-7200

HISTORICAL HIGHLIGHTS

1576 Martin Frobisher explores Baffin Island.

1610 Henry Hudson discovers Hudson Bay.

1670 The Hudson's Bay Company gets trade rights to much of the Northwest.

1845 Sir John Franklin sets off to find the Northwest Passage.

1858 Father Henry Grollier and Archdeacon James Hunter set up Roman Catholic and Anglican missions in the Mackenzie Valley.

1870 Britain transfers Hudson Bay Territory (Rupert's Land) and the North-Western Territory to Canada.

1903 The North West Mounted Police — precursors to the Royal Canadian Mounted Police — set up posts on Hudson Bay.

1903-06 Roald Amundsen navigates the Northwest Passage.

1921 Oil is discovered at Norman Wells.

1928 A flu epidemic decimates the Mackenzie Valley Dene.

1933 Gold is discovered at Yellowknife.

1975 The Northwest Territories get an elected council.

1993 Federal and Inuit representatives agree to create a new territory called Nunavut (Inuktitut for "our land") by 1999.

FAMOUS SONS AND DAUGHTERS

Georges Erasmus (1948 –).

A central figure in territorial politics, he has served as president of the Dene Nation and national chief of the Assembly of First Nations.

Gilbert LaBine (1890 – 1977). He discovered pitchblende, an ore containing radium and uranium, at Great Bear Lake.

Matonabbee (1736 – 82). A trader and Chipewyan leader, he guided Samuel Hearne overland to the Arctic Ocean in 1771.

John Howard Sissons (1892 – 1969). The Inuit called this first judge of the territorial court *Ekoktoegee* ("the one who listens to things").

ODDITIES AND SPECIALTIES

All compasses point to the north magnetic pole in the Northwest Territories. The pole, which moves constantly, is currently near Bathurst Island, northwest of Resolute Bay.

Permafrost (short for permanently frozen ground) in the Arctic islands is up to 500 m deep.

The Northwest Territories encompass four time zones (Atlantic Standard, Eastern Standard, Central Standard, Mountain Standard).

Numerous pingos (tundra-covered ice hills created by permafrost movement) dot the Mackenzie delta around Tuktoyaktuk.

There are few stoplights on Northwest Territories' highways, but you could come face to face with a black bear, wood bison, moose, or herd of caribou. Rivers are spanned by ferries in summer, ice bridges in winter.

PLACES TO VISIT, THINGS TO DO

Auyuittuq National Park (Baffin Island). Hikers and sea kayakers are rewarded with views of jagged mountain peaks presiding over sapphire-blue fjords, sheer rock cliffs, and monumental glaciers.

Canadian North Midnight Classic. Golfers at this Yellowknife annual June tournament tee off at midnight.

Caribou Carnival (Yellowknife). A Trappers' Ball, a Mushers' Banquet, and the Canadian Championship Dog Derby are among outdoor fun at this annual spring festival.

Festival of the Midnight Sun (Yellowknife). Northern artisans, galleries, and businesses join forces for a week-long celebration of northern art and culture.

Folk on the Rocks (Yellowknife). Inuit throat singers and Inuit and Dene folk-singers, dancers, and drummers are among performers at this annual July folk festival.

Great Northern Arts Festival (Inuvik). Art exhibitions and demonstrations, and workshops highlight this annual event.

Katannilik Territorial Park (Baffin Island). *Katannilik* is Inuktitut for "place where there are falls." The park stretches 1,500 km² between Lake Harbour and Iqaluit, and is renowned for its lush plants. Hikers can explore the park from the Itijjagiaq Trail.

Nahanni National Park (Fort Simpson). Adventurers rafting or canoeing on the South Nahanni River ride through challenging rapids and spectacular limestone canyons.

Northern Life Museum (Fort Smith). Territorial history is told through native and pioneer artifacts, and photos of explorers, traders, and missionaries.

Summer Solstice Celebrations (Inuvik and Yellowknife). Celebrations in both cities begin late in the evening of June 16 and include traditional music, songs, dances, food (including musk-ox and caribou burgers), and late night sales.

Sunrise Festival (Inuvik). In January, on the night before the first sunrise following a month of darkness, the city celebrates with bonfires and fireworks.

Toonik Tyme (Iqaluit, Baffin Island). This spring celebration features dogsled and snowmobile races, igloo-building, and traditional Inuit games.

Nova Scotia

*Where life's rhythms reflect a
bounteous but mercurial sea*

Nowhere is the surge of the sea
stronger than along the rugged, boulder-strewn shores of Nova Scotia.
Sailors plying these waters know all too well
how the mercurial Atlantic can change in
minutes from gentle sway to raging, white-
capped waves. The highest tides in the world
occur in the Bay of Fundy, where spring tides
at Burntcoat Head in Minas Basin can be
16 metres high.

Only the 26-kilometre-wide Chignecto
Isthmus keeps the province anchored to
mainland Canada. The remaining 7,600 kilometres of shoreline, and the fact that you are
never more than 56 kilometres from the sea,
make the Atlantic an inescapable presence.
The province's very outline resembles a giant
lobster — apt, considering that many local
livelihoods depend on the red crustaceans.

AMETHYSTS AND AGATES

The sea provides other legacies, too. From
Scots Bay on the tip of the Blomidon Peninsula, you can hike 14 kilometres atop forested Cape Split cliffs to a rocky beach where
Fundy's erosive tides expose amethysts and
agates. The grinding waves reveal other
"gems" across Minas Basin, where 300-mil-
lion-year-old fossils of the world's smallest
reptile were found at Horton Bluff along the
Parrsboro shore.

The waters here teem with shad, lobsters,
harbor porpoises, and finback, minke, pilot,
and humpback whales. North Atlantic right

*Brackish lagoons, sandy beaches, salt marshes, and
giant granite boulders highlight the rugged Seaside
Adjunct of inland Kejimkujik National Park.*

Great basalt cliffs known as the Giant's Causeway emerge from the sea at Brier Island just off Digby Neck. Brier is a stopping-off point for migrating birds.

SABLE: "GRAVEYARD OF THE ATLANTIC"

Few plants are permanent on tiny Sable Island, a crescent of sand in the North Atlantic some 290 kilometres southeast of Halifax. Hour after hour, northwesterly winds whip the sand into hills, then blow them down again. Crashing waves sweep the shore clean and deposit fresh sandbars along the coast.

Were it not for the abundant marram grass, most of the sand would have vanished by now. The sturdy marram, often called "sea hay," has long, stringy roots which help pin the grains down.

Sable is small by any standard — only 1.5 kilometres thick at its widest point and 38 kilometres long. The highest of two prominent dunes rises a mere 26 metres from the sea, and is barely visible in a storm. A strong push from Gulf Stream currents is slowly extending Sable's southern shore, and the north shore is moving southwest at an even slower pace, shifted by the Belle Isle Current.

Some 200 ships have been lost off this "Graveyard of the Atlantic," among them *Stella Maris, Ruby, Gondolier* and *Cora May.* The 400 or so wild horses galloping among the dunes today are said to be descended from ponies that survived shipwreck by swimming ashore.

whales, the world's most endangered cetaceans, also swim here. Atlantic puffins, sandpipers, Arctic terns, and razor-billed auks fly overhead.

Gentle hills and low ridges dominate the interior of "mainland" Nova Scotia. These hills are the remnants of ancient mountains, which Ice Age glaciers wore down to stubs. Rivers such as the LaHave, Shubenacadie, and St. Marys course past fields overgrown with wild blueberries, cranberries, mayflowers, and violets.

THE SEA'S ROAR

Local novelist Thomas Raddall has described how the sea "could get up and roar . . . and make you turn and run, afraid to look over your shoulder." Fishing crews heading out from Canso, Lockeport, and Yarmouth know that roar as well as they know the sea's bitter toll. Over 3,000 wrecks lie off Nova Scotia. One hundred ships have been lost at sea from Lunenburg alone.

Theresa E. Connor, the last Canadian schooner to fish the Georges Banks (1962),

Visitors to Peggy's Cove are enchanted by this tiny village where fishermen's houses perch bravely on wave-washed boulders beside the open sea.

The Cabot Trail, possibly the most beautiful marine drive in North America, skirts cove-sheltered fishing villages and sandy beaches in its loop around the rugged grandeur of Cape Breton Island.

which the area is famous. At any time, but especially in May when the 160-kilometre-long valley is awash in fragrant pink and white blossoms, it is hard to imagine this peaceful pocket was once the most contested land in the New World. British posts fell in 1613, 1632, 1667, and 1697, and the French in turn were ousted by the British in 1613, 1628, 1654, 1690, and 1710.

After the 1710 defeat, France urged the Acadians, now spread along Minas Basin and the Chignecto Isthmus, to move to French territory. Most declined. They were reluctant to leave their close-knit communities and the

farms they had wrested from the sea. Besides, they had no concern for their future having long gone about their farming and fishing independent of French or British rule. So they sidestepped the oath England demanded, promising they would swear allegiance when Britain guaranteed they would never have to take up arms against France or their Indian friends.

Then, on July 28, 1758, incredulous Acadians from Chignecto, Grand Pré, and Annapolis Royal were herded at bayonet point aboard British ships and scattered throughout British colonies to the south. The calamity is commemorated at Grand Pré National Historic Site, where there is a bronze statue of Evangeline, the heroine of Henry Wadsworth Longfellow's epic poem about the expulsions. Sculpted by Acadian Philippe Hébert, the figure appears young from one perspective, older and sadder from another. The site also has a stone church and formal gardens.

HAUNTING HIGHLANDS AND CRUEL COAST

One of North America's outstanding marine drives, the stunningly beautiful, 290-kilometre Cabot Trail encircles much of Cape Breton, an island linked to mainland Nova Scotia by a two-kilometre causeway spanning Canso Strait. The 1,098-square-kilometre saline Bras d'Or Lakes lie at the island's core.

Cape Breton's stark beauty appealed to Scottish Highlanders, who began to arrive after 1815. Reminded of their ancestral home, they settled in Whycocomagh, Iona, Inverness, and St. Ann's—and at Pictou, New Glasgow, and Antigonish on the mainland. Their descendants share their ancestors' love of fiddle music, storytelling, and traditional dance, and bagpipes and tartans are prominent when various communities celebrate their annual Highland Days.

Sydney, the island's largest city, is in coal-mining country. The rich bituminous coalfields of Sydney Mines, New Waterford, and Glace Bay are all nearby. The first coal mined on the continent was dug there by French troops from Louisbourg. Part of that massive bastion, razed by the British in 1760, has been painstakingly restored at Fortress of Louisbourg National Historic Park. Costumed guides give convincing portrayals of its 18th-century inhabitants, including its notoriously lax, undisciplined garrison.

For 37 years before Bell's death in 1922, Cape Breton was the summer home of the inventor of the telephone. Working models, artifacts, and photographs of his experiments with aeronautics, agriculture, deafness, genetics, marine engineering, and medical science are displayed at the Alexander Graham Bell National Historic Site near *Beinn Breagh,* his Baddeck estate.

A fisherman's boat rides at anchor as the sun sets over the Bras d'Or Lakes. Formed when the sea flooded a glacier-depressed valley, the mighty lakes are actually a land-locked sea.

A sparkling stream ripples through a sheltered valley in Cape Breton Highlands National Park. Hardwood-covered slopes plunge seaward from the rugged headlands surrounding the park's central tableland of shallow bogs and taiga barrens replete with granite-clinging reindeer moss and stunted spruce and tamarack.

Ontario

*Fringing a magnificent wilderness,
great cities and fertile farms*

Even though one in three Canadians lives in Ontario, nine-tenths of the vast province is uninhabited. Most Ontarians live in the chunk of land bounded by lakes Huron, Erie, and Ontario. About 5 million people, half the province's population, are centered in the Golden Horseshoe (an area encircling Lake Ontario from St. Catharines through Hamilton and Toronto to Oshawa), which produces half Canada's manufactured goods. Another 4 million make their homes in the Garden of Ontario, the fertile fruit lands and farmland separating lakes Huron and Erie, and in the industrialized cities of London, Kitchener-Waterloo, and Windsor, Canada's southernmost city.

With only 1 million people — one-third in Thunder Bay, Sudbury, Sault Ste. Marie, North Bay, and Timmins — Northern Ontario by comparison is almost empty. The region is Canada's largest producer of gold (found at Kirkland Lake, Timmins, and Porcupine) and an important source of nickel and copper (found at Sudbury).

Many northern towns have excellent fishing and hunting. The annual bear hunt is a spring highlight at Chapleau, a picturesque logging town. Hunting is prohibited, however, in the 7,000-square-kilometre Chapleau Crown Game Preserve nearby. Firearms, traps, and even slingshots are banned in the preserve, the largest in the Americas.

THE FIRST INLAND SETTLEMENT

Toronto, the provincial capital, is Canada's largest city. The commercial and industrial

*A full moon rides high over Manitouwabing Lake,
nestled amid pines and granite of the Muskoka area.*

Farm buildings snugly blanketed in snow are part of the winter landscape along Ontario's quiet rural roads. This farmhouse is near Newmarket (pop. 45,474), a growing community north of Toronto that began as a "new market" for aboriginal people, settlers, and fur traders.

Museum), Canada's Sports Hall of Fame, the Hockey Hall of Fame, the Ontario Science Centre, and the entertainment complex Ontario Place are just a fraction of its cultural and recreational assets.

Graceful architecture, including the gothic, stone Parliament Buildings, fine museums, tree-lined streets, flower gardens, and parklands set an elegant tone in Ottawa, the national capital. Until chosen for the honor in 1867, Ottawa (Bytown as it was then) was a center of the lumbering industry that flourished in the plains between the Ottawa and the St. Lawrence rivers. Today government is the chief employer.

The first European to tread the soil of what is now Ontario and see the sites where these cities stand was Étienne Brûlé, Champlain's rascally agent in the wilderness. Some years later, in 1615, Brûlé accompanied Samuel de Champlain up the Ottawa River, across Lake Nipissing, and down the French River into Lake Huron and Georgian Bay. At the Huron village of Carhagouha (present-day Lafontaine, a tiny community west of Midland), Champlain assisted a Recollet priest celebrate the first Mass in what is now Ontario, then wintered at the Huron nation's principal village of Cahiagué (present-day Warminster, southeast of Midland).

Encouraged by Champlain, Jesuit missionaries founded Sainte-Marie among the Hurons — Canada's first inland settlement (1634) — at what is now Midland. Before its destruction in 1649, North America's eight martyr saints served at Sainte-Marie. Of the five who died there, only Jean de Brébeuf, Canada's patron saint, is buried at the site. A re-creation of the palisaded mission contains 22 buildings — residences, stables, a forge, workshops, a church, a hospital and a pharmacy — staffed by costumed guides.

Boat cruises out of Midland follow the route taken by Brûlé and Champlain through a maze of narrow channels past the Thirty Thousand Islands. Some islands are nothing more than bare granite boulders. Others are topped with clusters of juniper, bearberry, and twisted white pine — images that inspired several Group of Seven artists. Fifty-

heart of the province, it encompasses various ethnic neighborhoods: Chinatown, Little Italy, and Greek and Portuguese communities. Its landmarks include the 553-metre CN Tower and the SkyDome Stadium, home of professional baseball and football. With 100 professional companies mounting performances, Toronto has almost as much live theater as London and New York. Canada's largest public museum (Royal Ontario

Twice a year, in late March and again in late October and November, thousands of migrating ducks and geese pause to rest and feed at Jack Miner Bird Sanctuary near Kingsville. Established in 1904, the sanctuary is one of North America's oldest refuges for migrating birds.

A CANOPY OF TREES FROM THE DEEP SOUTH

Point Pelee National Park boasts a forest like no other in Canada — a rare patch of Carolinian hardwood trees from the Deep South. Typically, Carolinian forests have tall, high-crowned trees. Their canopies arch into cathedral-like domes, which let in sun and rain.

Not long ago, such forests thrived in southern Ontario, but most were destroyed when settlers converted the land to agricultural use. The few remaining patches are found along the Erie shoreline and throughout the Niagara Peninsula — at Rondeau, Backus Woods, Catfish Creek, and Springwater Woods. But only Point Pelee offers an entire ecosystem at

work: a place where such rarities as the black gum, hop tree, and honey locust coexist with prickly pears and singing Carolina wrens.

Point Pelee, at the same latitude as northern California and Spain's Costa Brava, has one of the warmest climates in Canada. Tree branches in the national park hang heavy with Virginia creeper and wild grapevines. Sassafras, sycamore, hackberry, blue ash, and black walnut are at their northernmost range in the park, which contains stands of basswoods, Kentucky coffees, oaks, red ashes, silver maples, flowering dogwoods, and yellow-flowering tulip trees.

White limestone cliffs tower above boulder and cobblestone beaches and Georgian Bay's turquoise waters in Bruce Peninsula National Park near Tobermory. The park encompasses such diverse habitats as cedar swamps, sand dunes, and rocky barrens noted for their abundant crops of orchids and other wildflowers.

nine of the Thirty Thousand Islands are in Georgian Bay Islands National Park, which has more amphibians and reptiles than any other Canadian national park.

Some 25 ships have foundered on Georgian Bay's treacherous shoals, most in an area now bounded by Fathom Five National Marine Park. This scuba divers' mecca sits off the cedar- and birch-cloaked Bruce Peninsula separating Lake Huron from Georgian Bay. The adjoining Bruce Peninsula National Park encompasses some 270 square kilometres of the last unspoiled areas of southwestern Ontario and the most scenic parts of the Niagara Escarpment, the limestone spine extending from Tobermory to the Niagara River. The park's Lake Huron shoreline is characterized by marshlands and sandy beaches; its eastern boundary by dramatic

white cliffs, rocky headlands, and awesome boulder beaches. One of North America's great hiking trails, the 720-kilometre Bruce Trail, traverses all of these habitats on its way from Tobermory south to Queenston.

LOYALISTS LED THE WAY

There were only scattered trading settlements throughout what is now southern Ontario until colonists loyal to Britain fled north at the end of the American War of Independence. After 1784, more than 10,000 of these United Empire Loyalists settled in the Belleville/Kingston area. Some of the fine old homes they built there still stand in picturesque communities such as Bath, Picton, and Adolphustown, where a Loyalist museum displays quilts, butter churns, and china tea sets they used.

Some 80 percent of Canada's wine-making grapes come from the Niagara Peninsula, where numerous wineries offer tours and tastings.

WILD ORCHIDS ON A LIMESTONE PENINSULA

More than 40 orchid species — the largest concentration north of Florida — flourish on the northern tip of the Bruce Peninsula in Georgian Bay. The environment needed for orchid growth occurs when rainwater erodes the soft limestone of the peninsula, then collects into pools, when it cannot penetrate the harder dolomite layer underlying the limestone. Over time, minute particles of limestone settle in the standing water, altering its alkalinity and creating an excellent moisturizer and fertilizer for orchid roots.

Beauties in the Dorcas Bay Nature Reserve southwest of Tobermory include the grass pink, with its radiant, fuchsia petals, and the small purple-fringed orchid. One of the rarer finds is the calypso orchid, also known as fairy slipper. Sweetly fragrant, its main petal, the "lip," is yellow and white, with pink sepals. Other lady's slippers include the showy lady's slipper, pink lady's slipper, and ram's-head lady's slipper. These moccasin-shaped flowers grow 30 to 60 centimetres tall.

The lady's slippers and many of the showiest orchids rely solely on their beauty — their color and scent — to reproduce. The flowers contain no nectar with which to entice pollinating bees, wasps, or flies. Methods of pollination vary, but each species employs ingenious strategies to complete the task and ensure survival. Even then, some orchids may take up to 16 years to flower.

Other Loyalists settled along the Niagara River, which separates Canada from the United States, clearing away forests of white pine, birch, poplar, maple, and oak. Except for some patches of Carolinian forest left around Lake Erie, they also destroyed most of the rarer Kentucky coffee trees, sassafras, and magnolias. But in return, farms flourished in the area. The Niagara Peninsula is now a major fruitbelt, growing apples, peaches, plums, and grapes.

The War of 1812 brought more settlers, Scots and English soldiers and German mercenaries who decided to stay. Later the Irish poured in and waves of immigration continued throughout the 19th century — Eastern Europeans, Chinese, Italians, runaway slaves in the 1840's-1860's — through the Underground Railroad, which had terminals at Windsor, Niagara-on-the-Lake, and Dresden, where Uncle Tom's Cabin Historic Site is preserved — and Asian and southern European immigrants post-war.

AT THE WILDERNESS EDGE

Cottage country characterizes the Bruce Peninsula and the shorelines of the Muskoka Lakes, Lake of Bays, Kawartha Lakes, and Georgian Bay. All are at the edge of the Canadian Shield — a rugged canvas of green forests, white, quartzite hills, and twisted, Precambrian granite boulders that claims two-thirds of the province. Describing the rugged shores and windswept white pines of this landscape, A. Y. Jackson of the Group of Seven wrote: "I know of no more impressive scenery."

Several national parks and many of the province's 260 provincial parks safeguard this wilderness. Rounded, white quartzite hills, all that remains of the ancient La Cloche Mountains, frame stands of birch and pine at Killarney Provincial Park, a wilderness park on Georgian Bay's north shore. Archaeologists have uncovered evidence that the Plano People, northern Ontario's first inhabitants, camped in the area 9,000 years ago. Group of Seven artists Jackson, Arthur Lismer, Frank Carmichael, and A. J. Casson all painted in Killarney.

Superb canoeing is all but guaranteed on Ontario lakes such as this one bounded by yellow and orange streaked rock in Killarney Provincial Park.

Another renowned artist, Tom Thomson, was a summer fixture in Algonquin, the province's oldest and largest reserve, where he drowned in 1917. Algonquin, located between Ottawa and Sudbury, encompasses 7,600 square kilometres of such classic Shield elements as loon-frequented lakes, spruce bogs, and maple-covered granite hills. Moose, white-tailed deer, and black bears are readily spotted from trails and canoe routes.

Spruce and jack pine on the northern shores of Lake Superior mark the start of Ontario's boreal forest. At Pukaskwa National Park, an 1,878-square-kilometre expanse of rugged wilderness, boulder-strewn coves recall the billion-year-old volcanoes which shaped its shores. The Pukaskwa Pits, a sacred site of about 100 circular stone structures built by prehistoric Indians, are among the park's treasures.

In addition to supporting extensive dairy and livestock herds, southern Ontario farms produce a wide variety of mixed grain, corn, tobacco, soybean, fruit, and vegetable crops.

Spectacular rock formations, including the most dramatic heights and lookouts in the province, are found near Thunder Bay, the largest grain handling port in the world and Canada's third largest port. At nearby Sleeping Giant Provincial Park, a peninsula jutting into Lake Superior, four 244-metre-high mesas are said to be the reclining figure of the legendary Ojibwa giant, Nanibijou. Fragrant ferns are among several fern species in this park, which also has 24 species of orchid.

Quetico Provincial Park west of Thunder Bay is a canoeist's paradise. Barred owls, timber wolves, red squirrels, and lynx make their home there year-round. Only a few marked trails slice through this primeval wilderness, where Stone Age nomads hunted and fished 9,000 years ago.

The clay belts of the Rainy River valley support a rare stretch of northern farmland, with small farming towns at Rainy River (a border crossing point from Baudette, Minn.), Emo, Barwick, and Pinewood.

Nearby are the scenic bays and coves of the Lake of the Woods, Ontario's second-largest inland lake (after Lake Nipigon). From its reedy shores, flocks of pelicans fish for muskellunge, northern pike, and the magnificent walleye for which the area is renowned. Northern spruces, southern hardwoods, and Manitoba maples compete for space in Lake of the Woods Provincial Park, a peninsula in the lake. The park marks a transition zone for three distinct environments — northern, southern, and prairie. Kenora, a bustling, picturesque, pulp and paper town and outfitting center on the lake's north end, hosts a spectacular, international, seven-day, 14,500-island cruise and race each August.

THE FAR NORTH

Lumbering communities and small mining towns, such as Kirkland Lake and Cobalt — where the world's richest vein of silver was discovered in 1903 — dot the rocky, poorly drained hinterlands. Caribou, moose, and black bears graze on lichen-draped jack pine and spruce in Woodland Caribou Provincial

A visitor to Ouimet Canyon stands atop one of the mesas overlooking the 150-metre wide, 100-metre deep sunless chasm where subarctic plants cling to mossy crevices.

THE BEAUTY AND SPLENDOR OF NORTH AMERICA

Warmed by summer's sun, the tundra near Hudson Bay blooms briefly. This pond is on the Brant River in subarctic Polar Bear Provincial Park.

Park, a massive wilderness preserve on the Berens River plateau near Manitoba.

Civilization has barely touched the province's most northerly park, Polar Bear Provincial Park, at the mouth of the Winisk River. Seals, walruses, belugas, and white whales frequent coastal areas of the park, a November highway for up to 200 polar bears. At 24,087 square kilometres, the park is almost as large as the southern Ontario peninsula where 10 million people live. It connects with the Winisk River Provincial Waterway Park: mighty area rivers such as the Winisk, Albany, Ekwan, Attawapiskat, and Severn are among the world's longest waterways and, to novelist Hugh MacLennan, "the loneliest in the world."

Blessed with these and countless other waterways, with some 250,000 lakes including the Great Lakes, with Niagara's Horseshoe Falls on its southern boundary, and with James and Hudson bays framing it to the north, the province would indeed seem aptly named: Ontario is said to be derived from an Iroquoian term for "sparkling water."

A polar bear flounders in "The Great Swamp" adjoining James Bay. The swamp consists of thousands of square kilometres of green soupy bog that is treacherous except when frozen.

Prince Edward Island

In the "Garden of the Gulf," sandy beaches and red clay cliffs

White sand beaches and red clay cliffs hug the shores of Canada's smallest (224 kilometres long, 64 kilometres wide) and only island province. A 1,900-kilometre coastline separates the bounty of the ocean from the rich harvest of the interior. The sea teems with lobster, beds at Malpeque Bay yield 10 million oysters a year, and millions of kilograms of mussels cultured in island bays and inlets are sold worldwide. The red soil of the island — affectionately dubbed "Canada's Million-Acre Farm" — produces 32 varieties of its most famous export, the potato, and fields of blueberries, cranberries, raspberries, strawberries, and grain.

The island has three outstanding coastal drives — the Lady Slipper, which skirts the western region's secluded beaches and a 120-year-old operating lighthouse and guesthouse (at West Point); the Blue Heron, which explores *Anne of Green Gables* country and Prince Edward Island National Park; and the Kings Byway, where numerous lighthouses guard the heavily indented eastern coastline, and attractions, such as the Basin Head Fisheries Museum east of Souris, illustrate methods and materials of the inshore fishery.

CRADLED ON THE WAVES

To the Mi'kmaq Indians, who have lived there for 2,000 years, the island was *Abegweit* — "Land Cradled on the Waves." Jacques Car-

Marram grass-battened sand dunes and rolling farmland — green or gold according to the crop and the season — lapped by deep-blue waters are typical island vistas.

A full moon adds an eerie glow to the gleam from the Covehead lighthouse at the eastern section of Prince Edward Island National Park.

tier, on his 1534 voyage, called it ". . . the fairest land 'tis possible to see." Settlement, begun by Acadians in 1720, expanded in the 1780's when Loyalists fled the U.S.A. following the Revolutionary War. There was an influx of first Scots, then Irish, in the 1800's, all pinning their dreams of prosperity on the island's fertile soil. The 19th century was also the era of wooden ships, and island shipyards flourished. Some 3,100 vessels were built between 1840 and 1890 alone. Today, Green Park Provincial Park commemorates the glory days of shipbuilding.

A Charlottetown conference in 1864 was pivotal to the Confederation of 1867. Prince Edward Island, however, did not join until 1873, when its economy was faltering from railway debts, coupled with the disappearance of wooden ships.

Fox farming took off in the 1890's and was a major industry for decades. In its 1920's heyday, a pair of silver foxes sold for $35,000. The full story of fox farming is recounted in the International Fox Hall of Fame and Museum in Summerside, the island's second largest community.

Since the fox fur business declined in the 1930's, Islanders have relied on agriculture, fishing, and ever-burgeoning tourism. To its thousands of visitors, the island's absence of crowds, picturesque farming and fishing villages, gently rolling fields, ever-present wildflowers, and sheltered bays represent a kind of paradise.

No point on the island is more than 16 kilometres from the ocean. There are almost 800 kilometres of smooth beaches, and an ocean temperature of up to 21°C. Some of Canada's finest saltwater beaches are in the national park, which is also renowned for its dunes, red sandstone cliffs, salt marshes, and freshwater ponds. The great blue heron and the endangered piping plover, two of 315 species of bird on the island, nest there.

Courtesy comes naturally to Islanders, just as hospitality comes straight from their hearts. The island ambience is friendly, relaxed, unspoiled. With a population of just over 33,000, even Charlottetown, its largest and only city, has a small town air.

Water grinding into the underlying red sandstone has produced these irregular cliffs and overhanging rocks in the Cavendish area of Prince Edward Island National Park.

LAND OF AVONLEA

The central north shore was the inspiration for Avonlea in Lucy Maud Montgomery's books. The creator of Anne Shirley — *Anne of Green Gables*, arguably Canada's most famous fictional character — was raised in Cavendish, where Parks Canada has furnished the original Green Gables as it would have been in Anne's day (the late 1800's).

Apple blossom wallpaper and a puffed-sleeve dress adorn "Anne's bedroom." The Haunted Wood, Babbling Brook, Lovers' Lane, and other scenes from the book are nearby. Lucy Maud is buried in Cavendish cemetery.

Because Islanders still relish the gentle, unhurried, unpretentious way of life Montgomery described, they long rejected a fixed link to the mainland. Now that they have finally relented, they hope the $850 million toll bridge that will link Borden to Cape Tormentine, N.B., by 1998 will rejuvenate the economy.

Islanders joke that their province — the world's second largest producer (after Holland) of seed potatoes — consists of two beaches with a potato field in between.

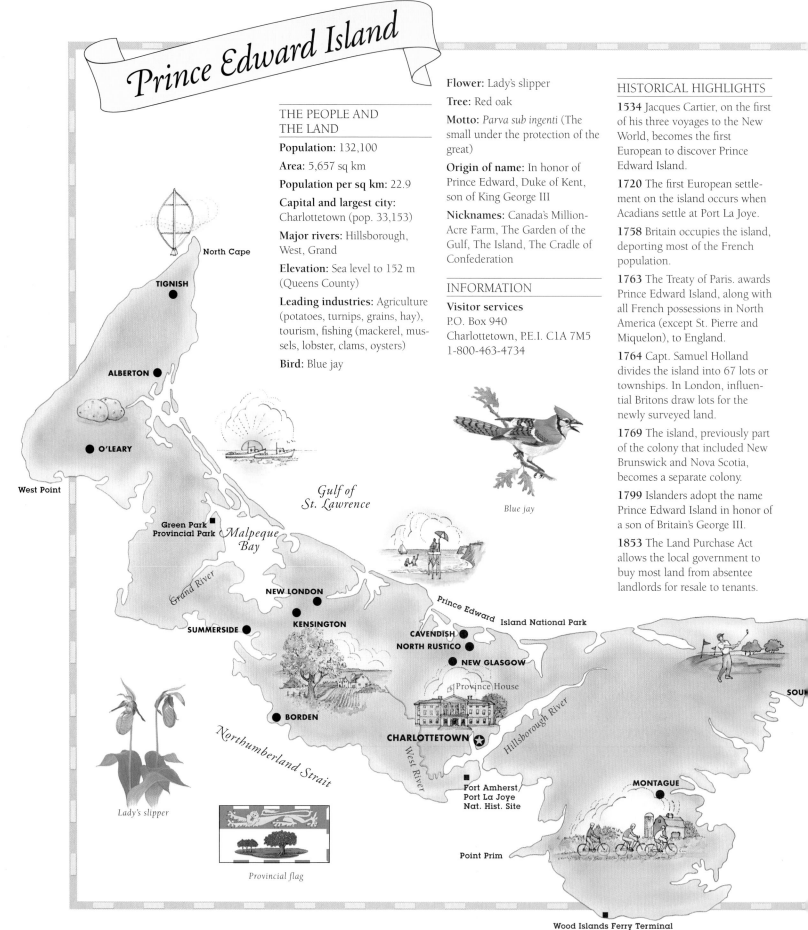

Prince Edward Island

THE PEOPLE AND THE LAND

Population: 132,100

Area: 5,657 sq km

Population per sq km: 22.9

Capital and largest city: Charlottetown (pop. 33,153)

Major rivers: Hillsborough, West, Grand

Elevation: Sea level to 152 m (Queens County)

Leading industries: Agriculture (potatoes, turnips, grains, hay), tourism, fishing (mackerel, mussels, lobster, clams, oysters)

Bird: Blue jay

Flower: Lady's slipper

Tree: Red oak

Motto: *Parva sub ingenti* (The small under the protection of the great)

Origin of name: In honor of Prince Edward, Duke of Kent, son of King George III

Nicknames: Canada's Million-Acre Farm, The Garden of the Gulf, The Island, The Cradle of Confederation

INFORMATION

Visitor services
P.O. Box 940
Charlottetown, P.E.I. C1A 7M5
1-800-463-4734

HISTORICAL HIGHLIGHTS

1534 Jacques Cartier, on the first of his three voyages to the New World, becomes the first European to discover Prince Edward Island.

1720 The first European settlement on the island occurs when Acadians settle at Port La Joye.

1758 Britain occupies the island, deporting most of the French population.

1763 The Treaty of Paris. awards Prince Edward Island, along with all French possessions in North America (except St. Pierre and Miquelon), to England.

1764 Capt. Samuel Holland divides the island into 67 lots or townships. In London, influential Britons draw lots for the newly surveyed land.

1769 The island, previously part of the colony that included New Brunswick and Nova Scotia, becomes a separate colony.

1799 Islanders adopt the name Prince Edward Island in honor of a son of Britain's George III.

1853 The Land Purchase Act allows the local government to buy most land from absentee landlords for resale to tenants.

North Cape

TIGNISH

ALBERTON

O'LEARY

West Point

Green Park Provincial Park

Malpeque Bay

Grand River

Gulf of St. Lawrence

Blue jay

SUMMERSIDE

NEW LONDON

KENSINGTON

BORDEN

Northumberland Strait

Lady's slipper

Provincial flag

Prince Edward Island National Park

CAVENDISH

NORTH RUSTICO

NEW GLASGOW

Province House

CHARLOTTETOWN

West River

Hillsborough River

Fort Amherst/ Port La Joye Nat. Hist. Site

Point Prim

MONTAGUE

SOU

Wood Islands Ferry Terminal

1864 Prince Edward Island hosts the Charlottetown Conference.

1873 Prince Edward Island becomes our seventh province.

1908 *Anne of Green Gables* is first published.

1992 Federal and all provincial delegates to the Charlottetown Conference agree to a constitutional reform package. The accord is later rejected in a cross-country referendum.

1992 P.E.I. approves a fixed link to the mainland.

FAMOUS SONS AND DAUGHTERS

"Stompin' Tom" Connors (1935 –). Skinners Pond was the childhood home of this country guitarist, who is known for such songs as *The Hockey Game* and *Bud the Spud*.

Sir Charles Dalton (1850–1933). He established the silver fox industry at Alberton in 1894 and was lieutenant governor from 1930 to 1933.

Robert Harris (1849–1919). The Welsh-born portrait painter is renowned for *The Fathers of Confederation* (burnt in the Ottawa Parliament Building fire in 1916). Many of his works are displayed at the Confederation Centre in Charlottetown.

East Point

William Critchlow Harris (1854–1913). Architect and brother of Robert Harris (see above), his designs can be seen throughout the Maritime provinces.

Angus MacEachern (1759–1835). The first Roman Catholic bishop of Charlottetown, he founded St. Andrew's College (1831), now part of the University of Prince Edward Island.

Sir Andrew MacPhail (1864–1938). A World War I medical officer and author, MacPhail was the founding editor of the *Canadian Medical Association Journal* (1911).

Lucy Maud Montgomery

(1874–1942). Prince Edward Island's most famous writer, Montgomery penned *Anne of Green Gables* (and seven successful sequels) as well as a number of adult novels, and hundreds of short stories and poems.

James Colledge Pope (1826–85). A shipowner and three-time Premier, he led P.E.I. into Confederation in 1873.

William Henry Pope (1825–79). A lawyer, journalist, and judge, he was a passionate advocate of Confederation.

James Yeo (1789-1868). In the 1840's, Yeo was P.E.I.'s most influential businessman — involved in shipbuilding, agriculture, and fishing — and a powerful politician.

ODDITIES AND SPECIALTIES

Thousands of harp seals are born each February 27 in the Gulf of St. Lawrence off the island. The seals' biological patterns are such that all baby harps are born within 48 hours of each other.

Lobster suppers are an island tradition at St. Ann's, New Glasgow, North Rustico, and New London.

"Fox houses" is the term used to describe certain luxurious homes built in the 19th century by those who had made fortunes from the silver fox industry.

An 18-metre lighthouse at Point Prim, a narrow tip of land west of Wood Islands, is Canada's only round brick lighthouse.

Before synthetic suspension agents became commonplace, almost half the world's supply of carrageenan — an emulsifier in toothpaste, wine, cough syrup, and ice cream — came from P.E.I. Its source was Irish moss.

PLACES TO VISIT, THINGS TO DO

Annual Outdoor Scottish Fiddle and Dance Festival (Richmond). Scottish concerts, step-dancing, fiddling, piping, singing and old-time square dancing are featured at this July celebration.

Annual Show and Shine Lobster Shanty North (Montague). Street rods, antiques, and special interest cars and trucks are displayed at this July event.

Charlottetown Festival. The musical *Anne of Green Gables* is among repertory theater presentations for all ages in the Confederation Centre of the Arts from June to September.

Confederation Centre Art Gallery and Museum (Charlottetown). Located in the Confederation Centre of the Arts, it contains works by Canada's

outstanding artists. Summer exhibitions include Lucy Maud Montgomery's manuscripts and scrapbooks and Robert Harris' sketchbooks.

Fort Amherst/Port La Joye National Historical Site. (Charlottetown). Just outside Rocky Point, it marks the first European settlement on the island.

Green Gables (Cavendish). This house, the setting for the *Green Gables* and *Avonlea* stories, has been restored to the 1890's, the period of the novels.

Green Park Provincial Park. Shipbuilder James Yeo's restored mansion is the centerpiece of this park, which has a re-created shipyard and audiovisual presentations of shipbuilding history.

Lucy Maud Montgomery Birthplace (New London). The author's wedding dress and veil are among memorabilia.

Racing. Harness races are held at Charlottetown, Summerside, and other tracks throughout the island.

Victoria Playhouse Summer Festival. Professional repertory theater and concerts are presented in July and August.

Woodleigh Replicas (Kensington). Large-scale replicas of York Minster, the Tower of London, and Glamis and Dunvegan castles are among historic buildings found there.

Quebec

A walled city, picturesque resorts, and giant hydroelectric dams

Three times the size of France, Canada's biggest province is home to 90 percent of Canadians of French origin and the only predominantly French-speaking territory in North America. (The French-speaking islands Saint-Pierre and Miquelon belong to France.) Its largest city, Montreal, is the third-largest francophone city in the world (after Paris and Kinshasa, Zaire), and the University of Montreal is the largest French-language university outside Paris.

THE QUIET REVOLUTION

Modern Quebec has been shaped by the Quiet Revolution, a 1960's surge of nationalistic pride. Governments of the day offered grants to encourage artistic expression, and that climate eventually produced confident, accomplished artists, sculptors, dancers, filmmakers, mimes, writers, orchestras, and music ensembles. It was in these circles that the term "Québécois" first began to replace "French-Canadian."

It was in this climate, too, that Quebec nationalized Hydro-Québec, and began building the giant hydro-generating stations that are a source of provincial pride and revenue today. Harnessing waterpower was a natural direction for a province whose vast territory — 1.6 million square kilometres — is covered by some 400,000 lakes — many as yet unnamed — strung together by a network of mighty rivers.

The greatest of these, the St. Lawrence, winds 3,700 kilometres from Lake Ontario to

The densely forested Laurentians are renowned for a bedazzling explosion of brilliant autumn colors.

Two out of every three farms in Quebec are involved in dairying. Some of the finest dairy farms lie along the St. Lawrence River east of Montreal.

the Atlantic Ocean, fed along the way by other great rivers, such as the Ottawa, the Saint-Maurice, the Manicouagan (site of some of the most impressive dams and the massive Manicouagan Reservoir), the Saguenay, and the Richelieu. All are alive with muskellunge, bass, eel, northern pike, and speckled and gray trout.

THE ST. LAWRENCE LOWLANDS

Early settlement took place along the St. Lawrence River, the main highway of New France from 1535, when French sea captain Jacques Cartier navigated upriver to what is now Montreal. These fertile lowlands remain the agricultural heart of the province. Close to 90 percent of Quebec's population is concentrated there. Almost half live in Montreal, a cosmopolitan industrial and commercial

center and Canada's second-largest city. An extensive network of restaurant- and shop-lined walkways — a sort of underground city — connects the Métro, the city's subway system, to offices and businesses at street level. Government offices, historic buildings, antique shops, art studios, bistros, and outdoor cafés hug cobblestone streets in Old Montreal, the city's historic district. The Old Port there is now a year-round center of recreation and entertainment.

Canada's first carriageway was built in the 1730's to link Montreal to Quebec City, the province's capital and one of Canada's oldest cities. The route, known as *le Chemin du Roy* (the King's Road), follows the north shore of the St. Lawrence. Some of the inns that served as relay stations, where travelers and horses rested, can still be seen at Batiscan, Portneuf, Neuville, and other villages along the way. North of Trois-Rivières, the route offers superb riverside views. La Pérade, a pretty village at the mouth of the Rivière Sainte-Anne, a tributary of the St. Lawrence,

The walled city of Quebec sprawls atop towering Cape Diamond, overlooking the historic Lower Town and the sudden narrowing of the St. Lawrence River that gave the city its name. Quebec is from an Algonquian word for "where the river narrows."

Church spires, such as this one at Saint-Ours, near Sorel, are part of the landscape in Quebec, where the church once was the focal point of every community. Many of these churches were designed and/or decorated by the province's greatest 18th- and 19th-century artists and craftsmen.

is a popular ice fishing spot. Anglers by the thousand converge there at tommycod time each spring, fishing and socializing in the cabins cluttering the frozen Sainte-Anne.

Because most of the walls that fortified Old Quebec (one-fifth of the present-day city) remain intact, Quebec City has been called the "Gibraltar of America." In declaring the historic district a World Heritage Site, the United Nations has classed it alongside such cities as Cairo, Florence, and Carthage. Quebec, the oldest city in North America, was established by Champlain in 1608 on cliffs overlooking the St. Lawrence River. Although defense works were started that year, the present walls are British reconstructions dating from 1820–32. The fortifications enclose the winding cobblestone streets and 17th-century buildings of Upper Town (once the center of administration and defense) and Lower Town (once the center of commerce) from the newer sections of the city.

The city's architectural treasures include steep-roofed stone houses (ca. 1684), which are among North America's oldest buildings. The star-shaped Citadel, a massive, gray fortress that is both the official summer home of Canada's governor general and home of the Royal 22nd Regiment (the Van Doos), is the largest fortification in North America garrisoned by regular troops.

The province is known for its beautiful churches and such religious shrines as St. Joseph's Oratory in Montreal and the Basilica of Our Lady of the Rosary at Cap-de-la-Madeleine. More than a million pilgrims a year also visit the town of Sainte-Anne-de-Beaupré, north of Quebec City. The village's immense Romanesque basilica, the largest shrine in North America, honors Saint Anne, the mother of Mary. Reports of miraculous cures have drawn pilgrims to the site since the 1600's. Many make the pilgrimage in late July for ceremonies marking the saint's July 26 feast day.

Each autumn and spring, hundreds of thousands of snow geese feast on bulrushes growing along the St. Lawrence estuary at

Autumn works its magic along Philippe Lake in Gatineau Park, 356 square kilometres of rocky forested hills and some 50 glacier-gouged lakes between the Gatineau and Ottawa rivers.

the Cap-Tourmente National Wildlife Area north of the shrine. The sanctuary is a stopover between their breeding grounds on Baffin Island and their wintering grounds in Virginia and Northern Carolina.

THE SPLENDID LAURENTIAN PLATEAU

Softwood forests cover most of the Laurentian Plateau, the region to the north of the St. Lawrence and the Ottawa rivers. The plateau, part of the Canadian Shield, comprises more than four-fifths of the province. Moose, white-tailed deer, beaver, and black bear make their home among the balsam fir, pine, spruce, and tamarack clothing the Laurentians, gently rounded remnants of an ancient mountain range.

This terrain, once a major forestry center, has a wealth of scenic parks plus the nature and wildlife reserves (réserves fauniques) of Plaisance, Papineau-Labelle, La Vérendrye, and Rouge-Matawin. Each fall, the maple-,

ash-, birch-, and oak-cloaked hills along the Ottawa River and nearby Gatineau Park blaze with brilliant red and burnished orange foliage.

Parc du Mont-Tremblant, the province's oldest reserve, remains Quebec's most popular destination. Scores of trails crisscross its forested hills. Seven fish-rich rivers and countless streams connect its 500 lakes. At 960 metres, Mont Tremblant is the highest peak in the Laurentians. Communities such as Arundel, Sainte-Adèle, Saint-Sauveur, and Sainte-Agathe-des-Monts nestle in the mountains, their economies built on the area's downhill skiing industry.

La Mauricie National Park to the east protects a 544-square-kilometre tract of the Laurentians and is a favorite spot of campers, canoers, and sailors. The park's lakes are filled with speckled trout. In summer, red trillium, asters, and insect-devouring pitcher plants carpet the forest floor.

Chair lifts take skiers and sightseers to the top of 960-metre-high Mont Tremblant, which overlooks a network of Laurentian year-round vacation areas.

The fir-covered Chic-Chocs Mountains cut a scenic swathe through the Gaspé Peninsula, where they slide terrace by terrace into the sea at Forillon National Park. The last herd of woodland caribou on the south shore of the St. Lawrence River inhabit an 803-square-kilometre Chic-Chocs reserve, Parc de la Gaspésie.

Much of the vast remote Réserve faunique des Laurentides, a wildlife reserve, has not yet been explored. Its vast wooded uplands are home to moose, black bear, deer, and wolves. The spectacular scenery of the adjoining Charlevoix region is at its best along the rugged coastline, which has been shaped over time by earthquakes and landslides. (Les Éboulements is named for *les éboulements de terre* — the landslides, which toppled nearby mountains in 1663 and 1830.) Because a rich variety of maples, giant elms, evergreens, Arctic tundra mosses, alpine flowers, and other plants grow there, large portions of Charlevoix have been designated a United Nations World Biosphere Reserve.

Fresh and salt waters mingle near Tadoussac, where the Saguenay River ends its journey from Lac Saint-Jean — famous for its landlocked salmon and wild blueberry harvests. Marine life where the Saguenay and St. Lawrence rivers meet includes the Greenland halibut, fin and blue whales, and belugas.

A severe climate is a fact of life in Quebec's sparsely populated Far North — homeland of the Cree and the Inuit. The Ungava Peninsula is frozen to a depth of 275 metres year-round. When the top of the permafrost thaws in summer, blackberry flowers, buttercups, and violet campanulas blossom on the tundra, where growth is ordinarily limited to isolated stands of stunted alder, birch, and willow, and the patches of lichens and mosses that attract large herds of caribou, and lesser numbers of musk-oxen, arctic foxes, otters, ermines, and polar bears. Seals, walruses, belugas, and the odd narwhal, identifiable by its single ivory tusk, swim in Hudson Bay.

HOME OF THE ATLANTIC'S FIERCEST FISHER

The red cliffs of Bonaventure Island off the Gaspé Peninsula's eastern shore are home to the largest colony of northern gannets in the world. Between March and October each year, about 15,000 of the fish-eating birds gather there, their nesting sites secure from such mainland predators as foxes and raccoons.

Courtship in the gannetry is noisy. Couples often bow to each other, rear up chest to chest, and clash their long, pointed bills as though in a fencing match.

The birds mate for life and return to the same nesting site year after year. Mating pairs build sloppy nests of dried seaweed and moss to shelter their single egg, which the female lays in May or June. Males bite their mates on the neck as a sign of greeting. And before leaving the nest, a gannet signals his departure — by pointing his bill skyward. Nests are often built on cliff tops or sheer ledges — so that the gannets can leap into the air without much effort. Because of their short legs and webbed feet, they are notoriously awkward, especially on takeoff.

Gannets are one of the Atlantic's fiercest fishers. In winter, they range from Massachusetts to Florida and the Gulf of Mexico. Dazzling in their white plumage, and supported by a 1.5-metre wingspan, they soar aloft on the lookout for schools of herring, mackerel, and capelin. When prey is spotted, they plunge seaward at speeds of up to 100 kilometres an hour. Impact is cushioned by a reinforced skull and air sacs in the neck and breast.

COVERED BRIDGES AND PEBBLE BEACHES

A succession of small mountains south of the St. Lawrence are remnants of an old mountain chain that extended from the Gaspé Peninsula south to the United States. Such scenic ski hills as mounts Orford, Sutton, and Bromont in the Eastern Townships (the region bounded by the St. Lawrence, Richelieu, and Chaudière rivers and the U.S. border) are part of these Appalachian uplands.

Many United Empire Loyalists settled in the Townships after the American Revolution, founding towns reminiscent of those they had fled in neighboring New England. Covered bridges, period homes, white church steeples, and flourishing dairy farms are part of the scenery around Hemmingford, Cowansville, Granby, and North Hatley. Tucked in the surrounding wooded hills are sugar shacks, where sap, tapped from the trees, is converted to maple syrup. Each spring there are visits to rustic *cabanes à sucre* for maple treats, a hearty meal, and dancing.

The Chic-Chocs Mountains form the backbone of the Gaspé Peninsula. Forests of black spruce, white birch, and balsam fir cling to the slopes of their highest peak, Mount Jacques-Cartier, in Gaspé Park. Above

The cove-indented, pebbly southern shore of Forillon National Park has been a fisheries site since the 17th century. Most of the early families came from the Channel Islands, but there were also some French Canadians, Irish, and Scots. The "Gaspé cure," a method of wind drying and salting fish, was famous internationally for its mild flavor. The museum (right) occupies the restored Anse-Blanchette home of one of the families here in the 1920's.

HAUNTING SCULPTURES AND RARE PLANTS

Centuries of wind and sea have carved the limestone islands of Mingan Archipelago National Park Reserve into haunting shapes — gargoyles, grooved cliffs, and solitary flowerpots. The 43 islands are scattered like pebbles along some 80 kilometres of the St. Lawrence River's north shore. Calcium and magnesium from the limestone have also created soil conditions conducive to the growth of many rare plants. Most of these are found along the shore, where they benefit from bright sunlight and occasional exposure to sodium-rich sea spray. The Greenland primrose, an arctic plant, and the red-leaved herb Robert, a southern species, are among the shore plants. Each July, the herb Robert's pink flower emerges briefly — it often blossoms and withers in the same day.

Some plants, such as limestone polypody and the Laurentian dandelion, a distant relative of the lawn weed, take root on steep slopes, between rocks, in fissures, and on damp ledges.

There are moorland and bog habitats, too. Mingan's moorland is a vast expanse of pebbled shore dominated by lichens and creeping shrubs and dwarfed and slanted trees that resemble bonsai. Arctic plants are at their southernmost range here. One such oddity, the alpine mouse-ear chickweed, flowers in June.

Moss, grasses, rushes and sedges thrive in the calcium-rich boggy areas, where water tends to stagnate. One of the plants found there is the broad-lipped twayblade, an orchid common to North America, but a find this far north.

the tree line, short-leaf willows cling to rocky terrain which shelters Virginia deer, moose, and even woodland caribou at their southernmost range.

Fishing village followed by fishing village make stretches of the 800-kilometre peninsula-encircling Gaspé Trail look like one long main street. Pebbled beaches lead to waters rich with shrimp, lobster, snow crab, and mackerel. Fishing for Atlantic salmon is a lazy pastime on the winding Matapédia, Bonaventure, and Cascapédia rivers.

Kittiwakes, herring gulls, and black guillemots can be seen darting and swooping near the cliffside nests, and gray harbor seals, and finback, minke and humpback whales dwell in the surrounding waters.

The town of Gaspé sits at the peninsula's tip: the name comes from *gaspeg*, an Indian word for land's end. Jacques Cartier sailed two ships into this natural harbor on July 24, 1534, erected a cross, and claimed the land for France. Percé Rock, Quebec's most famous landmark and one of Canada's most recognized natural attractions, is in the town of Percé. Artists and writers have long been fascinated by the sea-pierced, multicolored limestone mass, 475 metres long and 88 metres high, which attracts visitors from around the world.

At low tide, Gaspé visitors can walk to 438-metre-long, 88-metre-high fossil-rich Percé Rock, one of Canada's most recognized natural attractions.

Saskatchewan

Prairie, badlands, Mounties, and a majestic north

When people think of the Prairies, southern Saskatchewan is what they often see in their mind's eye. Its grain-covered plains ripple with many-colored harvests — green spring wheat ripening to autumn's gold; blue-petaled flax; bright yellow mustard and canola; magical sunsets streaked in brilliant purple, orange, and red.

As far as the eye can see in these southern regions of the province, great blue skies blend into horizons stretching to infinity. Here and there, a grain elevator silhouette breaks the skyline. Flocks of Canada geese and wild ducks soar above the grainfields, much as they did when bison roamed the plains. Ground squirrels, better known as prairie gophers, head for their burrows at the first sign of rain, and jackrabbits doze where tall green grasses shelter red prairie lilies and yellow honeysuckle.

BREADBASKET TO THE WORLD

This is the land Capt. John Palliser dismissed in 1859 as too arid ever to be farmed. The English explorer had not reckoned with later methods of irrigation and transportation, nor with the spirit of the settlers to come. And he could not conceive, as author Mary Hiemstra would a century later, "what an instrument of change a plough is."

By the turn of the century, homesteaders had turned the treeless grasslands into one big grainfield. Lured by posters proclaiming "Free homes for millions," they had poured in from Ontario, the Maritimes, the United

An overlook in the Cypress Hills reveals grass-covered, forest-streaked ridges undulating to ranchland beyond.

Trembling aspen borders the Spruce River Highlands Trail in Prince Albert National Park. The park has several distinctive forests, and trails are designed to let hikers sample this forest mosaic.

Transparent wings extended straight out from its body, a dragonfly drinks in the Big Muddy Badlands' morning dew.

States, and congested cities and lonely countrysides from Scotland to the Ukraine, having ridden west on the new transcontinental railway.

But the land did not give up its riches easily. The newcomers had to battle Saskatchewan's scorching summer heat, its grass fires, thunderstorms, hail, grasshopper plagues, flies, mosquitoes, and even the occasional tornado. Winter's assault was often brutal, heaping roof-high snowdrifts around their rough sod homes.

The rich prairie soil, however, provided more than adequate recompense, and the immigrants persevered. Today, Saskatchewan produces 54 percent of Canada's wheat, most of its rapeseed and rye, large quantities of barley, oats, and flax, and such specialty crops as lentils, peas, mustard, canary seed, sunflowers, faba beans, buckwheat, and triticale — a rye and wheat hybrid.

Although the province's economy is built on agriculture, there are mineral riches too. Towns with names like Eldorado and Uranium City betray their roots in the pursuit of precious resources. The world's largest exporter of uranium, Saskatchewan is also Canada's second-largest producer of crude oil. Swift Current, Lloydminster, and Este-

van are major oil exploration bases. Estevan is known both as Saskatchewan's "energy capital" (for the oil, natural gas, and coal deposits nearby) and as the "sunshine capital" of Canada (it averages more sunshine — 2,540 hours a year — than any other Canadian city). Some 40 percent of the world's potash reserves are found near Esterhazy. There is gold north of La Ronge, and gold, silver, copper, and zinc where Flin Flon straddles the Manitoba border.

BETWEEN TWO WORLDS

Provincially owned commercial forests extending across central Saskatchewan separate the farmland of the south from the other Saskatchewan, the land of the Canadian Shield. Prince Albert is both a center of this forest industry and a gateway to the

northern regions. This scenic city on the North Saskatchewan River lays claim to three prime ministers: its members of Parliament have included Sir Wilfrid Laurier, William Lyon Mackenzie King, and John Diefenbaker, whose home here is open to the public.

Prince Albert National Park, some 90 kilometres north of the city, straddles the divide between quarter sections and combines, traplines and timber. Wildlife in this 3,875-square-kilometre wilderness, the province's largest park, reflects the changing vegetation. Bison graze in the fescue grasslands of the southwest; badger, deer, and elk are found in the central aspen parklands; and caribou, moose, deer, and wolves roam the park's northern boreal forests. Bald eagles, loons, and white pelicans frequent the park's many lakes. Conservationist and writer Grey Owl

lived his last seven years in this park. A hiking trail leads to his Lake Ajawaan cabin and nearby grave.

Northern Saskatchewan has some 100,000 lakes and more than 300,000 square kilometres of forests. The Churchill River system contains a necklace of clear blue lakes, with names like Wapawekka, Peter Pond, and Trade. Wild, swift-flowing rivers entice weekend river runners and sport fishermen.

The mixed wood forests contain mostly trembling aspen, white spruce, and jack pine, with tamarack and balsam poplar in the lower areas. Muskrat, porcupine, and beaver hold sway here. Farther north, accessible only by air, a wilderness of muskeg, swamp, fish-rich rivers, and north country fishing lodges beckon only the hardiest adventurers.

Brightly painted, wooden grain elevators, like these south of Webb, gave prairie towns their distinctive skylines. Soon, however, they may be a thing of the past. In larger centers especially, they are being replaced by massive, high-output concrete models.

Yukon

Gold rush relics in a wildlife wonderland

The Klondike Gold Rush gave Yukon a history of intrepid prospectors, overnight millionaires, derring-do Mounties, and dance-hall queens. Nature on the other hand endowed the territory with an enduring cast of characters no less fascinating — Dall sheep browsing in alpine meadows; grizzly bears foraging river flats; and golden eagles spreading two-metre wingspans high among the mountains.

Numerous mountain chains run northwest to southeast across the Yukon, an area larger than France. In the south, glacial lakes sparkle among well-forested mountain valleys. In the north, the treeless arctic coastal plain slopes gently to the Beaufort Sea. A high interior plateau is cut by the mighty Yukon River down which 19th-century explorers, fur traders, and missionaries canoed.

By the late 1800's wood-powered stern-wheelers were plying the waterway, ferrying gold-hungry passengers north to Dawson City. Miles Canyon, which claimed many gold seekers, is now tamed and a tourist attraction of Whitehorse, home to 23,000 of the territory's 32,000 population.

THE CITY OF GOLD

Before George Carmack, Skookum Jim, and Tagish Charlie struck gold at Rabbit (later named Bonanza) Creek in 1896, there was little more than a miner's camp where the Yukon meets the Klondike. But by 1898, Dawson City had 30,000 people and enough saloons, casinos, and dance halls to sate the

The 165,000-strong Porcupine caribou herd nurtures its Alaskan-born calves in Ivvavik National Park.

appetites of the newly rich. For all who struck gold, however, far more declared defeat. Many never made it over the treacherous mountain passes and river rapids. Others were too late: the land that would yield more than $100 million in gold between 1896 and 1904 had already been staked.

Placer mining, a water sluicing method reminiscent of early panning, continues near Dawson City, where visitors mine the rich history preserved in wooden boardwalks and restored frontier buildings. Some retrace the Trail of '98, following the Klondike Highway 720 kilometres from Skagway, Alaska. Near Whitehorse, it skirts Lake Laberge, immortalized by Robert Service's *The Cremation of Sam McGee*. From Dawson City, the Top of the World Highway leads into Alaska and the 740-kilometre Dempster Highway crosses the Arctic Circle to Inuvik, N.W.T.

KLUANE AND IVVAVIK

The Alaska Highway travels 1,000 kilometres through the Yukon before entering Alaska. For one-tenth of the way, it skirts Kluane (pronounced kloo-wah-nee), a United Nations World Heritage site and one of Yukon's three national parks. Most of the way, rugged peaks form a mighty wall that hides the park's green valleys and plateaus where wolves and grizzlies roam. At Kath-

leen Lake and Sheep Mountain travelers glimpse a tiny smidgen of what Canada's second-largest park (after Wood Buffalo) has to offer: sparkling, turquoise water; wheeling gulls; and, through a telescopic lens, a view of Dall sheep grazing by the Slims River.

The great massifs of the St. Elias Mountains have kept Kluane locked in the grip of an ice age. A never-ending winter surrounds their Icefield ranges, which include 5,959-metre Mount Logan and 5,488-metre Mount St. Elias. In fact the St. Elias Mountains have North America's largest concentration of peaks above 4,420 metres. Some 2,000 glaciers, including the 112-kilometre Hubbard and the 72-kilometre Lowell, fill the valleys between. Altogether, the St. Elias region is the largest nonpolar ice mass on earth — an ice age landscape that survives because of its high mountains, northern location, and close proximity to Pacific moisture.

The lure of gold drew thousands in short-lived rushes from one creek to another before and after the turn of the century. The booms gave rise to communities of sod-and-log cabins with big hopes and big names, among them Silver City and Bullion City. But Kluane goldfields produced no Klondike.

Ivvavik ("the birthing place") straddles the Yukon's northern outreach to the Beaufort Sea and contains some of the territory's most

Flights over Kluane National Park Reserve afford glimpses of otherwise inaccessible areas. These "flightseers" enjoy an unobstructed view of Mount Logan, Canada's highest peak.

spectacular wildlife. In summer, shy, graceful Porcupine caribou share their cotton grass and dwarf-willow surroundings with a great variety of nesting waterfowl, including arctic tern, arctic loon, and whistling swans. Magnificent birds of prey such as gyrfalcons, peregrines, and golden eagles nest in the park's open areas as well as in the British Mountains.

People may have lived in this region throughout the last ice age. Much of what is now parkland was then part of the great Beringian Refugium, an arctic desert bordered by massive glaciers. This ice-free ground preserved many of our northern wildlife species, as well as the remnants of ancient cultures. Engigstciak, a bedrock outcropping on the plains near the Firth River delta, is a prime example. A natural site for Indian and Inuit hunters, its surrounding soils have preserved not only remnants of their nine successive cultures, but also the bones of animals such as wapiti, horse, bison, and some now extinct mammals that were hunted by early inhabitants.

The park also contains a particularly rich assemblage of plant species. The tundra teems with tiny flowers, and forests of white spruce and aspen that are characteristic of the taiga extend along river valleys toward the arctic coast.

The lacelike rocks and pinnacle formations of the Tombstone Range of the massive Ogilvie Mountains are reflected in Talus Lake, just off the Dempster Highway.

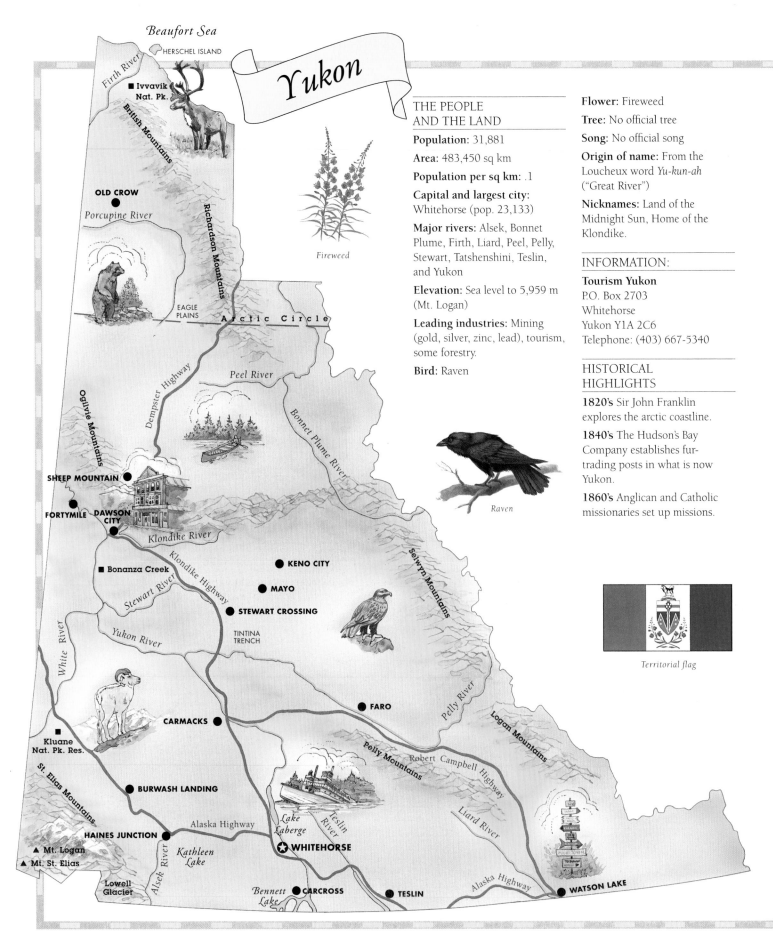

Yukon

THE PEOPLE AND THE LAND

Population: 31,881

Area: 483,450 sq km

Population per sq km: .1

Capital and largest city: Whitehorse (pop. 23,133)

Major rivers: Alsek, Bonnet Plume, Firth, Liard, Peel, Pelly, Stewart, Tatshenshini, Teslin, and Yukon

Elevation: Sea level to 5,959 m (Mt. Logan)

Leading industries: Mining (gold, silver, zinc, lead), tourism, some forestry.

Bird: Raven

Flower: Fireweed

Tree: No official tree

Song: No official song

Origin of name: From the Loucheux word *Yu-kun-ah* ("Great River")

Nicknames: Land of the Midnight Sun, Home of the Klondike.

INFORMATION:

Tourism Yukon
P.O. Box 2703
Whitehorse
Yukon Y1A 2C6
Telephone: (403) 667-5340

HISTORICAL HIGHLIGHTS

1820's Sir John Franklin explores the arctic coastline.

1840's The Hudson's Bay Company establishes fur-trading posts in what is now Yukon.

1860's Anglican and Catholic missionaries set up missions.

Fireweed

Raven

Territorial flag

Map labels

Beaufort Sea
HERSCHEL ISLAND
Firth River
■ Ivvavik Nat. Pk.
British Mountains
OLD CROW ●
Porcupine River
Richardson Mountains
EAGLE PLAINS
Arctic Circle
Dempster Highway
Peel River
Ogilvie Mountains
Bonnet Plume River
SHEEP MOUNTAIN ●
FORTYMILE ●
DAWSON CITY ●
Klondike River
■ Bonanza Creek
Stewart River
Klondike Highway
● KENO CITY
● MAYO
● STEWART CROSSING
Selwyn Mountains
White River
Yukon River
TINTINA TRENCH
■ Kluane Nat. Pk. Res.
● FARO
CARMACKS ●
Pelly River
Logan Mountains
St. Elias Mountains
● BURWASH LANDING
Pelly Mountains
Robert Campbell Highway
Alaska Highway
Lake Laberge
Teslin River
Liard River
▲ Mt. Logan
▲ Mt. St. Elias
HAINES JUNCTION ●
Kathleen Lake
Alsek River
★ WHITEHORSE
Lowell Glacier
Bennett Lake
● CARCROSS
● TESLIN
Alaska Highway
● WATSON LAKE

1894 Insp. Charles Constantine of the North West Mounted Police (precursor of the Royal Canadian Mounted Police) is dispatched to the Yukon.

1895 The Yukon's boundaries are defined, though the Yukon remains a district of the Northwest Territories. An NWMP post is established at Fortymile.

1896 George Carmack, Skookum Jim, and Tagish Charlie discover gold on Rabbit (now known as Bonanza) Creek, a tiny Klondike River tributary.

1897 News of the Yukon gold strike reaches the outside world when steamers carrying rich prospectors and their gold arrive at Seattle and San Francisco.

1898 Canada passes the Yukon Act, creating the Yukon Territory. Dawson City is the first capital.

1900 The White Pass & Yukon Route Railway links Skagway, Alaska, to Whitehorse, Yukon.

1913 Mining for lead and silver begins at Keno Hill.

1942 Fearing attack by Japan, and wanting an inland military route to Alaska, the U.S. builds the Alaska Highway which runs 2,200 kilometres from Dawson Creek, B.C., to Delta Junction, Alaska.

1942-44 The U.S. builds the 1,000-kilometre Canol Pipeline from Norman Wells to Whitehorse.

1953 Whitehorse becomes the territorial capital.

1979 The Dempster Highway is completed. Stretching 740 kilometres from Dawson to Inuvik, N.W.T., it follows a dogsled trail once used by the Mounties.

FAMOUS SONS AND DAUGHTERS

Pierre Berton (1920 –). *Klondike, The National Dream* and *The Last Spike* are among bestsellers by this Whitehorse-born author.

Martha Louise Black (1866 – 1957). Yukon's first (and Canada's second) woman MP hiked alone over the Chilkoot Pass and sailed down the Yukon River in a homemade boat during the 1898 gold rush.

"Klondike Joe" Boyle (1867 – 1923). The "King of the Klondike" is said to have negotiated a peace treaty between the Bolsheviks and Romania.

Edward "Ted" Harrison (1926 –). British-born Harrison has been painting Yukon landscapes since 1968.

Jack London (1876 – 1916). An American writer, London is famous for his Yukon adventure stories, *The Call of the Wild, The Sea Wolf,* and *White Fang.*

Audrey McLaughlin (1936 –). In 1989, she became the first Canadian woman to head a national political party (the New Democratic Party).

Robert William Service (1874 – 1958). "The bard of the Yukon," he gave the Klondike spirit a voice in books of poems such as *Songs of a Sourdough* and *Ballads of a Cheechako*. His Dawson cabin is now a national historic site.

ODDITIES AND SPECIALTIES

Yukoners celebrate Discovery Day in August in memory of the famous Klondike gold strike of Aug. 17, 1896.

During the gold rush, those who survived a Yukon winter from river freezeup to spring breakup were known as "sourdoughs." Newcomers were called "cheechakos." Sourdough was the fermented bread eaten by frontier folk; "Cheechako" was Chinook for "new to come."

Albert Johnson, the "Mad Trapper of Rat River," was said to kill prospectors for the gold in their teeth. He was killed on Feb. 17, 1932, following a lengthy manhunt.

An old glacial lake bed outside Carcross is known locally as the world's smallest desert.

The Thirty Mile, a 48-kilometre stretch of the Yukon River that flows past abandoned gold miners' shacks and skeleton paddlewheelers, has been designated a Canadian Heritage River.

A homesick American soldier working on the Alaska Highway is credited with erecting the first of 20,000 signposts in the "signpost forest" at Watson Lake.

Although the Yukon is known for its cold, several species of wild orchid grow there.

Part of the Dempster Highway, the only public road in North America to cross the Arctic Circle, cuts through the 960-kilometre Tintina Trench, the largest geological fault in Canada. The trench is up to 12 kilometres wide.

PLACES TO VISIT, THINGS TO DO

Discovery Claim-Bonanza Creek (Dawson City). Signs at this national historic site recount the gold discovery of 1896 and early mining days.

Dawson City. Visitors can gamble and see can-can dancers at Diamond Tooth Gertie's, pan for gold in local establishments, and take in a Klondike-style variety show at the Palace Grand.

George Johnston Museum (Teslin). Tlingit artifacts and photographs of native life from the 1920's to the 1940's are on display.

Ivvavik National Park (Arctic Coast). Homeland of the Inuvialuit people, the park protects calving grounds of the Porcupine caribou herd. Thousands of migratory birds nest in the coastal plains of this wilderness park.

Kluane National Park Reserve (Haines Junction). The park features valley glaciers, alpine tundra, and lush meadows, as well as grizzly bears, Dall sheep and moose.

Takhini Hot Springs (Whitehorse). These natural mineral hot springs feature year-round swimming, at 36°C, in a mountain setting.

W.D. MacBride Centennial Museum (Whitehorse). This museum traces Yukon history through exhibits on prehistoric mammals, early native culture, and the gold rush.

The White Pass and Chilkoot Trail. The narrow-gauge White Pass & Yukon Route Railway chugs over the precipitous White Pass as it did in gold-rush days.

The United States

Five broad regions, all generally running from north to south, define the landscape of the United States. In the east, the gently rolling terrain of the *Atlantic coastal plain* starts as a narrow band in New England and gradually widens to encompass the Gulf Coast.

Plunging southward from Maine, the *Appalachian Mountains* rise along the western edge of the coastal plain in the north and jut into the interior of the plain farther south. Once a lofty range, the pine-forested mountains are so old — more than 600 million years — that in most places they have been worn down to little more than 3,500 feet.

The *interior plain* stretches from the eastern Great Lakes westward to the Rocky Mountains. It narrows to the south, eventually merging with the Atlantic coastal plain near the Rio Grande. The vast interior plain has two major subregions. One is the central lowlands, where fertile fields of corn and cotton stretch to the horizon. The second major subregion is called the Great Plains and, as it moves west and becomes drier and higher, the High Plains. It is a major producer of wheat.

The *western mountain system* dominates the area west of the plains. The Rocky Mountains, with elevations of more than 14,000 feet, run from Alaska to Mexico. To the west rise the Cascades, the Sierra Nevada, and the Coast Ranges.

Between the Rockies and the far western ranges is the arid *intermountain plateau*, dominated by the Great Basin. This desertlike basin is an interior drainage system where rivers either dry up or empty into evaporating lakes, rather than running to the sea.

Beyond the continent, more than 2,000 miles to the southwest, lie the Hawaiian Islands, formed almost entirely by volcanic action.

U.S. flower: Rose

U.S. bird: Bald eagle

U.S. flag

Alabama

Water and woods in the heart of the South

Rushing brooks and streams slice through Alabama's dark forests, then join to form rivers and mighty waterways. Here, in the Heart of Dixie, is more navigable water than in any other state — a 1,350-mile system so much a part of Alabama's history that rivers form the dominant element in the state's Great Seal.

Here, too, are vast reaches of sweet gum, yellow poplar, and pine. After years of reforestation, the amount of land covered by trees remains the same — about 65 percent — as when Spanish explorers first arrived in 1519.

The north of Alabama is dominated by the green mountains and valleys of the Appalachian Highland. The once-wild Tennessee River loops through this part of the state, its fury tamed by a system of Tennessee Valley Authority dams. Farther south, the mountains soften into wooded hills, the hills into a gentle coastal plain. From this plain much of the continent's fresh water drains into the Gulf of Mexico, carried there by the Alabama and Tombigbee rivers. Along these rivers, stevedores once loaded cotton onto steamboats for shipment to the port of Mobile.

ALABAMA FEVER

In the early 1800's cotton lured hordes of settlers, mostly southerners who made their way to the state in a migration so fast and furious that "Alabama fever" was said to sweep Georgia, Virginia, and the Carolinas. Most of the new arrivals tilled the thin soil of the northern hills and southern plains. The center of the state, named the Black Belt for its

An ancient river sculpted sandstone into a natural bridge that still stands in northwest Alabama.

The deepest gorge east of the Mississippi was cut by the Little River in Alabama's northeast corner. Now called Little River Canyon, the craggy-walled chasm was inhabited by Cherokees when Hernando de Soto and his band of explorers came upon it in 1540.

THE BEAUTY AND SPLENDOR OF NORTH AMERICA

dark clay soil, became the domain of the legendary southern planter. There the still-potent myths of plantation life were born — of elegant homes, wealthy landowners, and southern belles who had little more to do than stroll among the azaleas — even though planters actually made up less than 1 percent of the state's white population by 1860.

Cotton ruled the Black Belt until boll weevils ravaged the fields and compelled farmers to diversify. Yet the land bestowed more than favorable soil for farming. Still more rivers snaked underground — not of water but of veins of coal that converged with deposits of iron in the north-central part of the state to provide the key ingredients for steelmaking. Only a few tiny villages stood in these ore-rich hills as late as 1871; then sharp-witted speculators bought up land and sold it off, lot by lot, to prospectors — and gave birth to Birmingham. Huge steel mills and foundries sprang up to turn the city into an industrial giant. Today the mills stand silent; but Birmingham, its industry now as diversified as the state's agriculture, remains a vibrant city.

South of Montgomery, closer to the coast, is the area that locals affectionately call L.A.: Lower Alabama, with its rolling hills thick with shortleaf and loblolly pines. To the southeast is the Wiregrass, named for the tall, stiff grasses that once covered the land and now a prime producer of peanuts. And still farther south, between Mobile Bay and the Florida border, lie the marshes, swamps, bayous, and white sand beaches of the coastal lowlands.

WHERE RIVERS MERGE

On the Gulf Coast stands Alabama's oldest city, Mobile. This is where the rivers merge, and where ships have set sail for foreign ports for almost three centuries. It remains an active seaport as barges ply the new Tennessee-Tombigbee Waterway that connects Mobile with the Ohio and Mississippi river systems farther north. Most of the state's other rivers, with names like Black Warrior, Cahaba, and Tallapoosa, carry no commerce today but still draw people to their peaceful banks — quiet and perfect places from which to savor this land of water and trees.

The marsh grasses of Mon Louis Island, on Mobile Bay, are home to alligators and great blue herons. Offshore, the waters teem with shrimps and blue crabs.

The sultry climate of the coastal lowlands feeds the Spanish moss that symbolizes the romantic South. An epiphyte, or air plant, the moss actually belongs to the pineapple family. After several years it grows long enough to brush the ground from the branches of its host trees, as it does from this venerable oak near Mobile.

Alaska

A wilderness of glaciers and mountains at the edge of the Arctic

Alaska, wild and immense, is one of the planet's treasures — a vast landscape of cloud-swept peaks, deep blue lakes, and mammoth glaciers. Between its mountain ranges stretch endless forests and tundra plains, where wolves howl from their lookouts and herds of migrating caribou flow like dark waves across the countryside.

Alaska is home to fewer than 600,000 people, more than half of whom are concentrated in two urban centers, Anchorage and Fairbanks. The rest live in isolated towns whose populations range from a few dozen to a few thousand. In the outlands and offshore roam Alaska's more numerous inhabitants — an estimated 600,000 caribou, 250,000 walruses, 150,000 moose, 150,000 sea otters, 25,000 beluga whales, and 3,000 polar bears.

"CLOSED DUE TO SUNSHINE"

Alaska begins with the protected waterways and forested mountains of the southeastern panhandle. Carved from the western edge of Canada, this rugged strip contains more than 1,000 islands. Winding through steep-sided fjords is the Inside Passage, the maritime highway for freighters and passenger ships.

This part of the state is rain country. Saturated winds from the Pacific bring constant clouds and a yearly rainfall that often exceeds 200 inches. Accustomed to the perpetual wetness, residents seldom bother with rain gear, although most wear the knee-high rubber boots they call Alaska sneakers. On the rare occasions that the weather turns clear, coastal towns take an unofficial holiday, and signs

Wreathed in mist, gargantuan Mount St. Elias looms over trekkers in southeast Alaska

Grizzly Lake is named for the bears that roam its woods. In the distance stand the Wrangell mountain range and snow-covered Mount Sanford.

THE BEAUTY AND SPLENDOR OF NORTH AMERICA

reading "Closed Due to Sunshine" may appear in shop windows.

Far to the west, across the Gulf of Alaska, the barren Aleutian Islands stretch more than a thousand miles across the northern Pacific. The westernmost of these volcanic outposts lies only 50 miles from Siberia. Scattered among the islands are villages of the Aleut people, whose culture is related to that of the Inuit but includes an overlay of traditions adopted from Alaska's early Russian settlers.

On the eastern side of the gulf stand the St. Elias Mountains, a maze of serrated peaks stretching into Canada and dominated by 18,000-foot Mount St. Elias. Rivers of ice twist down the valleys and coalesce into Malaspina Glacier. Farther along the gulf, near busy Prince William Sound, is Cook Inlet, its shores a wilderness until civilization looms up in the form of bustling Anchorage.

JACK LONDON COUNTRY

Inland from Anchorage is yet another great mountain wall, the Alaska Range, with Mount McKinley and Denali National Park as its centerpiece. Alaska's immense interior stretches north, to the Brooks Range.

The interior climate is marked by extraordinary extremes. In midwinter, when the sun appears for only a few hours a day, temperatures seldom rise above zero. In midsummer, the days last more than 20 hours, temperatures often reach the 70's, and residents cool off by waterskiing on the lakes and rivers.

This is a land of clear skies and vast horizons, of rambling mountains, wide valleys, and sinuous rivers. Mightiest of the rivers is the Yukon, which flows nearly 2,000 miles from northern Canada to the Bering Sea.

Jack London described the Yukon in *The Call of the Wild*, when it was peopled with hermitlike hunters, trappers, and prospectors. Even today you can find the same rugged types living in remote cabins and riverbank villages. But the days are gone when hordes of gold seekers followed the Yukon northward.

Most of today's adventurers come looking for wilderness rather than gold. Even residents of Fairbanks, the interior's largest city, get a taste of frontier life — when the ther-

mometer reads –50° F and the brilliant curtains of the aurora borealis dance across the night sky; when downtown streets are closed for dogsled races; and when moose drop in to browse the shrubbery in suburban backyards.

Beyond Fairbanks lie tracts of forest, swampy peat bogs, and a good number of Alaska's 3 million lakes. For millennia, Athabaskan Indians have inhabited this wild land, trapping game for subsistence. Nowadays they hunt with rifles, ride snowmobiles, and travel in motorboats.

THE NORTH SLOPE

Beyond the northern edge of Athabaskan country, the craggy peaks of the Brooks Range ease down to the North Slope. From the unbounded expanses of the Arctic Ocean, winter gales howl across a terrain so featureless that winter travelers may have difficulty telling where the land ends and the ice-covered sea begins. In some areas, permanently frozen soil, called permafrost, extends 2,000 feet below the surface. Yet, during the nine-week growing season, tundra plants burst into a glory of green, caribou gather in great herds on calving grounds, and throngs of sandhill cranes and tundra swans nest and raise their young.

Oil was discovered in this area in 1968. Today drilling rigs are strewn across the flatlands, and a huge industrial complex stands on the shore of Prudhoe Bay.

Glaciers form when snow accumulates over hundreds of years and crystallizes under pressure into glacial ice — a substance so dense that it is more like metamorphic rock than ice. Retreating glaciers terminate at the sea, their ice walls rising hundreds of feet. The warmer seawater causes huge chunks of ice to break away, or "calve"— thus are icebergs born.

HISTORICAL HIGHLIGHTS

1741 Vitus Bering, a Dane in the service of Russia, becomes the first European to reach Alaska.

1745 – 59 Russians, looking for sea otter furs, arrive in the Aleutian Islands chain.

1784 Russians establish a base on Kodiak Island.

1804 Sitka becomes the capital of Russian Alaska.

1867 Amid public protests over the purchase of an "icebox," U.S. pays $7.2 million for Alaska — about 2 cents an acre.

1899 Thousands of prospectors stampede into Nome after gold is discovered on the beach.

1900 Juneau is made the new capital. The move from Sitka involves three government employees and seven filing cabinets in one boat.

1912 Congress makes Alaska a U.S. territory.

1957 Oil is discovered near Swanson River on the Kenai Peninsula in southeastern Alaska.

1959 Alaska joins the Union as the 49th state.

1964 The most severe earthquake in North American history shakes Alaska, destroys most of Valdez, and kills 115 people.

1968 More oil is discovered near Prudhoe Bay in the Arctic Circle.

1971 The U.S. government grants 40 million acres and $962,500,000 in cash to Alaska's Inuit, Indians, and Aleuts.

1977 An 800-mile Alaska oil pipeline from Prudhoe Bay to Valdez is completed.

1989 A tanker runs aground in Prince William Sound, causing largest oil spill in U.S. history.

FAMOUS SONS AND DAUGHTERS

Alexander Baranov (1747 – 1819). Trained as a merchant in Siberia, this administrator of Russian Alaska's early fur trading company ruled Sitka like a provincial czar from 1799 to 1818. During that time he brought law and order to the rowdy colony.

Susan Butcher (1954 –). A sled dog trainer from the bush community of Manley, Butcher became Alaska's best-known "musher" by winning the 1,150-mile Iditarod Sled Dog Race four times in five years.

Ernest Gruening (1887 – 1974). Territorial governor from 1939 to 1953, Gruening was the force behind the drive for statehood. He then served as a U.S. senator for two terms.

Howard Rock (1911 – 76).

This Inuit painter and scrimshaw artist spurred the battle for native rights and lands when he established an activist intertribal newspaper, *The Tundra Times*, in Fairbanks in 1964.

Don Sheldon (1912 – 75). The legendary "glacier pilot" flew his small plane some 800 hours every year for 27 years, transporting mountaineers, skiers, and scientists to remote mountain ranges and using glaciers for airstrips. He went through 45 airplanes but never injured himself or a passenger.

ODDITIES AND SPECIALTIES

Seventeen of the 20 highest peaks in the U.S. are in Alaska.

In 1942 the Japanese occupied the Aleutian islands of Attu and Kiska, the only North American soil held by enemy forces in World War II.

Inuit, who carve household utensils and everyday objects from walrus tusk ivory, are the only Alaskans allowed to own the scarce commodity.

Eighty percent of Alaska's terrain is permanently frozen.

Barrow, the state's northernmost town, is only 800 air miles from the North Pole.

The Yupik and Inupiaq Inuit, who live on the coasts of the Bering Sea and Arctic Ocean, have almost 100 words for sea ice.

Alaskan Inuit make their traditional "ice cream" by mixing snow with seal oil and berries.

If it were not for a westward jog in the international date line, the far islands of the Aleutian chain would share a time zone with Russia and Japan.

PLACES TO VISIT, THINGS TO DO

Denali National Park and Preserve (125 miles northwest of Anchorage). This is the best place to view grizzlies, caribou, moose, and Dall sheep. Towering Mt. McKinley dominates the background.

Glacier Bay National Park and Preserve (Gustavus). Small planes or boats from Juneau take visitors to this meeting place of 16 glaciers, some of which tower 200 feet above the water.

Iditarod Sled Dog Race The famous dogsled race is held each March. Mushers and their teams of huskies travel from Anchorage to Nome in about 11 days.

Kenai Fjords National Park (Seward). Some of the world's most spectacular coastline can be viewed on day-long boat trips along the temperate Kenai Peninsula, called Alaska's Riviera.

Sitka The early capital of Alaska retains some of the flavor of its Russian origins. St. Michael's Russian Orthodox cathedral houses antique icons; Indian and Russian relics are on view at the Centennial Building.

Skagway Once the tumultuous gateway to the Klondike, this small town houses relics of the gold rush in its museums and restored buildings.

Tongass Historical Society Museum and Totem Heritage Center (Ketchikan). Unique totems, tools, baskets, and ceremonial objects of the Haida, Tlingit, and Tsimshian Indians are on display.

ALEUTIAN ISLANDS

Wrangell – St. Elias National Park (Glennallen). The largest national park in the U.S. is notable for its towering peaks and massive glaciers.

Alaska

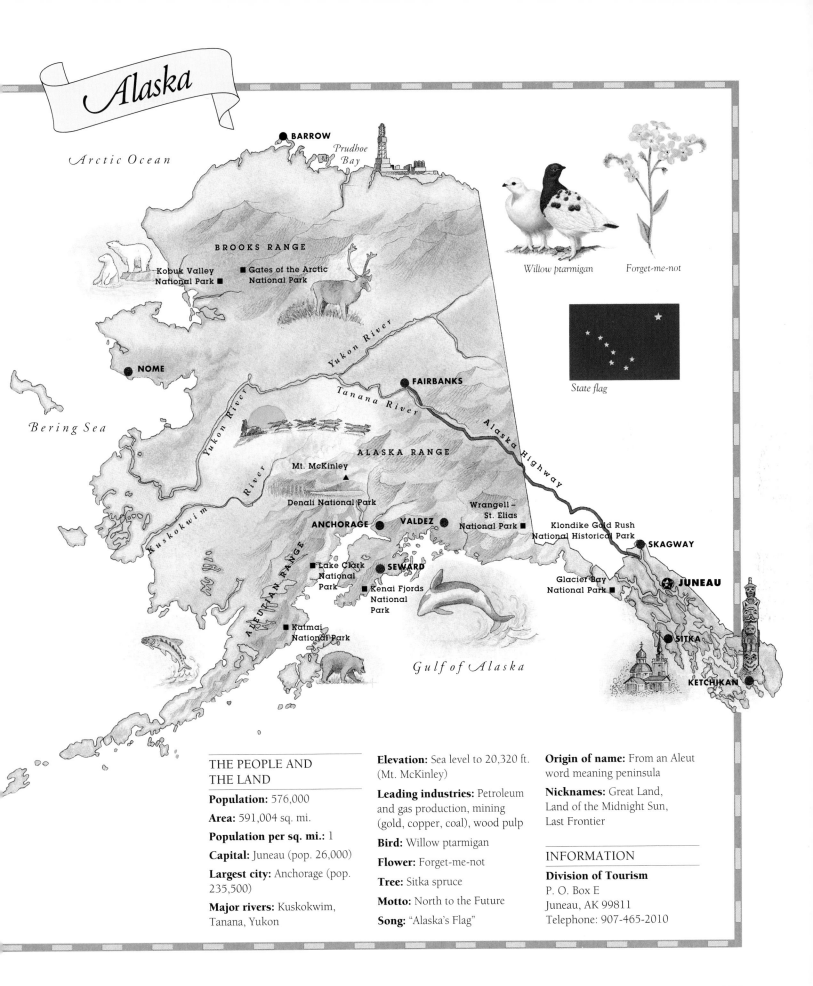

Arctic Ocean

● BARROW

Prudhoe Bay

BROOKS RANGE

Kobuk Valley National Park ■ Gates of the Arctic National Park

● NOME

Yukon River

Tanana River

● FAIRBANKS

Bering Sea

Yukon River

Kuskokwim River

ALASKA RANGE

▲ Mt. McKinley

Denali National Park

Alaska Highway

ANCHORAGE ● VALDEZ ●

Wrangell – St. Elias National Park ■

Klondike Gold Rush National Historical Park

SKAGWAY ●

ALEUTIAN RANGE

■ Lake Clark National Park

● SEWARD

Kenai Fjords National Park

Glacier Bay National Park ■

⊛ JUNEAU

■ Katmai National Park

Gulf of Alaska

SITKA ●

KETCHIKAN ●

Willow ptarmigan *Forget-me-not*

State flag

THE PEOPLE AND THE LAND

Population: 576,000

Area: 591,004 sq. mi.

Population per sq. mi.: 1

Capital: Juneau (pop. 26,000)

Largest city: Anchorage (pop. 235,500)

Major rivers: Kuskokwim, Tanana, Yukon

Elevation: Sea level to 20,320 ft. (Mt. McKinley)

Leading industries: Petroleum and gas production, mining (gold, copper, coal), wood pulp

Bird: Willow ptarmigan

Flower: Forget-me-not

Tree: Sitka spruce

Motto: North to the Future

Song: "Alaska's Flag"

Origin of name: From an Aleut word meaning peninsula

Nicknames: Great Land, Land of the Midnight Sun, Last Frontier

INFORMATION

Division of Tourism
P. O. Box E
Juneau, AK 99811
Telephone: 907-465-2010

Arizona

Harsh beauty
carved by water and time

Although much of Arizona appears barren, the state is rich in wildlife, vegetation, and minerals. Though dry, it was formed by ancient seas, and rushing rivers carved its breathtaking canyons. In the northern part of the state, the Colorado Plateau is flat and sparsely vegetated, even though most of it is elevated above 5,000 feet. Scorching heat, violent thunderstorms, stinging dust storms, and the occasional blizzard blast the landscape from season to season.

At Canyon de Chelly, on Navajo Indian reservation lands, are ruins left by the cliff-dwelling Anasazi people who lived there until some 700 years ago. Ancient paintings and carvings adorn the red sandstone cliffs that plunge down to crumbling pueblo houses, groves of golden cottonwoods, and flocks of sheep. Today Navajos occupy the canyon, with many of their tribal traditions intact. Women in velvet blouses bedecked with silver and turquoise jewelry still weave rugs, while men on horseback herd sheep and cattle.

Nearby, on the southern edge of Black Mesa, stand Hopi Indian villages. One of them, Oraibi, is believed to be the oldest continuously occupied spot in the United States.

CHASMS AND COOL MOUNTAINS

For all the mesas thrust upward from the Colorado Plateau, there are also chasms gouged deep — most notably, the fabled Grand Canyon. The rock of its inner gorge is 2 billion years old — some of the oldest exposed rock on earth — but the huge abyss is relatively

Giant saguaro cacti, some as tall as 50 feet and weighing up to 6 tons, rise from the floor of the Sonora Desert in southwestern Arizona.

THE ANCIENT ARCHITECTS

Nearly 2,000 years ago a mysterious people came to live on the Colorado Plateau. Called the Anasazi, or "Ancient Ones," today, the earliest of them were basket weavers who lived in homes of poles and brush in low-lying caves. But by the time they left the plateau 1,300 years later, they had progressed to the building of houses that remain the most intriguing feats of ancient North American architecture — the famous pueblo cliff dwellings.

The ruins of Anasazi villages are found from Arizona to Colorado. But none are more dramatic than those of Canyon de Chelly, positioned as they are within a labyrinth of sheer-walled sandstone passages. Built on ledges, within shallow caves, or nestled at the bottom of towering cliffs, the shadowy adobe houses grow so organically from their surroundings that they appear to be part of the earth itself. Three-story towers with stone walls rise above the round subterranean chambers (kivas) that were used for religious rituals. Other structures, some of them plastered with stucco, form intricate geometric shapes along the faces of the cliffs. Once occupied by several families, these multilevel buildings could be called early apartment houses.

Named *pueblos* ("villages") by the first Spanish explorers, the crowded settlements lent their name to a number of tribes that are now generically known as Pueblo Indians — tribes that include the Anasazi-descended Hopis but, surprisingly, not the Navajos who occupy Canyon de Chelly today.

With the Ajo Mountains as their backdrop, golden poppies spring to life in March and April in the southwestern Arizona desert. Fully adapted to a harsh environment, the flowers go to seed in a matter of days instead of the two weeks it takes for most poppies — in a rush to reproduce before the scorching summer heat can kill them off.

138

and here their chief Cochise eluded the U.S. Army from 1861 to 1871. Gun-toting outlaws also found a haven here.

To the southwest, beyond the booming city of Tucson, spreads the Sonoran Desert. Titan of this rust-colored land is the saguaro cactus. Towering in the air, arms reaching toward the sun, these plants probably more than any other are etched into the popular imagination as a symbol of the desert Southwest. Their accordion pleats expand and contract to maximize storage of precious water. Holes pecked out of the fleshy trunks provide many birds — elf owls, gilded flickers, Gila woodpeckers — with protected nesting sites. Atop the saguaro's trunk and arms (which appear only after the plant is about 75 years old), creamy white blossoms lasting only a day unfold in May and June.

Other cacti — prickly pear, fishhook, barrel, organ pipe, jumping cholla, pincushion — stand sheathed in needlelike bristles and, in some seasons, sprout brilliant, delicate flowers as if on cue. Wild gardens of purple owl clover, gold Mexican poppies, and blue lupine further paint the scene. Coveys of Gambel's quail and lone roadrunners dart among the varied vegetation. Wild pigs, coyotes, bighorn sheep, mule deer, and even mountain lions live in the desert, as do eight-eyed wolf spiders, tarantulas, scorpions, Gila monsters, and rattlesnakes.

Like the flower of the saguaro cactus, nothing seems to last long in the Arizona desert. A thin veil of snow descends overnight; by early the next morning, the slush has been swallowed up by the thirsty soil. Some black thunderclouds hover ominously over the land, only to dissipate without fanfare. Others cause flash floods, transforming dry, sandy washes into torrents of silt and roots and releasing the powerful fragrance of wet creosote bush. An hour later the washes run dry and the sweet smell is gone.

This is a place where nature is conspicuously in flux. And yet the varied and brilliantly colored desert landscape seems eternal. Twelve thousand years of human habitation notwithstanding, Arizona's beauty — stark, rugged, and mysterious — endures.

Bent by heavy snowdrifts, some stands of aspen saplings on the north rim of the Grand Canyon grow into crooked forests.

NATURE'S HEIRLOOMS

Two hundred million years ago, northeastern Arizona was a subtropical swampland studded with inland seas and active volcanoes. Giant salamanders inhabited a terrain forested with towering pine trees called *Araucarioxylon arizonicum,* long since extinct.

Most of the pines rotted away after they died. But some did not. Rivers flooding down from the mountains picked up the dead trees, tumbled them end over end, and stripped them of branches and roots. The trunks piled up in tremendous logjams on the lowlands, where they were gradually buried under layers of mud, sand, and volcanic ash.

Because this dense mixture contained little oxygen, the tree trunks decomposed extremely slowly. Water filtering down through the layers of sediment left a silica residue that leached into the cell tissues of the logs, where it turned into quartz crystals. Other minerals tinted the quartz in striking hues of red, yellow, orange, purple, and blue-green.

Over millions of years, the climate changed, the waters receded, and the soil that had entombed the trees eroded away, exposing the jewel-like fossilized trunks that lie strewn over more than 147 square miles — an area known today as the Petrified Forest.

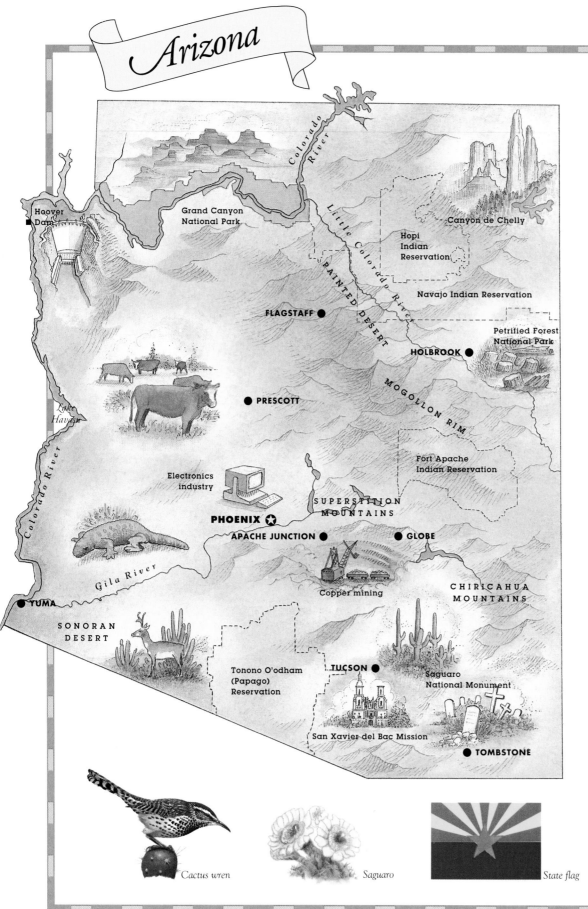

Arizona

THE PEOPLE AND THE LAND

Population: 3,752,000

Population per sq. mi.: 33

Area: 114,000 sq. mi.

Capital and largest city: Phoenix (pop. 2,073,600)

Major rivers: Colorado, Gila, Little Colorado

Elevation: 70 ft. (Yuma) to 12,633 ft. (Humphreys Peak)

Leading industries: Copper mining, agriculture (beef, cotton, citrus fruit, lettuce), electronics

Bird: Cactus wren

Flower: Saguaro

Tree: Paloverde

Motto: *Ditat Deus* (God Enriches)

Song: "Arizona: The March"

Origin of name: From a Papago word meaning small springs

Nickname: Grand Canyon State

INFORMATION

Arizona Office of Tourism
1100 West Washington
Phoenix, AZ 85007
Telephone: 602-542-8687

Owls call a saguaro cactus home.

Grand Canyon National Park

Hoover Dam

Colorado River

Little Colorado River

Canyon de Chelly

Hopi Indian Reservation

Navajo Indian Reservation

PAINTED DESERT

FLAGSTAFF

Petrified Forest National Park

HOLBROOK

Lake Havasu

MOGOLLON RIM

PRESCOTT

Colorado River

Electronics industry

Fort Apache Indian Reservation

SUPERSTITION MOUNTAINS

PHOENIX

APACHE JUNCTION

GLOBE

CHIRICAHUA MOUNTAINS

Copper mining

Gila River

YUMA

SONORAN DESERT

Tonono O'odham (Papago) Reservation

TUCSON

Saguaro National Monument

San Xavier del Bac Mission

TOMBSTONE

Cactus wren

Saguaro

State flag

HISTORICAL HIGHLIGHTS

1540 Spanish expedition under Coronado enters Arizona and discovers Grand Canyon.

1691 Jesuit Eusebio Francisco Kino begins missionary work in southern Arizona.

1752 First permanent Spanish settlement, a military post at Tubac, is established.

1821 When Mexico wins independence, Arizona passes from Spanish to Mexican rule.

1848 Mexico cedes Arizona north of the Gila River to U.S.

1853 With the Gadsden Purchase, rest of present-day Arizona is acquired by U.S.

1854 First Arizona copper ore is mined at Ajo.

1858 Gold is discovered at Gila City on the Colorado River.

1862 First Confederate, then Union troops occupy Tucson during Civil War.

1864 Some 9,000 Navajos surrender to U.S. troops after attack on Canyon de Chelly.

1881 In gunfight at O.K. Corral in silver-mining town of Tombstone, Wyatt Earp and two brothers gun down three men.

1886 Geronimo, leader of the Apache raiders, is exiled to Florida, and Indian raids on Arizona territory end.

1888 Copper production passes gold and silver in value.

1889 Capital of Arizona territory is moved from Prescott to 19-year-old city of Phoenix.

1912 Arizona enters the Union as the 48th state.

1919 Congress establishes Grand Canyon National Park.

1936 Hoover Dam starts supplying water for electricity and irrigation to Arizona, Nevada, and Southern California.

1950 – 60 Arizona's population increases 73.7 percent, faster than any other state.

1985 Central Arizona Project begins operation, directing water from Colorado River to arid rural areas and the cities of Phoenix and Tucson.

FAMOUS SONS AND DAUGHTERS

Geronimo (1829 – 1909). In the 1870's this skillful guerrilla fighter encouraged his fellow Chiricahua Apaches to desert their newly established reservation and resume their war against white settlers. In 1886 he gave himself up.

Barry M. Goldwater (1909 –). This U.S. senator (1952 – 64, 1968 – 87), known as Mr. Conservative, aroused national controversy as Republican presidential candidate in 1964 when he declared, "Extremism in defense of liberty is no vice."

Carl T. Hayden (1877 – 1972). This politician set a record for length of service in the U.S. Congress, as representative from 1912 to 1927 and senator from 1927 to 1969.

George W. P. Hunt (1859 – 1934). Hunt came to the territory as a gold prospector and later pioneered the development of irrigation systems during his four terms as governor.

Percival Lowell (1855 – 1916). Founder of the Lowell Observatory (1894), this astronomer predicted the existence and position of "Planet X." It was discovered 14 years after his death and named Pluto.

Sandra Day O'Connor (1930 –). A lawyer, O'Connor was appointed to the U.S. Supreme Court by President Ronald Reagan in 1981, making her the first woman justice.

ODDITIES AND SPECIALTIES

More telescopes (some 30 in all) are located near Tucson than anywhere else.

Blue corn, grown by Arizona's Hopi Indians for centuries, proved a boon to Indian farmers in the 1980's when it became a sought-after gourmet item.

In 1962 an enterprising American bought the London Bridge that since 1831 had spanned the Thames, and transported it to Lake Havasu in western Arizona, where it now stands.

Arizona has 37 kinds of lizards.

Hopi and Navajo Indians are among the best silversmiths in the U.S. Each tribe makes its own distinctive style of jewelry.

The United States' largest known meteor crater — almost a mile across — was formed some 30,000 years ago when a meteor weighing thousands of tons smashed into the Arizona desert.

True desert covers less than 1 percent of Arizona, but more than 40 percent is desert scrub.

PLACES TO VISIT, THINGS TO DO

Apache Trail (Apache Junction to Globe). This 78-mile road, once the route of raiding Apaches, affords good views of the Superstition Mountains.

Canyon de Chelly National Monument (Navajo Indian Reservation). This magnificent canyon of steep red cliffs contains Indian cliff dwellings dating back to A.D. 350.

Grand Canyon National Park The visitor standing on a rim of the breathtaking Grand Canyon is looking at 2 billion years of geologic history.

Monument Valley Navajo Tribal Park (Navajo Indian Reservation). Huge monoliths and spires of red sandstone loom high above the desert floor.

Painted Desert (northeastern Arizona). Intricately patterned by erosion, these badlands extend 300 miles from the Grand Canyon to the Petrified Forest.

Petrified Forest National Park (near Holbrook). The world's largest display of petrified wood lies at the southeastern edge of the Painted Desert.

Saguaro National Monument (nine miles east of Tucson). Thousands of saguaro cacti grow in this stark desert forest.

San Xavier del Bac Mission (nine miles southwest of Tucson). This mission serves the Papago Indians today. Completed in 1797, it is a fine example of early mission architecture.

Tombstone This town in southeastern Arizona, once the symbol of the lawless Old West, has been preserved so that tourists can still see the O.K. Corral, Bird Cage Theatre, and other sites in their original state.

Arkansas

Quiet hills and rivers preserved in timeless beauty

Drifting along the Buffalo River past towering limestone bluffs, negotiating the winding streets of Eureka Springs in the Ozark Mountains, following the Great River Road across the flat and verdant Delta, or standing in the evening darkness amid the pines of the Timberlands — throughout Arkansas one finds tranquillity and remoteness that seem inherent in the land.

Even native Arkansawyers are often unfamiliar with large stretches of the 53,000 square miles that make up their home, though they would argue that they are far from isolated. The state is, after all, bordered on the east by the Mississippi River, the nation's busiest waterway, and two interstates cross at the state capital of Little Rock.

When Arkansas was admitted to the Union in 1836, however, it barely had the 50,000 residents required for statehood. Most pioneers found its vast swamps along the Mississippi River too daunting a barrier and moved west by other routes. But as the swamps were drained and dammed the state grew, and by 1860 its population had increased tenfold.

BACK-COUNTRY ORIGINS

To most Americans, Arkansas means the Ozarks in the state's northwestern quarter, a peaceful land with steep hills and deep hollows. The Arkansas Ozarks were pioneered by small, independent farmers, who tended to keep to themselves in tucked-away communities scattered among the hills. Their

Year upon year of swirling springtime floodwaters have sculpted the limestone cliffs along the Buffalo River into unusual rock formations such as this vast hollow at aptly named Skull Bluff.

In the hilly Ozarks, level valleys often gave rise to small farms and towns like Boxley (above). The original Baptist church, now used as a community center, stands near the cemetery. The new church is across the road.

unchanging ways led to a century of stereotyping — an image of a hillbilly sitting on the sagging porch of a rough-hewn shanty, a scrawny, slouching hound nearby — but also kept alive old music and folk crafts that are celebrated today at the Ozark Folk Center in Mountain View. The peace and quiet have also made the Ozarks a magnet for retirees and others who simply would like a little distance from the hustle and bustle of city life. Today the Ozarks are among the fastest growing rural areas in America.

A FACE TO THE SOUTH

But not all of Arkansas is uplands. Along the flat and fertile floodplains of the Mississippi River — the Delta region — a different way of life developed. Cotton made this country, as it did so much of the antebellum South, bringing with it enormous plantations and a slow-paced, genteel society. Riverboats glided down the Mississippi into ports like Helena, which Mark Twain said had "one of the prettiest situations on the river." Now rice and soybeans have replaced cotton as the staple

crops, and Arkansas produces more rice than any other state. In the Delta town of Stuttgart, towering grain elevators often confuse out-of-towners, who think they are approaching a city filled with skyscrapers.

HOT SPRINGS AND PINELANDS

Southwest of the Delta lie the Timberlands, a region of gentle hills cloaked in dense pine forests. Spiritually, the region is more akin to the West than to the South. The town of Washington was a stopping place for Sam

HEATING THE HOT SPRINGS

Ghostly vapors rise in the Zig Zag Mountains of Arkansas, hovering above an eerie landscape encrusted in white. Their source, however, is far from otherworldly. The vapors rise where water from hot springs emerges after centuries inside the earth. The white crust surrounding the springs is tufa, a calcium carbonate deposit built up by the slow and endless flow of these steaming mineral-rich waters.

For centuries people have attributed marvelous healing powers to these springs. No less marvelous is the story of why they are hot and bubbly.

Whenever rain falls northeast of what is now the town of Hot Springs, it trickles down through the mountains' sedimentary rock, absorbing carbon dioxide and calcium carbonate, which gives the water its bubbles and distinctive taste. After 4,000 years the water reaches its maximum depth of 8,000 feet within the earth. Throughout this journey it has been warmed: as a result of the decay of radioactive elements, the average temperature in the earth's crust grows 3° to 5° F hotter every 100 yards.

Joints and fractures in the sandstone deep beneath Hot Springs allow the water to gush back to the earth's surface in as little as a year. Bubbling with gases that have been trapped within it for 40 centuries, the water bursts forth at 47 different springs at an average temperature of 143° F and a daily volume of 850,000 gallons.

Perched some 700 feet above the Buffalo River valley, Whitaker Point commands a magnificent view of the Upper Buffalo Wilderness Area. The spectacular vista from this crag overlooking an oak-hickory forest has attracted so many tourists in recent years that their very numbers have done damage.

Houston, Stephen Austin, and many of the other men who wrested Texas from Mexico in the 1830's. And here too, legend has it, Jim Bowie had a local artisan fashion his fearsome knife, dubbed the Arkansas toothpick. An oil boom in the 1920's around El Dorado further cemented the region's ties to Texas.

To the north, the craggy heights and steep valleys of the Ouachita Mountains initially discouraged permanent settlers, who often sought flatter lands for farming. However, the region's many natural springs, both hot and cold, were becoming a major tourist attraction as early as the first decades of the 1800's. Veiled in vapor, the bubbling hot springs here were hallowed by local Indians for their supposed healing powers long before white settlers built the bathhouses that made the town of Hot Springs a world-renowned health spa.

FRONTIER JUSTICE

Fort Smith was established in 1817 where the Ouachita Mountains met the Indian Territory that is now Oklahoma. It would become the state's most notorious town. Although tribal courts had legal authority over Indians, no one had jurisdiction over whites in the territory until Judge Isaac C. Parker arrived in 1875. Over the next 21 years Parker tried some 13,000 cases and sentenced 160 men to death, thus achieving a lasting place in western lore as the Hanging Judge.

But Arkansas is better known for its natural beauty than its history. It has been tagged the Wonder State and the Natural State, and both names fit. Nurtured by the natural barriers that once thwarted its development, Arkansas remains one of the most unspoiled sections of America.

Lying four miles west of the Mississippi River, Wapanocca National Wildlife Refuge is a major stopping place for ducks and geese during their north-south migrations. Some 600 of the refuge's 5,485 acres are covered with stands of cypress, like that above, which take root in the swamplands. Although many swamps have been drained, this terrain is typical of the landscape pioneers encountered along the river as they moved west into Arkansas in the early 1800's.

Arkansas

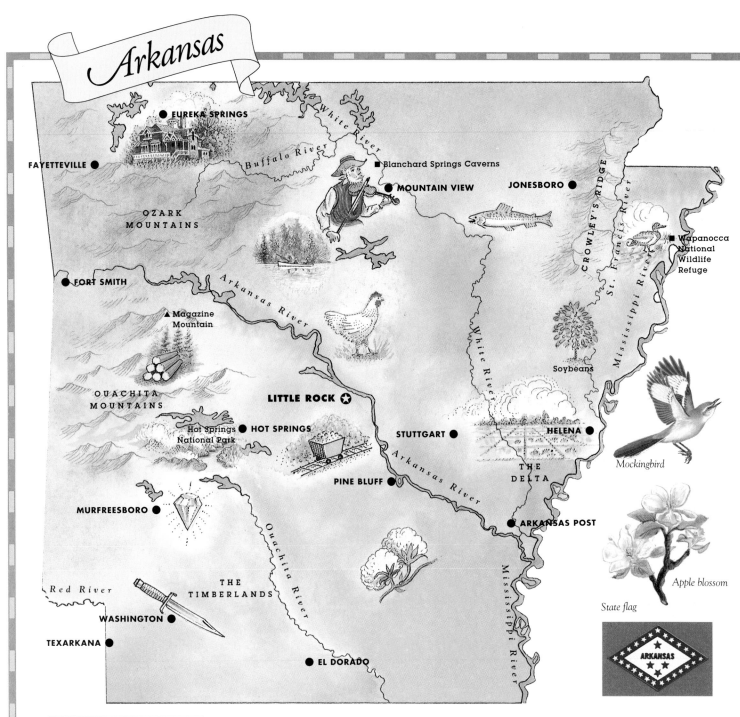

EUREKA SPRINGS

FAYETTEVILLE

Blanchard Springs Caverns

MOUNTAIN VIEW

JONESBORO

OZARK MOUNTAINS

Buffalo River

White River

FORT SMITH

Magazine Mountain

Arkansas River

CROWLEY'S RIDGE

St. Francis River

Wapanocca National Wildlife Refuge

Mississippi River

OUACHITA MOUNTAINS

Soybeans

White River

LITTLE ROCK ★

Hot Springs National Park

HOT SPRINGS

STUTTGART

HELENA

THE DELTA

Mockingbird

PINE BLUFF

Arkansas River

MURFREESBORO

ARKANSAS POST

Apple blossom

Red River

THE TIMBERLANDS

Ouachita River

State flag

WASHINGTON

TEXARKANA

EL DORADO

Mississippi River

THE PEOPLE AND THE LAND

Population: 2,427,000

Area: 53,187 sq. mi.

Population per sq. mi.: 46

Capital and largest city: Little Rock (pop. 201,000)

Major rivers: Arkansas, Mississippi, Ouachita, Red, St. Francis, White

Elevation: 55 ft. (Ouachita River) to 2,753 ft. (Magazine Mountain)

Leading industries: Chemicals, bauxite mining, petroleum and gas production, agriculture (broilers, rice, soybeans, cotton)

Bird: Mockingbird

Flower: Apple blossom

Tree: Pine

Motto: *Regnat Populus* (The People Rule)

Song: "Arkansas"

Origin of name: Derived from the name of a local Indian tribe, the Siouan Quapaw, meaning downstream people

Nicknames: Land of Opportunity, Natural State, Wonder State

INFORMATION

Arkansas Department of Parks and Tourism
1 Capitol Mall
Little Rock, AR 72201
Telephone: 501-682-7777

HISTORICAL HIGHLIGHTS

1541 Hernando de Soto crosses the Mississippi to become the first European on Arkansas soil.

1686 Frenchman Henri de Tonti founds Arkansas Post, the first white settlement in the lower Mississippi Valley.

1817 The U.S. builds Fort Smith to keep peace between Indian tribes and to protect westward-moving settlers.

1836 Arkansas is admitted to the Union as the 25th state.

1861 State conventions vote first to reject secession, then to secede. Some 9,000 whites and 5,000 blacks join Union Army.

1887 Bauxite is discovered near Little Rock; by 1918 Arkansas produces almost all bauxite mined in the U.S.

1921 Discovery of oil near El Dorado leads to a boom, and in 1924 Arkansas is fourth among states in oil production.

1927 Flooding of Mississippi River leaves one-fifth of state underwater.

1957 Defying a federal court order, Gov. Orval Faubus blocks integration of Central High School in Little Rock. President Eisenhower sends troops to enforce the order.

1971 After an expenditure of $1.2 billion to dredge and to build dams, the Arkansas River opens to commercial navigation from the Mississippi River to Tulsa, Okla., making Little Rock an inland port.

1985 Arkansas starts a national trend by requiring teachers to pass basic tests in reading and math to retain their jobs.

FAMOUS SONS AND DAUGHTERS

Hattie Caraway (1878 – 1950). The first woman elected to the U.S. Senate, Caraway won office in 1932, only 12 years after women got the right to vote.

Dizzy Dean (1911 – 74). The son of a sharecropper, Dean became one of baseball's great pitchers. He led the National League in strikeouts for four consecutive years (1932 – 35) and was elected to the Baseball Hall of Fame in 1953.

J. William Fulbright (1905 –). A longtime U.S. senator (1945 – 74), Fulbright chaired the Foreign Relations Committee from 1959 to 1974 and sponsored the act that established the Fulbright Scholarships for student exchange with other countries.

Douglas MacArthur (1880 – 1964). His most famous words were "I shall return" — a promise he made and kept to recapture the Philippines from the Japanese in World War II. Commander of U.S. forces in the Far East from 1941, he headed the Allied occupation of Japan and later the United Nations military forces in Korea.

Edward Durell Stone (1902 – 78). An architect of international fame, Stone designed the Museum of Modern Art in New York City, the Kennedy Center in Washington, D.C., and the U.S. Embassy in New Delhi.

Sam Walton (1918 – 92). Once the wealthiest man in America, Walton opened his first Wal-Mart store, in Rogers, in 1962.

ODDITIES AND SPECIALTIES

The oldest continuously published newspaper west of the Mississippi River is the *Arkansas Gazette,* founded in 1819.

As much as 500 feet high, 1 to 12 miles wide, and running half the length of the state, Crowley's Ridge was built up over millennia from fine windblown soil.

The city of Texarkana straddles the Arkansas-Texas border. So that neither state will feel slighted, the post office building is divided by the state line and has three doors, one leading to each state and a main door right on the boundary.

In 1925 the citizens of Winslow elected a woman, Maud Duncan, mayor and an all-female city council. Two years later, announcing that they had proved women could do the job as well as men, the women all resigned.

The only diamonds ever mined in the U.S. were discovered in Murfreesboro in 1906. Mined from 1908 to 1925, the site became part of Crater of Diamonds State Park in 1972.

At Hot Springs you can enjoy the purity of bottled spring water that fell as rain in the mountains here some 4,000 years ago.

Parking meters used worldwide are made in Harrison and Russellville.

PLACES TO VISIT, THINGS TO DO

Bass fishing The Arkansas River is among the best for bass anywhere in the U.S.

Blanchard Springs The limestone caverns of Blanchard Springs are filled with water-sculpted stalactites and stalagmites. The temperature remains a constant 58° F, and the relative humidity near 100 percent.

Buffalo River Flowing scenically through the Ozarks for 132 miles, the Buffalo was designated the country's first national river in 1972. It is ideal for canoeing, shoreline hiking, and small-mouth-bass fishing.

Eureka Springs With winding streets and Victorian homes, this popular Ozarks spa exudes the charm of the late 1800's.

Fort Smith Downtown Fort Smith is a national historic site. You can visit the old jail and the courtroom where "Hanging Judge" Isaac Parker presided.

Hot Springs National Park (Hot Springs). In 1832 part of the Hot Springs area was made the country's first national preserve. In the 1880's the park became a fashionable spa; in the 1940's the town was a gathering place for gangsters.

Ozark Folk Center (Mountain View). All the folk arts on display are handmade and reflect traditional skills. Local musicians play Ozark music.

California

Soaring mountains, vast deserts, and jagged cliffs at the continent's edge

When Spanish seafarers first sighted the golden hills of North America's western coastal range in 1532, the view reminded them of the mythical land described in *The Exploits of Esplandian*, a popular romance of the time — "an island called California, very near to the Terrestrial Paradise." The Spaniards' geography was imperfect — what they had found was not an island, but a 760-mile-long peninsula now called Baja (Lower) California. Nevertheless, the land that stretched north from those hills was indeed a paradise, undeniably blessed.

DIVERSE AND DRAMATIC

California is unmatched in its abundance and diversity. Its 500-mile-long Central Valley, lying between the Coast Ranges and the Sierra Nevada, is the most productive agricultural land in the entire Western Hemisphere, with an output of $11.5 billion in cash crops and livestock each year. The mist-covered forests of the north are home to the world's tallest living things: the coast redwoods (*Sequoia sempervirens*), which reach heights of more than 350 feet and can live for 1,000 years. A mere two hours' drive east from the balmy beaches of the Pacific is an enormous desert whose rock carvings are visual reminders of past civilizations that have disappeared as surely as the silver mines of a more modern era. Towering above all these wonders is the state's granitic spine, the Sierra Nevada, a range of rugged mountains larger in area than the Swiss, Italian, and French alps combined.

With tree lupines blooming in the foreground, the mountains and rolling pasturelands of the Coast Ranges meet the sea in Sonoma County.

A light fog cloaks a grove of California black oaks in Yosemite National Park.

Spring-flowering trillium adorns the woods of Humboldt County in northern California.

Equally grand is California's 760-mile coastline of jagged cliffs and sandy beaches. This dramatic rim of the continent has been a source of inspiration ever since Franciscan friars from Spain began building missions along the coast and linking them with the Camino Real (Royal Road) more than 200 years ago. Today the Pacific Coast Highway closely follows that early *camino,* and generations of poets and painters have traced every mile of it in their efforts to capture the beauty of Big Sur, the power of breakers crashing against the northern coast, and the twilight glow that transforms the evening sky above southern California into a palette of pastels.

California's population is as diverse as its landforms. The state's natural bounty has made it a 20th-century Ellis Island. One out of every four immigrants who enter the United States eventually settles here. Hispanics, mainly from Mexico and Central and South America, make up 28 percent of the population of Los Angeles County. And more than a third of all Asians living in the United States in 1990 called California home. The new arrivals have joined with native Californians to build a state that leads the nation not only in agriculture, but in computer science, aerospace, biotechnology, and entertainment.

A WORK IN PROGRESS

For most Americans, however, California is still defined by its scenery, from the lofty peak of Mount Whitney to the barren floor of Death Valley. Most of North America was molded eons ago by retreating Ice Age glaciers that scoured the Great Plains, scooped out the Great Lakes, and shaped the course of rivers. California, by comparison, remains a work in progress, a place where grinding pressures deep within the earth continue to uplift mountains, trigger volcanic eruptions, and rearrange the landscape.

Millions of years ago these tectonic forces brought forth the Sierra Nevada (called by Californians simply the Sierra or High Sierra), a bold 400-mile link in the mountain chain running from Central America to Alaska. The mountains contained the gold that drew a rush of miners and led to California's settlement and statehood. Though time has softened the wounds left by the hydraulic mining of gold rush territory, it has also claimed many of the towns cobbled together by fortyniners out to strike it rich. Those that have survived — places like Copperopolis, Chinese Camp, El Dorado, Jenny Lind, and Sutter Creek — are booming again because of a steady influx of retirees.

The coming of the "flatlanders" has not diminished the Sierra's sense of tradition. Saloons in the town of Columbia still offer a choice of whiskey or sarsaparilla just as they did a century ago, and the legendary Calaveras Jumping Frog contest has not changed since the days of Mark Twain. Nevertheless, gentrification is an undeniable and unavoidable fact of life. Old Wells Fargo offices more often than not sell designer cookies now, while hitching posts along Main Streets mark the spots where realtors park their cars.

But the Sierra offers a gift even greater than gold: water. In winter, moisture carried by prevailing westerlies blowing off the Pacific

Weathered sandstone bluffs tower over the ocean at Torrey Pines State Reserve near San Diego. The rare Torrey pine grows only here and on Santa Rosa Island, 175 miles away.

In a relatively peaceful stretch of California coastline, waves wash the beach at Drake's Bay, part of Point Reyes National Seashore north of San Francisco.

Giant sequoias rise from the western slopes of the Sierra Nevada. The species is one of the last survivors of an ancient family of trees that flourished in the time of the dinosaurs.

turns to snow when it hits the mountain range. Then, during the long months of summer, water from melting snow recharges the rivers, irrigates the Central Valley, and fills the swimming pools of Southern California, carried there by a system of aqueducts.

The heart of the Sierra is Yosemite National Park. Yosemite was originally carved out by streams cascading down the western face of the mountains. Later, glaciers moved through and ground away at the bedrock. The result is a breathtaking seven-mile-long valley from which rise sheer granite walls 3,000 to 4,800 feet high. Discovered by gold rush pioneers, the valley was saved from herdsmen and timber companies by John Muir, the pioneer environmentalist. Today Yosemite's exquisite alpine meadows, tumbling waterfalls, and trees that started life when ancient Greece was flourishing attract tens of thousands of visitors. Crowds and commercialization notwithstanding, the person who sees the mist hovering above Mirror Lake on an early autumn morning finds it is difficult to describe Yosemite as anything other than paradise.

VINEYARDS AND REDWOODS

West from Yosemite, across the Central Valley and beyond the capital city of Sacramento, lies the densely populated Bay area of northern California, with San Francisco as its cosmopolitan center. Just north of the city are the Napa and Sonoma valleys, home to hundreds of the vineyards that produce California's celebrated wines. Farther north, in Mendocino County, forests close in on the highway. Buffeted by salt winds and blanketed by fog, tiny towns cling to the barren coast or take shelter amid the towering redwoods.

Before man began cutting them down, the giant redwoods of California's northwest corner were virtually indestructible. Their wood is naturally resistant to water, their thick bark impervious to disease, parasites, and even fire. These qualities made the trees ready for the taking — for the wood used in Nob Hill mansions, for railroad ties, and for the planking in clipper ships carrying tea and silk from China to San Francisco. Today, to the alarm of conservationists, the demand is greater than ever, and many stands of old-growth trees are scheduled for cutting. The original 2 million acres of primeval forest have been reduced to less than 100,000. Fortunately, some 80,000 acres of the ancient forest are protected in Redwood National Park and elsewhere.

"A LOVELY AND TERRIBLE WILDERNESS"

For all of the favored green land of the north, most of California's south is arid. The stark mountains and plateaus east of the Sierra Nevada form part of the Great Basin, the largest and most desolate desert in North America. Nearby is the vast Mojave Desert, an area author Wallace Stegner described as "a lovely and terrible wilderness . . . harshly and beautifully colored, broken and worn until its bones are exposed."

Though home to the dry basin that early settlers named Death Valley, the Mojave is full of life, especially in the spring when flowers fed by winter rains bloom briefly before the heat of summer. Panamint chipmunks, Death Valley sage, turkey vultures, and sprucebush all call the Mojave home. Perhaps its most famous resident is the Joshua tree, a towering yucca that was named by a colony of Mormon pioneers who, while traveling west in search of a new Jerusalem, thought the plant's armlike branches beckoned to them like an Old Testament prophet.

But Southern California — especially the green, warm edge of the state that extends from Los Angeles southward to San Diego — has always beckoned to people. Los Angeles' vast network of towns exploded in mid-century into the U.S.A.'s second largest metropolis, and the city took its place as a symbol of the fast-living, car-based culture that typifies America in the eyes of much of the world.

Because growth continues unabated (California has been the U.S.A.'s most populous state since 1963), conservationists, like John Muir a century ago, seek to preserve their state's distinctive treasures: the virgin redwoods of the north, the haunting Mojave Desert of the south, the waters off the majestic rock-strewn coast. Enduring still, after a century of intense development, these treasures seem more valuable than ever.

JOHN OF THE MOUNTAINS

In 1863, John Muir, a native of Scotland, left the University of Wisconsin to explore the country's wilderness areas on his own. After treks through the Midwest, Canada, and into the Deep South, accompanied only by his knapsack, he made his way to California. There he was overwhelmed by the glory of the landscape — and outraged by the wholesale destruction of forests and meadows by timber companies and grazing sheep (animals he called "hoofed locusts").

In those days most Americans considered the land valuable only for the economic rewards it could offer. Muir, in writings and lectures, argued that the wilderness, its beauty, and the life it harbored were of value in themselves. And as his fame spread, so did his influence. Largely due to Muir's urgings, Yosemite was made a national park in 1890.

The bearded man whom Californians came to know as John of the Mountains continued to hike away for months at a time, only to return, like a Moses from Mount Sinai, to exhort Americans to preserve their remaining wilderness.

President Theodore Roosevelt invited the environmentalist on a camping trip to Yosemite in 1903. Muir, who by then had founded the Sierra Club, later said: "I stuffed him pretty well regarding the timber thieves . . . and other spoilers of the forests." Roosevelt must have listened, for by the time he left office his administration had created five national parks and added more than 140 million acres to the national forest system.

Cactus flowers bloom in Anza-Borrego Desert State Park, 90 miles east of San Diego.

Blanketed in grass and pine, the Santa Lucia range recedes into the mist along the ragged Big Sur coastline. The dramatic scenery, visible along Route 1 between San Simeon and Carmel, has long been an inspiration for writers and artists.

156

THE ACCIDENTAL SEA

Last century, the Salton Sink straddling the California-Mexico border was a desolate, furnace-hot basin choked with mesquite and tumbleweeds. Today the sink is the Salton Sea, the result of an accident on a massive scale.

In 1901, land developers, eager to see if the wasteland could be made to bloom, cut into the bank of the nearby Colorado River and built a short canal and a series of irrigation ditches to channel water into the basin. Their feat was immediately proclaimed a success. The newly irrigated land was so productive that speculators renamed the area the Imperial Valley.

For three years the towns of Brawley, Calexico, and El Centro boomed. No one, however, realized the power of the Colorado, an untamed 1,450-mile-long dynamo that, in those days, carried one of the heaviest silt loads of any river in the world. By the summer of 1904, silt was starting to plug the main irrigation canal along the Mexican border, and farmers were getting nervous as their water supply dwindled. To assure continued irrigation, a second cut was made in the riverbank. But when spring floods hit in the following year, the weakened embankment collapsed, sending the entire flow of the Colorado roaring into the basin and creating an instant sea almost 50 miles long and 15 miles wide.

Although the towns were spared, hundreds of farms were inundated. By 1907 the embankment was patched, and the Colorado resumed its regular course. But the Salton Sea, though now shrunk to 30 miles long and 10 miles wide, still laps at the desert — the curious result of man challenging nature and getting more than he bargained for.

Mount Ritter looms over a sylvan meadow in the Ansel Adams Wilderness, part of Inyo and Sierra national forests. The naturalist John Muir was the first to climb the mountain and study its glaciers.

Northern elephant seals can be seen up and down the California coast. Here, young seals lounge sociably on the beach. Elephant seals get their name from the large size of the males — up to 5,500 pounds — and for the elongated snouts the males will grow as adults.

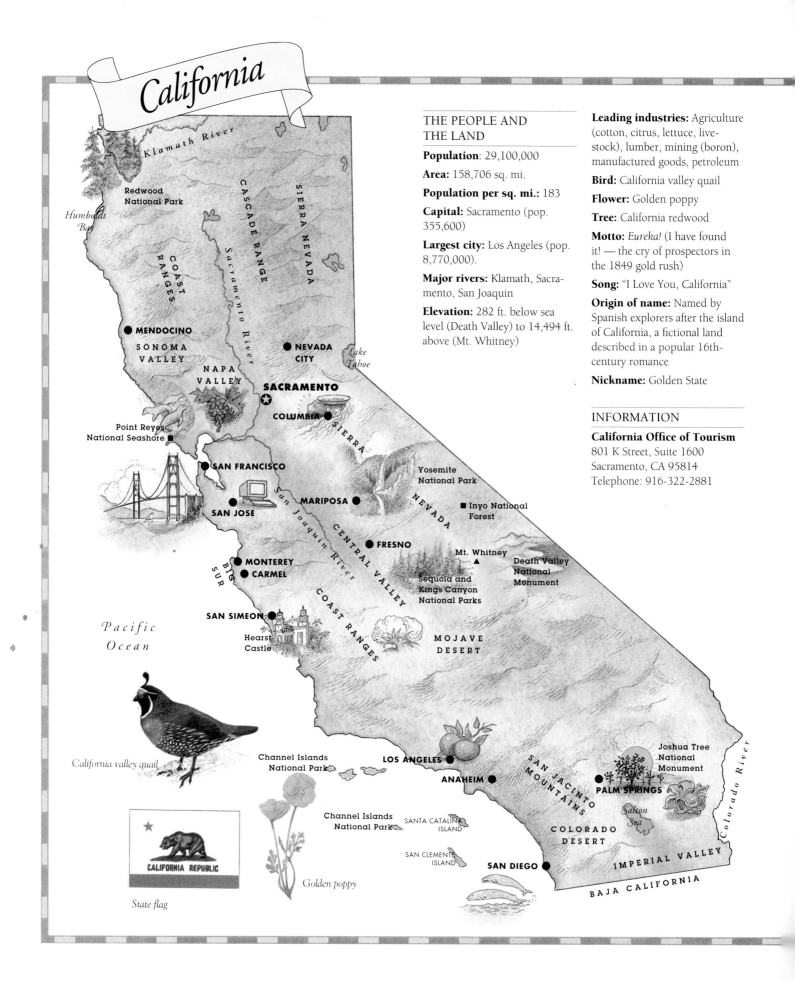

California

THE PEOPLE AND THE LAND

Population: 29,100,000

Area: 158,706 sq. mi.

Population per sq. mi.: 183

Capital: Sacramento (pop. 355,600)

Largest city: Los Angeles (pop. 8,770,000).

Major rivers: Klamath, Sacramento, San Joaquin

Elevation: 282 ft. below sea level (Death Valley) to 14,494 ft. above (Mt. Whitney)

Leading industries: Agriculture (cotton, citrus, lettuce, livestock), lumber, mining (boron), manufactured goods, petroleum

Bird: California valley quail

Flower: Golden poppy

Tree: California redwood

Motto: *Eureka!* (I have found it! — the cry of prospectors in the 1849 gold rush)

Song: "I Love You, California"

Origin of name: Named by Spanish explorers after the island of California, a fictional land described in a popular 16th-century romance

Nickname: Golden State

INFORMATION

California Office of Tourism
801 K Street, Suite 1600
Sacramento, CA 95814
Telephone: 916-322-2881

Map labels

Klamath River
Redwood National Park
Humboldt Bay
COAST RANGES
CASCADE RANGE
SIERRA NEVADA
Sacramento River
MENDOCINO
SONOMA VALLEY
NAPA VALLEY
NEVADA CITY
Lake Tahoe
SACRAMENTO
COLUMBIA
SIERRA
Point Reyes National Seashore
SAN FRANCISCO
Yosemite National Park
NEVADA
Inyo National Forest
MARIPOSA
SAN JOSE
San Joaquin River
CENTRAL VALLEY
FRESNO
Mt. Whitney
Death Valley National Monument
MONTEREY
CARMEL
BIG SUR
Sequoia and Kings Canyon National Parks
SAN SIMEON
COAST RANGES
Hearst Castle
MOJAVE DESERT
Pacific Ocean
California valley quail
Channel Islands National Park
LOS ANGELES
SAN JACINTO MOUNTAINS
Joshua Tree National Monument
Colorado River
ANAHEIM
PALM SPRINGS
Channel Islands National Park
SANTA CATALINA ISLAND
Salton Sea
COLORADO DESERT
SAN CLEMENTE ISLAND
SAN DIEGO
IMPERIAL VALLEY
BAJA CALIFORNIA
Golden poppy
CALIFORNIA REPUBLIC
State flag

HISTORICAL HIGHLIGHTS

1542 Juan Rodríguez Cabrillo, a Portuguese navigator sailing under the flag of Spain, arrives in San Diego Bay.

1579 Sir Francis Drake lands on California coast and claims the area for England.

1769 After Spain gains control of the region, Franciscan priest Junípero Serra founds a mission near present-day San Diego.

1821 Mexico revolts against Spain and the following year claims California as its own.

1848 Mexico cedes California to U.S. after the Mexican War. James W. Marshall finds gold at Sutter's Mill in the Sierra Nevada.

1849 Thousands of "forty-niners" rush to California in search of gold.

1850 California joins Union as 31st state.

1869 The first transcontinental railroad provides a direct link from West Coast to East.

1906 An earthquake destroys buildings and causes raging fires that devastate San Francisco. At least 3,000 people die.

1910 The first film made in Hollywood — D.W. Griffith's *In Old California* — is released.

1937 Golden Gate Bridge, connecting San Francisco and Marin County, opens to traffic.

1960 California Water Project makes it possible to direct water from northern mountains to arid areas, turning desert into productive farmland.

1965 Race riots break out in Los Angeles suburb of Watts. Before they end after five days, 34 people die.

1978 In a grass-roots taxpayers' rebellion, voters ratify Proposition 13, cutting property taxes by more than half.

1994 An earthquake with an epicenter near Northridge jolted Los Angeles, destroying freeways and causing 55 deaths.

FAMOUS SONS AND DAUGHTERS

Joe DiMaggio (1914 –). "Joltin' Joe" was a superb center fielder and hitter who hit safely in 56 consecutive games. He was elected to the National Baseball Hall of Fame in 1955.

Isadora Duncan (1878 – 1927). Duncan's expressionistic dancing, done barefoot in flowing garb, made her one of the best-known artists of her day.

William Randolph Hearst (1863 – 1951). Hearst became phenomenally wealthy and influential after amassing a huge empire of newspapers, magazines, and radio stations.

Jack London (1876 – 1916). The adventurous journalist, essayist, and fiction writer chronicled the Pacific Northwest in *The Call of the Wild* and other works.

Richard Milhous Nixon (1913 – 94). The 37th president, who resigned from office in 1974 after the Watergate scandal, grew up in Whittier and was graduated from Whittier College.

George S. Patton, Jr. (1885 – 1945). In World War II, Patton commanded the Third Army, which swept through Europe from Normandy to Czechoslovakia in 1944 – 45.

John Steinbeck (1902 – 68). This novelist won both the Pulitzer and Nobel prizes. His best-known work, *The Grapes of Wrath,* traced the migration of poor Okies to the promised land of the West.

ODDITIES AND SPECIALTIES

In only four years, 1848 – 52, the gold rush swelled California's population from 15,000 to 250,000 in one of the largest migrations in history.

If California were a nation, it would have the sixth strongest economy in the world.

North America's largest bird, with a wingspan of 10 feet, is the endangered California condor.

Yosemite Falls are 13 times higher than Niagara Falls.

With more than 25 million cars, trucks, and buses, California has the most motor vehicles per square mile in the world.

Inyo National Forest's bristlecone pine trees, estimated to be 4,600 years old, may be the earth's oldest living organisms.

PLACES TO VISIT, THINGS TO DO

Death Valley National Monument This parched desert basin of canyons, sand dunes, and salt flats is the lowest, hottest, and driest spot in the U.S.

Disneyland (Anaheim). The huge amusement park was the first to use high technology in exhibits and rides.

Gold Country (Mariposa to Nevada City on Highway 49). Visitors can pan for gold in the old mining towns that dot Highway 49, the road known as the Golden Chain.

Hearst Castle (San Simeon).

William Randolph Hearst's lavish and eccentric home, filled with art from around the world, is open daily for tours.

Point Reyes National Seashore This rugged peninsula north of San Francisco has scenic cliffs, meadows, lakes, woods, and long beaches pounded by surf.

Redwood National Park (near Crescent City). This park in the northwest corner of the state has 76,862 acres of old- and new-growth coast redwoods, the tallest trees on earth. Wild beaches edge the forests along the Pacific.

Sequoia and Kings Canyon National Parks (Three Rivers). The sequoias in these adjoining parks are not as tall as coast redwoods but are larger in sheer bulk. Looming above them is Mt. Whitney, tallest peak in the contiguous U.S.

Wineries (Napa, Sonoma, Lake, and Mendocino counties). Tastings are available throughout California wine country, which has more than 700 wineries.

Yosemite National Park This awe-inspiring stretch of the Sierra Nevada is a wonderland of waterfalls, granite formations, forests, cliffs, and mountains.

Colorado

America's rooftop,
the state nearest heaven

Colorado bestrides the Rocky Mountains with a foot in two different Americas. Its eastern edge is firmly planted in the rolling plains of the nation's agricultural heartland. Yet at its western border, 385 miles away, Colorado is a land of lonely buttes and mesas amid the picturesque plateaus of the desert. In between is the mountainous terrain where the Rockies, which stretch all the way from New Mexico into Canada, reach their greatest height. Colorado has an average elevation of 6,800 feet, with some 1,100 peaks soaring more than 10,000 feet high, and 53 peaks above 14,000 feet — making it literally the state nearest heaven.

GLINT OF GOLD

For many years Colorado seemed too stark and desolate to attract even the hardiest of explorers and settlers. As early as the 17th and 18th centuries, French trappers moved west from the Mississippi and Spaniards north from Santa Fe. But both groups were turned away by the proud and warring Indians of the Colorado plains and in the mountain valleys by the powerful Utes.

In 1858, gold was discovered in Cherry Creek at a site that is now in modern Denver. Within a year some 100,000 hopeful souls poured into the territory. By the 1860's the supposedly useless eastern part of the territory — dry plains covered with endless grasslands — was coming into its own as a cattle range. Herds were driven north from Texas into Colorado, and investors from the East

In a burst of beauty high in the San Juan Mountains, Ice Lake basin comes to life each summer with blue columbines, the Colorado state flower.

BLOWIN' IN THE WIND: COLORADO'S GREAT SAND DUNES

The tallest sand dunes in North America lie hundreds of miles from the nearest ocean — in the Colorado Rockies. When the glaciers melted at the end of the last ice age — about 12,000 years ago — the swollen Rio Grande carried millions of tons of silt and sand into the San Luis Valley. Once the waters subsided, the prevailing southwest winds blew the sand northward against the Sangre de Cristo Mountains in a process that continues to this day. As the wind collides with the mountains, it loses its speed and dumps the sand at their base. Today, these mammoth hills of sand are nearly 700 feet high and cover 55 square miles.

The wind also sculpts the crests of the dunes. Swirling upward across a dune, it gains speed and strength and picks up more sand. As the wind clears the peak, much of the sand drops suddenly, giving the dune a steeper far side.

Although the crests may shift several feet a day, the bulk of the dunes is stationary, in part because the mass of sand retains so much moisture that only the top few inches are dry enough to be carried off by the wind.

The bizarre rock formations of the Garden of the Gods, near Colorado Springs, were formed, the Ute Indians believed, when manitou, a supernatural force, turned the giants who invaded their land into stone. In the view at right, masses of weather-worn sandstone frame Pikes Peak in the distance.

The brilliant yellow of an aspen forest glows in Snowmass Canyon near the town of Aspen. Fall foliage is one of the splendors of the mountains.

and Europe, particularly England, put up huge sums to finance what was to become a thriving cattle industry.

Many of these investors came to inspect the territory where they were spending their money. Only then were the mountains appreciated for something more than their commercial potential — their astonishing physical beauty and the purity of their cool, dry air were enough in themselves.

While cattle barons and vacationers were civilizing the eastern plains and the Rockies, the part of Colorado west of the Rocky Mountains remained relatively untouched. Here, the convoluted land slopes down to the vast Colorado Plateau — a desolate but beautiful terrain of formidable gorges, jagged rock towers, and mesas jutting into a cobalt-blue sky.

Rocky Mountain meadows abound in fireweed and other wildflowers during the summer.

Sandstone pinnacles carved by thousands of years of erosion dominate the harsh wilderness of the Colorado National Monument, near Grand Junction. The highest of these natural spires is Independence Rock, pictured above, which towers to a height of 565 feet.

LAND OF THE GIANTS

Some 140 million years ago the desolate mountains on the Colorado-Utah border were a verdant plain crisscrossed with shallow rivers. Dinosaurs lived there then: the lumbering stegosaurus, with bony plates along its spine; the vegetarian camarasaurus (left); and the meat-eating allosaurus.

Millions of years later floods buried scores of these dinosaurs in muddy riverbanks. Slowly, the ocean inundated the plain and covered the dinosaur remains with thousands of feet of sediment that eventually turned to sandstone.

Then, about 65 million years ago, after the waters had retreated, the sandstone buckled upward, part of the same movement of the earth's crust that created the Rocky Mountains. Exposed as craggy ridges, the stone began to erode, ultimately revealing its fossil record.

Dinosaur remains have been found throughout western Colorado at such places as Grand Junction and Rangely. The best place to see them is at Dinosaur National Monument, which straddles the Colorado-Utah border north of the town of Dinosaur.

Ending in sagebrush flats that stretch into central Utah on the west, the land is host not only to the mighty Colorado River but also to the Gunnison, which has cut a startling 53-mile-long gash in the earth — the awe-inspiring Black Canyon of the Gunnison.

SCULPTING THE LANDSCAPE

For all of the stark beauty of western Colorado, the high ground of central Colorado is the state's real treasure. The Rocky Mountains were created when an older, worn-down mountain range was pushed upward, causing cracking and folding in the layers of sandstone, shale, and limestone that had formed in the bed of an ancient sea.

In some parts of the state, the land was shaped more abruptly. The San Juan Mountains, which extend over some 10,000 square miles of southwestern Colorado, were formed by volcanoes. This range presents some of the wildest beauty in the state, with vividly colored formations of striking, needlelike spires and jumbled piles of fallen rock.

The Colorado Rockies are actually five separate ranges: the Front, Park, and Sawatch ranges, and the San Juan and Sangre de Cristo mountains. The Front Range, the easternmost, runs in a north-south direction more than halfway down the center of the state. Some 80 percent of the state's 3.4 million inhabitants live east of this range, in a strip not much more than 30 miles wide and 150 miles long. Three of Colorado's most populous cities lie here: Colorado Springs, Pueblo, and Denver, the capital.

The Front Range is paralleled to the west by the Park Range, which is itself paralleled farther west by the Sawatch Mountains, where the resorts of Aspen and Vail nestle.

In the southwestern part of the state, the Sangre de Cristo Mountains and the San Juans enclose the San Luis Valley, the largest of Colorado's four "parks" — high valleys walled by mountains. The Rio Grande, which springs forth as a stream in the San Juans, meanders through the valley on its voyage to the Gulf of Mexico, providing drinking water for livestock and irrigation for sprawling fields of potatoes, sorghum, alfalfa, corn, and peppers.

The massive grandeur of the Rockies is most apparent from above, as in this early autumn view of Mount Sneffels near Ouray in the San Juan Mountains.

Connecticut

Rolling hills and old New England villages

T he only street in America more beautiful than North Street in Litchfield is South Street in Litchfield." So said writer Sinclair Lewis about two of the village's postcard-pretty streets. With their pleasant arrangement of clapboard houses, picket fences, steepled churches, and well-kept squares, Litchfield and other Connecticut towns are among New England's treasures. Puritans founded many of them, and even today the typical Connecticut village exemplifies order and simplicity — a legacy of the Puritan ways that prevailed in the state for more than 200 years, longer than anyplace else on the continent.

RELIGIOUS FREEDOM AND ELBOW ROOM

The quest for religious freedom is often said to have lured Thomas Hooker and his followers from Massachusetts Bay to the Connecticut Valley, but what the pioneers also sought was fertile soil and elbow room. Settling in Hartford, Wethersfield, and Windsor in the 1630's, the Puritans built their towns according to uniform plans, with a centrally located church and facing town green, or common, surrounded by the homes of the town's elite. Today Connecticut has 169 towns, many of them built on this pattern.

The third-smallest state, only 73 miles north to south and 100 miles east to west, Connecticut is shaped roughly like a rectangle, its jagged 253-mile southern boundary washed by Long Island Sound. In the densely populated southwestern corner, Darien, Greenwich, and other bedroom communities are home to

The pride of the reconstructed historic village at Mystic Seaport is the Charles W. Morgan, *an 1841 whaling bark that sailed to the Arctic and the South Pacific.*

Once part of a dense forest, the open fields of Connecticut's farmlands are a monument to the hard work of its early settlers. Orchards of pears, peaches, or apples, such as this one near Wallingford, are often seen amid the state's rolling hills. Fruit is Connecticut's fourth largest crop.

affluent suburbanites who commute to nearby New York City. Eastward, on the coast, are picturesque seafaring towns — Essex, Mystic, Stonington — where the pace is more leisurely and village life centers on boats.

STONE FENCES IN FORESTS

Rising from the busy coastal plain a series of low ranges and hills forms a classic rural setting. Stone fences solemnly mark property lines or retreat into forests — reminders of how mightily farmers once labored to clear the land. Even more bucolic is the far northwest corner, where the Litchfield Hills offer panoramic vistas into neighboring New York and Massachusetts. In fall, thousands of tourists, whom the locals call leaf peepers, journey to Litchfield, Kent, Cornwall, and their environs to see the dazzling red and yellow display offered by forests of maple and oak. Even today, more than half of Connecticut is forested, mainly with deciduous trees.

But the state's greatest natural asset is its splendid network of riverways that includes the Connecticut, Housatonic, Naugatuck, and Thames. Chief among them is the Connecticut, which rises in northern New Hampshire and sweeps down a 410-mile course to Long Island Sound, bisecting the state of Connecticut. The rich alluvial soil left in its wake was what the Puritans sought.

This fine river system, with its bounty of cheap water power, transformed Norwich, Waterbury, Bridgeport, and other towns into important manufacturing cities and made Connecticut a leading industrial state in the mid-19th century. Earlier, the people of Connecticut had discovered that most of the land outside the fertile river valleys was far too poor for farming. Industrious and enterprising, they turned to commerce — best represented by the Yankee peddlers who traveled across the young nation on wagons loaded with pots and pans, tools and nails, hats and

Throughout New England, stately maples line rural lanes, looking as if they have been standing on the land forever. In fact, most of the trees were planted as saplings to shade the byways after the forest was cleared. Many of these maples are now almost 200 years old.

Viewed from above on an autumn evening, Litchfield is the model of a well-ordered New England village centered on the Congregational Church and spacious town common.

THE CHARTER OAK — SYMBOL OF LIBERTY

In 1662 King Charles II of England granted Connecticut its own charter, entitling the colony to extensive self-government. Nonetheless, in 1687 not long after Sir Edmund Andros was appointed governor of all the New England colonies, he marched to Hartford and in the name of the new king, James II, demanded the charter back.

At the evening meeting where the document was to be relinquished, the lights suddenly went out. By the time they were relit, the charter had vanished. According to legend, Joseph Wadsworth, a Hartford resident, snatched the charter in the darkness and hid it in the hollow of a nearby oak.

The disappearance of the charter did not prevent Governor Andros from revoking it, but both his regime and that of James II were short-lived, and in 1689, after the Glorious Revolution in England, the colony's charter was restored to Connecticut.

The tree where Wadsworth had hidden the charter became a cherished local symbol of the struggle for self-government. Known as the Charter Oak, it had a circumference of 33 feet when it was felled by a storm in 1856. Afterward all sorts of objects were said to have been cut from its wood. Mark Twain once quipped that he had seen "enough Charter Oak to build a plank road from Hartford to Salt Lake City."

This painting of the oak was done about 1846 by Frederick Edwin Church, whose ancestors were among the original founders of Hartford.

combs. Still, it was not until the beginning of the American Industrial Revolution that Connecticut really came into its own.

YANKEE INGENUITY

Connecticut did not just benefit from the revolution; it helped create it. Hartford native Eli Whitney, inventor of the cotton gin, pioneered the use of interchangeable parts in the manufacture of firearms. His innovation was just one step away from the assembly line and mass production. American steel manufacturing began in Connecticut, and over the years Connecticut entrepreneurs invented or pro-

duced a mind-boggling number of other products: revolvers, clocks, bicycles, sewing machines, postage meters, shaving soap, jet engines, and nuclear submarines. Thus did Yankee ingenuity earn Connecticut a place among the nation's most prosperous states.

Hartford, the state capital since colonial times, has also been its economic center. Mark Twain made his home there, and although he traveled widely throughout the United States, Hawaii, Europe, and even to Egypt, he deemed Hartford "the prettiest town." Today its shiny glass and steel office towers are headquarters for some 50 companies whose business has

long been synonymous with the city — insurance. The city's insurance industry got its reputation for reliability in 1835, when a fire in New York City destroyed hundreds of buildings. Many insurance companies defaulted on their obligations, but one, the Hartford Insurance Company, paid every claim.

Connecticut residents, even those who live in Hartford or some other modern city, cherish their semirural surroundings and try to preserve them. That task has been easier since 1960, when local law was placed firmly in the hands of the villages and towns with which Connecticut is so closely identified.

Weathered farms like this one recall Connecticut's agricultural heritage. Although today Connecticut has only 3,800 farms — there were more than 20,000 fifty years ago — it has some 50,000 horses, giving it one of the greatest "equine densities" of any state, nearly 10 horses per square mile.

Delaware

A thimbleful of scenic beauty and serenity

Delawareans relish their state's nickname Small Wonder, taking as much pride in the small as in the wonder. Yellowstone National Park, they point out, is larger than diminutive Delaware, as are two Alaskan islands. Despite its tiny size, however — only Rhode Island is smaller — Delaware offers a wealth of beauty and a bonus of serenity. Even though it edges the populated corridor between Washington, D.C., and New York City, Delaware retains areas as unblemished today as they were a century ago.

UPSTATE, DOWNSTATE

In the north and west, Delaware is part of the hilly Piedmont province of the Appalachians. Here old fields break the rhythm set by rolling woodland knolls. During the 19th century, the rushing streams of these foothills powered flour and paper mills, whose efficiency prompted the Frenchman Éleuthère Irénée du Pont to set up a black gunpowder mill along the Brandywine Creek.

Today northern Delaware, in large part because of the Du Pont company's successes, is a bustling urban center with Wilmington at its hub. The outskirts of the city, however, offer the beauty of sprawling historic estates, many of which, like the Du Pont estate Winterthur, north of Wilmington, are now museums. This region, so like a quiet French watercolor, is called Château Country.

Northern Delaware comprises only one-sixth of the state. It is separated from southern Delaware by the Chesapeake and Delaware Canal, which links the Chesapeake Bay to the

A winter sun highlights snow-covered barrier dunes near Indian River Inlet, south of Cape Henlopen.

Giant bald cypress trees, which thrive in wet conditions, reach the northern limit of their range in Delaware's Great Cypress Swamp.

THE BEAUTY AND SPLENDOR OF NORTH AMERICA

Delaware River. Southward from this busy shipping channel spread the farming tracts of central Delaware. The modern poultry industry was born here in Sussex County in 1923, when Mrs. Wilmer Steele raised a brood of 500 chicks for quick sale.

Delaware's expansive farmland (50 percent of the state is still agricultural) ends in the east, where the waters of Delaware Bay lap into the fertile tidal marshes of the Atlantic flyway. In autumn, the piercing calls of migrating wigeons, teals, mallards, and geese fill the air above two national wildlife refuges, Bombay Hook and Prime Hook .

Tucked behind the barrier island that stretches along Delaware's Atlantic coast, the Rehoboth, Indian River, and Little Assawoman bays finger their way through low-lying land that offers tranquil sanctuaries for skyscraping loblolly pines and white-tailed deer. The waters of these bays are a playground, dotted with the colorful sails of pleasure boats.

THE DELAWARE COAST

Where the rolling waves of the Atlantic meet the more serene waters of Delaware Bay a crook of land called Cape Henlopen protrudes. It is the northernmost point of Delaware's 25-mile coastline. Each May, hundreds of thousands of migratory shorebirds stop here, lured by newly laid horseshoe crab eggs. Bobbing their long bills into the sand, they dart, stilt-legged and chattering, along the beach. Many have flown here nonstop from South American wintering grounds. Above pinelands and cranberry bogs, an observation tower in Cape Henlopen State Park overlooks the Great Dune — at 80 feet the highest sand dune between Cape Hatteras and Cape Cod.

Not far from Cape Henlopen, Rehoboth Beach, the "nation's summer capital," for years has provided a haven for refugees from the oppressive summer heat of Washington, D.C. Most Delaware beaches are state-owned — the creeping shadows of late afternoon are from protective dune fencing, not multistoried hotels. Laughing gulls fill the sky, while human visitors share the sands with cottontail rabbits and hermit crabs. It is something Delaware does well, packing a lot into a little.

Hand-gathered bundles of cornstalks surround an Amish farm west of Dover after the harvest.

Bombay Hook National Wildlife Refuge, near Smyrna, is a major stopping place for birds migrating along the Atlantic flyway. Hundreds of great egrets feed here each August as they travel from their northern summer haunts to winter homes in the Southeast.

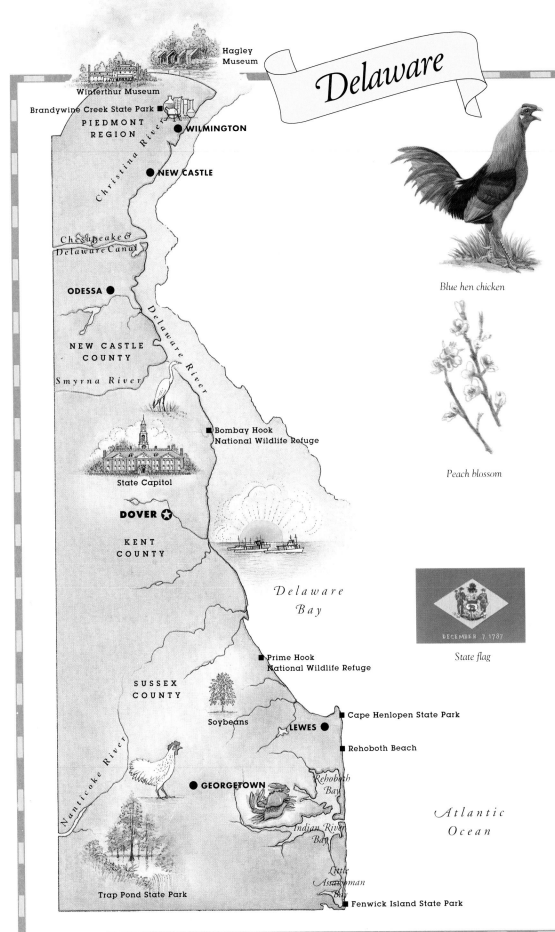

Hagley Museum

Winterthur Museum

Brandywine Creek State Park

PIEDMONT REGION

● **WILMINGTON**

Christina River

● **NEW CASTLE**

Chesapeake & Delaware Canal

● **ODESSA**

Delaware River

NEW CASTLE COUNTY

Smyrna River

■ Bombay Hook National Wildlife Refuge

State Capitol

DOVER ☆

KENT COUNTY

Delaware Bay

■ Prime Hook National Wildlife Refuge

SUSSEX COUNTY

Soybeans

Nanticoke River

● **GEORGETOWN**

■ Cape Henlopen State Park

LEWES ●

■ Rehoboth Beach

Rehoboth Bay

Indian River Bay

Atlantic Ocean

Little Assawoman Bay

■ Fenwick Island State Park

Trap Pond State Park

Delaware

Blue hen chicken

Peach blossom

State flag

DECEMBER 7, 1787

THE PEOPLE AND THE LAND

Population: 682,700

Area: 2,045 sq. mi.

Population per sq. mi.: 334

Capital: Dover (pop. 26,200)

Largest city: Wilmington (pop. 70,450)

Major rivers: Christina, Delaware, Nanticoke

Elevation: Sea level to 442 ft. (Ebright Road, near Centerville)

Leading industries: Chemical manufacturing, agriculture (chickens, soybeans, potatoes)

Bird: Blue hen chicken

Flower: Peach blossom

Tree: American holly

Motto: Liberty and Independence

Song: "Our Delaware"

Origin of name: Named after Lord De La Warr, first governor of colony of Virginia (1610 – 11)

Nicknames: Diamond State, First State, Peach State, Small Wonder

INFORMATION

Delaware Tourism Office
99 Kings Highway, Box 1401
Dover, DE 19903
800-282-8667 (in state)
800-441-8846 (out of state)

Howard Pyle's paintings of pirate ships were inspired by his visits to Rehoboth Beach.

HISTORICAL HIGHLIGHTS

1609 Searching for a trade route for a Dutch company, Henry Hudson explores Delaware Bay.

1631 A Dutch group establishes first European settlement on site of present-day Lewes.

1638 Swedes establish first permanent settlement, later taken over by the Dutch.

1664 English capture the Dutch holdings.

1682 The duke of York gives Delaware to William Penn. It becomes known as the Lower Three Counties of Pennsylvania.

1704 Penn lets Delaware have its own legislature.

1787 Delaware is first state to ratify U.S. Constitution.

1829 A canal connecting the Delaware River with Chesapeake Bay links Delaware farmers with urban markets.

1861 Though a slave-holding state, Delaware supports Union.

1935 Dr. W. H. Carothers, a Du Pont chemist, develops nylon.

1940 The Alfred I. du Pont Institute, one of the world's leading orthopedic hospitals, opens near Wilmington.

1951 Delaware Memorial Bridge links Delaware with New Jersey.

1971 Delaware passes Coastal Zone Act to protect wetlands against industrialization.

1983 University of Delaware celebrates its 150th anniversary.

FAMOUS SONS AND DAUGHTERS

Thomas Francis Bayard (1828 – 98). Like his grandfather and father, Bayard held office in the U.S. Senate (1869 – 85). He also served as Cleveland's secretary of state and as ambassador to Great Britain.

Henry Seidel Canby (1878 – 1961). A writer and critic, Canby was a founder of *The Saturday Review of Literature*. His books include *The Brandywine*.

Annie Jump Cannon (1863 – 1941). An astronomer known as the census taker of the sky, Cannon discovered and cataloged hundreds of stars while working at Harvard College.

John Dickinson (1732 – 1808). Called the penman of the Revolution, Dickinson wrote political articles and attended the Federal Constitutional Convention.

Éleuthère Irénée du Pont (1772 – 1834). A Parisian by birth, Du Pont started a gunpowder mill near Wilmington in 1802. His business developed into E. I. du Pont de Nemours & Company, now a leading manufacturer of chemicals and chemical products.

Thomas Garrett (1789 – 1871).

Garrett made his home part of the abolitionists' underground railroad that helped slaves travel to freedom.

Howard Pyle (1853 – 1911). A popular magazine illustrator, Pyle also wrote and illustrated books for young people. His work, which was inspired by the beauty of Delaware's piedmont, helped establish the Brandywine school of art.

Caesar Rodney (1728 – 84). Rodney rode all night to get to the Second Continental Congress in time to cast his tie-breaking vote for independence.

ODDITIES AND SPECIALTIES

The arc that bounds Delaware in the north was drawn in colonial days so that no part of Delaware's boundary with Pennsylvania would be closer than 12 miles to New Castle.

Wilmington's Old Swedes Church, built in 1698, is the oldest U.S. Protestant church still to hold regular services.

Swedish immigrants in southern Delaware built the first log cabins in the country.

Delaware was nicknamed the Peach State in the 1800's when orchards on the peninsula supplied nearby cities with the lush fruit. By 1900, however, the peach trees were gone, victims of a disease called the yellows.

In 1911 T. Coleman du Pont, fascinated by the automobile, spent $40 million to build a four-lane highway, then the most modern in the U.S., that ran the length of Delaware.

PLACES TO VISIT, THINGS TO DO

Bombay Hook National Wildlife Refuge (near Smyrna). More than 16,000 acres, mostly tidal salt marsh, are a haven for great egrets, snow geese, white-tailed deer, river otters, and other wildlife.

Brandywine Creek State Park (near Wilmington). Nature lovers can enjoy 784 acres of forests, meadows, and marshlands with a wide variety of flora and fauna, as well as the creek.

Fishing For saltwater fishermen Delaware Bay yields mackerel, bluefish, weakfish, and tautog. Rehoboth Bay and Indian River Bay are good for crabbing and clamming.

Hagley Museum and Eleutherian Mills (near Wilmington). The museum and E. I. du Pont's stone house are located on the banks of Brandywine Creek, on the site of Du Pont's first mill. Exhibits trace the evolution of industry in this region.

Lewes This historic city has a colorful historic district that includes the Zwaanendael Museum, a replica of a Dutch town hall.

Odessa Historic District Named for the Russian seaport, Odessa has fine examples of 18th- and 19th-century architecture, including the Brick Hotel with its famous collection of Victorian furniture.

Prime Hook National Wildlife Refuge (22 miles southeast of Dover). These coastal wetlands along Delaware Bay provide a breeding and winter habitat for migratory waterfowl.

Trap Pond State Park (Laurel). This park boasts the country's northernmost public natural stands of bald cypress.

Winterthur Museum and Gardens (near Wilmington). Henry Francis du Pont's exquisitely landscaped former country home has nearly 200 period rooms and a large collection of American decorative arts.

Florida

The exotic treasure of America's subtropics

Florida's destiny has been molded by water. Jutting into the Atlantic for 450 miles, this most celebrated of America's peninsulas has no point more than 60 miles from its coastline. Rainfall averages more than 50 inches a year, making Florida one of the wettest states. As a result, some 30,000 lakes are scattered throughout its interior, ranging from pint-sized ponds to the 700-square-mile Lake Okeechobee.

These warm and sheltered waters attract an astounding array of wildlife. Alligators, crocodiles, manatees, sea turtles, more than 350 species of birds, and 700 species of fish can be found in or around Florida's ponds and coastal waters.

AN 8,000-MILE COASTLINE

Curving 1,350 miles down the Atlantic and back up the Gulf of Mexico, Florida's coastline expands to over 8,000 miles when the shores of islands, bays, and lagoons are included.

The protected waters between these islands and the shore make an ideal habitat for wildlife, especially fish-eating birds such as herons, ibises, and pelicans. Coastal swamps, estuaries, and saltwater marshes create inviting environments for crabs, conches, clams, and oysters. Fertile shoals yield shrimps, lobsters, and scallops. Offshore waters also offer some of the world's best deep-sea fishing.

The Gulf Stream bestows its favors on Florida. A subtropical climate reigns over the southern end of the peninsula and the Keys, while the rest of the state is temperate.

Huge flocks of ibises and egrets — just two of Florida's more than 350 bird species — probe for fish and other food in the shallow waters of the Everglades.

Nine Mile Creek, above, is just one of the many waterways that wend through Ocala National Forest, a "wet desert" of porous sand that is covered with shallow pools and subtropical vegetation. The area offers outstanding largemouth-bass fishing.

Florida panthers, right, are the last cougars in the eastern United States. Equally at home in the pine forests, grassy wetlands, or tree-shaded hammocks of south Florida, they were hunted nearly to extinction before being protected as an endangered species. Today, they are rarely seen in the wild.

MIAMI, CITY AMONG THE PALMS

Just over 100 years ago, the site of present-day Miami was a jungle of alligator-infested swamps. Julia Tuttle, an ebullient woman from Ohio, owned considerable property in what is now downtown Miami. For years, she had tried unsuccessfully to persuade railroad magnate Henry Flagler to extend his rail lines south from the tony resort of Palm Beach. In 1894 disaster came to her aid.

An exceptionally harsh winter that year froze out tourists and blackened the citrus crop all the way down to Flagler's estate in Palm Beach. Farther south in Miami, however, fruit trees were still blooming. Cannily, Mrs. Tuttle sent Flagler a sprig of Miami orange blossoms and offered to give him half her property if he brought in the train. Within six years, Miami had its rail link.

THE DEEP SOUTH OF FLORIDA'S NORTH

Northern Florida exudes the leisurely aura of the Deep South, replete with pine forests and lofty oaks draped in Spanish moss above flowering dogwoods and brilliant azaleas.

The upper half of Florida's panhandle region is an area of gently rolling red clay hills where the state reaches its highest elevation — 345 feet above sea level. The Suwannee River rises in the north, in the Okefenokee Swamp on the Georgia border, and flows southwestward to the Gulf. When Stephen Foster composed his song about the "Old Folks at Home" on the "Swanee River," he never foresaw that in the next century more people would retire to Florida than to any other state.

From north to south, the interior is covered with lakes and swamps. In some places, underground rivers rise through caverns to create sparkling artesian springs.

THE RIVER OF GRASS

Covering almost the entire tip of Florida south of Lake Okeechobee, the Everglades are the largest subtropical wilderness in the United States. In fact, this is freshwater marshland and sloughs, a "river of grass" 100 miles long, 50 miles wide, and rarely more than a few inches deep. Standing a few feet above the high-water level are hammocks, small islands covered

FLORIDA'S UNLIKELY MERMAIDS

Even in a state renowned for its exotic wildlife, manatees are objects of curiosity. Distantly related to elephants, these large and lumpy gentle giants belong to the only order of mammals other than whales that spend their entire lives in the water. The average adult — about 10 feet long and weighing 1,000 pounds — spends as much as eight hours a day grazing, during which it devours about 100 pounds of sea grass and other aquatic vegetation. With their voluminous appetites, manatees have occasionally been pressed into service to clear weed-choked waterways.

Floating just below the surface, manatees can look almost human. When Christopher Columbus explored Caribbean waters he mistook them for mermaids, reporting with disappointment on their lack of beauty. A thick, wrinkled hide all but covers the manatee's small eyes, and bristly hair covers its lips. Nevertheless, beauty in manatees, too, is only hide deep, and these amiable sea cows are also known for their graceful movement.

Sensitivity to water temperature limits the manatee's range. Although a few are found as far north as the Carolinas in summer, winter's chill drives them south. Yet even during the colder months there are perhaps no more than 1,200 manatees in all of Florida. Since 1973 they have been officially designated an endangered species. The chief threat to these slow-moving mammoths comes not from any natural predator but from their collisions with barges and the propellers of powerboats.

The barred owl above is perched in its favorite habitat, a thick, wet woodland. Common in Florida, barred owls also are found as far away as western Canada. Generally, they feed on birds and small mammals, but they also may wade into pools to catch fish.

Among the most striking-looking of Florida's wading birds, roseate spoonbills hunt by touch rather than sight. Swinging their bills slowly back and forth in long arcs through the water, they scoop up small fish, shellfish, and crustaceans.

with trees and shrubs. Their slight elevation, which holds them above summer floods, is the key to their different environment. In an area often only a few feet square, gumbo limbo trees (called tourist trees because their bark is red and peeling) rise beside hardwoods such as mahogany and live oaks.

Everglades wildlife is diverse. Deer linger in the shade. The powerful cougar, or Florida panther, prowls the higher ground of the hammocks and pinelands. In sloughs and waterholes, stately great blue herons stalk frogs and fish, while white ibises probe the shallows. From heights up to 100 feet, ospreys and bald eagles swoop down to snatch some wriggling fast food.

Also fishing, but from below, is the powerful reptile known as the keeper of the Everglades — the alligator, which despite its fearsome reputation, helps preserve wildlife. During the dry winter season, alligators burrow into the boggy muck, clearing out debris and creating waterholes that serve other animals. Once headed toward extinction, alligators now flourish to the point where they often turn up as uninvited backyard guests.

On the south and west coasts, mangrove forests seem to clamber atop their tangled roots into the sea, their foliage bristling over the myriad islands that dot Florida Bay. Here bottle-nosed dolphins cruise, and 1,000-pound manatees graze contentedly in nearby sheltered waterways.

TROPICAL JEWELS

South of the mainland, a 150-mile-long necklace of islands curves between the Atlantic and the Gulf of Mexico. Known as the Keys from the Spanish word *cayo* meaning small island, the last of these landfalls peeks above the ocean only 90 miles from Cuba.

Commencing off Key Biscayne, the Florida Keys are North America's largest coral reef system. More than 40 species of coral thrive here together with hundreds of species of neon-hued tropical fish.

Here in the Keys, Florida literally wades out to sea — a fitting endpoint for a place whose beauty is so fully tied to the subtle balance between the land and water.

THE TREE THAT BUILDS NEW LAND

Throughout Florida's southern tip, dense mangrove forests blanket the coast, sheltering the shore from storm damage and serving as nurseries for fish, crabs, shrimps, and oysters. Unlike most trees, these broad-leaved evergreens are able to grow in salt water, making them ideal for the coastal environment. Of the three types of mangroves — red, black, and white — the red is the basis for their successful proliferation.

Called walking trees by the Seminole Indians, red mangroves seem to be marching along on a tangled bundle of roots. These not only provide the trees with food, water, and oxygen, they also build land. Each year, the average acre of red mangrove forest sheds about 7,000 pounds of leaves and twigs, which drop among the roots and are caught there. Shells and other ocean-carried debris are also swept in and snared. All of this organic material gathers around the dense root system and eventually decays, forming new land.

As the land builds up, the sturdy black mangroves take root, identifiable by the vertical tubes that grow from their roots. Farther inland, where the land is still higher and drier, the tall white mangroves find a home.

Since saltwater-hardy red mangrove seedlings can float unharmed for up to a year, experts believe that the Florida forests may have originated from seeds that drifted from Africa across the Atlantic.

At Cayo Costa, a barrier island on the Gulf coast outside Fort Myers, a lone whelk shell sparkles on the beach where the land and water gently merge to create a peaceful refuge. Even the clouds enhance the island's tranquil beauty.

HISTORICAL HIGHLIGHTS

1513 After landing on coast, the explorer Ponce de León claims Florida for Spain.

1564 French Huguenots build Fort Caroline on St. Johns River.

1565 Pedro Menéndez de Avilés drives out French and founds city of St. Augustine.

1763 Spain gives Florida to Britain in exchange for Cuba.

1783 Spain takes Florida from Great Britain.

1821 After years of dispute, Spain cedes Florida to U.S.

1832 Seminole Indians refuse to leave their homeland for reservations in the West. This leads to Seminole Wars, which Indians lose 10 years later.

1845 Florida enters Union as 27th state.

1920 – 25 Land speculation leads to an unprecedented real-estate boom and greatly increases state's population.

1947 Everglades National Park is established.

1950 Newly established space center at Cape Canaveral sends off its first rocket.

1969 *Apollo 11* astronauts, launched from Cape Canaveral's Kennedy Space Center, become first people to walk on moon.

1971 Walt Disney World opens.

1983 – 85 Freezing weather and a fungus ruin the citrus crops.

1986 Space shuttle *Challenger* explodes, killing the entire crew on board.

1988 Space shuttle *Discovery* is launched successfully.

FAMOUS SONS AND DAUGHTERS

Mary McLeod Bethune

(1875 – 1955). The 17th child of emancipated slaves, Bethune became cofounder of Bethune-Cookman College. During the 1930's and 1940's she organized the National Council of Negro Women and served as President Franklin Roosevelt's special adviser on minority affairs.

Osceola (c. 1800 – 38). A brilliant guerrilla fighter, Osceola led the Seminole Indians during the Second Seminole War. Lured to a peace meeting, he was arrested by U.S. military officers. He died in prison.

Claude Pepper (1900 – 89). A stalwart champion of the rights of the elderly, Pepper served in the U.S. Senate (1936 – 51) and in the House of Representatives from 1963 until his death.

Marjorie Kinnan Rawlings (1896 – 1953). After a career as a journalist, Rawlings settled in rural Florida. Her novel *The Yearling*, about a boy's love for his deer, won a Pulitzer Prize in 1939.

Joseph W. Stilwell (1883 – 1946). Known as Vinegar Joe for his bluntness, Stilwell fought in both world wars and became an army general. During World War II he was U.S. commander in the China-Burma-India theater.

ODDITIES AND SPECIALTIES

Florida has possibly the world's largest and deepest spring: Wakulla Springs, near Tallahassee.

Florida's weather is so consistently fair that the St. Petersburg *Evening Standard* did not charge for its newspaper if the sun was not shining by press time. This "sunshine offer" remained in effect from 1910 until the paper closed in 1986.

Key limes, which grow in the Keys and other tropical areas, are the tangy basis of Key lime pie, a creamy dessert.

Florida's tourist population outnumbers its year-round residents by more than 3 to 1.

PLACES TO VISIT, THINGS TO DO

Biscayne National Park (near Homestead). Visitors can explore this marine preserve, with its living coral reefs, from glass-bottomed boats, or make a short trip to Elliott Key for swimming or a nature walk.

Walt Disney World (near Orlando). Combining the Magic Kingdom, Epcot Center, and the Disney – MGM Studios Theme Park, this extraordinary amusement center offers scores of rides, shows, and pavilions.

Everglades National Park (near Homestead). A unique subtropical wilderness, the Everglades are larger than Delaware. Their southern section has been preserved in this park where boardwalks and tour boats provide easy access to varied habitats and an astounding array of wildlife.

Key West Famous for its sunsets, this tiny island has long been an artists' and writers' haven. The historic district includes the homes of Ernest Hemingway and John James Audubon.

Kennedy Space Center (near Titusville). Historic spacecraft and launch sites as well as exhibits and movies are on view.

John and Mabel Ringling Museum of Art (Sarasota). The legacy of circus owner John Ringling, the complex includes art and circus galleries, a mansion, and a playhouse.

St. Augustine Founded in 1565, the oldest permanent city in the U.S. has a living history museum in the Spanish Quarter.

Seashell collecting

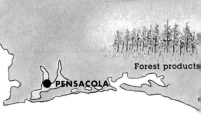
Forest products
PENSACOLA

Sanibel and Captiva islands along with the rest of the Gulf coast abound in unusual shells. Go at low tide.

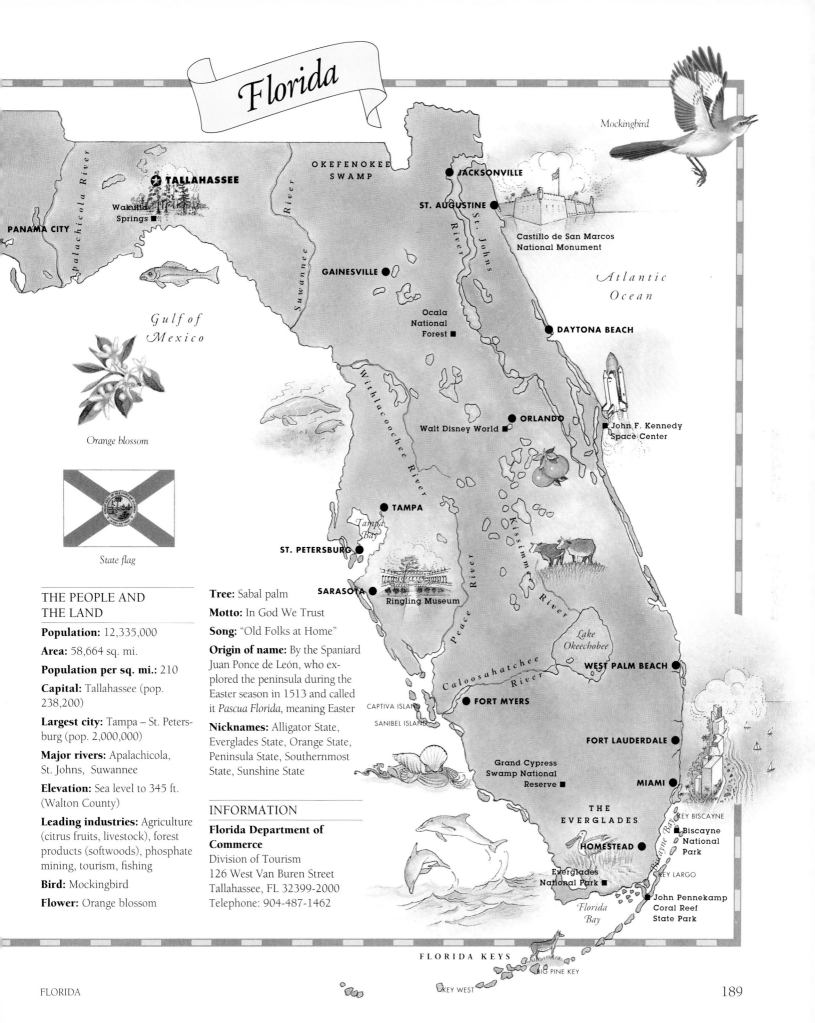

Florida

Mockingbird

OKEFENOKEE SWAMP

⊛ **TALLAHASSEE**

Wakulla Springs ■

PANAMA CITY

Apalachicola River

Suwannee River

● **JACKSONVILLE**

● **ST. AUGUSTINE**

Castillo de San Marcos National Monument

St. Johns River

Atlantic Ocean

GAINESVILLE ●

Gulf of Mexico

Orange blossom

Ocala National Forest ■

● **DAYTONA BEACH**

Withlacoochee River

ORLANDO ●
Walt Disney World ■

John F. Kennedy Space Center ■

● **TAMPA**

Tampa Bay

Kissimmee River

ST. PETERSBURG ●

State flag

SARASOTA ●
Ringling Museum

Peace River

Lake Okeechobee

THE PEOPLE AND THE LAND

Population: 12,335,000

Area: 58,664 sq. mi.

Population per sq. mi.: 210

Capital: Tallahassee (pop. 238,200)

Largest city: Tampa – St. Petersburg (pop. 2,000,000)

Major rivers: Apalachicola, St. Johns, Suwannee

Elevation: Sea level to 345 ft. (Walton County)

Leading industries: Agriculture (citrus fruits, livestock), forest products (softwoods), phosphate mining, tourism, fishing

Bird: Mockingbird

Flower: Orange blossom

Tree: Sabal palm

Motto: In God We Trust

Song: "Old Folks at Home"

Origin of name: By the Spaniard Juan Ponce de León, who explored the peninsula during the Easter season in 1513 and called it *Pascua Florida,* meaning Easter

Nicknames: Alligator State, Everglades State, Orange State, Peninsula State, Southernmost State, Sunshine State

INFORMATION

Florida Department of Commerce

Division of Tourism
126 West Van Buren Street
Tallahassee, FL 32399-2000
Telephone: 904-487-1462

WEST PALM BEACH ●

Caloosahatchee River

● **FORT MYERS**

CAPTIVA ISLAND

SANIBEL ISLAND

FORT LAUDERDALE ●

Grand Cypress Swamp National Reserve ■

MIAMI ●

THE EVERGLADES

KEY BISCAYNE

Biscayne National Park ■

HOMESTEAD ●

KEY LARGO

Everglades National Park ■

John Pennekamp Coral Reef State Park ■

Florida Bay

FLORIDA KEYS

BIG PINE KEY

KEY WEST

Georgia

Red clay hills and golden isles in the Empire State of the South

In 1733 the new colony of Georgia spread all the way from the marshy islands of the Atlantic coast to the banks of the Mississippi. James Edward Oglethorpe, an idealistic member of Parliament, had obtained a charter that would make the vast expanse of forested land a refuge for Britain's destitute and religious dissidents — a place for a second chance.

Exotic and virtually tropical in the eyes of the English, Georgia also held promise as a place to produce the spices, silks, and wines needed by the mother country. Soon it was evident that those commodities would never materialize — but the land was rife with other possibilities. The marshes along the coast were ideal for growing rice, and the land farther west would quickly yield a bounty of cotton and peaches. The earth would also give up marble, granite, and even gold (Dahlonega was the site of the nation's first gold rush in 1828, beating California by two decades).

BLUE RIDGE TO PIEDMONT

The city Oglethorpe laid out on the Savannah River was sultry and mosquito-infested, but it was also a model of town planning. Savannah's two-square-mile original quarter, with buildings clustered around leafy squares, remains one of the South's most romantic places. Spanish moss hanging from gnarled oaks brushes the sidewalks, and grand old houses suggest the graciousness with which the South, and Georgia in particular, are identified.

Not all of Georgia is so typically Southern. Cool mountains slope down into the northern reaches, part of the Blue Ridge of the

A live oak, heavy with vines and Spanish moss, frames a path through the forest on Wassaw Island.

Sharptop and Oglethorpe, two of the peaks in the Appalachian Mountains that reach into northern Georgia, blaze with color in autumn. Hollows and valleys in the mountains have been home to people of Scotch-Irish descent since the early 19th century.

Appalachians. Still more characteristic are the pine-covered red clay hills, known as the Piedmont, in the central part of the state. It was here that Georgians would eventually make good — both by mining the region's bedrock of granite and by turning its gentle slopes into the cotton fields that would become the basis for Georgia's first great industry.

A railway hub established in the Piedmont in the 1830's grew into the city of Atlanta. In the Civil War, Union General Sherman reduced most of it to ashes. Today, some 130 years later, the shimmering skyscrapers of the resurrected city rise like monuments to Georgians' initiative and enterprise.

Atlanta may be the pride of Georgia, but back roads fan out in every direction to what locals think of as the "real Georgia" — green expanses of field and forest interspersed with tiny towns with such remarkable names as Enigma and Between. Along the way, roadside entrepreneurs sell peaches, cold cider, and boiled peanuts, a Southern specialty served up from a bubbling caldron.

LAND OF THE TREMBLING EARTH

South of the Piedmont, the land becomes lower and flatter toward the coastal plain. Much of this part of the state is fertile farmland where wheat, soybeans, and still more cotton

A white water stretch of the Chattooga River challenges a kayaker in north Georgia.

are grown. Peach trees fill the flats south of Macon, while the town of Vidalia considers itself the onion-growing capital of the world.

THE GOLDEN ISLES

Sprinkled along the Atlantic coast are the barrier islands Georgians call the Golden Isles for the warm color of their sands. These languorous havens are a wonderland of constantly evolving marshes, beaches, and palmetto trees. Eight of the islands, still largely unspoiled, have been sold or donated to various government or conservation organizations. Four more are resorts, outfitted with golf courses and five-star hotels.

Near Springer Mountain, a hiker treks the southernmost portion of the Appalachian Trail, the mountain footpath that stretches 2,050 miles from Georgia to Maine.

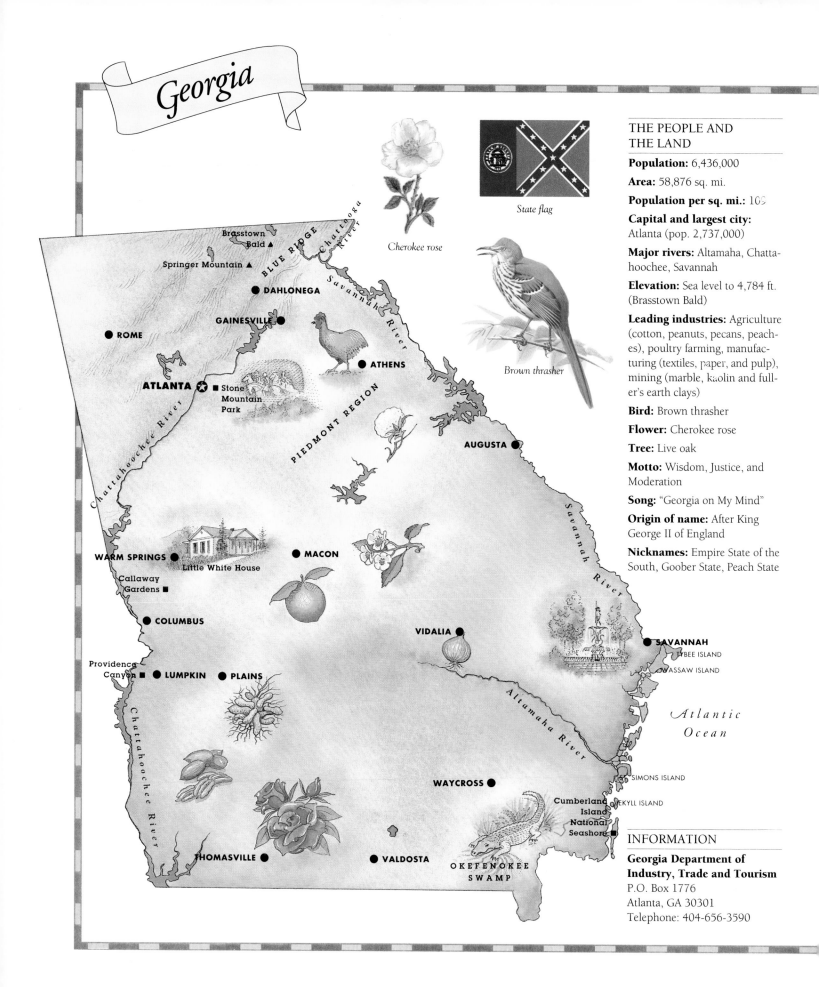

Georgia

State flag

Cherokee rose

Brown thrasher

Brasstown Bald ▲

Springer Mountain ▲

BLUE RIDGE

Chattooga River

Savannah River

● DAHLONEGA

● GAINESVILLE

● ROME

● ATHENS

ATLANTA ✪ ■ Stone Mountain Park

PIEDMONT REGION

● AUGUSTA

Chattahoochee River

WARM SPRINGS ● Little White House

● MACON

Callaway Gardens ■

● COLUMBUS

Providence Canyon ■ ● LUMPKIN ● PLAINS

VIDALIA ●

SAVANNAH ●
TYBEE ISLAND
OSSABAW ISLAND

Altamaha River

Atlantic Ocean

ST. SIMONS ISLAND

WAYCROSS ●

Cumberland Island National Seashore ■

JEKYLL ISLAND

THOMASVILLE ●

● VALDOSTA

OKEFENOKEE SWAMP

THE PEOPLE AND THE LAND

Population: 6,436,000

Area: 58,876 sq. mi.

Population per sq. mi.: 10?

Capital and largest city: Atlanta (pop. 2,737,000)

Major rivers: Altamaha, Chattahoochee, Savannah

Elevation: Sea level to 4,784 ft. (Brasstown Bald)

Leading industries: Agriculture (cotton, peanuts, pecans, peaches), poultry farming, manufacturing (textiles, paper, and pulp), mining (marble, kaolin and fuller's earth clays)

Bird: Brown thrasher

Flower: Cherokee rose

Tree: Live oak

Motto: Wisdom, Justice, and Moderation

Song: "Georgia on My Mind"

Origin of name: After King George II of England

Nicknames: Empire State of the South, Goober State, Peach State

INFORMATION

Georgia Department of Industry, Trade and Tourism
P.O. Box 1776
Atlanta, GA 30301
Telephone: 404-656-3590

HISTORICAL HIGHLIGHTS

1540 Hernando de Soto leads Spanish expedition into the area.

1732 King George II's charter establishes Georgia, the last of the 13 colonies.

1733 British colonists, led by James Edward Oglethorpe, found town of Savannah.

1742 The British defeat the Spanish, who have also claimed Georgia, on St. Simons Island.

1788 Georgia ratifies U.S. Constitution, becoming fourth state.

1793 Eli Whitney invents the cotton gin near Savannah.

1838 Last of Georgia Cherokees are forced to take "Trail of Tears" to reservations in the West.

1861 Georgia secedes from Union, joins Confederacy.

1864 General Sherman's troops burn Atlanta and ravage state in their "March to the Sea."

1881 Rebuilt, Atlanta holds International Cotton Exposition.

1921 Boll weevils destroy much of the state's cotton crop.

1943 Georgia becomes the first state in U.S. to give 18-year-olds the vote.

1973 Maynard Jackson, Jr., of Atlanta becomes first black mayor of a major southern city.

1986 Carter Presidential Center opens in Atlanta as museum, library, and think tank for international issues such as human rights and the environment.

FAMOUS SONS AND DAUGHTERS

Jimmy Carter (1924 –). Elected president in 1976, the peanut farmer from Plains brought an unaffected style to the White House. During his term Carter negotiated the Camp David accord between Israel and Egypt.

Ty Cobb (1886 – 1961). The phenomenal ability of this baseball player, known as the Georgia Peach, earned him a charter membership in the National Baseball Hall of Fame.

Joel Chandler Harris (1848 – 1908). Fascinated by black folklore, this newspaperman wrote the Uncle Remus tales. Many of the stories were inspired by slaves Harris had known as a young man.

Martin Luther King, Jr.

(1929 – 68). A Baptist minister, King became leader of the civil-rights movement and was awarded the Nobel Peace Prize in 1964. In 1968 he was assassinated in Memphis while there to support a strike.

Sidney Lanier (1842 – 81). One of the most accomplished poets of his time, Lanier took much of his inspiration from his home state, with such works as "Song of the Chattahoochee."

Juliette Gordon Low (1860 – 1927). Low started the Girl Scouts of America. Today there is an extensive collection of Girl Scout memorabilia on display at her Savannah home.

Carson McCullers (1917 – 67). This novelist and playwright wrote *The Heart Is a Lonely Hunter* and *The Member of the Wedding.*

Margaret Mitchell (1900– 49). Mitchell's story of Georgia in the Civil War, *Gone With the Wind,* is one of the most widely read novels in history and a motion picture classic.

Jackie Robinson (1919 – 72). Born in the town of Cairo, Robinson was the first black to play major-league baseball and the first to be inducted into the National Baseball Hall of Fame.

ODDITIES AND SPECIALTIES

Beneath modern Atlanta lies the original city, which was rebuilt in the 1960's as Underground Atlanta. It comprises 12 acres of museums, shops, restaurants, and nightclubs.

Gainesville, the self-proclaimed poultry capital of the world, has an ordinance against using utensils, instead of fingers, to eat the local fried chicken.

The Cherokee alphabet was invented in New Echota. Later, the first newspaper in an American Indian language, the *Cherokee Phoenix,* was printed there.

Macon boasts more cherry trees than any other U.S. city.

PLACES TO VISIT, THINGS TO DO

Callaway Gardens (Pine Mountain). This pine-swathed, 2,500-acre resort has hiking trails, lakes, and a huge greenhouse open for tours.

Stephen C. Foster State Park (Okefenokee National Wildlife Refuge). Boat tours and the Trembling Earth Nature Trail offer the best views of the 770-sq.-mi. Okefenokee Swamp, one of the largest freshwater wetlands in North America.

Jekyll Island Once the winter home of the nation's wealthiest families, including the Rockefellers and Vanderbilts, this barrier island is now a resort. Several of the former family homes are open to the public.

Savannah National Historic District The nation's largest urban historic district is made up of restored 18th- and 19th-century homes and public buildings, many of them facing picturesque squares. Old cotton warehouses along the Savannah River now house galleries, restaurants, and shops.

Stone Mountain Park

(Stone Mountain). The world's largest bas-relief sculpture — a tableau of Jefferson Davis, Robert E. Lee, and Stonewall Jackson on horseback — is carved into the face of the world's largest granite outcropping. Other attractions include a railroad, an antebellum plantation, and a riverboat.

Warm Springs After contracting polio, Franklin D. Roosevelt was a frequent visitor to this town's therapeutic springs. He built his home, the Little White House, nearby and died there in 1945. The house, now open to the public, is as he left it.

Hawaii

America's tropical paradise in the Pacific

More than 2,000 miles from the nearest continent, and on the same latitude as central Mexico, Hawaii is an exotic, tropical paradise. Plants and animals native to the islands are found nowhere else on earth.

About A.D. 300, a group of Polynesians arrived at this remote string of islands, and according to tradition named them after their homeland Hawaiki. Though the Hawaiians descended from these settlers now account for less than 20 percent of the state's population, their culture has made a distinct and permanent imprint. The warm and outgoing nature of Hawaiians has made this state a melting pot that works. While a movement is on to preserve the Hawaiian language, culture, and traditions, Polynesians, Orientals, Caucasians (*haoles* in Hawaiian), and other racial and ethnic groups live together harmoniously, with an intermarriage rate of more than 40 percent.

ISLANDS FROM THE SEA

Millions of years ago the Hawaiian Islands erupted from a hot spot on the Pacific Ocean floor. Layers of lava rose over time, formed undersea mountains, and 70 million years ago emerged from the sea as fiery volcanoes. They spread out in a line, northwest to southeast, more than 1,500 miles from end to end.

The youngest and least eroded of the volcanoes are the eight major islands that constitute the state of Hawaii — Hawaii, Maui, Oahu, Kauai, and Molokai; privately owned Lanai and Niihau; and uninhabited

The Kilauea Lighthouse crowns an isolated promontory on the north shore of Kauai. The adjoining parkland is a wildlife sanctuary for seabirds.

The remnant of an ancient volcanic crater, Hanauma Bay forms a perfect crescent 10 miles down the coast from Honolulu. Once the favored retreat for Hawaiian royalty, the picturesque bay is now a marine reserve whose waters support more than 90 species of fish.

Kahoolawe. The 124 smaller points of land are older, more eroded volcanoes.

Hawaii, the Big Island, lends its name to the entire state. Five volcanoes have contributed to its formation, two of which, Mauna Loa and Kilauea, remain active. Mauna Loa is the largest mountain in the world, a massive hunk of 10,000 cubic miles. Kilauea is the world's most active volcano. A third volcano, Mauna Kea, though its summit is a mere 13,796 feet above sea level, is the world's tallest mountain, measuring over 33,000 feet from the ocean floor.

Some parts of the island are drenched by constant rainfall while others are almost as dry as desert. Near Hilo lush stands of rain forest bloom with brilliant tropical flowers while waterfalls tumble into serene pools — exotic images that have long inclined people to think of Hawaii as paradise. On the other side of the island, a light blanket of snow may cover the summits of Mauna Loa and Mauna Kea. Meanwhile, the sun always shines on the dry, sunny beaches of the Kona Coast.

Despite its natural wonders and tourist attractions, the Big Island is largely agricultural. At the Parker Ranch, the largest individually owned cattle ranch in the United States, more than 50,000 head of cattle graze on nearly 225,000 acres in the shadow of old volcanoes. The island's rich soil also bears Kona coffee, macadamia nuts, orchids, and anthuriums.

OAHU: THE GATHERING PLACE

Archaeologists have been unable to pinpoint the first Hawaiian landing site, but some of the earliest identified settlements are on Oahu, long ago nicknamed the Gathering Place for its large population — which at more than 800,000 today is the largest of any Hawaiian island. Honolulu, on the southeastern coast, is the state's largest city, capital, and business center, as well as the site of Waikiki Beach.

While much of the island is a modern metropolis with urban skyscrapers, suburban homes nestled in mountains and valleys, and interstate highways (connected to no other state), Oahu retains its tropical allure. Overlooking Waikiki is Diamond Head, the extinct volcano that is Hawaii's most familiar landmark. Off Waikiki Beach are the waters where ancient Hawaiians developed the sport of surfing to an art, and 20th-century Hawaiians and *haoles* continue the search for the perfect wave. Up along the Windward Coast is idyllic Hanauma Bay, its peaceful waters a haven for tropical fish and a heaven for snorkelers. The steep green mountains of the Koolau Range drop into the Windward Coast in the east.

In downtown Honolulu stands a heroic bronze statue of Kamehameha the Great, one hand holding a spear and the other outstretched in a greeting of aloha. Around his shoulders is his royal cape, which was originally made from thousands of yellow feathers from the now-extinct mamo bird.

In 1795, Kamehameha united the islands (except Kauai and Niihau) and founded the Kingdom of Hawaii. He thus became the first of eight monarchs to rule Hawaii — the only American state to have been an independent kingdom.

Queen Liliuokalani, beloved by the Hawaiian people, was deposed in 1893 by American business interests and held virtual prisoner in her own Iolani Palace. A provisional government was established, which worked for annexation to the United States. Its efforts were finally successful in 1898. The Victorian palace, with its empty thrones, still stands.

KAUAI: THE GARDEN ISLAND

Kauai, the Garden Island, is known for its lush vegetation, the result of a potent mixture of sunshine and rainfall. Mount Waialeale, whose volcanic activity formed Kauai, is the wettest spot on earth, averaging more than 450 inches of rain a year. Rolling farmlands dominate the landscape, and sugarcane is the major crop.

Waimea Canyon — over 2,800 feet deep, a mile wide, and 10 miles long — is one of Kauai's most dramatic landforms. It is with beaches, however, that Kauai is associated in the popular imagination — this island was the setting for the motion picture *South Pacific*.

Just southwest of Kauai lies Niihau, the Forbidden Island, where all outsiders are barred and the Hawaiian language and culture

Irrigated fields of taro spread over the Keanae Peninsula on Maui. The starchy root vegetable, a staple in Hawaii and the rest of Polynesia, grows for seven months before being harvested.

A thicket of tulip trees and royal palms surrounds Nanaue Falls on the island of Hawaii.

Early morning sun strikes Iao Needle, a 1,200-foot volcanic cinder cone on Maui.

are preserved. The island is owned by a family who operate it as a cattle and sheep ranch.

MAUI: THE VALLEY ISLAND

Maui was formed from two volcanoes, connected by an isthmus, the "valley" in its nickname. In the eastern half lies the awe-inspiring Haleakala, whose crater is 21 miles in circumference, 19 square miles in area, and 3,000 feet deep.

Cattle graze and flowers and vegetables are grown on its cool slopes. Nearly 30 miles of trail wind down from the crater rim into the barren lava landscape (U.S. astronauts did some training here for their moon missions).

Highly developed, western Maui is often compared to California. But there is also a bit of New England on the western coast, where clapboard houses, widow's walks, and false-front buildings in the town of Lahaina recall the 19th-century influx of Yankee whalers and New England missionaries.

West of Maui lies Lanai, site of a large pineapple plantation. Kahoolawe, the smallest of the major islands, lies southwest of Maui and is uninhabited.

MOLOKAI: THE FRIENDLY ISLAND

Molokai adopted its nickname, not just because its people are friendly, but to bury its past. It was here, during the 1860's, that the government started shipping leprosy patients into exile on the Kalaupapa Peninsula, separated from the rest of Molokai by steep perpendicular cliffs. The recent history of Kalaupapa is dominated by the saintly figure of Father Damien, a Belgian priest who served the colony from 1873 to 1889.

Molokai is the only island, except Niihau, whose population is mainly Hawaiian. Everywhere remnants of Hawaiian culture are evident. Temple ruins, petroglyphs, and derelict ponds once stocked with fish for kings are historic reminders of the Hawaiian heritage that happily still pervades the islands.

The Koolau Range parallels the eastern coast of Oahu for 37 miles and forms a dramatic backdrop for the city of Honolulu. Suburbs creep right up into foothills of the mountains.

Idaho

*From wilderness to farmland,
a grand mix of western scenery*

Geographers cannot seem to agree on whether to call Idaho part of the Pacific Northwest, the Rocky Mountain West, or the Intermountain West — not surprising, since a topographical map of the state looks something like a crazy quilt patched together with odd pieces of mountain and prairie, desert and lakeland, forest and plain.

First part of Oregon Country, then Washington Territory, present-day Idaho — home to only about a million people — is what was left over when Montana was eventually shorn away. But if Idaho is a scrap, it is a gloriously scenic one, from its 45-mile-wide panhandle on the Canadian border to its mountainous wilderness areas and vast plains farther south. Cobbled in along the way are rolling prairies, snowy peaks, and sage-covered flatlands.

BRIGHT FIELDS OF THE GRASSLAND

Hugging the western edge of the panhandle and curving partway down the Snake River is Idaho's grassland — Camas Prairie (named for the star-shaped blue flowers whose bulbs were a staple food of the region's Nez Perce Indians) and the fertile Palouse Hills. The cultivated fields in this part of Idaho could have been lifted from Pennsylvania Dutch country. Rustic barns dot oceans of rippling wheat and flowering rape, while poplars edge bright green fields of barley, beans, and peas. (Potatoes, Idaho's most famous commodity, belong to the Snake River Valley, a distant 300 miles to the south). The city of Lewiston, market center for the prairie and once the capital of

A country road in the Palouse Hills cuts a swath between fields of peas and flowering yellow rape.

Although typical of the yawning chasms of the West in this section of its 70-mile length, Bruneau Canyon narrows to only 30 feet wide in some places.

wildflowers bloom on the open slopes. Also nestled in the northern ranges is Lake Pend Oreille, 43 miles long, more than 1,000 feet deep, and an irresistible lure for fishermen.

Blanketing these northern ranges are western white pines — some of them 200 feet tall. Relentless logging, a disastrous fire in 1910, and the ravages of blister rust have reduced much of the virgin growth to a memory, but 80 percent of northern Idaho is still forested. The cedar-hemlock forest of the Selkirks shelters the country's last remaining herd of woodland caribou. And from many overlooks in this lakeland, only the wake of a holiday fisherman's boat suggests that anything has changed in the last 200 years.

In central Idaho, the Salmon River cuts through the loftier Lemhi, Lost River, and Sawtooth ranges. This storied "River of No Return" was the one that Indians convinced Lewis and Clark to detour. From its birthplace in the Sawtooths — mountains sharpened to points by glaciers — the 400-mile Salmon traverses a 2-million-acre wilderness. Today adventurous river runners in kayaks, canoes, and rafts test its waters and give new life to isolated towns like Stanley and Salmon.

LAND OF ABRUPT CHANGE

South of the Sawtooths the land is arid and flat, with the Snake River swinging in a graceful arc across sagebrush-covered plains. But irrigation of the Snake River Valley has turned more than 2 million acres into flourishing farmland. Seventy percent of all Idahoans live within 50 miles of the river; most are concentrated in the cities of Boise, Pocatello, and Idaho Falls, but many live on farms, growing sugar beets, beans, and enough potatoes to account for a full quarter of the nation's output.

With fertile fields cheek by jowl with arid plains, southern Idaho is not easily categorized. But that is true of the rest of the state as well, where the land is wont to change all the more abruptly — from plain to mountain, from prairie to forest. Within the jigsaw borders of this piece of western terrain, nature has created a splendid patchwork.

With the sunlit Sawtooth Mountains in the background, a solitary sculler glides through the mist on Little Redfish Lake.

Illinois

The spirit of the prairie, the heart of America

Illinois was the place where the sky began, the place where new settlers emerged from the shadows of the eastern woodlands into a vast, sun-drenched plain. Here, standing at the edge of an ocean of grass, Americans got their first, awestruck glimpse of the immense fertility of the continent, the abundance that lay like God's promise over the land. At last freed of the forest, the sky unfurled and the land rolled on to infinity — flat, free, destined for the plow. Here, they knew, the East ends and the West begins.

PROSPECT OF THE PRAIRIE

"One of the most delightful prospects I have ever beheld," wrote an amazed traveler describing the prairie in 1791, "all the low grounds being meadow, and without wood, and all of the high grounds being covered with trees and appearing like islands; the whole scene seemed an Elysium." The land was then thickly covered with tall grass, the big bluestem that rises higher than a man can reach, with roots lodged 15 feet into the earth. The depth of the grass roots was the key to the life of the prairie. Periodic fires raged over the land, burning off dead grass on the surface and leaving the roots intact to sprout anew from the ashes.

Over thousands of years this process of fiery death and regrowth created soil of unsurpassed fertility. From A.D. 900 to 1450 the land nurtured an advanced American Indian culture, known to us today by the fascinating remnants of a large city, the Cahokia Mounds, near present-day Collinsville. The largest urban Indian settlement north of Mexico, this

The rocky land at the southern tip of Illinois remains wooded, as in this scene at Ferne Clyffe State Park.

The rolling midwestern prairie, its tough grass tamed by the plow, presents a classic American panorama. The farms shown here lie in the northwest corner of Illinois.

city and its surrounding communities housed some 20,000 people who had an extensive trading and agricultural economy. The 70-odd surviving earthworks, most of them burial mounds, cover six square miles.

So rich was the soil of the prairie that the first white settlers who farmed it did not have to work very hard to survive. It took only 50 days of plowing, planting, cultivating, and harvesting to bring in a 10-acre corn crop. One traveler thought that Illinoisans "do the least work I believe of any people in the world." In Illinois in 1837, a transplanted Vermonter named John Deere made farming still easier, manufacturing a steel plow that cut through the tough grass roots and became known as "the plow that broke the plains."

Deere's plow ushered in the age of large-scale agriculture. Today, 80 percent of the state's land is devoted to farming, and Illinois produces much of the nation's corn, soybeans, and wheat. The taming of the prairie has not

Streams feeding the Illinois River eroded 18 canyons through Starved Rock State Park, near Utica. The park takes its name from the 125-foot butte where, according to legend, a band of Illinois Indians died of hunger after a battle with the Ottawa-Potawatomi tribes.

Geese wander the grounds at Lincoln's New Salem State Historic Site, a re-creation of the village where Abraham Lincoln lived in the 1830's. The village, with its rustic log buildings, is located near the central Illinois town of Petersburg.

come without cost (huge amounts of topsoil are washed away each year), but it has brought a different kind of beauty to Illinois — the sight of impeccably straight rows of corn stretching to the horizon across a patchwork of farms, the very image of abundance.

A MINGLING OF NORTH AND SOUTH

The first lands to be settled in Illinois were the less arable plains along the rivers in the south. Cairo, the city that grew up at the confluence

The dramatic sweep of the prairie inspired not only the poetry of Carl Sandburg and the paintings of realists like Grant Wood, but also an architecture that is emphatically American in style. Frank Lloyd Wright, who lived and worked in Chicago for some 30 years, saw in the prairie a particular kind of beauty that he believed its dwellings should reflect. The result was his elegantly simple design for "prairie houses," countless examples of which sprang up in Illinois and neighboring states. The houses were particularly prized in the more affluent suburbs of Chicago, where the specimens that remain true to their original designs are given landmark status today.

With their low, horizontal lines and expansive rooms, prairie houses blended into the endless horizon of the plains. Porches, terraces, and balconies served to bring the outdoors inside, and indigenous construction materials and mellow earth colors further integrated the houses with their surroundings.

Wright constructed his most famous example of the style, Robie House, in Chicago in 1909. Now open to the public, the graceful structure stands as a telling reminder of Wright's lasting influence on American domestic architecture, and, in turn, of his primary inspiration — the distinctive landscape of the great American Midwest.

Blanketed by a late snow, frozen Lake Springfield begins its spring thaw. By mid-May the lake, in central Illinois, will be abuzz with motorboats and waterskiers.

of the Mississippi and Ohio rivers — the arteries that carried foodstuffs and manufactured goods through inland America — seemed destined for greatness as a marketplace. But Cairo waned, while a city on a patch of marshland to the north grew to splendor — Chicago. Railroads, meatpacking, steel, banking, commerce, and a host of other enterprises drew millions of immigrants, creating the mighty "City of the Big Shoulders."

This contrast between industrialized north and rural south is one of the aspects that gives Illinois its dynamism. From its early days this midwestern state has been a crossroads of cultures, politics, religions, and economic forces. Not only was it the meeting place of East and West, it was the place where the people and attitudes of North and South mingled. Chicago is almost as far north as Boston, Cairo as far south as Richmond. And Illinois is so long that it has the climate and flora of both North and South — fir trees flourish in the cool northern reaches while peaches grow in the warmth of the south.

ORCHARDS AND WILDFOWL

Not all of Illinois is prairie. A glacier-made ridge in the southernmost part of the state, the Shelbyville moraine, marks a dividing line between the grasslands and forests. South of the ridge the hills are thick with trees. Farmers cultivate lush orchards of plums, apples, peaches, cherries, and pears, and the landscape is dotted with crystalline lakes that sustain rare and endangered wildfowl. The wild turkey, once virtually extinct in Illinois, has been coming back in increasing numbers in the southern counties. And near Shawnee National Forest, more than 100,000 Canada geese come to spend the winter each year at Crab Orchard National Wildlife Refuge and Horseshoe Lake Wildlife Refuge.

Still, for all the beauty of the southern counties, it is the spirit of the state's northern rolling prairie that suffuses Illinois. Carl Sandburg, a native of the state, evoked that spirit in one of his poems:

The prairie sings to me in the forenoon and I know in the night I rest easy in the prairie arms, on the prairie heart.

Tower Rock is the highest of the limestone bluffs that loom over the Ohio River in southern Illinois. The scenic overlook is part of the 263,000-acre Shawnee National Forest.

Indiana

Historic, homey, and Hoosier

At a turkey shoot during pioneer days, the typical Indiana frontiersman would hang back, leaning on his long rifle, while the visitors and city folk did all the talking. Then he would prime his piece, step up to the line, and win the turkey. Hoosiers, as Indianans like to be called, remain much the same today: calm, competent, and competitive — colorful, too, just not flamboyant.

The same can be said of the state that is their home. It is a green, leafy, unpretentious sort of place, with plenty of trees in the cities and towns, patches of woods scattered here and there across the rural countryside, and dense forests in the south.

FROM FOREST TO FARMLAND

When Indiana entered the Union in 1816 almost the entire state was part of a great hardwood forest stretching from the Mississippi River to the Appalachians. Today only 19 percent of the state is wooded and three-quarters of the land is devoted to agriculture.

The southern hills were the first part of Indiana to be settled as backwoodsmen, mainly from similar areas in Tennessee, Kentucky, and Virginia, crossed the Ohio River in search of new land. Typical of these yeoman farmers were Abraham Lincoln's parents, who arrived from Kentucky in 1816, the year Indiana became a state and the future president was seven years old. Even today the region retains its heritage, giving Indiana perhaps the most southern character of any northern state.

Glimpses of the original landscape can still be seen in southern Indiana, especially its

The East Fork of the White River wends its way across Hoosier National Forest south of Bedford.

Circular barns like the one above became the rage in Fulton County around 1900 as farmers sought to lessen their labors by using a central feeding area for livestock. The barns proved difficult to heat and light, however, and the last one was built in 1924.

Brown County is pretty all through the year, but each autumn the colorful foliage of mixed hardwoods turns this unspoiled terrain into one of nature's grand spectacles. Generally, people flock to Brown County State Park, which comprises some 15,500 acres and has 27 miles of picturesque country roads. Also in the county are Yellowwood State Forest and Hoosier National Forest, equally beautiful and not as crowded.

central part — an area of steep bluffs and scenic outlooks, tranquil river bottoms, limestone caves, and wandering deer.

By contrast, the northern half of the state is flat, dotted with lakes and crossed by an intertwining system of rivers that served the Indians and early explorers as highways. The Miami Indian stronghold of Kekionga, for example, stood on the site of present-day Fort Wayne, guarding the short overland portage between the Maumee River and a tributary of

the Wabash and ultimately connecting Lake Erie with the Gulf of Mexico.

Settlers from the East began entering Indiana in significant numbers during the 1830's, when the National Road (the main pioneer roadway west, now paralleled by Route 40) reached Indianapolis. Their first task was to clear the vast tracts of level, fertile land for farms. After the Civil War, lumbering operations began, and in a matter of decades the great forest had disappeared, to be replaced by the farms, country roads, quiet villages, and amiable tree-lined streets that have become Indiana's hallmarks.

A TREACHEROUS SWAMP

The wetlands of Indiana's northern plains were among the last places to be cleared. It was here that the young writer and naturalist Gene Stratton Porter came in the late 1890's, encountering what she called "a treacherous swamp and quagmire filled with every plant,

Sixty-foot-high Big Clifty Falls is the most spectacular of the many cascades in Clifty Falls State Park near Madison. The most thrilling time to hike the trails of this hilly, 1,360-acre preserve is during the spring, when the water level is highest.

animal, and human danger known in the worst of such locations in the Central States." Yet it was also, as she realized, a place of surpassing beauty, teeming with birds, moths, butterflies, and wildflowers — and it was vanishing as lumbermen felled trees and developers pushed through drainage ditches.

In best-selling novels published between 1903 and 1923, Porter brought national attention to the fragility and transient loveliness of this world. Today, Indiana protects its northern wetlands with a series of fish-and-wildlife preserves where migrating mallards, blue herons, and sandhill cranes still swoop down to rest among the cattails and water hemlock, just as they did in Porter's time.

HOOSIERS ALL

Occupying a patch of flat land in the exact geographic center of the state is Indianapolis, the state capital. Laid out in 1820, the planned city is the epitome of tree-lined urban orderliness in its older neighborhoods and downtown. Cornfields and orchards lie well within its borders — the result of a move to extend the city's boundaries in 1969 — while residents enjoy such urban amenities as art museums, a symphony orchestra, and professional sports, as well as the running of the world-famous Indianapolis 500-mile auto race.

Its big-city ways notwithstanding, Indianapolis is typically Hoosier, and it is Hoosier character that gives this state its style. These days that character is no longer exemplified by the cool and competent frontiersman at the turkey shoot, but it still may have much to do with sharpshooting. Every March in cities and towns throughout Indiana, excitement mounts as Hoosiers breathlessly follow the playoffs for the statewide high-school basketball championship. It always seems to come down to a tie score with only seconds left on the clock. Then some lanky Hoosier calmly steps to the line and drops in a free throw — and, like the pioneers before him, wins it all. It is a ritual Indianans never tire of.

Flat-topped black buggies are a sign of devotion to tradition in the Amish villages of northeastern Indiana.

AMERICA'S QUARRY

Walk around New York, Chicago, Washington, D.C., or many other American cities and you will be looking at bits of Indiana. Much of the architectural limestone used on building exteriors in this country comes from a strip of Indiana ground 50 miles long, a few miles wide, and 60 feet deep near the towns of Bedford and Bloomington. Stone from this belt — the Salem Outcrop — was used in Rockefeller Center and the Empire State Building in New York City, the Tribune Tower in Chicago, the Pentagon and the Lincoln Memorial in Washington, and in 14 state capitols.

The limestone was created some 330 million years ago when water covered the Midwest. Like most limestone, it is made from the decomposed bodies and shells of ancient sea creatures. But the Indiana beds are especially free of other ocean debris, which would have flawed the rock. This purity makes the Hoosier stone prized building material. It can be worked in smooth architectural slabs of 10 to 20 tons and quarried in mammoth blocks weighing up to 10 times that much.

Autumn brings both bounty and beauty to Conner Prairie, a 55-acre restoration of an 1830's pioneer village and farm north of Indianapolis.

Iowa

*Cornfields green and gold,
proclaiming a fertile land*

In the popular movie *Field of Dreams,* a long-dead legendary baseball player returns to life and steps onto a baseball diamond a farmer has built on his cornfield. Surveying the scene of agrarian beauty, the baseball player asks, "Is this heaven?"

"No," the farmer replies. "It's Iowa."

In Iowa movie theaters this brief exchange produced bursts of applause as well as hoots of laughter. The mixed reaction reflects the two-sided feeling Iowans have for their state: on the one hand, a self-deprecating awareness of Iowa's reputation as a place where corn and hogs reign supreme, and on the other, a deep conviction that Iowa, a magnificently fertile land between two great rivers, really is the next thing to heaven.

RURAL HEART AND SOUL

The very word *Iowa* stands as a virtual synonym for America's agricultural heritage and bounty. Only California and Texas, which are several times Iowa's size, exceed the state in the value of farm products. And more than any other state, Iowa still represents Thomas Jefferson's ideal nation of well-educated farmers. It boasts both the greatest number of farms of any state except Texas and the highest literacy rate in the nation.

Despite its image as a state of farmers, Iowa's town- and city-dwellers outnumber farm residents by almost 10 to 1. They live in places like Des Moines, Iowa's capital and a major center for the insurance industry; Cedar Rapids, home of one of the nation's largest

Cattle and cornfields under a broad Iowa sky are the picture of American agriculture. This farm is in the eastern part of the state, near Iowa City.

Plowing furrows across the slope of the land helps to prevent water erosion.

In full bloom during summer, lavender wild bergamot brightens a thicket near Decorah.

cereal mills; and Dubuque, a picturesque Mississippi River town where one can find both a greyhound track and a monastery nearby. But the heart and soul of Iowa resides in its rural towns — more than 1,000 of them, scattered more or less uniformly across the state.

THE GREAT AMERICAN BICYCLE RIDE

A rolling celebration of Iowa's small towns occurs each July, when about 10,000 bicyclists from all over the country ride clear across the state. The week-long event, called Ragbrai (an acronym for the sponsoring Des Moines Register's Annual Great Bicycle Ride Across

Iowa), serves up a smorgasbord of midwestern specialties. Ragbrai riders are apt to encounter, say, a pig roast in Pisgah, Danish pancakes in Kimballton, a beer tent in Belle Plaine, and corn on the cob in Exira.

The Ragbrai route changes every year, but always proceeds from west to east, along with the prevailing breezes. Near the western border, most of it formed by the Missouri River, looms a newcomer's first sign that Iowa (to quote one bicyclist) "is emphatically *not* flat." Grassy ridges, called loess hills, rise 100 to 200 feet above the surrounding landscape. Indians and French fur trappers once gath-

ered in these hills to trade goods. This pre-pioneer era is memorialized in the name of Iowa's seventh-largest city, Council Bluffs, situated just across the Missouri from Omaha.

The Iowa landscape east of Council Bluffs rolls up and down through dense networks of streams and rivers. Here, in river valleys lacing the eastern and southern sections of the state, are most of Iowa's woodlands — some 1.5 million acres forested mainly with hardwoods such as elms, oaks, maples, hickories, and walnuts.

The topography flattens out suddenly as one travels northeast. An invisible boundary

Dry, golden stalks of corn glisten in the sunlight at harvest time. Iowa's fertility is legendary. Poet Robert Frost, who had struggled to farm less generous ground in New England, said that Iowa soil "looks good enough to eat without putting it through vegetables."

Dusted with snow, a farm in Clayton County in northeastern Iowa sparkles in the clear, cold winter air. The sunlight reflected on the clouds creates such vivid colors that they seem almost painted.

THE RIGS THAT WORKED THE PRAIRIE

The conversion of Iowa's prairie into productive farmland in the mid-19th century coincided with rapid advances in the implements used to plow, reap, and thresh. In addition to John Deere's famous steel plow, new machines drawn by horses (but still requiring a man to operate the moving parts) provided a level of efficiency that only a couple of decades before had been unimaginable.

The new horse-drawn rake did the work of 10 men with hand rakes. Horse-drawn reapers processed six times more acreage than men with handheld grain cradles or scythes could. And a mechanical hay loader, such as the one shown here, did the work in a fraction of the usual time.

Some of these old rigs are still working in Iowa today — not on the modern farms seen from the highway, but at a unique outdoor museum, Living History Farms, on the edge of Des Moines. This 600-acre site includes three working farms that rely entirely on implements used, respectively, in 1700,

1850, and at the turn of the century. Visitors can mark the progression of 19th-century agriculture as farmers in period clothing use the vintage machines to perform tasks exactly the way their forebears did a century or more ago.

delineates a peninsulalike lobe extending down from the north and deep into central Iowa, as far south as Des Moines. This region, the Des Moines Lobe, is where the Wisconsinan glacier lopped off the hills and filled in the valleys of north-central Iowa some 20,000 to 25,000 years ago. This is Iowa as the world knows it, relatively flat and very fertile.

FROM PRAIRIE TO FARMLAND

The Woodland and Plains Indians knew the territory that became Iowa as a vast, rolling expanse carpeted with prairie vegetation. This included such native grasses as big and little bluestem, switchgrass, sideoats grama, and buffalo grass. The grasses mingled with scores of wildflowers, such as pasqueflowers, prairie violets, gentians, blazing stars, and asters. All told, some 300 different plant species supported a similar diversity of insects and animals, from honeybees to bison. Here and there groves of burr oak trees dotted the grasslands.

Fewer than 10,000 of the original 30 million acres of Iowa prairie remain, much of it in railroad rights-of-way, abandoned pioneer cemeteries, or state-maintained prairie preserves.

Iowa's earliest pioneers, who made their homes in wooded bottomlands near the Mississippi in the 1830's, had no idea of the agricultural potential that the prairies held. But when John Deere's all-steel plow became available to them, farmers were able to penetrate the thick prairie loam, and the region was settled in a quick burst of westward expansion. The most enduring images of Iowa may be those created by the artist Grant Wood, who ranks among Iowa's most famous natives. Wood chose the land and people of his native state as his subjects in such paintings as "Fall Plowing" and "American Gothic."

Iowa has changed a great deal since Wood painted his popular canvases of the state in the 1930's. Iowans have endured the worst family-farm crisis in their history, and are now struggling to bring industrial farming practices into line with environmental and food-safety concerns. But through it all, Iowa holds fast to its special place in the American imagination as the quintessence of rural life, symbol of the nation's bounty.

An east coast wildflower, New Jersey tea, is well established in Turin Loess Hills Preserve.

Kansas

*A windswept state of prairies,
wheat fields, and cottonwoods*

The original inhabitants of this land called themselves the *Kansa,* "people of the south wind." So when the name of the Indian tribe was applied to the whole territory that became Kansas, it was appropriate. Far from the gentling influence of any ocean, Kansas is beset by extremes of weather brought in by constant wind. Hot southerly winds ripple the prairie grasses all summer, until autumn reverses them and the winds sweep back through as freezing blasts from the north.

A GENTLY RISING STATE

The rectangle that is Kansas is on a slant, sloping upward from the southeastern corner toward the northwest, rising at an average of about eight feet per mile. The Chautauqua Hills of southeastern Kansas are covered by forests of oak and hickory. During the warmer months rose-red summer tanagers sing from the blackjack oaks all day, and the nighttime woods echo with the throaty chants of the chuck-will's-widow.

Along rivers everywhere, the typical tree is the cottonwood. Tough, and with deep taproots, it can grow along rivercourses where the flow is far underground in dry seasons.

These southern sounds were unfamiliar to the pioneers who rushed to Kansas from New England in the 1850's, making haste to help install enough antislavery voters to ensure that Kansas would become a free state. They, like later settlers, were people of strong convictions, leaders in a variety of causes: abolition, prohibition, and woman suffrage.

Almost ready for the October harvest, sunflowers grow in a farmer's field in eastern Kansas. The plants' seeds will be used for foodstuffs and oil.

On the plains south of Dodge City, a wheat field is whipped by wind as clouds churn overhead. Kansas is given to extremes of weather because it is located midway across the continent, where warm southerly air collides with cold currents from the north.

TURKEY RED WHEAT AND BLUESTEM GRASSES

Across the state, the land supports some 200 varieties of native grasses, and a few introduced species too. Chief among the imports is the hardy winter wheat, brought in by Mennonite immigrants from Russia. Arriving in 1874, the Mennonite farmers had packed in each family's luggage some handpicked Turkey Red wheat, a choice variety that is well adapted to the hard conditions of the Great Plains. Winter wheat transformed central Kansas into the breadbasket of America and created many typical Kansas scenes: wheat fields stretching to the horizon; tall grain elevators, visible for miles around; combines clanking across the fields at harvesttime.

Designed for the aerial view, the works of artist Stan Herd are planted into Kansas farmland. The "canvas" for the piece above is the soil of Douglas County, near Eudora.

But little wheat grows in the most distinctive of Kansas landscapes: the Flint Hills, a rocky, rugged region running north and south through the middle of the eastern half of the state. Too formidable even for tough and resourceful Kansas farmers, much of the land here was never broken by the plow, and it remains one of the largest tall-grass prairies in North America.

Konza Prairie in the Flint Hills is part of the largest remaining tall-grass prairie in the country.

Kentucky

*Surpassing beauty in the
land of Daniel Boone*

Kentucky was one of America's legendary frontiers, thrown open when Daniel Boone blazed the Wilderness Road through Cumberland Gap just as the American Revolution was beginning. Until then, the formidable Appalachian Mountains had discouraged the colonists from even attempting to explore the virgin territory extolled by a few intrepid trappers and hunters — a land of deeply forested hills and valleys roamed by bears, buffaloes, and elk.

Kentucky was also a land of surpassing beauty and natural abundance, and Boone's expedition suddenly made it attainable. Following his trail or traveling down the Ohio River, settlers poured into the new frontier from Virginia, the Carolinas, and Pennsylvania — 12,000 of them by the end of the Revolutionary War.

BLUEGRASS AND PENNYROYAL

Pushing on past the jagged ridges and narrow valleys of the Cumberland and Pine mountains, many of the early pioneers planted their corn and hemp in the promising bluegrass meadows of north-central Kentucky. Others farmed the fertile Pennyroyal, or "Pennyrile," to the south, a region named for the aromatic herb that flourishes there. Civilization advanced so rapidly in the Bluegrass region that prospering farmers soon replaced their sturdy log houses with elegant Georgian and Greek revival estates, where they grew fine tobacco, bred fast horses, and distilled bourbon whiskey. Lexington, founded in 1775, was proudly pointed out as the "Athens of the West" to such

*Few horse farms are as handsome as those in the
Bluegrass, where Thoroughbreds are raised for racing.*

Fog settles in the hollows of the western foothills of the Appalachian Mountains. This view is from Pilot Knob, a lookout near Berea.

19th-century tourists as the marquis de Lafayette, who may well have thought the whole of Kentucky was as aristocratic as its Bluegrass.

KENTUCKY CONTRASTS

In fact, Kentucky was then and is today a region of extreme contrasts created by the state's unique geography. The Bluegrass owes its prosperity both to the Ohio River, which made Louisville an important port, and to the rich limestone soil that nourishes the famous blue-tinged grasses so relished by Thoroughbreds. The beautiful farmland of the Pennyroyal, with its rolling hills and rivers —the Green, the Cumberland, the Tennessee —is dotted with geological oddities: sinkholes, subterranean streams, and a vast labyrinth of caverns culminating in Mammoth Cave.

In the west, the hilly land of the western coalfield region is rich in mineral deposits and dotted with hardscrabble mining towns. Yet the Purchase — a tract of alluvial bottomlands and loess uplands at the extreme western tip of Kentucky that was purchased from the Chickasaws in 1818 — was settled by southern planters and still looks like a remnant of the romantic Old South today.

At the other end of the state, the eastern highlands are another world. With spectacular waterfalls, towering hardwood forests, and cliffsides scarred by strip-mining but massed with rhododendrons, the highlands reflect both the heartbreaking beauty and backbreaking challenge of Appalachia. Here weathered cabins cling to ridges, swaying bridges span dizzying heights across gorges, Canada warblers sing from shady thickets, and the sound of the dulcimer drifts through the hollows on summer evenings.

But this, too, is Kentucky, as authentic a part of the state's heritage as the Bluegrass horse farms. It was from these mountains the settlers first saw the land they would call home. "Stand at Cumberland Gap," wrote historian Frederick Jackson Turner in 1893, "and watch the procession of civilization, marching single file — the buffalo following the trail to the salt springs, the Indian, the fur-trader and hunter, the cattle-raiser, the pioneer farmer — and the frontier has passed by."

Sky Bridge, a rock arch spanning 90 feet, is one of more than 80 natural arches in the Red River Gorge Geological Area. The area, part of Daniel Boone National Forest in eastern Kentucky, was overlaid with erosion-resistant sandstone millions of years ago. Arches were created when weaker rock underneath the narrow sandstone ridges was gradually worn away.

Louisiana

A spicy potpourri of people, cultures, and wildlife

Louisiana is nothing less than exotic — a land of steamy swamps and lazy bayous, regal old mansions and tumbledown fishing shacks. Its lush landscapes — fields engulfed by honeysuckle, kudzu, and wisteria, endless marshes, swamps where towering bald cypresses are veiled in Spanish moss — are just as remarkable as Louisiana's culture. Though largely the legacy of the region's French past, Louisiana's language, folklore, and cuisine, particularly in the southern half of the state, are strongly seasoned by other influences — Spanish, African, West Indian, American Indian — and each lends its own special accent to Louisiana's cultural potpourri.

ON THE BANKS OF THE MISSISSIPPI

The state's unique character also owes much to its lakes, bayous, lagoons, marshes, swamps — and, above all, the majestic, meandering Mississippi River. (Even Shreveport, far to the west and north, connects to the Mississippi via the Red River.) As it snakes down from Arkansas, the Mississippi serves as Louisiana's eastern border, flowing past cottonfields, stands of loblolly pine, and oxbow lakes formed from the river's own abandoned loops. Farther south, near Baton Rouge and New Orleans, the river sweeps by the impressive lawns and white columns of plantation homes built two centuries ago by cotton and sugarcane planters. Farther along, the river skirts Lake Pontchartrain, with its sailboats and shining causeway, and swings around New Orleans.

The city began in 1718 as a neat square which French engineers laid out in the river's

Sunbeams streaming through morning mist accent the mysterious beauty of the luxuriant Atchafalaya swamp.

Lavish displays of azaleas grace 4,700-acre Hodges Gardens in west-central Louisiana.

Hundreds of lazy bayous meander through the lush, soggy swampland of southern Louisiana.

swampy curve — an area known today as the Vieux Carré, or French Quarter. Here the French and Spanish built their charming houses and courtyards, decorated them with lacy wrought iron, entertained at balls and banquets, intermarried, and over the years created the rich culture known as Creole.

New Orleans remains diverse and intriguing — a city where life is one marvelous parade. During the world-famous Mardi Gras season the city hosts colorful festivities that culminate in a raucous, gorgeous parade. And in this town, even such solemn occa-

sions as funerals call for a parade, led by a jazz band playing dirges.

SWAMPS AND BAYOUS

West of New Orleans, in the south-central part of the state, lies Acadiana, a unique region of bayous. It was named for the Acadians who made their way there via the Mississippi River after being exiled from present-day Nova Scotia in 1755 for refusing to swear loyalty to the British crown. Called Cajuns (from "Acadians"), the people clung to their own language and customs, but adapted to their swampy home by living in raised cottages, growing what crops they could on higher ground, and carving dugouts called *pirogues* to explore the giant Atchafalaya swamp.

Although abundant in the swamps, bird life is most spectacular in Louisiana's coastal wetlands — a vast sea of marshland stretching from the Texas border to the Mississippi delta. Here migratory birds of every kind — waterfowl, shorebirds, songbirds, and birds of prey — gather to spend the winter months in such great wildlife refuges as Sabine, Lacassine, and Rockefeller.

An elegant allée *(or alley) of overarching, 200-year-old oaks frames the long approach road at Rosedown Plantation. On either side of the road, paths wind through gardens adorned with statues and fountains.*

Maine

The land that greets the sunrise

Katahdin ("highest land, nearest to the gods") is the Abnaki Indian name for Maine's loftiest mountain. And the name is apt, for Katahdin, nearly a mile high, dominates the surrounding hills and is the centerpiece of the state's vast woodlands.

This majestic peak is but one example of Maine's natural beauty — a beauty that does indeed seem near to the gods, or at least divinely inspired. Seven chains of lakes, more than 2,500 in all, spill across dark green forests like sparkling blue sapphires. In the northeast, vast fields of potato plants carpet the earth with white blossoms. In the southeast, the coastline twists and turns through an intricate network of coves, inlets, and islands at the edge of the indigo sea. And in the center of the state, densely forested mountains, Katahdin among them, cut an awe-inspiring profile against the azure sky.

DOWN EAST

Maine's jagged coast meets the Atlantic Ocean with long peninsulas, spray-soaked granite cliffs, and more than 2,000 off-shore islands. Some of these islands are no more than rocky resting places for gulls. Others, such as Vinalhaven, have sizable and flourishing communities, and the largest, Mount Desert Island, contains the town of Bar Harbor and much of Acadia National Park. The names of the islands often provide a clue about the origin of the people who lived there: Monhegan was named by American Indians, Isle au Haut by the French, and Beals Island by Yankees.

Crashing surf at craggy Portland Head creates a quintessential image of Maine. Built in 1791, the lighthouse here rises more than 100 feet above the shore.

The tranquillity of a sunlit cove at Acadia National Park belies the violence of its history. Maine's jagged coastal cliffs are the legacy of glaciers that passed over the region 20,000 years ago. Moving southward, the massive ice sheets smoothed slopes that faced north and tore rock from those that faced south, leaving the southward-facing coast rough-hewn and rugged.

It seems reasonable to say that Maine is located "up north," but ever since early New England mariners sailed downwind in an easterly direction from Boston to reach its coast, Maine has been dubbed Down East. Earlier residents, the Abnakis, called the region Dawnland because they saw it as near the rising sun. More realistic than poetic was the Algonquian name, which translates as Land of the Frozen Ground. Its truth is echoed by present-day Mainers, who joke that their state has two seasons: July and winter.

The Maine coast is a world of quiet, sea-worn villages tucked into sheltered harbors where sailboats are moored. From Kittery north to Eastport, lobstermen ply their trade, and kayakers explore the rocky coves of protected archipelagoes. When the fog rolls in, it can be so thick that the ocean seems to disappear. At moments like this, the coastal cottages have a timeless charm, their shuttered windows, weathered clapboard siding, and gabled roofs seeming to peek through the mist from yesteryear. Often the only sounds are the cries of gulls and the forlorn moaning of a distant foghorn.

At other times, the sun shines so brightly and the air is so clear and crisp that the whole coast seems to sparkle. It is not hard to understand why so many painters — among them Winslow Homer, Rockwell Kent, Edward Hopper, John Marin, and three generations of Wyeths — have sought inspiration here for more than a century.

DEEP IN THE WOODS

From its border on the Atlantic Ocean, the state extends north to Canada, embracing vast woodlands that become increasingly wild and undisturbed the farther north one goes. This is the domain of moose, deer, bears, and owls, where humans are merely intruders in a primeval land that still belongs to nature.

Nearly 90 percent of Maine is still blanketed with forest — maple, oak, spruce, fir, hemlock, and especially white pine, the state's official tree. When explorer Henry Hudson sailed into Penobscot Bay in 1609 with a broken mast, he found that a white pine, with its tall, straight trunk, made a perfect replacement. In 1691 the British government decreed that all white pines more than 24 inches in diameter growing within three miles of the shore belonged to the British navy.

Surprisingly, in this century of vanishing wilderness, the forests of Maine are still so undeveloped that over half the woodland is divided into large townships identified solely by numbers and often accessible only by the deeply rutted, unpaved roads connecting isolated logging camps. No wonder, then, that the wry advice of Maine natives to lost motorists is "You can't get there from here."

In this wild domain — stretching from Rangeley Lakes near the New Hampshire border northeast to Fort Kent — people are scarce and moose can seem as common as squirrels. The forest seems to go on forever, ornamented by rocky outcrops, glistening lakes, and winding rivers. Moosehead Lake, Maine's largest, lies here, and not far away are Mount Katahdin and the scenic trails of Baxter State Park.

Solitude and serenity reign in the Maine woods. Camped by a sun-dappled stream, where a gentle breeze brings the scent of pine and the chirping of songbirds, the visitor cannot help but feel that Maine is the place to rediscover the world as nature made it.

Fog invades Monhegan Island with stealth, robbing it of sunshine but not serenity.

Lean and stark, the trunks of paper birches contrast sharply with the vibrant palette of autumn foliage at Grafton Notch State Park in Maine's western mountains.

A purity accompanies winter on the Maine coast, as the coves are dusted with snow, shrouded in mist, and abandoned by their summer visitors.

THE BEAUTY AND SPLENDOR OF NORTH AMERICA

CLOWN PRINCE OF THE NORTH ATLANTIC

One of Maine's most colorful residents is the puffin, or sea parrot. With black and white feathers, triangular orange bills, and short, plump bodies, puffins look like a cross between a parrot and a penguin. In fact they are members of the auk family, which includes other deep-diving seabirds.

Puffins are superb fishermen. They dive underwater and "fly" after fish, propelled by their strong, stubby wings. When they emerge on the surface, they often carry their catch — as many as 30 small fish at a time — clamped firmly in their bills.

When it comes to flying in the air, however, puffins are less successful. Unless there is a brisk wind to give them a boost, the portly birds splash along in the water, wings flapping madly, in order to get aloft. Once airborne, they continue their arduous pumping in a clumsy flight that has been called a triumph of will over physique.

Puffins nest in colonies by burrowing into seaside cliffs. The female generally lays only one egg, and after it hatches both parents care for the offspring until it is about six weeks old. Then the chick is abandoned in the protection of the burrow. A week later, driven by instinct and, presumably, hunger, the young bird flutters off the cliff and into the sea, where it develops the skills to fish and fly.

Mount Katahdin dominates Baxter State Park, a 200,000-acre wilderness named for Gov. Percival P. Baxter, who donated the land to the state.

Maryland

A pocket-size portrait of America

Small though it is, Maryland has such a dazzling variety of natural and man-made features — remote mountains, crowded urban areas, fertile farmlands, scenic shorelines, modern industrial centers, old tobacco plantations — that the state has been called an America in miniature. It seems fitting, then, that America's national anthem, "The Star-Spangled Banner," was written in Maryland, and that its capital, Washington, D.C., was built on land donated by the state.

THE BOUNTIFUL CHESAPEAKE BAY

The most striking of Maryland's natural features — and a great national treasure in itself — is the Chesapeake Bay. This 200-mile-long estuary, which bisects the state, has so many arms, inlets, and islands that its total shoreline is greater than the distance from Maryland to California. It is also a mammoth nursery and feeding ground for wildlife, so replete with birds, fish, shellfish, and other creatures that Baltimore writer H. L. Mencken once facetiously dubbed it a protein factory.

A giant peninsula (called the Delmarva Peninsula because it is shared by Delaware, Maryland, and Virginia) separates the Chesapeake Bay from the Atlantic Ocean. While throngs of vacationers are drawn to beaches in and around Ocean City, on the Atlantic, the rest of Maryland's share of the peninsula, called the Eastern Shore, manages to preserve the flavor of its agricultural and maritime past. On the Bay side, major highways pass through expansive fields of wheat, corn, and

At this exhilarating overlook in western Maryland's Garrett County, mountains surround the Cove, a natural amphitheater of rolling, contour-plowed fields.

As the light of dawn creeps eastward from the Chesapeake Bay Bridge in the distance, a sloop makes its way down Whitehall Creek toward open water.

soybeans, and smaller country roads wind through old villages whose names — Oxford, Cambridge, St. Michaels — reflect the area's British heritage. The countryside's gracious brick mansions and venerable churches, some more than 200 years old, cannot, however, match the age of a local tree, the magnificent Wye Oak, which has been casting its ample shade for some four centuries.

When the Wye Oak was a mere century old, a visiting Dutchman remarked on "a great storm coming through the trees," a thunderous sound made by the flapping wings of thousands of ducks. He was, of course, an early witness to one of the huge migrations of waterfowl, shorebirds, and songbirds that —

attracted by the abundant food, water, and shelter provided by the Chesapeake Bay — pause here every spring and fall.

GRACEFUL MOUNTAINS, GENTEEL TOWNS

Western Maryland, a narrow strip of land bordered by the historic Mason-Dixon line on the north and the Potomac River on the south, contrasts dramatically with the flat coastal plain. Here the scenic Blue Ridge and Allegheny mountains, where wealthy Americans once built idyllic retreats, now draw hikers, skiers, and white-water rafters.

In southern Maryland, just west of the Chesapeake, are miles of tobacco fields that have been a part of the landscape since colo-

Catoctin Mountain Park, west of Thurmont, contains 25 miles of scenic woodland trails. It is also the site of Camp David, the presidential retreat.

Wild ponies are among the most charming and conspicuous residents of Assateague Island, situated on the Atlantic Coast south of Ocean City. Though the precise origin of the ponies is uncertain, they have lived on the island for centuries and are believed to be descended from small domestic horses kept here by early settlers.

nial days. The tobacco crop built the elegant town houses and mansions of Annapolis, just to the north, which in its 18th-century hey-day was called the genteelest town in North America by an English visitor.

In the next century it was Baltimore that grew and prospered, becoming a preeminent center of shipping and manufacturing. Even so, the city retained what visiting author Henry James called a perfect felicity. Though linked by commerce to the North and to ports throughout the world, Baltimore even today manages to preserve the gentle airs of the South — not surprising in a state where so many contrasting elements blend to form a miniature America.

Massachusetts

Sandy shores, gentle hills, and a nation's heritage

Massachusetts abounds in images that have helped to form the Americans' sense of their past: the Pilgrims landing at Plymouth Rock, the first Thanksgiving, the Boston Tea Party, the midnight ride of Paul Revere, the minutemen at the battles of Lexington and Concord. Yet the state that looms so large in that nation's story is not very big at all.

THE CAPES

Massachusetts seashores are among New England's finest, with rocky coves and inlets as well as vast stretches of sandy beach. Some of the best beaches are preserved in the 44,000-acre Cape Cod National Seashore, which covers almost the entire outer cape from Orleans north to Provincetown. Its eastern shore is pummeled by the swirling surf of the open Atlantic, while its western coast is swept by the gentler waves of sheltered Cape Cod Bay.

Walking the streets of the cape's seaside villages evokes a rich sense of the area's maritime past, from the stately captains' houses in Sandwich to the fishing shanties on Sandy Neck in Barnstable and the colorful harbors at Chatham and Provincetown. Nowhere is this feeling of nautical history stronger than on Martha's Vineyard and Nantucket, the islands just south of the cape whose fortunes were founded on 19th-century whaling. It was Nantucket that Herman Melville depicted in his classic novel *Moby Dick*.

North of Boston lies another maritime center — Cape Ann, where the town of Gloucester stands, the nation's oldest active fishing

As the Green Mountains of Vermont stretch southward into Massachusetts, they become the Berkshire Hills, where scattered farms recall New England's past.

The marshes along the Ipswich River are not only picturesque, but ecologically important because they offer a resting spot for migrating birds.

THE BEAUTY AND SPLENDOR OF NORTH AMERICA

Much of the farm country in western Massachusetts is a patchwork of ridges and valleys where meadows intermingle with woodlands.

port. Boats from here still head out to Georges Bank in search of cod and haddock, just as they have since the time of the Pilgrims.

THE RIVER AND THE HILLS

Inland, beyond the broad coastal plain, lies a wide swath of uplands — a southward extension of the White Mountains of New Hampshire. From these heights, the land slopes gently down to the banks of the Connecticut River. To the west of the Connecticut Valley the land rises again to form the Berkshire Hills. They are not imposing by most standards. Mount Greylock, the tallest peak, tops out at 3,491 feet. But their gentle slopes are among the most beautiful areas in the state, drawing droves of vacationers not just to the scenery but to the summer arts colonies that present theater, music, and dance. Beyond the Berkshires the land rolls down to a narrow valley before rising once again in the Taconic Range along the Massachusetts-New York border. Most of this area is woodland.

SQUANTO, PLAGUE, AND THE PILGRIMS

When the Pilgrims landed in Massachusetts in December 1620, they had few of the practical skills needed to survive in the North American wilderness. Fortunately for them, Squanto, a Pawtuxet Indian, came to their settlement at Plymouth and served the newcomers as guide and mentor, showing them, among other things, the Indian trick of using dead fish as fertilizer when planting corn.

Squanto had little trouble communicating with the Pilgrims because, unlikely as it may seem, he already spoke English. He had been kidnapped several years earlier by a British adventurer and sold into slavery in Spain. Escaping, he made his way to London, where he lived for a time before hiring on as a hand on a ship bound for New England.

By late 1619 Squanto had made his way back to his home village at Plymouth, where he found that the entire Pawtuxet tribe had been wiped out by the plague — one of many epidemics that rat-infested European ships brought to North America. According to one estimate, 90 percent of the coastal Indians from Rhode Island to Maine succumbed to disease in the early 1600's. Finding himself the last of the Pawtuxets, a man without a tribe, Squanto joined the Pilgrims who now inhabited his homeland.

From the 1880's through the 1920's, the village of Magnolia — now part of Gloucester — was a summer haven for the wealthy, who built mansions along its rocky shore. Although most of these grand estates have now been converted to condominiums, the area's magnificent vistas of the open ocean remain unchanged.

RECYCLED CITIES

Massachusetts is one of the most urbanized and industrialized regions in the United States. From Lowell and Fall River to Worcester and Springfield, its cities have persevered by adapting to changing times.

Few places better illustrate this than New Bedford, which once ranked among the most prosperous whaling ports in the world. In the mid-19th century, when whale oil gave way to kerosene for lighting, New Bedford transformed itself into a busy textile-manufacturing center. Some hundred years later, when most of the great mills had closed or moved away, New Bedford was reborn as home port to the largest fishing fleet on the East Coast. Since then the city has gained new luster by restoring its historic district, where the streets are lined with mansions that once belonged to well-to-do sea captains and the ambience of the 19th century still prevails.

WALKING THROUGH HISTORY

Massachusetts residents everywhere have learned to live in comfortable proximity with history, and many places are so authentically preserved and restored that they bring the past to life. In Salem, site of the notorious 17th-century witch trials, a walking tour highlights a happier era in the city's history — the days when three-masted ships called East Indiamen, designed and built by Salem shipwrights, sailed around the globe.

In Boston the Black Heritage Trail features landmarks of the city's black community, and the Freedom Trail winds among such landmarks as Paul Revere's home, the oldest surviving house in the city; King's Chapel, an Anglican church that became the first Unitarian church in the nation; and Faneuil Hall, a meeting place for revolutionaries in colonial times and now part of a bustling new commercial center called Quincy Market.

THE SACRED COD

In Massachusetts, the Sacred Cod, as residents still call it, is no ordinary fish; in fact, since 1784 a golden replica of a codfish has hung in the State House in Boston as a memorial to "the importance of the Cod-fishery to the welfare of the Commonwealth."

As early as the 1490's, John Cabot and other explorers had alerted Europeans to the existence of vast schools of cod in the North Atlantic. By 1580 there was a veritable armada of fishing vessels off the North American coast — as many as 350 ships in a single season.

Early settlers were quick to note this natural bounty: the rocky soil of New England convinced many that fishing would be far better than farming as a way of life. Three years after the Pilgrims landed in Plymouth, an outpost was established at Gloucester, and by the 1770's it was one of New England's busiest fishing ports. Indeed, fishing and transatlantic trading became the bases of many early New England fortunes.

The typical Cape Cod cottage, like this one on Nantucket, has well-weathered cedar shingles and a white picket fence festooned with flowers.

HISTORICAL HIGHLIGHTS

1620 Pilgrims on the *Mayflower* land at Plymouth.

1630 Puritans found Boston.

1676 Settlers defeat Indians in King Philip's War.

1692 Twenty people executed at Salem Village for witchcraft.

1775 The Revolutionary War begins at Lexington and Concord.

1788 By ratifying Constitution, Massachusetts becomes sixth state to enter Union.

1831 William Lloyd Garrison publishes antislavery newspaper, the *Liberator*, giving birth to abolitionist movement.

1891 Basketball is invented by Dr. James Naismith at Springfield School for Christian Workers.

1897 Nation's first subway system opens in Boston.

1903 Boston hosts first baseball World Series.

1927 After a sensational trial, anarchists Nicola Sacco and Bartolomeo Vanzetti are executed for murder.

1942 Fire at Cocoanut Grove nightclub in Boston kills 492 people and leads to improved fire laws nationwide.

1960 Senator John F. Kennedy is elected president.

1974 – 75 Boston erupts in racial violence over busing to achieve racial balance in schools.

1980's Growth of computer industry revives state's economy.

FAMOUS SONS AND DAUGHTERS

The only father and son U.S. presidents, **John Adams** (1735 – 1826) became the second U.S. president in 1797 and his son **John Quincy Adams** (1767 – 1848) became the sixth in 1825.

Leonard Bernstein (1918 – 90). The dashing musical director (1958 – 70) of the New York Philharmonic also left a legacy of compositions, including the musical *West Side Story*.

Emily Dickinson (1830 – 86). Often brief, Dickinson's poems are filled with insights and imagery. She lived her entire life in her father's house in Amherst.

W.E.B. Du Bois (1868 – 1963). A distinguished scholar, Du Bois helped found the National Association for the Advancement of Colored People in 1909.

Nathaniel Hawthorne (1804 – 64). Descended from a judge at the Salem witch trials, Hawthorne criticized the Puritan past in such works as *The Scarlet Letter*.

Oliver Wendell Holmes, Jr. (1841 – 1935). Known as the Great Dissenter, Holmes served on the U.S. Supreme Court from 1902 to 1932.

John F. Kennedy (1917 – 63).

At the age of 42, Kennedy became the youngest person to be elected president. He was assassinated in Dallas.

Edwin H. Land (1909 – 91). Inventor of the instant camera, Land founded the Polaroid Corporation in Cambridge in 1937.

Norman Rockwell (1894 – 1978). Technical skill and a wry sense of humor made Rockwell one of America's favorite illustrators. His studio in Stockbridge is now a museum.

Henry David Thoreau (1817 – 62). An iconoclast who championed individual integrity and the beauty of nature, Thoreau is best remembered for the time he spent living alone at Walden Pond and for his essay "Civil Disobedience."

ODDITIES AND SPECIALTIES

Cape Cod and the area around Plymouth produce nearly half of the nation's cranberries.

Massachusetts is famous for its colleges — 106 in all. Harvard, the oldest college in the nation, was founded at Cambridge with a colonial government grant in 1636. Mount Holyoke, the oldest women's college, was established at South Hadley in 1837.

Boston baked beans, made with molasses, have been a staple since colonial times.

A lake near Webster has the remarkable Indian name of *Chargoggaggoggmanchauggagogg-chaubunagungamaug,* which means "I fish on my side of the lake, you fish on yours, and no one fishes in between." The fainthearted call it Lake Webster.

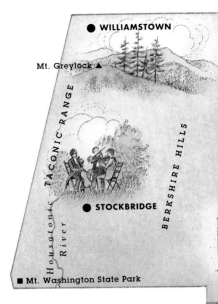

PLACES TO VISIT, THINGS TO DO

Cape Cod National Seashore (South Wellfleet). Preserving nearly 50 miles of Cape Cod's shoreline, as well as marshland, the refuge is a haven for wildlife and beach lovers alike.

Mt. Greylock State Reservation (North Adams). Mt. Greylock's summit, which can be reached by car, offers a view of five states. Enjoy the autumn foliage here.

Mt. Washington State Park (Mt. Washington). Hiking through the woodlands of the Taconic Range offers stunning vistas of surrounding farmlands. Eighty-foot-high Bash Bish Falls is one of the state's most spectacular sights.

Old Sturbridge Village (Sturbridge). Forty historic buildings have been moved to this 200-acre site to re-create a New England village in the early 1800's.

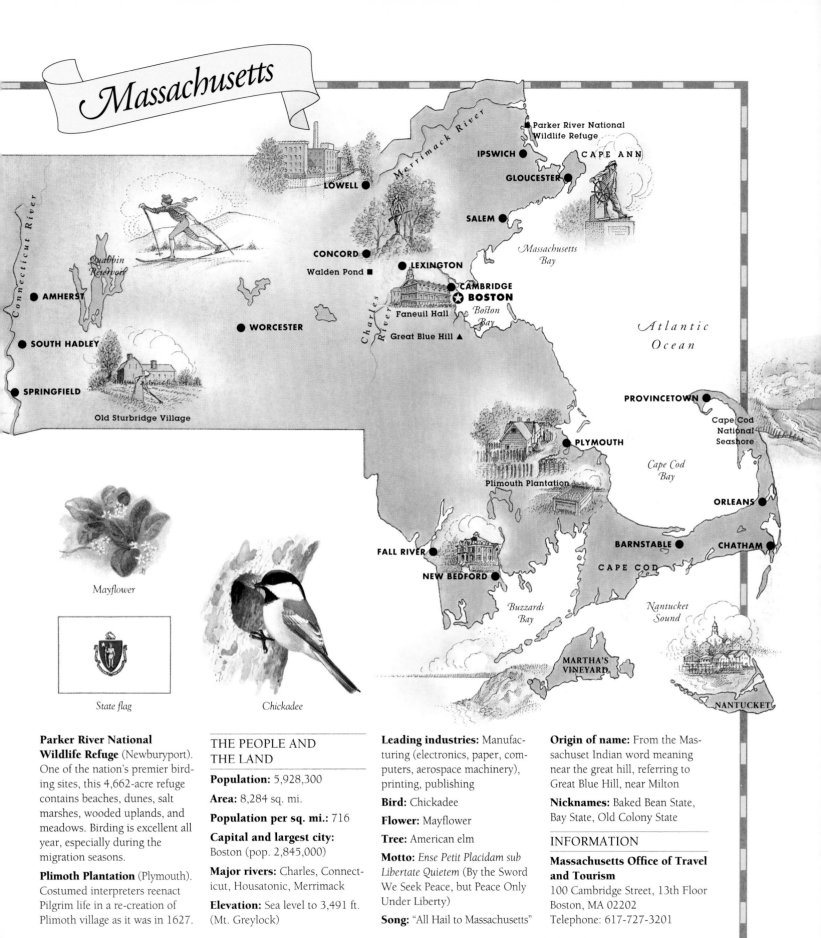

Massachusetts

Parker River National Wildlife Refuge
IPSWICH
CAPE ANN
GLOUCESTER
LOWELL
SALEM
Massachusetts Bay
CONCORD
LEXINGTON
Walden Pond
CAMBRIDGE
BOSTON
Faneuil Hall
Boston Bay
AMHERST
WORCESTER
Charles River
Great Blue Hill ▲
Atlantic Ocean
SOUTH HADLEY
Quabbin Reservoir
Connecticut River
SPRINGFIELD
Old Sturbridge Village
PROVINCETOWN
Cape Cod National Seashore
PLYMOUTH
Cape Cod Bay
Plimouth Plantation
ORLEANS
FALL RIVER
BARNSTABLE
CHATHAM
NEW BEDFORD
CAPE COD
Buzzards Bay
Nantucket Sound
MARTHA'S VINEYARD
NANTUCKET
Merrimack River

Mayflower

State flag

Chickadee

Parker River National Wildlife Refuge (Newburyport). One of the nation's premier birding sites, this 4,662-acre refuge contains beaches, dunes, salt marshes, wooded uplands, and meadows. Birding is excellent all year, especially during the migration seasons.

Plimoth Plantation (Plymouth). Costumed interpreters reenact Pilgrim life in a re-creation of Plimoth village as it was in 1627.

THE PEOPLE AND THE LAND

Population: 5,928,300

Area: 8,284 sq. mi.

Population per sq. mi.: 716

Capital and largest city: Boston (pop. 2,845,000)

Major rivers: Charles, Connecticut, Housatonic, Merrimack

Elevation: Sea level to 3,491 ft. (Mt. Greylock)

Leading industries: Manufacturing (electronics, paper, computers, aerospace machinery), printing, publishing

Bird: Chickadee

Flower: Mayflower

Tree: American elm

Motto: *Ense Petit Placidam sub Libertate Quietem* (By the Sword We Seek Peace, but Peace Only Under Liberty)

Song: "All Hail to Massachusetts"

Origin of name: From the Massachuset Indian word meaning near the great hill, referring to Great Blue Hill, near Milton

Nicknames: Baked Bean State, Bay State, Old Colony State

INFORMATION

Massachusetts Office of Travel and Tourism
100 Cambridge Street, 13th Floor
Boston, MA 02202
Telephone: 617-727-3201

Michigan

Romantic landscapes at the heart of the Great Lakes

Perhaps because the waters that virtually surround Michigan lack the salty tang of the ocean, most people do not think of it as a place defined by water. And yet it is. Lying at the heart of the Great Lakes, the state is embraced by four of these five inland seas — Lakes Michigan, Superior, Huron, and Erie.

The lakes are everywhere an inescapable presence: no point in Michigan is more than 85 miles from one of their shores. And the waters also divide the state into two distinct parts. The five-mile-wide Straits of Mackinac separate the Lower Peninsula, with its familiar mitten shape, from the lushly forested Upper Peninsula, which juts out from the northeastern border of Wisconsin.

LEGACY OF THE GLACIERS

The Great Lakes were formed at the end of the last ice age, when meltwater from a vast continental ice sheet filled five enormous basins that had earlier been hollowed out by the ice. The glaciers also left smaller watery scars throughout Michigan. Scattered across the state are more than 11,000 lakes, many of them laced together by miles of sparkling rivers that slice through dark forests and spill over countless rapids and waterfalls. The largest falls, Tahquamenon, are the centerpiece of a state park northwest of Sault Ste. Marie. A torrent of dark water stained by tannin from a tamarack swamp upstream, they tumble down in a cascade 48 feet high and 200 feet wide.

Another souvenir of the Ice Age, though of quite a different sort, is preserved at Sleeping Bear Dunes National Lakeshore. There, on

Pictured Rocks is the name given to the fantastic sandstone cliffs that run along part of Lake Superior's shore.

Indian legend says that this arch on Mackinac Island was formed when the tears of a maiden pining for her lover washed away the stone.

THE BEAUTY AND SPLENDOR OF NORTH AMERICA

In the wilds of the Upper Peninsula, the Presque Isle River winds through a gorge at Porcupine Mountains State Park.

the eastern coast of Lake Michigan, winds have piled up enormous dunes of glacier-made sand. Some of the dunes tower more than 450 feet above the lake and command majestic views of the twin Manitou Islands far offshore. According to Indian legend, the area took shape when a mother bear and two cubs tried to flee a forest fire by swimming across Lake Michigan. The mother, it is said, made it to shore, where, transformed into a gigantic dune, she still awaits her offspring. But the hapless cubs drowned before reaching land, and can be seen today as the two islands.

FORESTS AND FARMLANDS

Most of Michigan's lake-strewn terrain is gently rolling. Virtually all of it used to be covered with dense forests that long ago attracted the attention of loggers, who began arriving in Michigan in the mid-19th century.

Especially prized were the stands of towering white pines, which could easily be milled into building material. Huge amounts of pine were harvested to build houses, first for French settlers in Detroit (later to become one of the most industrialized cities in the world), then for settlers who poured into Michigan from the East after the opening of the Erie Canal in 1825. The pines also supplied building material for the cities that began to spring up on the treeless Great Plains. By the turn of the century, the state's woodlands started to disappear. Timber barons soon transferred operations to the Pacific Northwest and left the exposed earth of Michigan to the farmers.

But some areas proved to be unsuitable for anything but forest. The farmers departed too, leaving much of the woodland to restore itself. Only in the southern half of the Lower Peninsula did agriculture thrive. Farmers who

The red squirrels that inhabit Michigan's woods store pine and spruce cones for the winter.

Forming a delicate veil of water, Munising Falls are among the most exquisite of the 150 waterfalls of the Upper Peninsula. Visitors can walk on a ledge behind the falls.

had abandoned the thin soil of New England settled here and built Yankee farmhouses. Thus visitors to the area may feel they have somehow strayed into a corner of Vermont.

LAND OF HIAWATHA

The Upper Peninsula remains a place apart, even though it has been linked to the Lower Peninsula since 1957 by a bridge that gracefully leaps the Straits of Mackinac (pronounced Mackinaw). If the peninsula is bitterly cold for much of the year, the languorous summers there are enchanting. The romantic landscape became one of the most famous locales in American literature as the "shores of Gitche Gumee," the setting for Longfellow's narrative poem *The Song of Hiawatha,* which he based in part on the legends of Indians in this region.

A highlight of the area is also one of Michigan's greatest natural splendors — Pictured Rocks National Lakeshore. Extending for miles along the southern coast of Lake Superior, it is a realm of spectacular, multi-colored rock cliffs sculpted by the elements into caves, arches, and other fantastic shapes.

Poised between the two peninsulas is Mackinac Island. The British built a fort, now restored, on the island in 1780, and after the War of 1812 John Jacob Astor's fur company established a post there. In the words of the poet William Cullen Bryant, "the manifest destiny of Mackinac Island is to be a watering place." In the second half of the 19th century Mackinac did indeed become one of the nation's premier resorts, attracting the cream of midwestern society. Their favorite stopping place was the Grand Hotel, which opened in 1887 and is noted especially for its 880-foot-long veranda overlooking Lake Huron and the Straits of Mackinac.

With spectacular vistas rivaling those of the seaboard states, Mackinac Island is a place where the vastness of the Great Lakes is most apparent. But there is another spot with an equally commanding view — although it is a bit less accessible than the Grand Hotel's veranda. Astronauts traveling to the moon discovered that among the few terrestrial features visible to them were these five lakes, earthly mirrors shining into the infinity of space.

Icy winds from Lake Michigan turn the North Pier Lighthouse at St. Joseph, near the southwest corner of the state, into a winter sculpture.

AN ECOLOGICAL BALANCING ACT

Isle Royale, the largest island in Lake Superior, is more than a scenic national park. It is also a unique natural laboratory where animals, cut off from the mainland, play out the drama between predator and prey and, in the process, enable scientists to observe nature's ecological balancing act.

As late as the 1940's, foraging herds of moose on the island had no natural enemies. As a result, they multiplied so rapidly that they almost wiped out the stands of yew and balsam that provided their food.

When the animals' very existence seemed threatened, salvation came along in an unexpected form: a pack of predatory wolves that crossed the frozen lake to the island around 1949. Since then, wolves have consistently thinned the moose population, usually attacking those weakened by age or disease. At the same time, healthy moose have kept the wolves in check with their lethal hooves. The result: naturally controlled populations of moose and wolves, with survival assured for both.

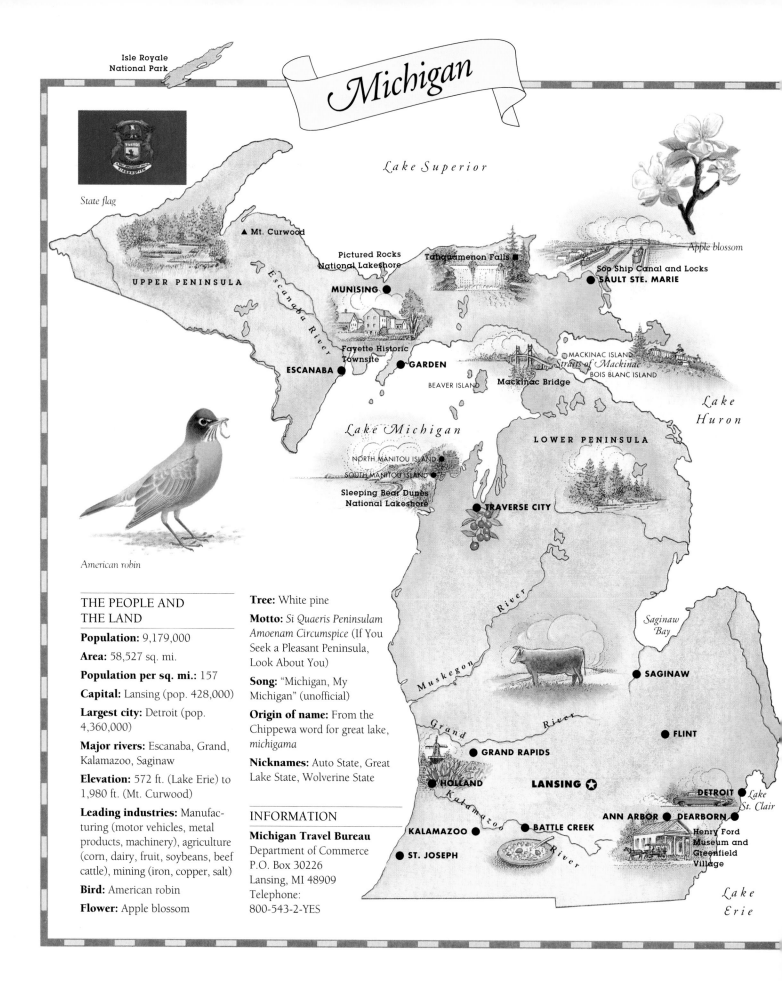

Isle Royale National Park

Michigan

Lake Superior

State flag

▲ Mt. Curwood

UPPER PENINSULA

Escanaba River

Pictured Rocks National Lakeshore

Tahquamenon Falls ▪

MUNISING ●

Soo Ship Canal and Locks
SAULT STE. MARIE ●

Apple blossom

Fayette Historic Townsite

ESCANABA ● ● **GARDEN**

MACKINAC ISLAND
Straits of Mackinac
BOIS BLANC ISLAND

BEAVER ISLAND   Mackinac Bridge

Lake Huron

Lake Michigan

NORTH MANITOU ISLAND
SOUTH MANITOU ISLAND

Sleeping Bear Dunes National Lakeshore

LOWER PENINSULA

TRAVERSE CITY ●

American robin

River

Saginaw Bay

Muskegon River

● **SAGINAW**

● **FLINT**

Grand River

GRAND RAPIDS ●

HOLLAND ●

LANSING ✪

Kalamazoo River

DETROIT ● *Lake St. Clair*

ANN ARBOR ● ● **DEARBORN**

Henry Ford Museum and Greenfield Village

KALAMAZOO ●

BATTLE CREEK ●

ST. JOSEPH ●

River

Lake Erie

THE PEOPLE AND THE LAND

Population: 9,179,000

Area: 58,527 sq. mi.

Population per sq. mi.: 157

Capital: Lansing (pop. 428,000)

Largest city: Detroit (pop. 4,360,000)

Major rivers: Escanaba, Grand, Kalamazoo, Saginaw

Elevation: 572 ft. (Lake Erie) to 1,980 ft. (Mt. Curwood)

Leading industries: Manufacturing (motor vehicles, metal products, machinery), agriculture (corn, dairy, fruit, soybeans, beef cattle), mining (iron, copper, salt)

Bird: American robin

Flower: Apple blossom

Tree: White pine

Motto: *Si Quaeris Peninsulam Amoenam Circumspice* (If You Seek a Pleasant Peninsula, Look About You)

Song: "Michigan, My Michigan" (unofficial)

Origin of name: From the Chippewa word for great lake, *michigama*

Nicknames: Auto State, Great Lake State, Wolverine State

INFORMATION

Michigan Travel Bureau
Department of Commerce
P.O. Box 30226
Lansing, MI 48909
Telephone:
800-543-2-YES

HISTORICAL HIGHLIGHTS

c. 1620 Étienne Brulé is believed to be the first European explorer to reach Michigan.

1668 Father Jacques Marquette establishes a permanent settlement at Sault Ste. Marie.

1701 Antoine Cadillac establishes the fur-trading post that will eventually become the city of Detroit.

1763 Britain acquires Michigan from France in treaty that ends French and Indian Wars.

1796 American flag is raised in Michigan for the first time as British leave Detroit.

1805 Congress establishes Michigan as a territory.

1837 Michigan joins Union as the 26th state.

1855 Soo Ship Canal and Locks, linking Lakes Huron and Superior, open at Sault Ste. Marie.

1900 Detroit's first automobile plant is built.

1914 Automobile industry accounts for 37 percent of state's manufacturing.

1942 Automobile factories convert to war production.

1957 Mackinac Bridge, between towns of St. Ignace and Mackinaw City, joins Upper and Lower Peninsulas.

1974 Coleman A. Young becomes first black mayor of city of Detroit.

1987 People Mover monorail, spanning almost three miles, opens in downtown Detroit.

FAMOUS SONS AND DAUGHTERS

Ralph Bunche (1904 – 71). A political scientist, Bunche became the first black division head at the U.S. State Department. His work on the United Nations Palestine Commission earned him the 1950 Nobel Peace Prize.

Edna Ferber (1887 – 1968). Born in Kalamazoo, Ferber wrote novels about American life. Her books include *Show Boat*, the basis for the famous Broadway musical, and the Pulitzer Prize-winning *So Big*.

Gerald R. Ford (1913 –). Longtime congressman, then vice president, Ford succeeded Richard M. Nixon as president in 1974. A candidate for the office in 1976, he was defeated by Jimmy Carter.

Henry Ford (1863 – 1947). Ford revolutionized the auto industry when he began mass-producing the moderately priced Model T in 1913.

Ring Lardner (1885 – 1933). Lardner's fine ear for the vernacular contributed to his success as a writer and satirist. Among his best-known short stories are "Haircut" and "Champion."

Sojourner Truth (1797? – 1883). Born Isabella Baumfree in New York, the evangelist spent the last 30 years of her life in Battle Creek, counseling freed slaves and working for women's rights.

ODDITIES AND SPECIALTIES

When Dr. John H. Kellogg of Battle Creek created cornflakes to serve as a nutritious dish for sanitarium patients, he started an industry. Today Battle Creek is the world's leading producer of breakfast cereals.

The southwest Michigan town of Holland is the only place in the U.S. where Dutch-originated delftware pottery is made.

Northern Michigan is the site of the National Mushroom Hunting Championship every May, when mushroom fanciers take to the woods to search out the prized morel mushrooms that grow there in profusion.

Despite its novelty, the reason for the naming of the Be Good to Your Mother-in-Law Bridge (built in 1880 across the Black River in Croswell) has been lost in the mists of time.

Although Michigan is nicknamed the Wolverine State, the small, bearlike creatures are exceedingly rare there. The only ones most Michiganders ever see are in the Detroit Zoo.

PLACES TO VISIT, THINGS TO DO

Fayette Historic Townsite (Garden). This iron-smelting village on Lake Michigan was abandoned more than a century ago. Restored buildings, including the opera house, are open for tours.

Henry Ford Museum and Greenfield Village (Dearborn). This 14-acre museum chronicles the nation's shift from agriculture to industry, with exhibits of cars, trains, furniture, and machinery. Adjacent is Greenfield Village, a collection of historic structures, some reconstructed. Included is the courthouse where Lincoln practiced law.

Hiawatha National Forest (Escanaba). The landscape immortalized in Henry Wadsworth Longfellow's poem, *The Song of Hiawatha*, has islands, swamps, and pine forests.

Isle Royale National Park (Houghton). The isolation of Lake Superior's largest island, 9 miles wide and 45 miles long, has made it a naturalist's paradise. Among the wildlife are moose, wolves, beavers, and loons.

Mackinac Island Rising from Lake Huron like the great turtle it was named for, this island is home to caves, natural bridges, and historic Fort Mackinac.

National Cherry Festival (Traverse City). This eight-day event, held every July, celebrates Michigan's status as the nation's leading cherry producer. Parades, live entertainment, sporting events, and cherry pies are the main attractions.

Pictured Rocks National Lakeshore (Munising). As well as beaches and waterfalls, the Lake Superior shoreline boasts 15 miles of dramatic rock cliffs that have been eroded into unusual shapes.

Sleeping Bear Dunes National Lakeshore (Glen Arbor, Glen Haven, Empire). Part of Lake Michigan's shoreline, this scenic area has two islands, vast sand dunes, beaches, and forests.

Minnesota

Cool forests, fertile farms, and a multitude of lakes

A remote lake in northern Minnesota, so hidden by the surrounding wilderness that it took explorers 130 years to find it, is the serene but rather unspectacular origin of the longest river in North America — the mighty Mississippi. When at last a party of indefatigable searchers led by Henry Rowe Schoolcraft and an Ojibwa Indian guide found the boggy headwaters of the great river in 1832, they named the lake Itasca.

It sounds like an American Indian word, but *Itasca* is in fact Latin — or truncated Latin, anyway — for the name was created by lopping off the first and last syllables of the phrase *veritas caput,* or "true source." Today the true source — together with the surrounding area of lakes, bogs, and evergreen forests — is protected and enshrined in beautiful Itasca State Park.

FROM TOPSOIL TO TWIN CITIES

Some 10,000 years ago, the glacial ice that bulldozed its way across the land deposited tons of rich, virgin topsoil. From the 1850's to the early 1900's, news of this bountiful soil, ideal for farming, attracted swarms of Scandinavians, Germans, and other immigrants seeking a new life.

Rich farmland is not the only legacy of the ancient glaciers. Their enormous bulk gouged out pits that became the myriad lakes Minnesota is famous for. The figure 10,000 is usually touted by Minnesotans, but the true number of lakes is far greater. In any case, their sheer quantity has made Minnesota a

Serenity prevails at Cherokee Lake, one of thousands of idyllic lakes and ponds that make up the Boundary Waters Canoe Area in northeastern Minnesota.

Brightened by the dawning light, the labyrinthine waters of Kabetogama Lake snake through miles of evergreen forest in remote Voyageurs National Park.

"land of lakes," where one out of six people owns a boat, one out of three has a fishing license, and nearly everyone spends at least some part of the year relaxing by a lake.

Lakes are found even within the city limits of Minneapolis and St. Paul — the Twin Cities area, which is the home of more than half the people of Minnesota. Located where the Mississippi and Minnesota rivers join together — a spot convenient for travel and trade — the Twin Cities were built on land first occupied by prehistoric Indians. Some of their burial mounds can be seen today, as can the original Fort Snelling, a frontier outpost established in 1819. This fortress was the seed from which the Twin Cities took root.

LAND OF TIMBER WOLVES AND VOYAGEURS

In northeastern Minnesota, which is called the Arrowhead because of its triangular shape, lakes also take center stage. Largest of all — a virtual inland sea — is mammoth Lake Superior. Its shoreline, parts of which are lined with spectacular cliffs, serves as Minnesota's eastern border north of Duluth. (This great port city is connected to the Atlantic Ocean via the St. Lawrence Seaway.)

Inland from the giant lake lies one of Minnesota's greatest natural treasures: the maze of rivers and streams, glacial lakes, and deep boreal woods that make up Superior National Forest and, to the northwest, Voyageurs National Park. This vast wilderness provides a

JEWELS OF MINNEAPOLIS

On a bright summer day, the six sparkling lakes in the heart of Minneapolis — Cedar Lake, Lake of the Isles, Lake Calhoun, Lake Harriet, Lake Hiawatha, and Lake Nokomis — seem as blue as lapis lazuli, their shimmering surfaces spangled with rowboats, canoes, and sailboats. In winter, the lakes harden into diamonds, where bundled-up skaters slice figure eights across the glistening ice.

Fashioned by ancient glaciers, the lakes and their shores were once the domain of Dakota Indians. A sign near Lake Calhoun, which the Indians called Lake of the Loons, marks the location of one of their villages. By the 1850's the Indians were gone, but the lakes and their settings, thanks to wise city planning, were beautifully preserved as Minneapolis expanded around them.

Today a stroll along one of the winding lakeside paths offers a visual commentary on urban fitness, fashion, and courtship. But with a little imagination one can picture the Dakota Indians in their canoes, gathering wild rice in the shallows.

---

refuge for moose, bears, and a large population of timber wolves. But it is known mainly for its network of waterways — given such peculiar names as Stump, Fiddle, Stickle, Temperance, and Vermilion —which were for 200 years the thoroughfares of commerce and conflict for Dakota and Ojibwa Indians and their clients, the French, British, and Canadian fur traders.

The routes once taken by voyageurs, the scrappy souls who hauled beaver pelts out of the wilderness, are still intact today. These historic paths and waterways continue to be traversed — not by voyageurs, but by adventurous hikers, campers, canoers, and city-weary vacationers.

At dawn and dusk, white-tailed deer forage for weeds, twigs, and nuts. The deer are common in Minnesota woodlands, but this particular sight — twin albino does — is rare indeed.

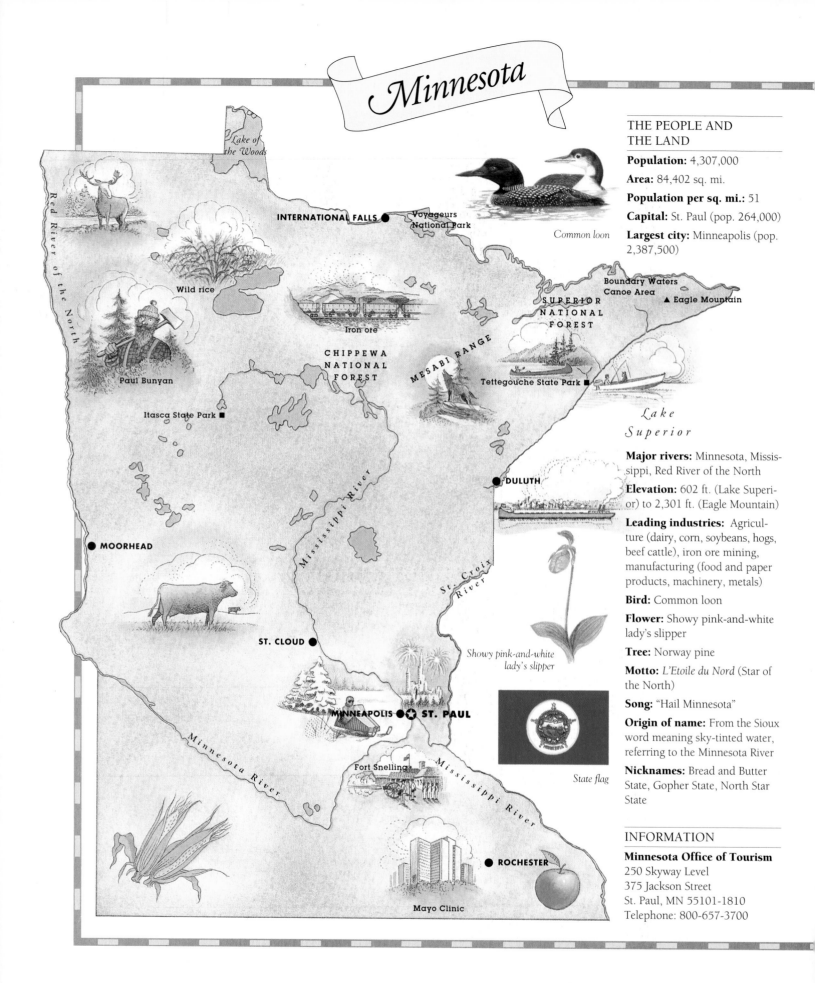

Minnesota

Population: 4,307,000

Area: 84,402 sq. mi.

Population per sq. mi.: 51

Capital: St. Paul (pop. 264,000)

Largest city: Minneapolis (pop. 2,387,500)

Common loon

Major rivers: Minnesota, Mississippi, Red River of the North

Elevation: 602 ft. (Lake Superior) to 2,301 ft. (Eagle Mountain)

Leading industries: Agriculture (dairy, corn, soybeans, hogs, beef cattle), iron ore mining, manufacturing (food and paper products, machinery, metals)

Bird: Common loon

Flower: Showy pink-and-white lady's slipper

Tree: Norway pine

Motto: *L'Etoile du Nord* (Star of the North)

Song: "Hail Minnesota"

Origin of name: From the Sioux word meaning sky-tinted water, referring to the Minnesota River

Nicknames: Bread and Butter State, Gopher State, North Star State

Showy pink-and-white lady's slipper

State flag

INFORMATION

Minnesota Office of Tourism
250 Skyway Level
375 Jackson Street
St. Paul, MN 55101-1810
Telephone: 800-657-3700

Map labels

Lake of the Woods

Moose

Wild rice

INTERNATIONAL FALLS

Voyageurs National Park

Paul Bunyan

Iron ore

CHIPPEWA NATIONAL FOREST

Itasca State Park

MESABI RANGE

Boundary Waters Canoe Area

▲ Eagle Mountain

SUPERIOR NATIONAL FOREST

Tettegouche State Park

Lake Superior

Red River of the North

● MOORHEAD

● DULUTH

St. Croix River

● ST. CLOUD

MINNEAPOLIS ✪ ⊛ ST. PAUL

Minnesota River

Fort Snelling

Mississippi River

● ROCHESTER

Mayo Clinic

HISTORICAL HIGHLIGHTS

1679 Daniel Greysolon, sieur du Luth, explores area near present-day Duluth.

1783 U.S. acquires eastern Minnesota from Great Britain as part of Treaty of Paris.

1803 U.S. gains the western portion from France as part of the Louisiana Purchase.

1816 Congress passes law to ensure U.S. control of its fur trade.

1832 Henry Rowe Schoolcraft discovers source of the Mississippi at Lake Itasca.

1849 Congress creates Minnesota Territory.

1858 Minnesota becomes the 32nd state.

1862 U.S. troops squelch a bloody Sioux revolt.

1890 Huge iron-ore deposits are found in the Mesabi Range.

1959 St. Lawrence Seaway opens, making Duluth the westernmost Atlantic port.

1968 Minnesotan Hubert Humphrey loses presidential election to Richard Nixon.

1976 Native son Walter Mondale is elected vice president under Jimmy Carter.

1984 Mondale loses presidential election to Ronald Reagan.

FAMOUS SONS AND DAUGHTERS

Warren E. Burger (1907 –) This St. Paul lawyer became assistant U.S. attorney general and a U.S. judge before serving as chief justice of the United States from 1969 to 1986.

William O. Douglas (1898 – 1980). Appointed to the U.S. Supreme Court by Franklin D. Roosevelt in 1939, Douglas served as an associate justice until he resigned in 1975.

Bob Dylan (1941 –). Beginning in the early 1960's, Dylan's songs of social protest made him an icon of America's counterculture and one of the most magnetic performers of his generation.

F. Scott Fitzgerald (1896 – 1940). Fitzgerald spoke for the generation of the 1920's Jazz Age. His widely acclaimed novels include *The Great Gatsby* and *Tender Is the Night*.

Judy Garland (1922 – 69).

A child singer, Garland earned enduring fame as Dorothy in the motion picture *The Wizard of Oz*. As an adult she entertained millions of fans with her films, records, and concerts.

Hubert H. Humphrey (1911 – 78). After serving as mayor of Minneapolis, Humphrey became Minnesota's first Democratic senator. A champion of arms control and civil rights in the U.S. Senate, he later served as Lyndon Johnson's vice president and in 1968 ran for president himself.

Sinclair Lewis (1885 – 1951). The author of such novels as *Main Street*, *Babbitt*, and *Elmer Gantry*, Lewis waged war on parochialism and hypocrisy. He was the first American to win the Nobel Prize for literature.

Charles A. Lindbergh (1902 – 74). The shy aviator was celebrated worldwide after piloting the *Spirit of St. Louis* on the first nonstop solo flight from New York to Paris in 1927.

ODDITIES AND SPECIALTIES

Minnesota abounds in water — nearly 5,000 square miles of it, including well over 10,000 lakes and about 90,000 miles of lake and river shoreline.

Minnesota lumberjacks once entertained each other with tales of the mythic hero Paul Bunyan and his blue ox, Babe, whose gigantic feet and tail were said to have created the lakes and rivers.

Northern Minnesota grows about three-fourths of the world's native wild rice, and the southern part of the state produces over a dozen varieties of apples.

The abundant snow and ice in this state inspired the unusual sport of "smooshing," in which teams race not on skis but on two-by-four beams — four brave people to a pair.

Pipestone, quarried by Indians in southwestern Minnesota, is used to make the ceremonial peace pipes that were once smoked to seal treaties.

PLACES TO VISIT, THINGS TO DO

Fishing The lakes, rivers, and marshlands of Minnesota have an abundance of trout, walleye, muskellunge, and largemouth bass. Several rivers, such as the Baptism, Cascade, and French, have Chinook salmon.

The Guthrie Theater (Minneapolis). Founded by British director Tyrone Guthrie and opened in 1963, the theater, with its three-sided "thrust" stage and its remarkable productions, has received nationwide acclaim.

Itasca State Park (Lake Itasca). Here are the headwaters of the Mississippi River, as well as over 150 lakes and bogs, Indian mounds, and the forested Wilderness Sanctuary, which can be seen from Wilderness Drive.

Mayo Clinic Buildings National Historic Landmark (Rochester). This world-renowned clinic began as a family enterprise in 1889. Tours are available, and visitors may also view the Mayo Medical Museum and the mansion built by Dr. Charles Mayo in 1910 – 11.

St. Paul Winter Carnival Attracting thousands of visitors every year, the carnival features beautiful sculptures fashioned from blocks of ice and, every few years depending on the weather, the fabulous Ice Palace.

Superior National Forest (Duluth). This immense wilderness in the Arrowhead section of Minnesota contains millions of acres of lakes, streams, and woodland, including the Boundary Waters Canoe Area, which abuts the Canadian border.

Voyageurs National Park (International Falls). Just northwest of Superior National Forest, the park is crisscrossed with trails and waterways used by 18th-century fur traders.

Mississippi

Magnolias and mockingbirds in a land nobody wants to leave

Lovely and languorous, Mississippi is the most traditionally southern of all the Deep South states. Here the legendary cotton fields sprawl in the sun beside sloping green levees. Here stand cool white-columned mansions shaded by magnolias that bear huge, creamy blossoms. Mockingbirds sing deliriously from the treetops and Confederate cemeteries are still decorated with fresh flowers.

Although Hernando de Soto had explored the region as early as 1540, disputes among the French, Spanish, English, and Indians discouraged settlement for most of the 18th century. Not until the turn of the 19th century did things begin to happen. The cotton gin was invented just as planters were giving up on tobacco and indigo farming; and, in 1798, the U.S. Congress formally organized Mississippi as a territory. Then, as the Choctaw and Chickasaw Indians were sent to Oklahoma, leaving vast tracts of land behind, settlers poured in founding such towns as Vicksburg, Tupelo, Yazoo City, Holly Springs, and Le Fleur's Bluff — soon to be renamed for Andrew Jackson and made the state capital.

FROM COTTON COUNTRY TO GOLDEN COAST

Perhaps the most distinctive region of the state is the Delta, an elliptical floodplain lying between the Mississippi and Yazoo rivers in northwestern Mississippi. This is cotton country — flat, nearly treeless, home of the very rich and the very poor. It was this fertile land that made possible the leisurely and luxurious plantation lifestyle for which Mississippi has been both envied and censured.

Tangles of heavenly scented wisteria adorn a footbridge in Jackson's Mynelle Gardens.

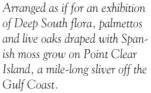

Arranged as if for an exhibition of Deep South flora, palmettos and live oaks draped with Spanish moss grow on Point Clear Island, a mile-long sliver off the Gulf Coast.

Gulf Islands National Seashore is made up of six barrier islands a few miles off the Mississippi and Florida coasts. Here, sea oats sprout from the dunes of Horn Island.

East of the Mississippi floodplain, much of the state is a mix of undulating hills and prairies, forests, and farmland, interrupted here and there by ancient Indian mounds. The highest elevations, in the northeastern corner of the state, are found among the outcroppings of the Tennessee River Hills, the southernmost ridges of the Appalachian Mountains. The best known of the prairie regions, just west of these hills, is the long,

narrow Black Belt, so named for its dark and extremely fertile soil.

Most of the lower third of the state is known as the Pine Hills, or the Piney Woods. Once a forest of virgin longleaf and slash pines, it was severely cut during the early 1900's. Replanted since then, the area accounts for much of the state's 17 million acres of forestland.

Driving through these silvery-green pine woods, one comes at last to the coastal low-lands, where the Old Spanish Trail, now U.S. Highway 90, runs for 26 miles between the wide sandy man-made beaches of the Gulf of Mexico and the elegant antebellum and Victorian vacation homes of Bay St. Louis, Pass Christian, and Biloxi. Tall palms and ancient live oaks line the beach boulevard, shrimp boats crowd the harbors, black skimmers and least terns nest among the sea oats, and laughing gulls wheel noisily overhead.

Travelers come upon landscaped driveways like this one as they explore the countryside around Natchez. This alluring tunnel of live oaks and azaleas arouses fantasies of what lies at the end — perhaps a glimpse of the Old South in the form of a white-columned mansion or a gazebo on a manicured lawn.

Missouri

A serene landscape traversed by two mighty rivers

Missouri is a study in contrasts: mountain mists and prairie grasses, surging rivers and cloistered caves, genteel St. Louis and down-to-earth Kansas City, President Harry Truman and outlaw Jesse James. It is also a natural crossroads, for Missouri, located in the very heart of America, serves as a link between East and West, North and South.

PLAINS AND MOUNTAINS

Much of the state consists of rich farmland. North of the Missouri River, which bisects the state as it flows from Kansas City to St. Louis, fertile, rolling plains in a region once buried under glaciers are now covered by expanses of golden grain. South of the Missouri River and to the west lie the Osage Plains, where gentle streams meander through fields of wildflowers and where wheat and corn share the land with protected tracts of the original prairie.

In contrast, most of the state south of the Missouri River is taken up by the varied landscapes of the Ozark Mountain region — an area of forests, lakes, rivers, rugged hills, and low mountains that extends into neighboring Arkansas. The Ozarks contain some 10,000 springs, many of which gush with more than a million gallons of water per day. The area is also honeycombed with thousands of caves carved out of limestone by underground streams. These mysterious netherworlds, where labyrinthine passageways twist and turn for miles, are filled with beautiful rock formations and bizarre creatures, such as blind white cave fish, that spend their lives in total darkness.

The tortuous shoreline of mammoth, man-made Lake of the Ozarks is longer than the coast of California.

Rising above the eroded limestone bedrock of the Mississippi River near Altenburg is massive, fortresslike Tower Rock.

THE BEAUTY AND SPLENDOR OF NORTH AMERICA

THE WRY SAGE OF HANNIBAL

Samuel Langhorne Clemens was born in the little town of Florida, Missouri, but Mark Twain was born — fittingly enough — on the Mississippi River. The writer took his pen name from the words used by men on riverboats to call out the depth of the water. "Mark twain," which means two fathoms deep, was heard so often by Clemens during his exhilarating years as a steamboat pilot that he deemed it an apt nom de plume.

Later Mark Twain traveled around the world, speaking and writing on a dazzling variety of subjects, but he was considered at his best when reminiscing about his early years spent on the river.

Twain's connection with the Mississippi began when he was a small boy and his family moved to Hannibal, where the ever-present river shaped every aspect of life. Below the bluffs flowed "the great Mississippi, the majestic, the magnificent Mississippi, rolling its mile-wide tide along, shining in the sun." As a child, Twain could not have anticipated how significant his adventures on the river would become. Without them, Tom Sawyer would not have become a river "pirate," Huckleberry Finn would never have rafted the river with his friend Jim, and life on the Mississippi would be a much dimmer memory in the mind of America.

In the southeast corner a section of the state called the bootheel juts into Arkansas (when Missouri entered the Union, a few wealthy plantation owners from the region lobbied successfully to have it included in the state). Here the Mississippi alluvial plain, once covered by lush bald cypress swamps, was drained to expose its rich dark soil. The land now yields tons of soybeans and rice, as well as the most southern crop of all — cotton.

THE GATEWAY STATE

From the outset, the Mississippi and Missouri rivers, coursing through the state from top to bottom and from side to side, attracted explorers and fur traders. Early river towns such as St. Charles (the state's first capital) and the Town of Kansas (now Kansas City) became busy ports. In the 19th century the steamboats that chugged up and down the Mississippi were immortalized by Hannibal's own Mark Twain.

During America's years of exploration and growth, Missouri was the starting-off point to the vast, beckoning West. Lewis and Clark began and ended their famous expedition to the Pacific in St. Louis; both the Santa Fe and Oregon trails started in Independence; and the hardy riders of the pony express galloped out of St. Joseph toward Sacramento.

North and South also converged in Missouri. Abolitionists and slaveholders alike lived in the state, and during the long and bloody Civil War Missourians fought on both sides — some, tragically, against their own kin.

Delicate, downy seedballs catch the fading light in a field of thistles not far from Kansas City.

Missouri

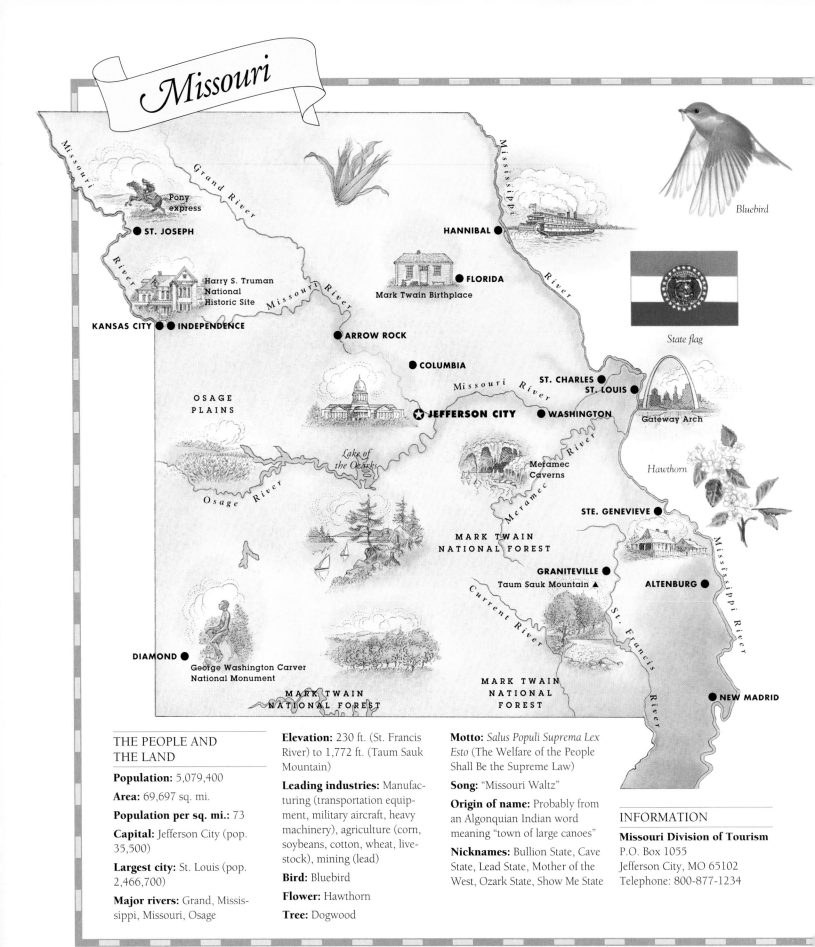

Bluebird

State flag

Pony express

● ST. JOSEPH

Grand River

Missouri

River

Harry S. Truman
National
Historic Site

KANSAS CITY ● ● INDEPENDENCE

Missouri River

● ARROW ROCK

HANNIBAL ●

● FLORIDA
Mark Twain Birthplace

Mississippi

River

● COLUMBIA

OSAGE
PLAINS

ST. CHARLES ●
Missouri River   ST. LOUIS ●

☆ JEFFERSON CITY   ● WASHINGTON

Gateway Arch

*Lake of
the Ozarks*

Osage River

Meramec
River

Meramec
Caverns

Hawthorn

STE. GENEVIEVE ●

MARK TWAIN
NATIONAL FOREST

GRANITEVILLE ●
Taum Sauk Mountain ▲

ALTENBURG ●

Current River

St. Francis River

DIAMOND ●
George Washington Carver
National Monument

MARK TWAIN
NATIONAL FOREST

MARK TWAIN
NATIONAL
FOREST

Mississippi River

● NEW MADRID

THE PEOPLE AND
THE LAND

Population: 5,079,400

Area: 69,697 sq. mi.

Population per sq. mi.: 73

Capital: Jefferson City (pop. 35,500)

Largest city: St. Louis (pop. 2,466,700)

Major rivers: Grand, Mississippi, Missouri, Osage

Elevation: 230 ft. (St. Francis River) to 1,772 ft. (Taum Sauk Mountain)

Leading industries: Manufacturing (transportation equipment, military aircraft, heavy machinery), agriculture (corn, soybeans, cotton, wheat, livestock), mining (lead)

Bird: Bluebird

Flower: Hawthorn

Tree: Dogwood

Motto: *Salus Populi Suprema Lex Esto* (The Welfare of the People Shall Be the Supreme Law)

Song: "Missouri Waltz"

Origin of name: Probably from an Algonquian Indian word meaning "town of large canoes"

Nicknames: Bullion State, Cave State, Lead State, Mother of the West, Ozark State, Show Me State

INFORMATION

Missouri Division of Tourism
P.O. Box 1055
Jefferson City, MO 65102
Telephone: 800-877-1234

HISTORICAL HIGHLIGHTS

1673 Explorers Marquette and Jolliet discover mouth of Missouri River.

1682 Robert Cavelier, sieur de La Salle, claims area for France.

c. 1735 Ste. Genevieve is the first permanent settlement.

1762 France yields Missouri region to Spain.

1763 Pierre Laclède selects site for St. Louis.

1800 Spain returns Missouri area to France.

1803 U.S. receives Missouri as part of Louisiana Purchase.

1804 Lewis and Clark set out on their famous western expedition from St. Louis.

1811 – 12 Three massive earthquakes hit sparsely populated New Madrid, permanently altering the southeastern Missouri landscape.

1812 Congress organizes the Missouri Territory.

1820 Missouri Compromise paves way for Missouri to enter Union as a slave state and Maine as a free state.

1821 Missouri becomes 24th American state.

1836 Platte Purchase adds six counties to the state.

1857 The U.S. Supreme Court denies freedom to Missouri slave Dred Scott, fueling controversy that leads to Civil War.

1860 Pony express service starts in St. Joseph.

1904 Louisiana Purchase Exposition (also known as the St. Louis World's Fair) opens in St. Louis.

1931 Bagnell Dam is completed, forming the Lake of the Ozarks.

1945 Harry S. Truman is inaugurated as 33rd president.

1965 Gateway Arch is completed in St. Louis.

1983 Dioxin, a toxic by-product of chemical manufacturing plants, contaminates Times Beach, forcing residents to leave.

1988 A severe drought causes major difficulties with river transportation.

FAMOUS SONS AND DAUGHTERS

Josephine Baker (1906 – 75). A black entertainer living in France, Baker achieved fame when she performed at the Folies-Bergére. By the late 1920's she was the toast of Paris.

Dale Carnegie (1888 – 1955). A lecturer and former salesman, Carnegie drew on experiences in his own life to write the hugely successful *How to Win Friends and Influence People*.

George Washington Carver (c. 1864 – 1943). Born a slave, Carver became an important scientist who discovered hundreds of uses for the peanut and sweet potato. His birthplace in the town of Diamond is now a national monument.

Jesse James (1847 – 82). Together with his brother Frank, Jesse James led a notorious outlaw gang that robbed banks and trains for more than a decade.

John J. Pershing (1860 – 1948). West Point graduate and former Indian fighter, Pershing was commander of the American Expeditionary Forces in World War I, during which he transformed the ill-prepared U.S. troops into effective combat units.

Joseph Pulitzer (1847 – 1911). Pulitzer, an immigrant from Hungary, published the St. Louis *Post-Dispatch* and the New York *World*. He also endowed the prestigious Pulitzer Prizes.

Virgil Thomson (1896 – 1989). A major figure in contemporary music, Thomson was an organist, composer, author, and music critic. His works include operas, ballets, chamber music, and scores for films.

Harry S. Truman (1884 – 1972). Raised in Independence, Truman served in the U.S. Senate before his election as vice president. When Roosevelt died in 1945, Truman became president.

ODDITIES AND SPECIALTIES

Missouri's central location and navigable rivers — notably the Mississippi and Missouri — made the state an important transportation center. Today St. Louis and Kansas City continue to serve as two of the nation's busiest inland ports.

More corncob pipes are produced in Washington, Mo., than anywhere else in the world.

A spelunker's heaven, Missouri in 1990 reported a record of 5,000 caves within its borders. Some of the creatures that live in them, such as the grotto salamander, can be found nowhere but in the Ozarks.

The ice-cream cone is believed to have been invented at the St. Louis World's Fair in 1904, when a vendor used a folded waffle to hold ice cream.

PLACES TO VISIT, THINGS TO DO

Arrow Rock An outfitting point for the Santa Fe Trail, this river town features a number of 19th-century buildings that have been carefully preserved.

Gateway Arch (St. Louis).

Located at the center of the Jefferson National Expansion Memorial, the 630-foot arch is the nation's tallest monument. It is also the highest freestanding arch ever built.

Hannibal The spirit of Mark Twain lives on in his childhood hometown, where one can visit his family home, a museum, and the famous Mark Twain Cave.

Lake of the Ozarks (60 miles southwest of Jefferson City). Covering 58,000 acres, with a shoreline of over 1,300 miles, this artificial lake is one of the world's largest. Set amid dense oak and hickory forests, the lake offers boating, fishing, and other recreational activities.

Mark Twain National Forest (Rolla). The rivers, springs, lakes, and caves of the Ozark woods create some of the most striking scenery in the state. Visitors can view it while hiking, driving, horseback riding, or taking a "float trip" down a river.

Meramec Caverns (Stanton). Once the hideout of Jesse James, the cave contains five levels of unusual rock formations.

Montana

Fifty mountain ranges at the edge of the Great Plains

Although most of Montana belongs to the Great Plains, it is mountains that give the state its extraordinary beauty. More than 50 majestic ranges — among them the colorfully named Beaverhead, Big Belt, Crazy, Flathead, and Tobacco Root — make up Montana's share of the Rocky Mountains, strung down the western third of the state.

The mountains also helped give Montana its Wild West image, for this was the territory of rough-and-ready prospectors and opulent copper barons. A gold strike in 1862 at Grasshopper Creek first drew the miners, who eventually found silver, coal, and copper as well — and called Butte, the town they founded on one of the world's largest copper deposits, "the richest hill on earth."

Each of Montana's mountain ranges is a scenic wonder in itself. The two-lane highway that crosses the Beartooth range, for example, has been called the most beautiful drive in the United States. This 69-mile route, on U.S. 212, starts in the little town of Red Lodge and traces a series of steep zigzags, or switchbacks, along the Montana-Wyoming border to 10,974-foot-high Beartooth Pass and beyond. The drive ends at Cooke City, a gateway to Yellowstone National Park.

GOING TO THE SUN

Many other scenic ranges and subranges sweep down from northwestern Montana. Along the crest of some 20 of them — including the Boundary, Lewis, Anaconda, Mission, Bitter-

Rocky Mountain goats live in places so remote and precarious that the beasts have little to fear from predators. These two wander the rough terrain of Haystack Butte in Glacier National Park.

The Musselshell River, here looking as tidy as an English stream, moves through the undulating terrain of central Montana.

THE BEAUTY AND SPLENDOR OF NORTH AMERICA

PAINTER OF THE PLAINS

No one documented the life of Montana's great northern plains better than Charles M. Russell, who was born in St. Louis, Missouri, in 1864. Drawn by the irresistible romance of the West, Charlie arrived in Montana as a 16-year-old; once there, he herded sheep, lived with a trapper, rode the range, and dwelled among the Indians. He also produced some 4,500 works of art before his death in 1926.

The self-taught artist's famous "Waiting for a Chinook," depicting the hard winter of 1886 – 87 that brought death to thousands of cattle, launched his career. His oil paintings, murals, watercolors, drawings, and bronze sculptures portray virtually every aspect of cowboy life, and his renderings of the Plains Indians are so detailed they can serve as historical records. But no matter how successful Charlie Russell became — a mural commission earned him $30,000 — his log-cabin studio was always open to his cowboy friends, with whom he indulged his legendary gift for storytelling. The studio and artist's house are now part of the C. M. Russell Museum Complex in Great Falls.

root, Centennial, and Swan — runs the Continental Divide. Centered squarely on the divide at the northern border of the state is Glacier National Park, a breathtaking preserve of sharp peaks and icy lakes. The best view of the park's vast vertical walls of glacier-polished rock is from the Going-to-the-Sun Highway, a 55-mile-long road that traverses the park and crosses the divide at Logan Pass.

With every 1,000-foot gain in elevation, the traveler encounters a climate equivalent to that 300 miles north; hence the presence of five life zones in the park — grassland, deciduous forest, coniferous forest, alpine tundra, and glacial ice. This range has endowed the park with an extraordinary variety of flora and fauna.

BIG SKY COUNTRY

Mountains give Montana its name and its grandeur, but the larger portion of the state is given over to sweeping plains — the majestic Big Sky Country. As in other parts of the West, a procession of immigrants put the land to different uses. Some succeeded and stayed, others failed and departed.

First, the Indians came for buffalo. The Blackfoot, Crow, and other Indian tribes tracked huge herds across the plains, using the animals for food and clothing, and sheathing tepees with their skins. Then, in the 1870's, white ranchers arrived to make use of the open range and its native grama and bunch grasses, which provide ideal food for cattle.

Wagon wheels of old are brought to mind by the water pipes in a Montana wheat field. Grain covers much of the vast plain that lies east of the mountain ranges.

Nowhere is the beauty of Glacier National Park more apparent than at St. Mary, one of the largest of the park's 650 lakes. Visible in the center is tiny Wild Goose Island.

Soon after came professional buffalo hunters in search of animal hides to ship back east. By 1885 the seemingly inexhaustible buffalo herds had all but disappeared, and Montana's dozen-odd native Indian tribes, deprived of the animals that gave them sustenance (and now almost entirely dependent on the government), were relegated to six reservations by the end of the century.

The vast open range went the way of the buffalo in the early 20th century when hordes of sodbusters arrived to farm the land offered by the U.S. government. After staking out the range with barbed wire and bringing in a few good wheat crops in a run of unusually rainy years, most of the sodbusters abandoned their farms by 1920, defeated by grasshopper plagues, drought, and windstorms that blew away the topsoil.

Today many visitors come to Montana to enjoy a venerable western institution — the dude ranch. Such ranches got their start when railroads began bringing tourists to Yellowstone Park in the 1880's and nearby ranchers

At the National Bison Range, 400 bison share the land with pronghorns, sheep, and elk.

welcomed the strangers into their homes, charging a fee as a way to help keep things together in tough times. Later, in the 1920's, a few drought-threatened cattle ranches were revived by doubling as vacation spots.

Some city dwellers choose working ranches where they can become part of the crew for a few days; others want only a little horseback riding or fishing. But all appreciate the truth in western artist Charlie Russell's words: "You have to get on a horse to see what God has made."

Bear grass blooms at the Chinese Wall, a 13-mile-long cliff along the Continental Divide.

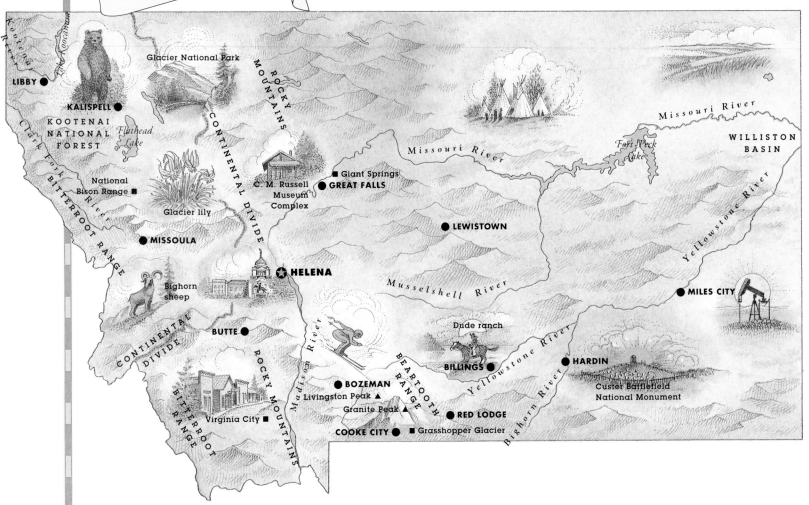

Montana

Libby ●
Kalispell ●
K O O T E N A I N A T I O N A L F O R E S T
Flathead Lake
Glacier National Park
National Bison Range ■
Glacier lily
Missoula ●
Bitterroot River
Clark Fork
B I T T E R R O O T R A N G E
Kootenai River
Lake Koocanusa
R O C K Y M O U N T A I N S
C O N T I N E N T A L D I V I D E
C. M. Russell Museum Complex
Giant Springs ■
GREAT FALLS ●
Missouri River
Bighorn sheep
★ **HELENA**
BUTTE ●
C O N T I N E N T A L D I V I D E
Virginia City ■
Madison River
R O C K Y M O U N T A I N S
B I T T E R R O O T R A N G E
BOZEMAN ●
Livingston Peak ▲
Granite Peak ▲
COOKE CITY ●
Grasshopper Glacier ■
RED LODGE ●
B E A R T O O T H R A N G E
LEWISTOWN ●
Mussel shell River
Dude ranch
BILLINGS ●
Yellowstone River
HARDIN ●
Bighorn River
Custer Battlefield National Monument
Missouri River
W I L L I S T O N B A S I N
Fort Peck Lake
Yellowstone River
MILES CITY ●

THE PEOPLE AND THE LAND

Population: 794,300

Area: 147,046

Population per sq. mi.: 5

Capital: Helena (pop. 23,900)

Largest city: Billings (pop. 116,400)

Major rivers: Clark Fork, Kootenai, Missouri, Yellowstone

Elevation: 1,800 ft. (Kootenai River) to 12,799 ft. (Granite Peak)

Leading industries: Agriculture (cattle, wheat), timber, mining (gold, silver, copper)

Bird: Western meadowlark

Flower: Bitterroot

Tree: Ponderosa pine

Motto: *Oro y Plata* (Gold and Silver)

Song: "Montana"

Origin of name: From the Spanish word for mountainous

Nicknames: Big Sky Country, Bonanza State, Land of the Shining Mountains, Mountain State, Treasure State

INFORMATION

Montana Department of Commerce
Travel Montana
1424 9th Avenue
Helena, MT 59620
Telephone: 800-541-1447

State flag

Western meadowlark

Bitterroot

HISTORICAL HIGHLIGHTS

1743 French explorers Pierre and François de La Vérendrye sight what they call the Shining Mountains, perhaps the Bighorn Mountains.

1803 With Louisiana Purchase, eastern Montana comes under jurisdiction of U.S.

1805 – 06 Lewis and Clark explore region on their way to and from Pacific Ocean.

1807 Manuel Lisa builds trading post at confluence of Yellowstone and Bighorn rivers.

1846 Treaty with Great Britain gives northwestern portion of Montana to U.S.

1862 Discovery of gold at Grasshopper Creek brings in thousands of prospectors.

1864 Congress passes bill declaring Montana a territory.

1876 Indians defeat George Armstrong Custer's cavalry troops in Battle of Little Bighorn.

1877 Indian fighting in Montana ends with surrender of Chief Joseph and Nez Perce Indians to federal troops.

1880 Railway line reaches Montana for first time.

1889 Montana enters Union as 41st state.

1910 Congress establishes Glacier National Park.

1940 Fort Peck Dam, the country's largest earth-filled hydraulic dam, is completed on Missouri River in northeastern Montana.

1951 Oil boom begins in Williston Basin in eastern Montana.

1975 Libby Dam, which created 90-mile-long Lake Koocanusa, begins operation.

1983 The Anaconda Company, whose mines yielded copper and other minerals worth nearly $4 billion, closes after a century of production in Butte.

FAMOUS SONS AND DAUGHTERS

John M. Bozeman (1835 – 67). This pioneer blazed the Bozeman Trail, a shortcut from the Overland Trail to the Montana goldfields. Today Bozeman Pass and a city are named after him.

Gary Cooper (1901 – 61).

The actor who epitomized the strong, silent type made more than 90 films and won Oscars for his performances in *Sergeant York* and *High Noon*.

A. B. Guthrie, Jr. (1901 –). After growing up on the Montana frontier, Guthrie wrote about the West in such works as the novel *The Big Sky* and the screenplay for *Shane*.

Mike Mansfield (1903 –). A U.S. representative for 10 years before being elected senator, Mansfield, a Democrat, was majority leader for a record 16 years. He served as ambassador to Japan from 1977 to 1988.

Jeannette Rankin (1880 – 1973). An outspoken pacifist who argued against U.S. participation in World Wars I and II, Rankin was the first woman to serve in the House of Representatives. She was the only legislator to vote against declaring war on Japan after the raid on Pearl Harbor in 1941 — a vote that effectively ended her political career.

ODDITIES AND SPECIALTIES

Only 201 feet long, the Roe River near Great Falls may be the shortest river in the world.

Millions of grasshoppers that were entombed in ice long ago can still be seen at Grasshopper Glacier in the Absaroka-Beartooth Wilderness.

An estimated 20 million buffalo roamed the Montana plains in the 1860's. Some 25 years later, hunters in pursuit of buffalo hides had reduced the population to fewer than 100.

In one of the greatest land rushes ever, the number of acres under cultivation in Montana jumped from 886 acres in 1900 to 30 million acres in 1919.

PLACES TO VISIT, THINGS TO DO

Custer Battlefield National Monument (near Hardin). Custer's Last Stand took place on this site in 1876, when Indians annihilated U.S. troops in the valley of the Little Bighorn River.

Flathead Lake (near Kalispell). The largest natural freshwater lake west of the Mississippi, Flathead reflects the surrounding mountains and forest in its waters, which offer fishing, boating, and swimming.

Giant Springs (near Great Falls). Located on the banks of the Missouri River, these springs are among the largest in the world, with a daily flow of nearly 390 million gallons of water.

Glacier National Park (West Glacier). This spectacular park in the Rocky Mountains features lofty peaks, sharp-edged ridges, clear lakes, dense forests, and alpine glaciers. Its streams are a favorite with fishermen; no license is required.

Kootenai National Forest (Libby). Rising above rivers, lakes, and evergreen trees are the snowy peaks of five mountain ranges in this vast forest.

Miles City Jaycee Bucking Horse Sale (Miles City).

Among the events centered on this annual sale of bulls and unbroken horses, held the third weekend in May, are pari-mutuel horse racing, dances, barbecues, and a rodeo.

National Bison Range (Moiese). The buffalo roam over some 19,000 acres of grassland at the base of the Mission Range. Visitors can either watch the bison in designated pastures or, in summer, take the 19-mile self-guided auto tour.

Virginia City This restored ghost town, now a national historic landmark, was the center of gold rush activity in the 1860's. Open for tours in the summer are an assay office, saloon, blacksmith shop, hotel, Wells Fargo office, general store, and the building that served as the territorial capitol from 1865 to 1875.

Nebraska

*Clear skies, rolling hills,
and the river road west*

Nebraska sweeps to the horizon in broad, gently undulating hills and open, sun-drenched vistas. These treeless expanses perplexed some of the first white people who ventured onto the prairie in the 19th century. Maj. Stephen H. Long, after exploring the region in 1819, concluded that it was "destined by the barrenness of its soil, the inhospitable character of its climate, and by other physical disadvantages, to be the abode of perpetual desolation." The lack of trees, however, belied the fruitfulness of the plain. Nebraska in actuality pulses with life.

RICHES OF THE PRAIRIE

Meriwether Lewis and William Clark on their 1804 expedition through this region were astonished by the immense herds of elk and antelopes they saw. Prairie potholes — shallow basins filled intermittently with water — supported untold numbers of ducks and geese, and the nutritious native grasses fed enormous herds of bison, or American buffalo.

What had been called "the abode of perpetual desolation" developed instead into the Cornhusker State, a realm of farms and ranches, livestock feedlots and towering grain elevators, where 95 percent of the terrain is given over to the production of corn, soybeans, wheat, sorghum, and other crops, and to the raising of beef cattle and hogs.

In the eastern part of the state nature provides enough rain to sustain these crops and livestock. In the western reaches, however, where the rainfall dwindles, the water supply

Winter frost bedecks the trees at the base of Scotts Bluff. A landmark for pioneers, the bluff was named for Hiram Scott, a fur trader who died nearby in 1828.

Little changed from the way the early settlers found them, the Sandhills exude the vastness and solitude of open rangeland. The rolling hills here are in fact sand dunes held in place by grasses. Covering an area nearly the size of West Virginia, the Sandhills are the largest stable dune system in the Western Hemisphere.

depends on human ingenuity. Networks of canals bring water from huge reservoirs in far western Nebraska and Wyoming, and deep wells tap underground aquifers for irrigation rigs that loom in the fields west of Cozad.

North-central Nebraska remains uncultivable, a 19,000-square-mile region of ancient sand dunes stabilized by the tenacious roots of prairie grass. These Sandhills of Nebraska, as they are called, were once the domain of nomadic Great Plains Indian tribes — especially the Cheyenne, Pawnee, and Sioux. Today the Sandhills are a kingdom of cattle ranches, for although the soil is too porous

for irrigation, the dunes do support enough grass to feed cattle on the open range. Far removed from the din of urban civilization, the Sandhills are exquisitely quiet, empty, and vast — a place of clear skies, stunning dawns and dusks, and jet black nights pricked with quadrillions of stars.

THE RIVER ROAD WEST

The name Nebraska comes from the Oto Indian word *nebrathka*, which means flat water. This is what the Otos called the great river that flows west to east across the state. It was a suitable name: before the river was harnessed for agri-

Each summer, the bold orange of wild sunflowers brightens the prairie vistas near Alliance.

THE PIONEERS' LANDMARK

On the level land of the Great Plains, occasional geological irregularities — a towering rock spire or an unexpected canyon — provided unmistakable and welcome landmarks for pioneers headed

cultural purposes, it was wide — three miles in places — and shallow, and rarely riled into swells or whitecaps. French traders concurred with the Oto assessment of this distinctly flat river and called it the Platte.

An estimated 350,000 people headed westward through the Platte Valley between 1840 and 1866. The procession of wagon trains came to an end with the completion of the transcontinental railroad in 1869, which followed the same path along the Platte as the preceding pioneers. Today Interstate 80 parallels this pioneer route most of the way across Nebraska.

west. The sight of these natural features not only assured the wagoners that they were on the right course, but also told them how far they had come and how far they had to go.

One such landmark on the Oregon Trail was mentioned more often in the diaries of pioneers than any other — Chimney Rock, the clay-and-sandstone spire that towers 470 feet above the North Platte Valley in Nebraska. Westward migrants, jostling across the plains in covered wagons at a speed of little more than a mile an hour, could see this steeplelike formation for days before they reached it. When they arrived, they knew that they had traveled 650 miles from St. Joseph, Missouri, and had 1,400 more to go before reaching the Pacific Ocean. They also could enjoy a pleasant campsite, for a reliable spring spouted from the base of the rock.

Nevada

Beauty in the desolate wasteland of the Great Basin

Well into the first half of the 19th century, the lonely land just east of the Sierra Nevada remained an enigma. While some explorers returned with stories of snow-covered mountains, pine forests, and rushing trout streams, others described the land as hell's antechamber.

People also wondered what became of all the snow from the Sierra Nevada when it melted. The first Spaniards to arrive in the region believed the snow drained into a mighty river that crossed present-day Nevada and linked the heart of the continent with the Pacific Ocean. But the hoped-for waterway, which they called the San Buenaventura, was never found. It was left to John Charles Frémont, assigned in 1844 to chart the desolate land between the Rocky Mountains and the Sierra Nevada, to discover the disappointing truth. Instead of feeding a great river, the snow from the Sierra Nevada drained onto the salt flats below, creating instant lakes and small rivers, many of which evaporated by summer. Left behind were shallow depressions filled with spiraling alkali dust. The enigma, it seemed, was solved: this land was little more than a forbidding desert.

GOLD AND SILVER

"I believe God never made anything without a purpose," said newspaper editor Horace Greeley after taking the Overland Trail through Nevada in 1859. "But the wilderness I have just crossed is certainly worthless for agriculture. Unless there shall prove to be great mineral wealth there, it has been created in vain."

The unearthly peaks of the Ruby Mountains smolder in the afternoon sun. This scene is at Liberty Lake.

Lake Tahoe, Nevada's oasis of water and woodland, is the largest alpine lake in North America. Its crystalline waters are cupped by the granite peaks of the Sierra Nevada on the Nevada-California border.

Nevada's mineral wealth became uncontested fact that same year when two miners prospecting outside present-day Reno discovered what later became known as the Comstock Lode. Not only was there gold aplenty, but the bluish sand that kept clogging the miners' sifters that separated nuggets from sand turned out to be high-grade silver sulfide.

Gold and silver still contribute to Nevada's economy today. But the state's most valuable asset is its allure for tourists — the neon-lit casinos of Las Vegas, the resorts of Lake Tahoe, and the beauty of the very desert that early explorers deemed a wasteland.

The arid Great Basin within which Nevada lies extends into parts of California, Oregon, Idaho, Wyoming, and Utah. Once the basin was the bottom of a vast prehistoric sea called Lake Lahontan. As the lake evaporated, repeated volcanic convulsions uplifted and fissured the earth, leaving more than 100 jagged mountain ranges running from north to south.

Only a few of the mountain valleys still contain viable lakes. Pyramid Lake and Walker Lake, once the deepest parts of ancient Lake Lahontan, today are recreation areas, blue-green bodies of water eerily terraced with spongy calcium-based deposits called tufa. Many of the rivers in Nevada are shallow, and frequently run dry. Yet, despite receiving less than 10 inches of rain a year, Nevada has an amazing diversity of plants and wildlife.

It is Lake Tahoe, however, that is Nevada's most precious gem. Set amid alpine meadows in the Sierra Nevada, the lake is surrounded by stands of ponderosa pine, piñon, and juniper. In 1861 Samuel Clemens (who would adopt the name Mark Twain a year later) arrived from Missouri to look for gold and discovered that Nevada's real treasure was the beauty and serenity of Lake Tahoe. "So singularly clear was the water . . . that the boat seemed floating in the air," he later reminisced in *Roughing It*.

The gold mines Twain wrote about are little more than rubble today. But the raw majesty of the snowcapped mountains and the stark drama of the desert remain undiminished.

Indigo blooms in the brick-red sands of southeastern Nevada, near Las Vegas.

Nevada

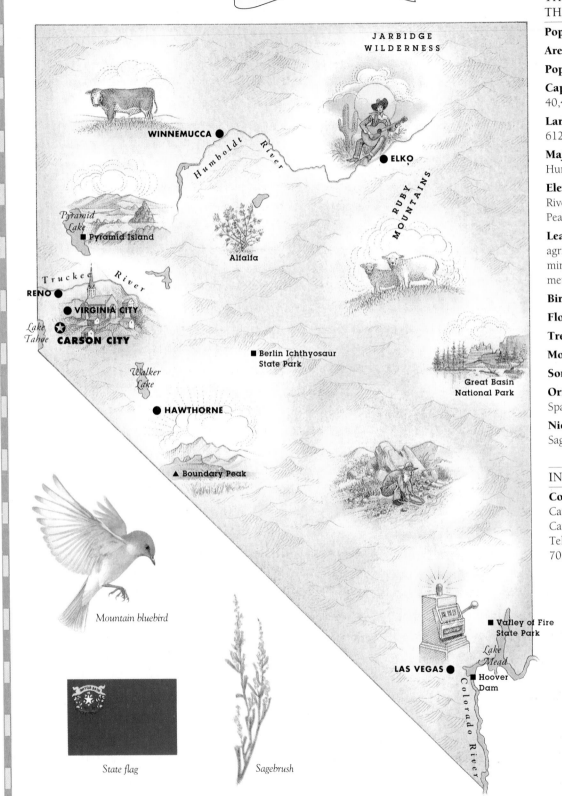

WINNEMUCCA

ELKO

JARBIDGE WILDERNESS

Humboldt River

Pyramid Lake
■ Pyramid Island

Alfalfa

RUBY MOUNTAINS

Truckee River

RENO

VIRGINIA CITY

Lake Tahoe

★ CARSON CITY

■ Berlin Ichthyosaur State Park

Walker Lake

Great Basin National Park

● HAWTHORNE

▲ Boundary Peak

Mountain bluebird

Sagebrush

State flag

■ Valley of Fire State Park

Lake Mead

LAS VEGAS ●

■ Hoover Dam

Colorado River

THE PEOPLE AND THE LAND

Population: 1,193,000

Area: 110,561 sq. mi.

Population per sq. mi.: 11

Capital: Carson City (pop. 40,400)

Largest city: Las Vegas (pop. 612,600)

Major rivers: Colorado, Humboldt, Truckee

Elevation: 400 ft. (Colorado River) to 13,140 ft. (Boundary Peak)

Leading industries: Tourism, agriculture (cattle, sheep, alfalfa), mining (gold, silver), processed metals, processed foods

Bird: Mountain bluebird

Flower: Sagebrush

Tree: Single-leaf piñon

Motto: All for Our Country

Song: "Home Means Nevada"

Origin of name: From the Spanish word for snowcapped

Nicknames: Mining State, Sagebrush State, Silver State

INFORMATION

Commission on Tourism
Capitol Complex
Carson City, NV 89710
Telephone: 800-NEVADA
702-687-4322 in Nevada

HISTORICAL HIGHLIGHTS

1826 – 27 Fur trader Jedediah Smith and his party cross Nevada on their way to California.

1828 Peter Ogden, a Hudson's Bay Company employee, begins exploration of northern Nevada and discovers Humboldt River.

1844 John Frémont, with Kit Carson as his guide, begins to map Nevada.

1848 Mexico cedes Nevada to U.S. after Mexican War.

1849 Mormon Station, a trading post later renamed Genoa, is first permanent white settlement.

1859 With discovery of Comstock Lode, a rich silver and gold deposit, prospectors rush to the settlement that will become Virginia City.

1861 Congress establishes Nevada Territory.

1864 Nevada joins Union as the 36th state.

1868 Transcontinental railroad crosses Nevada.

1869 Gambling is legalized.

1873 Mining industry begins to wane as federal government limits use of silver in coins.

1874 Two Indian reservations, Pyramid Lake and Walker River, are created for Northern Paiutes, who were defeated in the Indian War of 1860.

1880 Population begins a 10-year decline as gold and silver mines peter out.

1907 Newlands Irrigation Project turns parts of west-central Nevada into agricultural land.

1909 State legislature declares gambling illegal.

1931 State legalizes gambling and lowers residency requirement for divorce to six weeks.

1935 Boulder Dam (now Hoover Dam), then the largest dam in U.S., is completed.

1951 Atomic Energy Commission tests nuclear weapons at Yucca Flat.

1970 U.S. census shows Nevada to have been fastest growing state in previous decade.

1980 State legislature passes antipollution laws to protect Lake Tahoe.

1986 Great Basin National Park, the first national park in Nevada, is established.

FAMOUS SONS AND DAUGHTERS

Walter van Tilburg Clark (1909 – 71). This writer set his psychological novels and short stories in the Old West. His most famous work, *The Ox-Bow Incident*, is the story of the lynching of three innocent men.

John W. Mackay (1831 – 1902). A "silver king," Mackay made his fortune mining the Comstock Lode. In 1886 he organized the Postal Telegraph Cable Company, which broke Western Union's monopoly in the U.S.

William Morris Stewart (1827 – 1909). As one of Nevada's first two U.S. senators, Stewart was author of the 15th Amendment, which guarantees equal voting rights, without regard to "race, color, or previous condition of servitude."

Sarah Winnemucca (1844? – 91). Daughter of a Paiute chief and wife of a U.S. Army officer, this interpreter and guide became one of the first Indians to write about Indian grievances. Her book was called *Life Among the Paiutes*.

Wovoka (1858? – 1932). This Paiute Indian was a leader of the 19th-century Ghost Dance religious movement, which sought to resurrect ancestors and restore a waning culture.

ODDITIES AND SPECIALTIES

Taxes from gambling provide nearly 40 percent of Nevada's general revenues.

The driest of all the 50 states, Nevada relies on a number of man-made lakes and underground sources to augment its meager water supply.

Outside of Alaska, the federal government owns more of Nevada than any other state — more than 85 percent.

Each year in Elko, thousands of cowboys and other ranch hands gather to perform poems and songs they have written to pass the time on the range.

Las Vegas is not only the nation's gambling capital but its marriage capital as well; the city boasts some 50 wedding chapels.

PLACES TO VISIT, THINGS TO DO

Berlin Ichthyosaur State Park (near Gabbs). This park has two attractions: the ghost mining town of Berlin and the fossils of ichthyosaurs, colossal reptiles that swam in an ancient inland sea.

Great Basin National Park The most spectacular part of the Great Basin is in this park — the southern part of the Snake mountain range, with forests (including ancient bristlecone pines), limestone caves, and Nevada's only glacier.

Lake Tahoe (near Carson City). Center of a year-round resort area, Lake Tahoe is renowned for the clarity of its water. Snowcapped mountain peaks surround the 72-mile shoreline.

Pyramid Lake (near Reno). A remnant of the prehistoric waters that covered northwest Nevada, this lake contains a pyramid-shaped island and abundant cutthroat trout.

Valley of Fire State Park (near Las Vegas). Striking sandstone formations of many colors stand in this desert valley.

Virginia City Looking almost as it did in 1870, when it was a rich mining town, Virginia City features boardwalks, Victorian mansions, churches, and an historic shortline railway.

New Hampshire

An old Yankee home, New England to the core

Nestled between Maine and Vermont, and extending from Massachusetts to the Canadian border, New Hampshire lies in the heart of New England. Since it is endowed with all the natural beauty of its neighbors — unspoiled forests, mammoth mountains, shimmering lakes, and scenic coastline — and is imbued with some 300 years of Yankee heritage, New Hampshire could easily lay claim to being the state most representative of New England.

WHITE MOUNTAIN WILDERNESS

Nature prevails in its northern reaches, where people are scarce and wildlife is not only plentiful but relatively undisturbed. Bears, moose, and bobcats roam the dense woods, while minks, beavers, and otters frolic in streams and ponds. In White Mountain National Forest, myriad trails wind through more than 1,000 square miles of woodland. Stands of pines, spruces, maples, and birches skirt breathtaking gorges and dramatic cliffs. One such craggy outcrop, at Franconia Notch, forms the famed profile of the Old Man of the Mountains. Nearby, the highest peaks in New England bear the names of American statesmen and presidents: Adams, Eisenhower, Franklin, Jackson, Jefferson, Madison, Monroe, Webster — and, most majestic of all, 6,288-foot Mount Washington.

South of White Mountain National Forest, in the state's midsection, lie many of New Hampshire's more than 1,000 crystal-clear lakes. Their names — Kanasatka, Winona,

Looming over snow-covered buildings in Franconia are the massive slopes of the White Mountains, which extend from west-central New Hampshire into western Maine.

Spotlighted by sunbeams, winter hikers make their way along the Signal Ridge Trail on Mount Carrigain, located almost exactly in the center of gigantic White Mountain National Forest. A soupy mist envelops the mountainside to the rear of the hikers.

Winnisquam, Ossipee — conjure up visions of the Indians who once plied their waters with birchbark canoes. Largest of the lakes is Winnipesaukee, whose name means "smile of the Great Spirit." Just northwest of Winnipesaukee lies elegant Squam Lake, where Henry Fonda fished from his speedboat and, with Katharine Hepburn, contemplated old age in the celebrated film *On Golden Pond.*

COVERED BRIDGES AND SALTY PIERS

The southwestern corner of New Hampshire is a serene and scenic land that time forgot, where classic New England villages, with

general stores and white-steepled churches, are separated by miles of rolling countryside punctuated by red barns and covered bridges. Of all the covered bridges in New England, New Hampshire has more than half. It also has the longest — the 460-foot structure that spans the Connecticut River at Cornish.

Peterborough, not far from the Massachusetts border, could be called a typical, well-preserved New England town. In a sense it also represents the world at large, since it served as the model for Thornton Wilder's *Our Town,* the renowned play about life, death, and the human condition. Not far from Peter-

From late September to early October, maple trees break out in a conflagration of color.

borough, 3,165-foot Grand Monadnock rises from the plain. Because its resistant rock held fast when, eons ago, the surrounding rock was worn away, it now stands alone.

Southeastern New Hampshire — between the Merrimack Valley and the Atlantic Coast — is where most of the state's residents live and work. Some are descended from the original British settlers; others, from European or Canadian immigrants. Whatever their ancestry, however, they proudly uphold the Yankee traditions of thrift, conservatism, and especially independence — as evidenced by the state's motto: "Live Free or Die"!

This granite basin in Franconia Notch State Park was sculpted during the last ice age.

New Jersey

Hidden pleasures
off the beaten path

Some visitors, racing along the turnpike between Philadelphia and New York, might agree with Benjamin Franklin, who quipped that New Jersey was like "a barrel tapped at both ends" by these two major cities just across its borders. But, like Franklin, highway speedsters miss the hidden pleasures that are uniquely New Jersey's. The state is filled with secret splendors that are readily apparent to those who pause to explore and savor.

Perhaps New Jersey's best-kept secret is that it is a peninsula, bounded on the west by the Delaware River and on the east by the Hudson River and the Atlantic Ocean. Throughout its history, this position has made it the crossroads of the East Coast.

As early as colonial times New Jersey's rich farmlands — today among the most productive in the United States — attracted immigrants from Germany, Scandinavia, and the British Isles. The Philadelphia – New York corridor has always been the state's area of greatest growth. A canal and a railroad in the mid-1830's and the New Jersey Turnpike in 1952 provided ever more efficient transportation along this route. But the wonders of New Jersey lie off this heavily beaten path.

HILLS AND PINE BARRENS

Only 35 miles west of the turnpike is the 7,000-acre Great Swamp National Wildlife Refuge, where pink lady's slippers bloom along the boardwalks. Another 50 miles farther north the land opens up to farmland, and to forested hills. These are the Kittatinny Moun-

A tugboat moving past the towering cliffs of the Palisades proclaims that commerce is thriving along the lower Hudson River.

Completed in 1834, the 44-mile-long canal connecting the Delaware and Raritan rivers was built across New Jersey's narrow waist to speed shipments between Philadelphia and New York. Today sections of it are preserved as a state park enjoyed by canoeists and hikers.

tains, New Jersey's section of the Appalachian chain. In the south of the state lies an area unlike any other: the Pine Barrens. One million acres of pine and oak forests, white cedar swamps, cranberry bogs, sand roads, and 17 trillion gallons of some of the cleanest water on earth (in the Cohansey aquifer) have been preserved here under the Pinelands Protection Act. The most celebrated inhabitant is the Pine Barrens tree frog, a two-inch-long green amphibian with lavender stripes and a voice as loud as a duck's. In addition, more than 850 species of plants have been found here.

COASTAL TREASURES

New Jersey's 127-mile shoreline on the Atlantic Ocean is best known for the boardwalks of Asbury Park and Wildwood and the casinos of Atlantic City, but here too are hidden places where quiet still rules. Much of the shore is a ribbon of barrier beaches, whose sheltered waters attract a magnificent array of wildlife. Snowy owls occasionally spend the winter at Island Beach State Park, and diamondback terrapins come ashore each summer to lay their eggs in the sand above the water line. Each spring and fall hundreds of thousands of waterfowl pause on the New Jersey shore during their migration along the Atlantic flyway.

Cape May, New Jersey's southernmost point, extends into the Atlantic Ocean like a welcoming hand, beckoning migrating birds northward at winter's retreat and also providing a jumping-off point for their autumn migration south. As early as the 1760's the cape also welcomed vacationers. More than 600 preserved Victorian buildings now recall the resort's golden age in the late 1800's.

The Red Mill at Clinton Historical Museum Village ground both grain and graphite before it was closed in 1920.

White-tailed deer, like other New Jersey residents, enjoy the woodlands.

A spelunker gazes into a pool at Lechuguilla Cave, the most recently discovered portion of the immense Carlsbad Caverns system.

THE BEAUTY AND SPLENDOR OF NORTH AMERICA

Jemez Canyon, blessed with hot springs, has been inhabited since the 14th century. Coronado counted seven thriving pueblos there in 1540.

now protected as a national park: Carlsbad Caverns. When the labyrinthine caverns were first discovered, they were considered little more than a source of the fertilizer called guano — nutrient-rich droppings from the millions of bats that occupied the upper cave (as many as 500,000 bats still live there today). It was not until the early 1900's that a few brave souls ventured into the more remote caverns and discovered some of the most astonishing limestone formations ever seen. Today visitors are led through the ancient chambers to view such wonders as the giant stone columns of the Big Room, a 14-acre cavern with a ceiling so high that a 40-story building would fit inside.

INDIAN COUNTRY

Southwest of the eastern plains lies a vast, arid region of stark, sun-blasted mountains and sprawling desert, split down the center by the Rio Grande. The Continental Divide runs through this part of the state, cresting the dry slopes of the Animas Mountains, the Rocky Mountains' last gasp before they melt into Mexico's Sierra Madre.

In a clear turquoise sky, turkey vultures circle high over the harsh landscape. But the muddy waters of the Rio Grande, dammed at Elephant Butte in 1916, now bring life and industry to some isolated pockets of this desert. Huge, irrigated fields of chili peppers are grown around the tiny town of Hatch,

An adobe oven, or horno, occupies a corner at Taos Pueblo. To the left is a stairway, clearly for use only by the surefooted.

ART OF THE PUEBLOS

For centuries, the Pueblo Indian tribes of New Mexico — among them the Santa Clara, Acoma, and San Ildefonso — have used the warm-hued clay of the Southwest to fashion pottery that ranks among the most artistic on earth. Many potters create vessels the traditional way — not with a potter's wheel but by hand, then painting them with a brush made from a short piece of yucca stem. Pigments for paints come from the soil or from plants. Black is obtained by boiling tansy mustard or mesquite bark; red and yellows by powdering ocher dug from the earth.

Much of the distinctive decoration on Pueblo pottery relates directly to the topography and weather of the Southwest. The finely painted lines that form steps symbolize the mountains that rise from the desert. Mesas and canyons are represented with a crenellated pattern, while inverted pyramids stand for the dust devils, or whirlwinds, that blow across the canyon floors. Whirlwinds that move across the plains are sometimes shown as spirals or circles.

Water and cloud symbols are used as a friendly incantation to the deities. A double staircase pattern represents clouds; forked or zigzag lines show lightning; and a straight line placed over shorter, slanted lines symbolizes the rainfall so welcome in this arid land.

A Spanish ruin stands at Pecos National Monument, its adobe bricks slowly melting away.

groves of pecan trees shade the desert near Las Cruces, and vegetables are harvested for market in the little truck gardens that spread north from El Paso, Texas, into New Mexico.

Gradually, the desert rises northward to the foothills of the Black Range and the Mogollon Mountains, where great forests of ponderosa pines, Douglas firs, junipers, and blue spruces shelter the large elk, mule deer and bighorn sheep herds of the Gila Wilderness high country. Atop a lofty mesa stands the ancient pueblo of Acoma, continuously inhabited for perhaps 13 centuries. The pueblo, also known as Sky City, was so difficult to reach before a road was built, and the ascent so steep, that Coronado reported in 1540 that he and his men "repented as we climbed to the top." Nearby, a number of other pueblos are preserved at Gila Cliff Dwellings National Monument.

More Indian land spreads northward from Gallup, the town that, with the exception of reservations, is home to the country's largest population of American Indians. This arid region, the Four Corners, where the borders of New Mexico, Arizona, Utah, and Colorado converge, is a place of wind-twisted buttes, sand-carved mesas, and sage-blanketed deserts. It is also the site of an isolated, 1,500-foot-high volcanic neck with sheer vertical walls. Pioneers named the massive formation Shiprock because its two jagged spires resemble sails; the Navajos called it "the rock with wings" and considered it sacred.

THE BEAUTY AND SPLENDOR OF NORTH AMERICA

Sandwiched between the eastern plains and western deserts is the place where New Mexico's essential character resides — the mysteriously lovely Sangre de Cristo Mountains, jutting down from Colorado and named by the Spaniards after the blood-red color of the peaks at sunset. Two famous towns in the shadow of the mountains, Santa Fe and Taos, attract ever-growing numbers of visitors from around the world to sample the region's intriguing blend of Indian, Hispanic, and Anglo-American cultures and a landscape as starkly beautiful as any in the Southwest.

The historic districts of Santa Fe and Taos are also repositories for one of the most unusual architectural styles on the North American continent: free-form adobe houses, built with the local soil and aglow with soft earth colors. For centuries, Indians mixed sandy clay with stones to make the cementlike adobe material, which they formed into walls, a handful of adobe at a time. The Spaniards strengthened the adobe with straw and molded it into the bricks with which they built their houses, missions, and churches.

Some centuries-old adobe buildings in Santa Fe and Taos seem to be sculpted from the earth on which they stand. In the late 20th century, their timeless design has enjoyed new appreciation, with modern public buildings and private houses in the fashionable Santa Fe style cropping up in other parts of the Southwest and elsewhere.

Taos, a few miles from the Taos pueblo that was built by Indians around 1190, sits on a broad plateau at the foot of Mount Wheeler, the highest peak in New Mexico. Modern Taos traces its reputation as an artist's colony back to a group of New York painters and illustrators who began to move there just before the turn of the century. Since then, painters, sculptors, and writers have made the town their home. No doubt they are attracted by the special quality of the light, the isolation, the mix of cultures, and a terrain so dramatic that at times it seems almost unreal. They would be hard pressed to find a more inspiring setting, even in the magical land that is New Mexico.

Erosion has created a startling landscape at the Bisti Badlands Wilderness Area in northwestern New Mexico. Geologists call these vertical formations toadstool rocks, hoodoos, or earth pillars.

Most cactus flowers fold their petals in darkness, but the brilliant blooms of the claret cup hedgehog will stay open through the night.

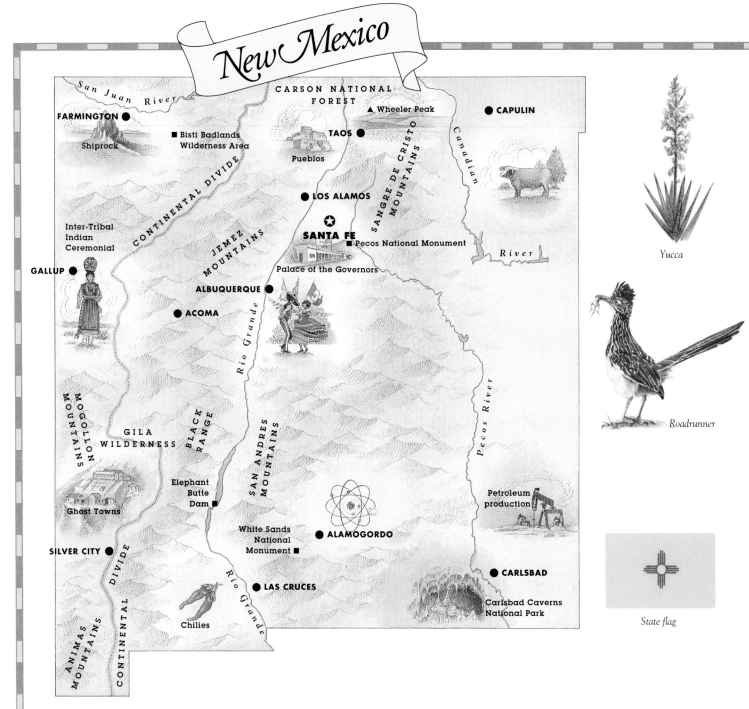

New Mexico

San Juan River

FARMINGTON ●

Shiprock

■ Bisti Badlands
Wilderness Area

CARSON NATIONAL
FOREST

▲ Wheeler Peak

CAPULIN ●

TAOS ●

Pueblos

Inter-Tribal
Indian
Ceremonial

CONTINENTAL DIVIDE

JEMEZ MOUNTAINS

LOS ALAMOS ●

✪ **SANTA FE**

■ Pecos National Monument

SANGRE DE CRISTO MOUNTAINS

Canadian

River

GALLUP ●

Palace of the Governors

ALBUQUERQUE ●

ACOMA ●

Rio Grande

MOGOLLON MOUNTAINS

GILA
WILDERNESS

BLACK RANGE

SAN ANDRES MOUNTAINS

Ghost Towns

Elephant
Butte
Dam ■

Pecos River

Petroleum
production

SILVER CITY ●

CONTINENTAL DIVIDE

White Sands
National
Monument ■

ALAMOGORDO ●

CARLSBAD ●

Rio Grande

LAS CRUCES ●

Chilies

ANIMAS MOUNTAINS

CONTINENTAL DIVIDE

Carlsbad Caverns
National Park

Yucca

Roadrunner

State flag

THE PEOPLE AND THE LAND

Population: 1,490,400

Area: 121,593 sq. mi.

Population per sq. mi.: 12

Capital: Santa Fe (pop. 112,000)

Largest city: Albuquerque (pop. 493,100)

Major rivers: Canadian, Pecos, Rio Grande, San Juan

Elevation: 2,817 ft. (Red Bluff Reservoir) to 13,161 ft. (Wheeler Peak)

Leading industries: Mining (petroleum, potash, copper, coal), natural gas production, tourism, agriculture (cattle, dairy products, hay)

Bird: Roadrunner

Flower: Yucca

Tree: Piñon

Motto: *Crescit Eundo* (It Grows as It Goes)

Song: "O Fair New Mexico"

Origin of name: Named by the first Spanish settlers in honor of Mexico, the country from which they came

Nicknames: Cactus State, Land of Enchantment, Spanish State

INFORMATION

New Mexico Department of Travel and Tourism
Joseph M. Montoya State Building
1100 St. Francis Drive
Santa Fe, NM 87503
Telephone: 800-545-2040

HISTORICAL HIGHLIGHTS

1540 Francisco Vásquez de Coronado begins his exploration of New Mexico.

1598 Juan de Oñate establishes first Spanish settlement near present-day Española.

1610 Second Spanish governor, Pedro de Peralta, founds Santa Fe.

1680 Pueblo Indian tribes rebel against Spanish settlers, who flee to Mexico.

1692 Diego de Vargas reconquers province for Spain.

1706 Albuquerque is founded.

1821 With Mexico's independence from Spain, New Mexico comes under Mexican rule. William Becknell blazes Santa Fe Trail from Missouri.

1846 In the Mexican War, U.S. government gains control of New Mexico.

1848 Defeated in Mexican War, Mexico cedes New Mexico and other parts of the West to U.S.

1850 Congress establishes New Mexico as a territory.

1862 In the Civil War, Union soldiers win Battle of Glorieta Pass and force Confederate troops from New Mexico.

1879 Atchison, Topeka, & Santa Fe Railroad links New Mexico with the eastern U.S.

1912 New Mexico enters Union as 47th state.

1916 Mexican renegade Pancho Villa raids town of Columbus.

1945 First atomic bomb is tested in the desert at Trinity Site near Alamogordo.

1970 Congress gives Taos Pueblo Indians title to 48,000 acres in Carson National Forest, including the Blue Lake the Pueblos consider sacred.

1986 Governor proclaims New Mexico a sanctuary for Central American refugees.

FAMOUS SONS AND DAUGHTERS

Billy the Kid (1859 – 81). This notorious outlaw, whose real name was William H. Bonney, grew up in Silver City. Said to wear an eternal smile, the Kid nevertheless committed five known murders.

Kit Carson (1809 – 68). As a teenager, Carson ran away from Kentucky and joined an expedition going to Santa Fe. He gained fame as a trapper, guide, Indian agent, and Union general.

Conrad Hilton (1887 – 1979). Hilton's career started in his family's inn in San Antonio, N.M. He eventually became "king of the innkeepers" with his international hotel chain.

Jean Baptiste Lamy (1814 – 88). The life of this hardworking French-born priest, archbishop of Santa Fe, was the inspiration for Willa Cather's novel *Death Comes for the Archbishop.*

Bill Mauldin (1921 –). Mauldin's award-winning cartoons, focusing on the day-to-day lives of American soldiers in World War II, were internationally acclaimed.

Georgia O'Keeffe (1887 – 1986).

This painter, who lived much of her life on a ranch in Abiquiu and came to be identified with the Southwest, derived inspiration from New Mexico's landscape.

Pope (? – 1688). The leader of the Pueblo Indians masterminded the successful revolt against the Spanish in 1680.

ODDITIES AND SPECIALTIES

One of New Mexico's culinary specialties is the red chili pepper. After the fall harvest, peppers are hung outside houses in decorative strings, called *ristras*, to dry.

New Mexico produces nearly half of the nation's uranium.

Santa Fe is not only the oldest capital city in the U.S.— founded in 1610 — but the highest, at almost 7,000 feet.

The state's many ghost towns attest to the boom-and-bust quality of mining in frontier times. Some of the "ghosts" in these places are legendary — Judge Roy Bean, Butch Cassidy, Lillian Russell.

Los Alamos National Laboratory developed the first atomic and hydrogen bombs. Today the laboratory focuses on nuclear research and development.

PLACES TO VISIT, THINGS TO DO

Bandelier National Monument (Los Alamos). Ancient Indians carved rooms out of canyon walls and built pueblo villages here. The ruins can be seen from a trail along the canyon floor.

Capulin Mountain National Monument (Capulin). Once an active volcano, Capulin is now clothed in dense forest. From its summit, visitors have a sweeping view of five states.

Carlsbad Caverns National Park (27 miles south of Carlsbad). Among the caverns that can be viewed by the public is the Doll's Theater, its ceiling massed with delicate stalactites. Another, the Hall of the Giants, has columns that rise 60 feet.

Chaco Culture National Historical Park (45 miles southeast of Farmington). These ruins, in 15-mile-long Chaco Canyon, include the huge Pueblo Bonita and 10 other major pueblos.

Inter-Tribal Indian Ceremonial (Gallup). This five-day marathon of arts-and-crafts displays, rodeos, and Indian ceremonial dances is held every August. Some 25 tribes from the U.S. take part.

Old Town (Albuquerque).

Albuquerque's original plaza, which dates from 1779, has a number of historic buildings. Among them is the "folk Gothic" Church of San Felipe de Neri.

Palace of the Governors (Santa Fe). The oldest government building in the U.S. was built in 1610. Now a museum, it includes re-creations of reception rooms and offices with period paintings, rugs, and pottery.

New York

A realm of solitude, far from Manhattan

Traveling through the Finger Lakes region of western New York in 1833, the English actress Fanny Kemble found it to be a realm of "beautiful solitudes" that were "blessedly apart from the evil turmoil of the world." Unwittingly, she had described the dual nature of the Empire State, which possesses one of the world's capitals of frenzy and haste, New York City, as well as rural solitudes in endless variety. New York State is very nearly the size of England. And upon it nature has mapped out her own brand of dukedoms and baronies — the Adirondack and Catskill mountains, the Finger Lakes, the valley of the Hudson River — each a world unto itself, with its own mood, myths, and varied charms.

FRONT DOOR TO AMERICA

With its glitter and wealth, its tense human dramas, and its relentless pace, New York City draws all eyes to itself and dismisses the territory north of the Bronx as "upstate," unreachable by subway. To the east, Long Island is the site of two of the city's five boroughs (Brooklyn and Queens), then stretches in 80 miles of fertile farmland and sandy beaches to the Hamptons, the onetime fishing villages that have become chic retreats for the rich.

New York City sees itself as a center, but it has always been a gateway too, the front door to America for immigrants and for commerce. The Hudson River, the western boundary of Manhattan, was and is the start of a corridor to the heartland of the continent. It was named for Henry Hudson, who explored it in

Forty miles north of New York City, the peaceful Hudson winds through the wooded Hudson highlands. To the right is Bear Mountain Bridge.

The phloxlike blooms of dame's rocket fill the woods with a heady fragrance on spring evenings. The plant, a Eurasian perennial, has become naturalized in the forests around the Finger Lakes.

1609. In 1825, when the 363-mile-long Erie Canal was opened, the Hudson was linked with the Great Lakes.

From its source in the Adirondacks to its mouth in New York Harbor, the Hudson flows for 315 miles. The broad expanse of river moving placidly through looming immensities of granite is one of the greatest of all American landscapes, a dramatic spectacle that inspired the Hudson River school of paint-

ers and scores of writers. The bright, hazy light of the river was captured in the canvases of artists Jaspar Cropsey and John Frederick Kensett in the style known as luminism. Washington Irving, author of "Rip Van Winkle" and "The Legend of Sleepy Hollow," wrote his short stories and books in a comfortable cottage by the river; and the painter Frederick E. Church built his home and studio on a hill overlooking it.

LIFE IN THE PARK

Amid the steel and glass towers of New York City there flourishes a surprising oasis of nature — Central Park. Ornate fountains, clipped lawns, and well-kept flower beds to the contrary, some parts of this 843-acre preserve look like untamed countryside or dense woodland, thick with oaks, maples, and black cherries and blooming with wild asters.

Several species of birds and animals occupy the park. Some — warblers, gray squirrels, woodchucks, and bats — have lived there since soon after the park took shape in the mid-19th century. Others, like the cottontail rabbits that hop across the meadows, have taken up residence more recently, establishing a foothold in the park after urban dwellers released them there. Raccoons, too, have been spotted by the lakes in the woods.

The wildlife that most visitors to the park encounter, however, is behind the gates of the Central Park Zoo, a beloved Manhattan institution in operation since 1864. Here polar bears swim behind huge glass walls, face to face with delighted children, before lumbering out of the pool to lounge in the sun. Squawking penguins play tag in the Edge of the Icepack section, while tamarin monkeys swing from vines in the Tropic Zone. In both the zoo and the open spaces of Central Park, wildlife has found a place in the heart of Manhattan.

Jewel of the Finger Lakes region is Watkins Glen, a two-mile gorge at the southern tip of Seneca Lake. A foot trail through the chasm takes visitors past 19 glistening waterfalls spilling into deep pools shaded by hemlock, yew, and mountain maple trees.

North Carolina

From highlands to Hatteras,
a green and unspoiled land

North Carolina claims the loftiest mountain east of the Mississippi (6,684-foot Mount Mitchell), the longest chain of barrier islands (the Outer Banks), the highest sand dune (140-foot Jockey's Ridge), and the greatest natural diversity in the East (in this one state are more kinds of trees than in all of Europe).

North Carolina is also a land of many firsts: the first three attempts to colonize America, the first birth of an English child on American soil, the first American gold rush, the country's first school of forestry, and the first successful airplane flight. And, in 1776, North Carolina was the first colony to instruct its delegates to the Continental Congress to vote for independence from Great Britain.

THE CRUEL AND BEAUTIFUL COAST

Unlike most coastal states, North Carolina was settled from its interior because its coastline offered no suitable ports. Its gleaming strands of barrier islands both tempted and thwarted 16th-century seamen as they tried to navigate the cruel shoals off Cape Hatteras (the "graveyard of the Atlantic") or to steer through tricky inlets into the quiet waters of Albemarle or Currituck sounds.

Two early attempts at colonization, in 1526 and 1585, failed utterly. A third attempt, in 1587, Raleigh's famous Lost Colony, ended in mystery when its 119 men, women, and children vanished without a trace except for one word — CROATOAN — carved on a tree. Although by 1710 settlers from the Virginia

The ancient Blue Ridge Mountains, where blossoming rhododendrons reach their peak in mid-June, roll into the distance like huge swells on an azure sea.

Fog blankets fields near Valle Crucis in the Blue Ridge Mountains. The lower slopes in this area, which have a more temperate climate than is found higher in the mountains, have been used for generations to raise cattle and tobacco.

colony had founded such tidewater towns as Bath, Beaufort, and Edenton, the Outer Banks remained sparsely populated until well into the 20th century.

Today these lovely islands are North Carolina's crown jewels. Hang gliders soar over the dunes not far from where the Wright brothers first proved man could fly. Surfers ride the waves near the treacherous shoals that sank so many ships (parts of their wrecked hulls are still visible in the sand). From Bodie Island in the north, through Pea Island National Wildlife Refuge, where thousands of shorebirds and waterfowl converge during migration, the wide protected beaches of Cape Hatteras National Seashore stretch some 70 miles to the picturesque village of Ocracoke. Nearby, the infamous pirate Blackbeard met his death at the hands of the British in 1718.

Inland, across brackish marshes and inlets teeming with fish, crabs, and snowy egrets, lies the tidewater land of swamps, lazy rivers, and Carolina bays. Here are found such botanical rarities as the insect-devouring Venus flytrap, native only to the Carolina lowlands. To the west of this wide coastal plain rises the Piedmont, a region of gentle slopes and low ridges that has become the most populous and progressive part of the state. Nevertheless, the industrial Piedmont manages to balance its bustling cities with pleasantly rural, rolling landscapes.

HIGH IN THE MISTY MOUNTAINS

West of the Piedmont are the beautiful North Carolina mountains — Blue Ridge, Great Smokies, Black, Unaka, Bald, and others — their craggy peaks vaulting to 6,000 feet. Lush forests and fields of wildflowers soften their slopes. Ascending from foothills to summit, one may pass through several different zones of climate and vegetation. Cove hardwood forests dominate the lower altitudes. The higher reaches are the domain of the red spruce and Fraser fir, evergreens similar to those found in the boreal forests of Canada. Here such "northern" birds as saw-whet owls, red crossbills, and black-capped chickadees make their home all year round.

The mountain country was settled after 1770 by farmers from Pennsylvania, Virginia, and Maryland who were looking for new land. Many were of Scotch-Irish descent, and decided to move deeper into the rugged terrain that reminded them of their ancestral home. Later the whole Asheville area became a summer retreat for wealthy Charleston and Savannah residents seeking to escape the torpid coastal climate, as well as for the Rockefellers, Fords, Roosevelts, and Vanderbilts. One magnificent monument to this opulent era is George Vanderbilt's colossal Biltmore House, a 250-room mansion set on some 8,000 acres of gardens, reflecting pools, and woodland.

Today North Carolina's mountains, traversed by the splendidly scenic Blue Ridge Parkway and including about half of Great Smoky Mountains National Park, are prime vacationland with luxurious resorts. Yet simple rustic cabins, mountain music, and traditional crafts such as dollmaking, rug weaving, and fiddlemaking are also found throughout the highlands, and the natural beauty of the land remains refreshingly unspoiled.

Spanish moss, draped over the boughs of trees in this coastal bottomland forest, is a familiar sight along the banks of the South River. In colonial times, flat-bottom boats plied the river, carrying goods across the southern coastal plain to Wilmington.

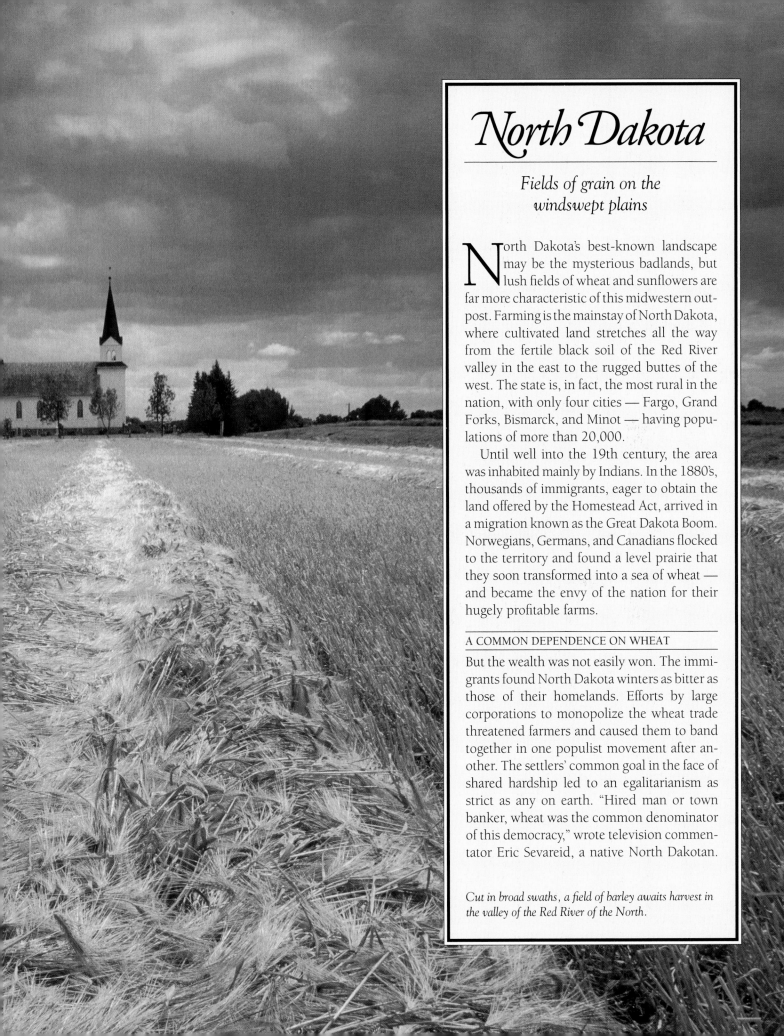

North Dakota

Fields of grain on the windswept plains

North Dakota's best-known landscape may be the mysterious badlands, but lush fields of wheat and sunflowers are far more characteristic of this midwestern outpost. Farming is the mainstay of North Dakota, where cultivated land stretches all the way from the fertile black soil of the Red River valley in the east to the rugged buttes of the west. The state is, in fact, the most rural in the nation, with only four cities — Fargo, Grand Forks, Bismarck, and Minot — having populations of more than 20,000.

Until well into the 19th century, the area was inhabited mainly by Indians. In the 1880's, thousands of immigrants, eager to obtain the land offered by the Homestead Act, arrived in a migration known as the Great Dakota Boom. Norwegians, Germans, and Canadians flocked to the territory and found a level prairie that they soon transformed into a sea of wheat — and became the envy of the nation for their hugely profitable farms.

A COMMON DEPENDENCE ON WHEAT

But the wealth was not easily won. The immigrants found North Dakota winters as bitter as those of their homelands. Efforts by large corporations to monopolize the wheat trade threatened farmers and caused them to band together in one populist movement after another. The settlers' common goal in the face of shared hardship led to an egalitarianism as strict as any on earth. "Hired man or town banker, wheat was the common denominator of this democracy," wrote television commentator Eric Sevareid, a native North Dakotan.

Cut in broad swaths, a field of barley awaits harvest in the valley of the Red River of the North.

The Little Missouri River meanders through Wind Canyon in the South Unit of Theodore Roosevelt National Park, established in 1978.

358

"Perhaps it was our common dependence upon wheat that made all men essentially equal."

The settlers brought all three of North Dakota's distinct geographic regions into cultivation. The valley of the Red River of the North (so called to distinguish it from the Red River in the south-central United States), a 40-mile-wide strip along the Minnesota border, is blanketed with fields of sugar beets, potatoes, beans, and more sunflowers than even Kansas grows. To the west, the Drift Prairie, named for the deposits of fertile drift — clay, sand, and other earth materials — left behind by glaciers, is now a prime producer of wheat, barley, and oats.

Dotting the gentle hills of the prairie are innumerable small bodies of water called potholes, where flocks of migrating waterfowl nest. Bird watchers gather at Audubon, Long Lake, and other wildlife refuges to observe piping plovers and sharp-tailed grouse. Nature lovers make their way to the prairie's northern edge to fish and hike in the forested Turtle Mountains (average height only 700 feet).

Wheat is also grown in the western portion of the state that lies within the Missouri Plateau. Mineral discoveries here have helped diversify the economy, with lignite mined near Beulah and oil pumped around Williston.

The Missouri Plateau boasts the state's most dramatic scenery: the badlands. Three separate sections of this extraordinary terrain are now a national park named for Theodore Roosevelt, who became enamored of the loneliness and vastness of the landscape when he first saw it as a young man.

The park is a fantastic world of canyons, buttes, and spires that the Little Missouri River, rain, and wind have carved out of the plain. Flowing mud, baked into a bricklike mass by the heat of smoldering lignite — a woody-textured coal that is often ignited by lightning — make some of the hillsides look like the work of an abstract sculptor. Wildflowers cling to slopes scored deeply by erosion. It is a rugged and mysterious place that, unlike the rest of North Dakota, has been changed not by the hand of man but only by the elements.

A red sandstone bluff in western North Dakota overlooks the grassy plains that spread from the banks of the Missouri River. Wild prairie roses bloom in the foreground.

North Dakota

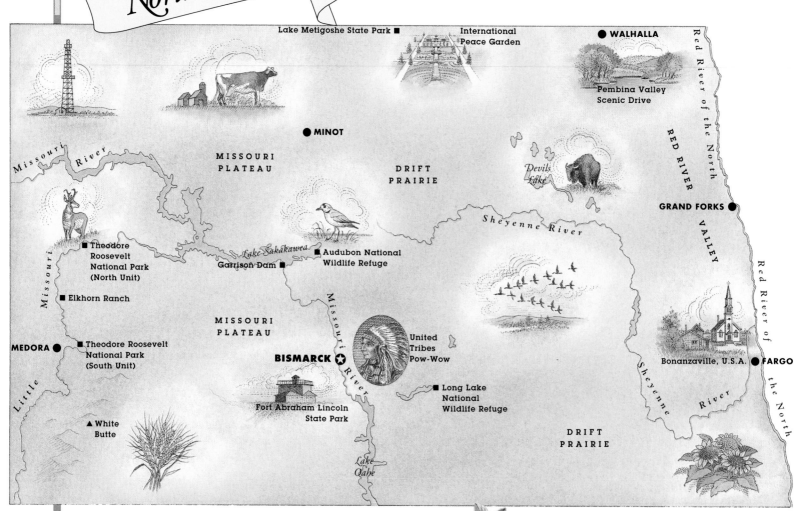

Lake Metigoshe State Park ■

International Peace Garden

● WALHALLA

Pembina Valley Scenic Drive

Red River of the North

RED RIVER

● MINOT

MISSOURI PLATEAU

DRIFT PRAIRIE

Devils Lake

RED RIVER VALLEY

GRAND FORKS ●

Missouri River

Lake Sakakawea

Audubon National Wildlife Refuge

Garrison Dam ■

Sheyenne River

Red River of the North

Theodore Roosevelt National Park (North Unit) ■

■ Elkhorn Ranch

MISSOURI PLATEAU

Missouri River

MEDORA ●

■ Theodore Roosevelt National Park (South Unit)

BISMARCK ☆

United Tribes Pow-Wow

Bonanzaville, U.S.A. ● FARGO

Sheyenne River

Little

Fort Abraham Lincoln State Park

■ Long Lake National Wildlife Refuge

DRIFT PRAIRIE

▲ White Butte

Lake Oahe

Western meadowlark

Wild prairie rose

State flag

THE PEOPLE AND THE LAND

Population: 634,200

Area: 70,702 sq. mi.

Population per sq. mi.: 9

Capital: Bismarck (pop. 85,800)

Largest city: Fargo (pop. 148,400)

Major rivers: Missouri, Red River of the North, Sheyenne

Elevation: 750 ft. (Red River of the North) to 3,506 ft. (White Butte)

Leading industries: Agriculture (wheat, beef cattle, barley, sunflower seeds), mining (oil, lignite), manufacturing (processed foods, farm machinery)

Bird: Western meadowlark

Flower: Wild prairie rose

Tree: American elm

Motto: Liberty and Union, Now and Forever, One and Inseparable

Song: "North Dakota Hymn"

Origin of name: From the Sioux word meaning friend or ally

Nicknames: Flickertail State, Land of the Dakotas, Peace Garden State, Sioux State

INFORMATION

North Dakota Tourism Promotion
604 East Boulevard
Bismarck, ND 58505
Telephone: 701-224-2525

HISTORICAL HIGHLIGHTS

1682 Robert Cavelier, sieur de La Salle, claims region for France.

1738 Pierre La Vérendrye explores area that will become the central part of North Dakota.

1797 Trading post for furs is established at Pembina.

1803 With Louisiana Purchase, U.S. acquires southwestern North Dakota.

1804 Lewis and Clark build Fort Mandan on the Missouri River and spend the winter.

1812 Scottish and Irish colonists establish a settlement at Pembina.

1818 Through an agreement with Britain, U.S. gains remainder of North Dakota.

1861 Congress establishes Dakota Territory.

1863 Land becomes available under the Homestead Act.

1871 Northern Pacific Railroad reaches Fargo.

1883 Bismarck becomes capital of the territory.
University of North Dakota opens at Grand Forks.

1889 North Dakota joins Union as 39th state.

1915 Farmers create Nonpartisan League to fight for state control over wheat trade monopolies.

1929 Seven-year drought begins, bringing dust storms and hardship to farmers.

1947 Theodore Roosevelt National Park is authorized.

1951 Oil is discovered near town of Tioga.

1956 Garrison Dam, on the Missouri River, begins to produce electric power.

1968 Garrison Diversion Project, to increase state's water supply, is begun.

1988 Drought kills much of North Dakota's wheat crop.

FAMOUS SONS AND DAUGHTERS

Louis L'Amour (1908 – 88). One of the best-selling authors of all time, the prolific L'Amour wrote 86 western novels. Many were made into movies.

William Langer (1886 – 1959). As governor and U.S. senator, Langer endeared himself to his constituents — and made a number of political enemies in Washington — with his tactics to help farmers.

Peggy Lee (1920 –). After touring with Benny Goodman's band, Lee recorded a series of hit songs. Though known primarily for her distinctive singing style, she is also a songwriter and an actress.

Eric Sevareid (1912 –). Sevareid, who rose to fame as a news commentator, became interested in journalism while still a child in Velva. Newspaper reporting led to his long career in radio and television.

Vilhjalmur Stefansson

(1879 –1962). Born in Canada and raised in North Dakota, Stefansson was a dedicated explorer who spent more than five years mapping the Arctic. He later wrote a number of books about his experiences.

Lawrence Welk (1903 – 92). Welk transformed the accordion music played in North Dakota's German communities into the "champagne music" of his dance bands. His television show ran for more than 15 years.

ODDITIES AND SPECIALTIES

President Benjamin Harrison signed the papers admitting North and South Dakota to the Union at the same time, covering the names so that no one would know which was admitted first.

To call North Dakota's weather extreme is to understate the case. During one year, 1936, the temperature ranged all the way from −60° F to 121° F.

Flickertails are ground squirrels that thrive in central North Dakota — hence its nickname, the Flickertail State.

Theodore Roosevelt lived on his North Dakota ranch, Elkhorn, from age 26 to 28. The ranch is now part of the national park that bears his name.

In the early 19th century, Lewis and Clark took note of the abundance of waterfowl in North Dakota. Modern observers still do: more of these birds nest in this state than in any other.

PLACES TO VISIT, THINGS TO DO

Bonanzaville, U.S.A. (West Fargo). Named for North Dakota's profitable 19th-century "bonanza" farms, this period village includes a town hall, a rural church, and a sod house.

Fort Abraham Lincoln State Park (near Mandan). Beauty and history are the dual attractions at this park, which contains a fort and Indian village.

International Peace Garden

(Dunseith). Dedicated in 1932 and situated on the U.S.-Canadian border, this colorful, 2,339-acre garden commemorates the pledge of lasting peace between the two countries.

Lake Metigoshe State Park (near Bottineau). This wooded recreation area lies along the shores of a beautiful lake in the Turtle Mountains.

Pembina Valley Scenic Drive (Walhalla). State Highway 32 offers one of the loveliest forest drives in the state, following the Pembina River through a 30-mile chasm.

Theodore Roosevelt National Park (headquarters at Medora). North Dakota's only national park, set in the harshly beautiful badlands, pays tribute to the 26th president's conservation efforts. Colorfully striped buttes and gorges are home to buffaloes, pronghorns, and prairie dogs.

United Tribes Pow-Wow (Bismarck). Every September, thousands of people come to watch this singing and dancing competition among Sioux, Chippewa, and other Indian tribes. Indian food and crafts are featured.

Ohio

A cherished land between a great lake and a long, winding river

Before 1800, Ohio was a rugged frontier, the gateway to the Northwest Territory and the scene of ferocious battles between white men and Indians. Over the years it evolved into a land of farms, where life centered on the Bible and the plow. Later, smokestacks became as familiar as silos with the growth of sprawling cities such as Cleveland, Columbus, Toledo, and Cincinnati.

Today the character of Ohio is perhaps best reflected in the state's "40 towns" — small cities with populations of 10,000 to 25,000, usually including a Main Street, a brick courthouse, and a town square with a band shell for summer concerts. White Victorian houses, their wide wooden porches furnished with gliders and wicker chairs, line tree-shaded streets named Elm or Maple. This familiar and cherished part of America is often called, affectionately, the Heartland.

ERIE'S SHORES TO AMISH COUNTRY

Bustling cities and tranquil towns predominate across the Ohio landscape, but the state has a generous share of natural wealth — secluded forests, deep caverns, extensive marshlands, and glistening lakes. Most notable of the lakes is Erie, whose shores, stretching from Toledo in the west to Conneaut in the east, form most of Ohio's northern border. Between Toledo, the third-largest port city on the Great Lakes, and Sandusky Bay some 30 miles to the east, the lake's vast marshy shoreline serves as a temporary home for Canada geese, great blue herons, and le-

At Warner's Hollow in northeastern Ohio, gentle Phelps Creek flows through a mile-long gorge, its base carpeted with the lush growth of midsummer.

Some 87,000 farms are found all across Ohio. This one, located south of Cleveland, is run by an Amish family. Since their religion forbids the use of modern machinery, the Amish till their fields as their ancestors did — with horse-drawn plows.

gions of other migrating birds. At the end of the long, fingerlike peninsula above Sandusky Bay is Marblehead, where magnified candlelight once beamed from Ohio's oldest lighthouse.

Farther east the shoreline is dominated by greater Cleveland. Moses Cleaveland was a Connecticut Yankee who in 1796 led a band of surveyors to Ohio's Western Reserve — a tract of land "reserved" by King Charles II for settlers from Connecticut. Here they cleared the land and laid out a town much like the ones they left behind in New England.

Ohio's rich farmland drew a group of people for whom farming was not just a livelihood but a way of life. The Amish — Swiss and German followers of the religious leader Jacob Amman, who faced persecution in their homelands — took up residence in Wayne, Holmes, and other counties south of Cleveland. There they have preserved the ways of their ancestors to the present day. Dressed in

old-fashioned clothes, the Amish travel by horse and buggy, hitching their reins to parking meters in the towns where they shop. Their country stores stock nonelectrical tools and appliances (such as gas-run refrigerators) for their own use, while visitors come to buy the exceptional Amish cheeses, honeys, and handmade quilts. Such products are never in short supply, for some 60,000 Amish live in Ohio — more than in any other state.

Another devout group to settle near Cleveland was the United Society of Believers in Christ's Second Appearing. Sometimes called Believers, they were commonly known as Shakers because of the bodily quivering and shuddering that took place during their moments of religious fervor. Though the Shakers' adherence to celibacy led to their demise in Ohio by the early 1900's, their community is memorialized at its original site by the elegantly planned town of Shaker Heights.

A SERPENT FROM THE DISTANT PAST

In a remote part of southern Ohio near Locust Grove stands an ancient and mysterious earthen monument known as the Great Serpent Mound. About 5 feet high, 20 feet wide, and a quarter mile long, the sinuous mound was named for its snakelike appearance. The tail coils into a spiral and the head has wide open jaws that grasp a giant oval egg.

Exactly when the Great Serpent Mound was built is not known, but archeologists believe it was the work of the Adena people, prehistoric Indians who lived in southern Ohio between 800 B.C. and A.D. 400. Many of the mounds found in Ohio — some towering as high as 60 feet — were used for burial or fortification, but the Great Serpent Mound, it is supposed, played some significant role in Adena religious ceremonies.

In 1887 this remarkable site was almost destroyed, but Frederic Ward Putnam, the Harvard professor who first excavated the mound, raised enough money to save it. In the following year Ohio passed the first law in the country to preserve such archeological wonders for posterity.

BY THE BEAUTIFUL OHIO

Far below Cleveland, in the southeastern part of the state, lie the Appalachian foothills, which contrast dramatically with the rest of Ohio's flat to rolling landscape. This area embraces some of Ohio's most beautiful countryside, and includes gigantic Wayne National Forest, consisting of about 176,000 acres of dense woodland, rocky outcrops, white-water streams, and plunging waterfalls. Much of the wilderness here looks the same today as it did when the first settlers arrived two centuries ago.

The Ohio River, which serves as the state's southeastern border near Marietta, forms the southern border once it swings westward. The "Beautiful Ohio" celebrated in song passes the little river towns of Pomeroy, Gallipolis, Portsmouth, Ripley, and eventually, in Ohio's southwestern corner, the genteel city of Cincinnati. Here barge traffic has long since replaced the stern-wheelers that once chugged up the Mississippi River from New Orleans, but a few of the old-time steamboats still ply the waters along Cincinnati's shores, often within earshot of the roaring crowds assembled at Riverfront Stadium.

Between the Ohio River and Columbus — the state capital, positioned like a bull's-eye in the center of the state — thousands of square miles of rich farmland are interspersed with reminders of Ohio's Indian past. History comes alive in the labyrinthine passages of the Olentangy Indian Caverns, where the Wyandot Indians used to hide from enemy tribes.

In central and southwestern Ohio, the ancient Adena and Hopewell Indians built earthen mounds at hundreds of sites, which they used for fortification, burial, or ceremonial purposes. A number of the monuments have survived to this day. Though very little is known about these people of antiquity, they probably spent their lives fishing, hunting, and gathering wild plants, and no doubt felt a tranquil kinship with the land. For their successors, on farms and in small towns all across Ohio, the tranquillity endures.

In Crane Creek State Park on Lake Erie are two plants named for their wet habitat: swamp rose mallow, with large pink blossoms, and swamp milkweed, with clusters of small, star-shaped blossoms.

Oklahoma

Where the face of America changes

Oklahoma stands where North America changes from shady woodlands to stark desert buttes. In the eastern part of the state, lush, green, wooded hills and valleys, spilling over from Missouri and Arkansas, are so reminiscent of the South that Oklahomans call this area Little Dixie. At the state's center, vast grasslands stretch southward from the great American prairie. Farther west, in the panhandle, stark silhouettes of lonely buttes dominate the flat, dry High Plains terrain.

The weather also can change dramatically here. Cool, dry air from the north colliding with southern breezes gives the state nearly constant winds and violent storms. Within days, streams change from ribbons of sand to gushing torrents. High winds flatten fences and whip up tornadoes. When a stranger asks, "Does the wind blow this way all the time?" a native Oklahoman is likely to reply, "No. Half the time it blows the other way."

A VOLATILE PAST

As if taking a cue from the weather, the state itself has had a volatile past. Oklahoma was home to the Plains Indians when, in 1825, the U.S. government declared the region Indian Territory. During the next half century more than 60 tribes from the East and the northern Plains were forcibly moved to reservations there. Then, under pressure from homesteaders, the government took back reservation lands. At noon on April 22, 1889, the territory was instantly transformed as white settlers raced to claim homesteads in the first of Okla-

In the northwest corner of the panhandle, dark clouds over Black Mesa, Oklahoma's highest point, portend the momentary violence of a gathering storm.

In the Chickasaw National Recreation Area, Rock Creek wends through an ecological transition zone where woodlands meet grasslands. Cardinals of the eastern woods and roadrunners of the arid Southwest are among the birds that can be seen here.

homa's land rushes. By evening whole cities of tents had sprung up on the grassy plains.

When these homesteaders arrived, the Oklahoma tallgrass prairie was a waving sea of green that sometimes towered over their covered wagons. But within 40 years the soil was so overtilled that it was waiting for disaster, and in the 1930's tragedy struck in the form of drought. As vegetation died, the dry soil was blown away by the winds. Oklahoma and much of the southern Great Plains turned into America's Dust Bowl.

After World War II, however, Oklahomans harnessed their abundant system of rivers to

build mammoth water-management projects aimed at preventing disaster in future droughts. Today, with some 1,800 reservoirs and nearly 200,000 farm ponds, the state has a greater ratio of water to land than Minnesota, the Land of Ten Thousand Lakes.

UNEXPECTED LANDSCAPES

To outsiders who think of Oklahoma as flat prairie, its mountains come as a surprise. In the east the Ouachitas and the Ozarks boast idyllic valleys with crystalline streams. To the southwest, part of the Wichita Mountains are included in a large national wildlife refuge.

In the far west, in the panhandle, the landscape is stark and arid. With rainfall less than 16 inches a year, trees are so scarce that early settlers burned buffalo chips for fuel, calling them prairie coal.

Since the 1880's, the oil boom has sped Oklahoma's development, so that today the rocking arms of oil well pumps are familiar sights in fields, on farms, and even on city streets. Amid the incongruities of this rapidly changing landscape, however, the character of Oklahoma somehow remains constant in its rocky eastern hills, waving fields, and the limitless horizons of its western plains.

The granite hills of southwestern Oklahoma in and around Quartz Mountain State Park were once sacred ground for the Kiowa and Comanche Indians. Today sweeping fields of grain are nestled among their craggy outcroppings. Bald eagles frequent the area in winter.

Pennsylvania

Gentle vistas in the cradle of independence

Pennsylvania is rock-ribbed. The steely mountain ranges of the Appalachian chain lock the state's midsection in a series of ridges and valleys not unlike a rib cage. But plant life and the hand of man have gradually softened the rough terrain. Few vistas in the eastern United States are more bucolic than the cultivated fields of Pennsylvania Dutch country, and few forests offer a more verdant display than those of the Allegheny Plateau.

THE PEACEFUL EAST

Farmers have tilled the fertile soils of southeast Pennsylvania since the 1600's. As soon as William Penn proclaimed "the foundation of a free colony for all mankind," his Quaker brethren arrived from England and Wales to clear the land for crops. An official policy of religious tolerance then drew Germans, including Amish, Mennonites, and Dunkers. So industrious were these "Pennsylvania Deutsch" that southeastern Pennsylvania became one of colonial America's most important breadbaskets. Today the patchwork of fields in Lancaster County is among the most pleasing sights in the state, with quaint barns and silos — often decorated with hex signs — sitting against a backdrop of wooded hills.

Philadelphia was and is the metropolis of eastern Pennsylvania. Overlooked today by a statue of William Penn high atop City Hall, the city was laid out in 1682 in a grid — a new idea at the time that was later copied in many of the cities built across the West. The orderly "greene Countrie Towne" that Penn

Classic pastoral landscapes can be seen from one end of Pennsylvania to the other. This farm is near the town of Export, just east of Pittsburgh.

A profusion of ironweed and goldenrod blooms in a clearing at Erie National Wildlife Refuge in northwestern Pennsylvania.

THE BEAUTY AND SPLENDOR OF NORTH AMERICA

founded became America's preeminent city of the 18th century and the birthplace of its independence.

THE HARD WAY WEST

Pennsylvania's Appalachians are not as lofty as most stretches of the range. Still, for centuries they proved to be a formidable barrier. Settlers who crossed the seemingly infinite expanse of crests and troughs named the range the Endless Mountains — a name that still sticks in the northeastern part of the state. Traveling in central Pennsylvania remained difficult well into the 20th century, with roads so steep and winding that trucks usually detoured to longer but safer routes farther north.

If crossing Pennsylvania by land was difficult, it was impossible by water: no east-west river system crosses the state. Nature's oversight was remedied in the 1840's, with the completion of a system of canals and railroads linking Philadelphia and Pittsburgh.

Nonetheless, rivers have been of critical importance to Pennsylvania. The Delaware gave Philadelphia access to the sea; the Lehigh carried coal and iron ore from the Appalachians to the foundries of Bethlehem; the Susquehanna linked Pennsylvania farmlands with Chesapeake Bay. But perhaps the most important water route is at Pittsburgh, where the Allegheny and the Monongahela rivers come together to form the Ohio River, the great migration and trade route to the West.

Pittsburgh was the "Gateway to the West" until the frontier shifted and St. Louis inherited the title. When its role in the migration of pioneers was finished, the city gained greater renown and wealth as the foremost manufacturer of steel. Until the 1970's, factories lined the banks of its three rivers for miles on end.

The gentle meadows and brooks of Lancaster County beckoned the first Pennsylvania Dutch settlers, who turned the countryside into productive farmland.

Pine Creek Gorge, in the north-central part of the state, is called the Grand Canyon of Pennsylvania. The gorge winds through dense woodlands for 50 miles.

A MINGLING OF ELEMENTS

Pittsburgh sits on the Allegheny Plateau, a land of broad ridges and deep valleys north and west of the Allegheny Mountains, an Appalachian subrange. The beautiful hardwood forests, fields, bogs, and streams of the plateau, once the home of the Seneca Indians, now draw hikers, fishermen, and photographers. In autumn, old stands of beech, birch, and maple set the woods aflame with color; in June, mountain laurel bursts forth with delicate pink blossoms.

Also on the plateau, some 70 miles southeast of Pittsburgh, is situated one of the finest man-made works in Pennsylvania — the celebrated house called Fallingwater, which Frank Lloyd Wright designed for the Pittsburgh businessman Edgar J. Kaufmann in 1936. Built of local sandstone and concrete, it perches on a craggy waterfall in a forest setting. When Kaufmann gave the property to a conservation group he said that Wright had created it "as a declaration that in nature man finds his spiritual as well as physical energies." The house is a mingling of elements that express the character of Pennsylvania: an energetic combination of natural and man-made, rugged and refined.

AMERICA'S FIRST BOTANIST

The oldest surviving botanic garden in the United States is the legacy of native-born botanist John Bartram of Pennsylvania. In 1728, at a farm he purchased on the Schuylkill River in what is now southwestern Philadelphia, Bartram laid out a five-acre plot where he cultivated specimens he collected in the region. He also conducted experiments in cross breeding. Later he made collecting expeditions into New York, west to the Ohio River, and in the South. On a trip to Georgia with his son, Bartram discovered a rare tree with beautiful white flowers resembling camellias. He named it *Franklinia* after his friend Benjamin Franklin.

Although he had only a fourth-grade education, Bartram, born in 1699, learned enough Latin to read the books of the renowned Swedish botanist Linnaeus, and eventually gained recognition as a botanist himself. In 1765 King George III appointed him King's Botanist, and Linnaeus lavished praise on Bartram, calling him "the greatest natural botanist in the world."

During the Revolutionary War British soldiers made camp at the farm, but they treated the famed plantings with respect. Later, Bartram's heirs and the subsequent owners of the property took care to maintain the garden. In 1891 it was acquired by the city of Philadelphia and flourishes today as Bartram's Garden, open for the public to enjoy.

In east-central Pennsylvania, forests of sugar maples turn a brilliant yellow in October. In late winter the trees can be tapped for their sweet sap.

Rhode Island

A jewellike corner of New England, steeped in history

The smallest state in the country, and proudly so, Rhode Island measures a modest 47 miles from north to south and only 40 miles from east to west. But given the surprising variety of destinations within its borders — emerald forests, eye-soothing farmland, dynamic cities, spectacular seasides — Rhode Island's compact size is a traveler's blessing, for no one place is ever more than a short drive from any other. It is possible to tour historic city streets in the morning, picnic by a lazy country stream in the afternoon, and stroll beside the moonlit surf in the evening.

PROVIDENCE PLANTATIONS

In northwestern Rhode Island, forests of birch and cedar are dotted with shining lakes and ponds. Country roads pass by sprawling dairy and poultry farms, recalling the early years when outlying towns were called plantations and the state was given the official name State of Rhode Island and Providence Plantations.

In the northeastern part of the state, the Blackstone River courses south to Pawtucket. Here Samuel Slater built the first water-powered cotton mill in 1790, ushering in an industrial revolution that drew legions of immigrants to Rhode Island. Slater himself came from England, where cloth manufacturing secrets were so jealously guarded that textile workers were forbidden to leave the country. To get out, Slater disguised himself as a farmer.

South of Slater's restored mill in Pawtucket lies Rhode Island's cosmopolitan capital, Providence. Roger Williams, who left strictly Puri-

Block Island's admirers have called it the Bermuda of the North. One of the island's most prominent landmarks is Southeast Lighthouse, built in 1873.

The harbor at Warren, off Narragansett Bay, was an important center for whaling, oystering, and shipbuilding in the 19th century.

THE BEAUTY AND SPLENDOR OF NORTH AMERICA

tan Massachusetts in search of religious freedom, founded the city in 1636, and in the next two centuries it became one of the East Coast's busiest ports. Here flourished the infamous triangular trade — West Indies molasses for New England rum for African slaves.

The Providence of today, though a busy urban center, is filled with reminders of the past. Dozens of elegant 18th-century homes, each with a bronze plaque recording the date it was built and the name of its first owner, are found along Benefit Street and the area surrounding Brown University on College Hill.

"THE OCEAN STATE"

Sweeping from the Atlantic Ocean all the way inland to Providence is Rhode Island's most impressive natural treasure — gigantic Narragansett Bay, which endows the tiny state with a staggering, 400-mile coastline (without the bay the coastline would be only 40 miles long). On the bay are some 35 islands, known by such quaint and quirky names as Hog,

Hen, Rabbitt, Patience, Hope, and Despair. The largest is named Rhode Island, aptly enough, but to avoid confusion residents use the island's Indian name, Aquidneck.

On the southern end of Aquidneck lies the celebrated resort town of Newport. Its prim colonial churches, brick squares, and weathered wharves recall the Newport of 200 years ago, when it was an active port and a center for shipbuilding. But in the last century Newport has become a symbol of opulence, with luxurious yachts bobbing at anchor and palatial turn-of-the-century mansions. Called "cottages" by their owners, they have housed such astronomically wealthy Americans as the Astors, Morgans, Dukes, and Vanderbilts.

Off the mainland lies another, more solitary island. A tranquil, treeless place of rolling moors and towering bluffs, Block Island is, except for a few vintage Victorian hotels, refreshingly undeveloped. Only seven miles long, the island — like the state of Rhode Island itself — is both compact and beguiling.

From Cliff Walk, a seaside footpath in Newport, strollers can steal glimpses of sumptuous mansions built from the Gay Nineties to the Roaring Twenties.

This 200-year-old windmill at Prescott Farm in Middletown still grinds corn.

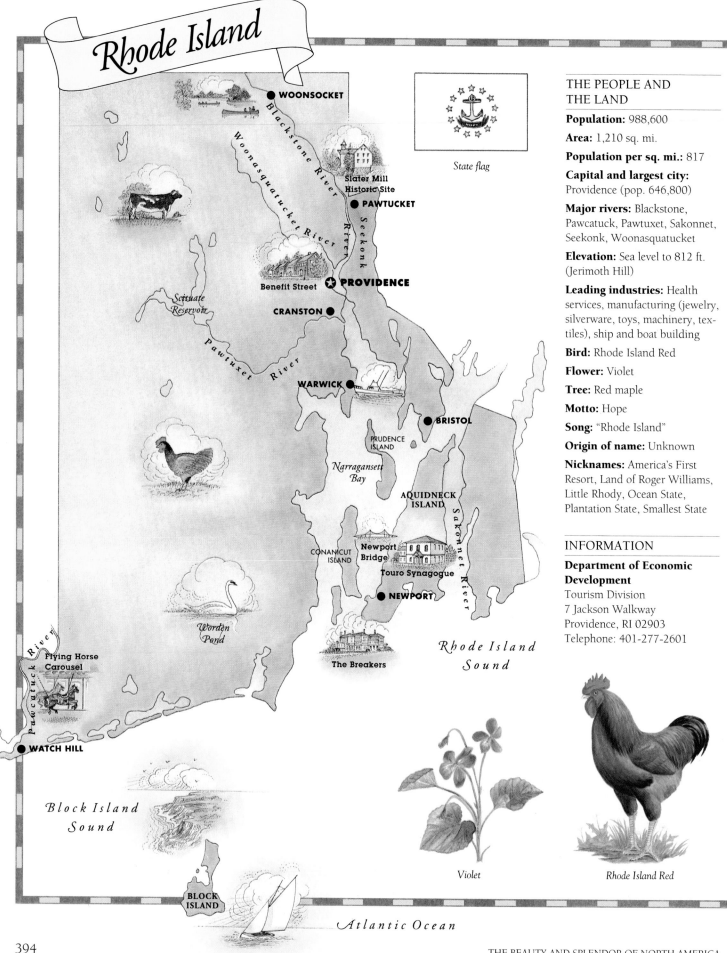

Rhode Island

WOONSOCKET

Slater Mill
Historic Site

PAWTUCKET

Blackstone River

Woonasquatucket River

Seekonk River

Benefit Street

★ **PROVIDENCE**

Scituate Reservoir

CRANSTON

Pawtuxet River

WARWICK

BRISTOL

PRUDENCE ISLAND

Narragansett Bay

AQUIDNECK ISLAND

CONANICUT ISLAND

Newport Bridge

Touro Synagogue

NEWPORT

The Breakers

Rhode Island Sound

Sakonnet River

Pawcatuck River

Flying Horse Carousel

Worden Pond

WATCH HILL

Block Island Sound

BLOCK ISLAND

Atlantic Ocean

State flag

THE PEOPLE AND THE LAND

Population: 988,600

Area: 1,210 sq. mi.

Population per sq. mi.: 817

Capital and largest city: Providence (pop. 646,800)

Major rivers: Blackstone, Pawcatuck, Pawtuxet, Sakonnet, Seekonk, Woonasquatucket

Elevation: Sea level to 812 ft. (Jerimoth Hill)

Leading industries: Health services, manufacturing (jewelry, silverware, toys, machinery, textiles), ship and boat building

Bird: Rhode Island Red

Flower: Violet

Tree: Red maple

Motto: Hope

Song: "Rhode Island"

Origin of name: Unknown

Nicknames: America's First Resort, Land of Roger Williams, Little Rhody, Ocean State, Plantation State, Smallest State

INFORMATION

Department of Economic Development
Tourism Division
7 Jackson Walkway
Providence, RI 02903
Telephone: 401-277-2601

Violet

Rhode Island Red

394

HISTORICAL HIGHLIGHTS

1524 Giovanni da Verrazzano, sailing on behalf of France, enters Narragansett Bay.

1614 Dutch mariner Adrian Block lands on the island that will bear his name.

1636 Roger Williams founds Providence, the first permanent settlement.

1663 Charles II of England grants Rhode Island a charter.

1772 Colonists protesting trade restrictions burn a British revenue ship, the *Gaspee.*

1774 Rhode Island prohibits importation of slaves.

1776 Rhode Island is the first colony to declare its independence from England.

1790 Rhode Island joins the Union as the 13th state.

1842 Dorr's Rebellion leads to more liberal state constitution.

1938 A devastating hurricane and tidal wave cause more than 250 deaths and about $100 million in property damage.

1969 Newport Bridge links Jamestown and Newport, spanning Narragansett Bay.

1971 The legislature approves a state personal income tax.

1976 Operation Sail sends tall ships to Newport and New York for the Bicentennial.

1980 Voters approve a referendum pledging $87 million to protect Narragansett Bay.

FAMOUS SONS AND DAUGHTERS

George M. Cohan (1878 – 1942). The versatile Broadway entertainer wrote, directed, and produced most of the shows in which he danced, sang, and acted. He wrote such classic songs as "Over There" and "The Yankee Doodle Boy."

Nathanael Greene (1742 – 86). Greene became an important general in the Revolutionary War. A superb strategist, he served as commander in the decisive Carolina campaign.

Anne Hutchinson (1591 – 1643). An outspoken religious leader, Hutchinson helped found present-day Portsmouth, R.I., in 1638 after being banished from the Massachusetts Bay Colony for her dissident views.

Matthew Calbraith Perry (1794 – 1858). In 1854, the distinguished naval officer succeeded in convincing Japan to open its ports to world trade.

Oliver Hazard Perry (1785 – 1819). Like his brother Matthew, Perry had a great naval career. Upon defeating the British in the Battle of Lake Erie, he sent the famous message: "We have met the enemy, and they are ours."

Gilbert Stuart (1755 – 1828). A portrait painter with an elegant style, Stuart is best known for his portraits of George Washington.

Roger Williams (c. 1603 – 83). The founder of Providence and father of Rhode Island, clergyman Williams held strong views on the separation of church and state, which later influenced the framers of the U.S. Constitution.

ODDITIES AND SPECIALTIES

More than 20 percent of the nation's registered historic landmarks are in Rhode Island.

The state capitol's self-supported marble dome is second in size only to that of St. Peter's Basilica in Rome.

Watch Hill claims America's oldest carousel, called the Flying Horse because the horses, hung from chains, swing outward.

Newport's Touro Synagogue, built in 1763, is the country's oldest Jewish house of worship.

Newport is well known for its yachting events, including the Newport-to-Bermuda race and the America's Cup race.

The ledges and sandbars off Block Island have sunk more than 1,000 ships. A long time ago plunderers, hoping to loot cargo, lured vessels toward the rocks by waving lanterns. The wrecks are memorialized by such place-names as Cow Cove, where shipwrecked cows once made their way to shore.

Developed in Little Compton in 1854, the Rhode Island Red was so superior to other chickens both in its egg-laying ability and the quality of its meat that it turned poultry-raising into a major U.S. industry.

The tiny town of Bristol swells to many times its population every Fourth of July, when it hosts the nation's oldest Independence Day parade and celebration, dating back to 1785.

PLACES TO VISIT, THINGS TO DO

Block Island Accessible by ferry, the island is known for its timeless charm, with lovely beaches, cliffs, ponds, and Victorian inns.

Cliff Walk (Newport). Along this three-mile coastal path are a number of opulent mansions, including The Breakers, built by Cornelius Vanderbilt. Several of these palatial homes are open to the public.

Discount shopping Factory outlets, many located in former textile mills, are found in the Blackstone River Valley, where the country's first factory outlet opened in 1954.

Fishing Narragansett Bay teems with striped bass, bluefish, cod, tuna, and a variety of shellfish.

Great Swamp Management Area (next to Worden Pond). In this island-dotted swamp, deer and mute swans live among some 4,000 kinds of plants, including orchids and arctic moss.

Mile of History (Providence). Along Benefit Street are restored 18th- and 19th-century buildings, among them the elegant John Brown House, which contains a magnificent collection of antique furniture.

Slater Mill Historic Site (Pawtucket). Here, on the banks of the powerful Blackstone River, is Samuel Slater's restored cotton mill, along with a museum tracing the development of industrial technology.

South Carolina

Uplands, lowlands, and a gracious sense of the past

South Carolinians like to say that Charleston is the place where the Ashley and Cooper rivers join to form the Atlantic Ocean. The enormous pride embodied in the joke seems oddly incongruous with this quiet Atlantic seaboard state tucked between the mountains of North Carolina and the red clay hills of Georgia. South Carolina's beauty is subtle rather than spectacular, emanating from grassy savannas and shady pinewoods, lonely marshlands and windswept beaches.

PLANTERS AND FARMERS

The English and Barbadian colonists who settled near Charles Town in 1670, and the French Huguenots who arrived a few years later, discovered that the swampy lowlands surrounding them were ideal for rice paddies. Starting with a single bag of Madagascar rice bought from a sea captain in about 1685, the colonists were exporting their own crop by 1690. By 1700 a complex plantation system was established.

Meanwhile, the hilly and forested Piedmont above the lowlands was being settled by arrivals from the northern colonies. Mostly hardscrabble farmers, they resented the airs and influence of the coast-dwelling aristocrats. Conflicts between up-country and low country arose early and persisted even after the state's capital was moved, as a compromise, to Columbia, midway between the two areas. Regional distinctions began to blur only when the cotton craze swept the entire state in the late 1700's. Vast tracts of forest fell to make

With more than 1,000 species of plants, including 250 varieties of azaleas and 900 varieties of camellias, Magnolia Plantation and Gardens near Charleston is in colorful bloom throughout the year.

Stands of gangling palmetto trees proliferate along the boggy shores of South Carolina's many coastal rivers and canals.

THE BEAUTY AND SPLENDOR OF NORTH AMERICA

way for the new crop. The shot fired on Fort Sumter on April 12, 1861, was aimed at protecting South Carolina's "white gold."

UPLANDS AND LOWLANDS

In the rugged northwestern corner of the state, the Cherokee Foothills Scenic Highway winds close to such impressive sights as craggy Caesar's Head, Table Rock Mountain, and 420-foot Raven Cliff Falls. In boggy Ashmore Tract Heritage Preserve, botanists have found such rare plants as the carnivorous mountain sweet pitcher plant, which grows only in the Carolina highlands. Although the hilly Piedmont region forms the industrial core of the state, the countryside is still pleasantly dotted with lakes, horse farms, golf courses, peach orchards, and fields of soybeans.

To the southeast lies the low country, including the 60-mile sweep of beach known as the Grand Strand; the historic towns of Georgetown, Beaufort, and Charleston; and the marshy wetlands where Francis Marion, the Swamp Fox, baffled the redcoats during the American Revolution. Here also are the fabled Sea Islands. Hilton Head, with tasteful contemporary homes and 20 golf courses, exudes wealth and leisure. On Daufuskie blacks still preserve the Gullah language and lore of their forebears, early American slaves. On Cape Romain, loggerhead sea turtles crawl up the beaches to lay their eggs.

Charleston, lying in the heart of the coastal lowlands, is a city of infinite charms. Its citizens were alert to its uniqueness so early that in 1929 it became the first city in America to protect its historic district. Today the city has more than 70 buildings predating the American Revolution, 200 built before the War of 1812, and 850 before the Civil War. To walk among these old houses lining the battery along the harbor is to step back into the gracious elegance that rice and cotton created at the mouth of the Ashley and Cooper rivers.

According to an ancient Cherokee legend, flat-topped Table Rock Mountain, above, served as a dining table for a giant chief who sat on a smaller nearby hill called The Stool.

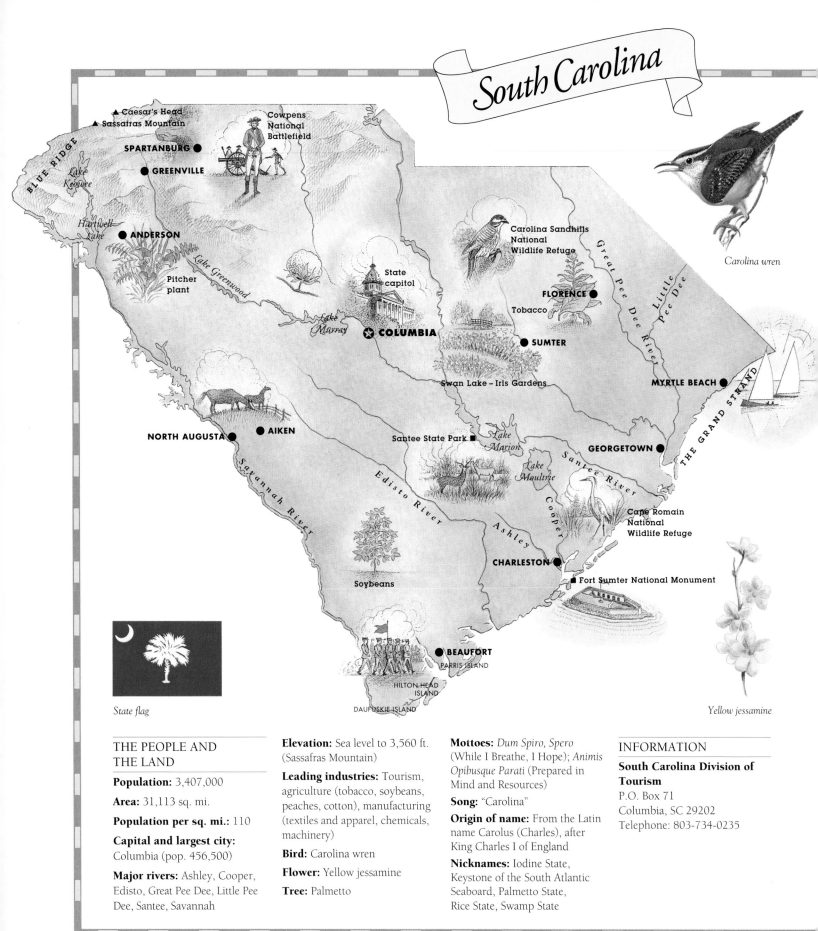

South Carolina

Caesar's Head ▲
Sassafras Mountain ▲
SPARTANBURG ●
Cowpens National Battlefield
BLUE RIDGE
Lake Keowee
● **GREENVILLE**
Hartwell Lake
● **ANDERSON**
Pitcher plant
Lake Greenwood
Lake Murray
State capitol
Carolina Sandhills National Wildlife Refuge
Great Pee Dee River
Little Pee Dee
FLORENCE ●
Tobacco
☆ **COLUMBIA**
● **SUMTER**
Swan Lake – Iris Gardens
MYRTLE BEACH ●
THE GRAND STRAND
Savannah River
NORTH AUGUSTA ●
● **AIKEN**
Santee State Park ■
Lake Marion
Edisto River
GEORGETOWN ●
Lake Moultrie
Santee River
Cooper
Ashley
Cape Romain National Wildlife Refuge
Soybeans
CHARLESTON ●
Fort Sumter National Monument
BEAUFORT ●
PARRIS ISLAND
HILTON HEAD ISLAND
DAUFUSKIE ISLAND

Carolina wren

Yellow jessamine

State flag

THE PEOPLE AND THE LAND

Population: 3,407,000

Area: 31,113 sq. mi.

Population per sq. mi.: 110

Capital and largest city: Columbia (pop. 456,500)

Major rivers: Ashley, Cooper, Edisto, Great Pee Dee, Little Pee Dee, Santee, Savannah

Elevation: Sea level to 3,560 ft. (Sassafras Mountain)

Leading industries: Tourism, agriculture (tobacco, soybeans, peaches, cotton), manufacturing (textiles and apparel, chemicals, machinery)

Bird: Carolina wren

Flower: Yellow jessamine

Tree: Palmetto

Mottoes: *Dum Spiro, Spero* (While I Breathe, I Hope); *Animis Opibusque Parati* (Prepared in Mind and Resources)

Song: "Carolina"

Origin of name: From the Latin name Carolus (Charles), after King Charles I of England

Nicknames: Iodine State, Keystone of the South Atlantic Seaboard, Palmetto State, Rice State, Swamp State

INFORMATION

South Carolina Division of Tourism
P.O. Box 71
Columbia, SC 29202
Telephone: 803-734-0235

HISTORICAL HIGHLIGHTS

1526 Spanish adventurer Lucas Vásquez de Ayllón establishes a short-lived settlement.

1663 English king Charles II grants region to eight lords proprietors for colonization.

1670 Colonists from England and Barbados settle near present-day Charleston.

1729 After a rebellion against the proprietors, the Carolinas become a British royal province.

1780 – 81 Defeat of loyalist troops at battles of Kings Mountain and Cowpens are turning points in American Revolution.

1788 South Carolina joins Union as eighth state.

1790 State capital is moved from Charleston to Columbia to ease tension between low-country and up-country inhabitants.

1822 Slave uprising suppressed.

1832 State legislature nullifies a federally imposed tariff, leading to a crisis over states' rights.

1860 South Carolina is first state to secede from Union.

1861 Confederate attack on Fort Sumter begins Civil War.

1865 Union troops led by Gen. William Tecumseh Sherman burn Columbia.

1868 South Carolina is readmitted to Union.

1877 Federal troops leave state as Reconstruction ends.

1886 Earthquake rocks Charleston, killing 92 people.

1895 State revises constitution, disenfranchising most blacks by denying them right to vote in Democratic Party primaries.

1921 Boll weevil destroys cotton crop, forcing diversification.

1947 Federal court ruling upholds blacks' right to vote in Democratic Party primaries.

1951 Atomic Energy Commission builds Savannah River Plant near Aiken to refine plutonium.

1964 Desegregation of public schools begins.

1989 Hurricane Hugo devastates coastal area.

FAMOUS SONS AND DAUGHTERS

Bernard Baruch (1870 – 1965). Born in Camden, Baruch made a fortune on Wall Street. Later he served as an adviser to every president from Wilson to Eisenhower.

John C. Calhoun (1782 – 1850).

Secretary of war, U.S. vice president (1825 – 32) and later a powerful U.S. senator, Calhoun was an eloquent and energetic defender of states' rights.

Althea Gibson (1927 –). Gibson was the first black to become an international tennis champion, winning at Wimbledon in 1957 and 1958. After retiring, she became a professional golfer.

Strom Thurmond (1902 –). Governor of South Carolina from 1947 to 1951, Thurmond has been a U.S. senator since 1955. He ran for president in 1948 as a states' rights democrat.

Charles H. Townes (1915 –). Townes's work in maser and laser research earned him a share of the 1964 Nobel Prize in physics.

ODDITIES AND SPECIALTIES

Nearly all the Marine Corps recruits in the eastern U.S. are trained at Parris Island.

The first Reform Jewish congregation in America was established at Charleston in 1824.

The poinsettia gets it name from South Carolinian Joel Poinsett, who discovered the flower in Mexico while serving as U.S. ambassador there.

DuBose Heyward and George Gershwin based their opera *Porgy and Bess* on Heyward's novel *Porgy*, which is set in Charleston.

Among the state's culinary delights is she-crab soup, made with white crabmeat and roe.

Although South Carolina's most famous dance may be the Charleston, its best-loved is the shag. A kind of swing dance step dating back to the 1930's, the shag became the state's official dance in 1984.

PLACES TO VISIT, THINGS TO DO

Aiken Three historic districts preserve the opulent architecture and atmosphere of Aiken in the 1890's, when it was a winter colony for wealthy northerners. This is the heart of South Carolina's horse-breeding country.

Cape Romain National Wildlife Refuge (Awendaw). Stretching over three islands, this 35,000-acre refuge of marshes and beaches attracts wintering waterfowl and shorebirds.

Carolina Sandhills National Wildlife Refuge (McBee). These wooded hills protect a large population of the endangered red-cockaded woodpecker.

Gardens (Charleston area). *Cypress Gardens* offers a unique blend of cypress trees, bright flowers, and lagoons. *Magnolia Plantation and Gardens* features masses of azaleas and camellias, and boat tours through a 125-acre wildlife refuge. *Middleton Place,* an 18th-century plantation, includes what may be the nation's oldest landscaped gardens.

Myrtle Beach Besides swimming and fishing, this seaside resort offers 60 golf courses.

Santee State Park (Santee). With cottages, campsites, and nature trails, this is an ideal base from which to explore Lake Marion and Lake Moultrie. Santee National Wildlife Refuge is a short drive away.

Savannah River Scenic Highway This scenic route wends its way for more than 100 miles along the Savannah River north of Augusta, Georgia.

Swan Lake – Iris Gardens (Sumter). Six of the world's eight species of swans have been gathered here on a 45-acre lake surrounded by a 150-acre garden planted with 25 varieties of irises.

South Dakota

Black Hills, Badlands, and wide open spaces

South Dakota is a land of bewildering variety and breathtaking extremes. Here are limitless expanses of space and very few people, sweeping treeless plains and steep forested mountains, sunny skies and torrential rains, rich farmland and uninhabitable badlands, scorching heat and bone-chilling cold, soothing silence and historic strife.

Writers rhapsodize about South Dakota's vastness. They speak of "the smell of distance," "the pull of horizon," and the "great quietness broken only by the wind." Even so, this giant land — the size of Ohio and Indiana combined — is so thinly populated that cattle outnumber people five to one.

In South Dakota the sun shines brightly and cheerfully almost every day; yet monstrous thunderstorms can appear out of nowhere, hammering the land unmercifully. In summer 100-degree temperatures are not uncommon, but in winter the thermometer plunges well below zero, ushering in ground-splitting frosts and arctic blizzards.

EAST AND WEST OF THE MISSOURI RIVER

Rectangular South Dakota is sliced through the middle by the mighty Missouri River, which makes its way through the state from north to south for some 550 miles. From the air the river looks like a jagged blue scar, shimmering and zigzagging across the land. No longer the much-feared, rampaging Big Muddy of earlier times, the Missouri — thanks to its many modern dams — is now a series of long, sinuous reservoirs. Called the Great Lakes

The otherworldly landscape of Badlands National Park is composed of sedimentary rock that has been eroded by wind, rain, and frost for some 35 million years.

of South Dakota, they have transformed the river into a mecca for fishing and boating.

The river also draws droves of bird watchers. They come to steal glimpses of cormorants, tundra swans, great blue herons, sandhill cranes, red-tailed hawks, and other regional and migrating birds. Plant life thrives near the river too. The surrounding hills and plains bloom with black-eyed Susans, prairie buttercups, and the pasqueflower, South Dakota's purplish, fur-petaled state flower.

George Fitch, a 19th-century humorist, wrote that the Missouri "rearranges geography" and "dabbles in real estate." That was before the age of dams, when erosion and flooding drastically altered both the form and value of the land. Still, the great river does cut the state into two distinct halves. To the east are low hills, small lakes, and endless stretches of fertile cropland — the legacy of glaciers — where wheat, corn, oats, and hogs are raised. Called East River, this half of the state is where 70 percent of South Dakotans live — in Sioux Falls, Watertown, Huron, and Aberdeen, and on the farms in between.

The land west of the river (or West River), untouched by the mammoth glaciers that bulldozed the east, is laced with deep canyons, ragged badlands, cathedrallike mountains, and rolling plains. Buttes rise 600 feet above the green grasslands, their burnt red contours set against the bright blue sky. Here legions of buffalo once grazed, blackening the land as far as the eye could see.

The western half of South Dakota is steeped in frontier history. In the early days, intrepid explorers and fur traders fought the elements, and the 19th century saw frenzied gold rushes

A dusting of snow on granite boulders adds a bracing note to the serenity of Sylvan Lake in the Black Hills. In the 1920's sculptor Gutzon Borglum considered the area as a possible site for the sculptures that now adorn Mount Rushmore.

and bloody battles with the proud Sioux, who defended their territory against the encroaching white man. Today vast Indian reservations and sprawling cattle ranches share the land.

LANDS BOTH BAD AND BEAUTIFUL

To the southwest are the hauntingly beautiful Badlands. Here, over millions of years, wind, rain, snow, and ice have carved out an eerie, lifeless moonscape of gorges, mesas, ridges, pyramids, knobs, and spires. As the sun moves across the sky, the myriad formations change their hues from pastel pinks and tans to deep reds and browns. At dusk they loom from the earth like phantoms in a land bewitched.

So forbidding was this geological obstacle course, where travel was aggravatingly slow and water dangerously scarce, that the Sioux called it *mako sica* ("bad land"), and wary French trappers dubbed the region *les mauvaises terres à traverser* ("bad lands to travel across"). The name was kept by modern geologists, who view the Badlands as examples of erosion gone berserk.

Skirting the state's western border are the Black Hills, so named by the Sioux because they look dark and somber when viewed from the distant plains. In the 1870's the stampede for gold saw white men by the thousands invade the Black Hills, which the Sioux regarded as the sacred home of the Great Spirit. The Sioux rose in outrage, ushering in the 15-year-long Indian wars. They ended in 1890 with the death of some 200 Indians, shot by U.S. troops near Wounded Knee Creek.

Today travelers flock to the scenic Black Hills — which are actually mountains towering to heights of up to 7,200 feet — for recreation. The land below contains miles of mazelike caves, and the hills themselves are blanketed with pine and spruce trees and ornamented with spectacular outcrops.

While the hand of nature has sculpted dizzying granite pinnacles atop these impressive mountains, the hand of man has carved gigantic presidential faces into the side of Mount Rushmore. The many-faceted Black Hills, like the rest of South Dakota, make it abundantly clear why the state has been nicknamed the Land of Infinite Variety.

Buffalo still roam in Custer State Park, where thunder from the sky sometimes seems to echo the thundering of the great herds that stampeded here a century ago. Sharing the grassy slopes today are deer, elk, antelope, and an occasional coyote.

The yellow-headed blackbird nests in freshwater marshes and nearby fields.

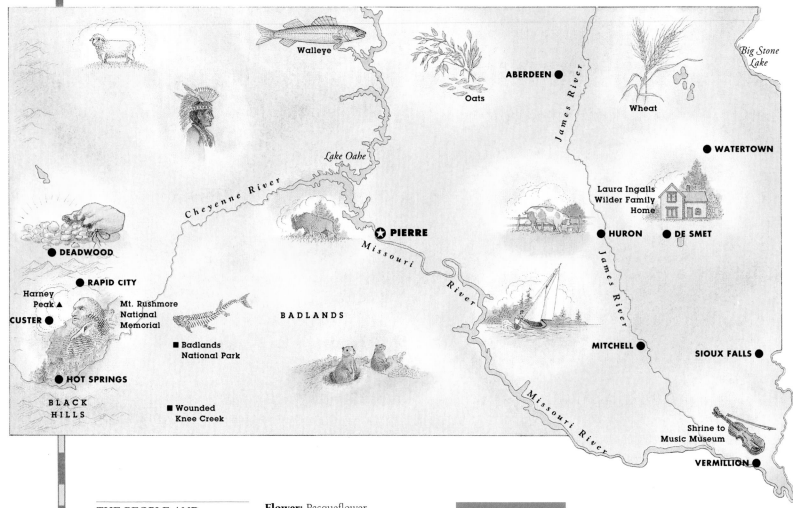

Walleye

Oats

ABERDEEN

James River

Big Stone Lake

Wheat

WATERTOWN

Laura Ingalls Wilder Family Home

Lake Oahe

Cheyenne River

HURON

DE SMET

PIERRE

Missouri River

James River

DEADWOOD

RAPID CITY

Harney Peak ▲

Mt. Rushmore National Memorial

CUSTER

BADLANDS

MITCHELL

SIOUX FALLS

■ Badlands National Park

HOT SPRINGS

BLACK HILLS

■ Wounded Knee Creek

Missouri River

Shrine to Music Museum

VERMILLION

THE PEOPLE AND THE LAND

Population: 693,300

Area: 77,116 sq. mi.

Population per sq. mi.: 9

Capital: Pierre (pop. 14,000)

Largest city: Sioux Falls (pop. 128,000)

Major rivers: Cheyenne, James, Missouri

Elevation: 962 ft. (Big Stone Lake) to 7,242 ft. (Harney Peak)

Leading industries: Agriculture (cattle, corn, wheat), gold mining, food processing

Bird: Ring-necked pheasant

Flower: Pasqueflower

Tree: Black Hills spruce

Motto: Under God the People Rule

Song: "Hail, South Dakota"

Origin of name: From the Sioux word for friends or allies

Nicknames: Artesian State, Blizzard State, Coyote State, Land of Infinite Variety, Sunshine State

INFORMATION

South Dakota Department of Tourism
711 East Wells Avenue
Pierre, SD 57501-3369
Telephone: 800-843-1930

State flag

Ring-necked pheasant

Pasqueflower

HISTORICAL HIGHLIGHTS

1743 François and Louis-Joseph La Vérendrye are first white men to explore South Dakota.

1803 U.S. acquires most of Dakota region from the French with the Louisiana Purchase.

1809 St. Louis Fur Company begins trade in the upper Missouri valley.

1831 The *Yellowstone*, the first steamboat on the upper Missouri River, reaches banks of present-day Fort Pierre.

1858 Yankton Sioux cede vast lands to U.S.

1861 Congress establishes the Dakota Territory.

1874 Gold is discovered in the Black Hills.

1877 Sioux are forced to surrender the Black Hills.

1878 A land rush initiates Great Dakota Boom.

1889 South Dakota joins Union as 40th state.

1890 Federal troops kill some 200 Sioux at Wounded Knee Creek, ending the Indian wars.

1927 Gutzon Borglum begins carving Mt. Rushmore National Memorial.

1944 The Flood Control Act authorizes dam construction on Missouri River.

1963 Minuteman intercontinental ballistic missiles are positioned at town of Wall.

1972 Flooding causes more than 200 deaths in Rapid City area.

1973 American Indian Movement members and sympathizers occupy village of Wounded Knee for 71 days.

1980 U.S. Supreme Court orders federal government to pay Sioux tribes more than $205 million to compensate for 1877 forced surrender of Black Hills.

FAMOUS SONS AND DAUGHTERS

Crazy Horse (c.1840 – 77). This Oglala Sioux chief led his people against white encroachment in the Black Hills.

Gall (c.1840 – 94). An ally of Sitting Bull at the Battle of Little Bighorn, this Sioux chief later helped improve relations between his people and whites.

Hallie Flanagan (1890 – 1969). During the 1930's Flanagan headed the Federal Theatre Project of the Works Progress Administration. She staged over 1,000 productions nationwide.

Ernest O. Lawrence (1901 – 58). Lawrence won the 1939 Nobel Prize in physics for his atomic research, including the development of the cyclotron.

George McGovern (1922 –). McGovern represented South Dakota in the U.S. House (1958 – 62) and Senate (1962 – 80). In 1972 he ran for president against Richard Nixon.

Sitting Bull (c.1834 – 90).

Born on the Grand River, Sitting Bull became an esteemed Hunkpapa Sioux chief and medicine man. His refusal to move to a reservation led to the Battle of Little Bighorn, an important victory for the Sioux and the scene of Custer's last stand.

ODDITIES AND SPECIALTIES

Thousands of bushels of corn make up the murals, redone annually, on the Corn Palace in Mitchell. Moorish domes and minarets add to the building's whimsical appearance.

De Smet, known as the Little Town on the Prairie, was the home of Laura Ingalls Wilder in the 1880's. Her children's books tell of life on the Great Plains.

Gold lured such colorful Old West figures as Wild Bill Hickok, Calamity Jane, and Poker Alice to the mining town of Deadwood. In 1876, while holding what has since been called the "deadman's hand" of aces and eights, Hickok was killed by Jack "Crooked Nose" McCall in Deadwood's Saloon No. 10.

The Badlands have yielded a wealth of fossils, including those of rhinoceroses and camels.

Beginning in 1927, sculptor Gutzon Borglum labored for 14 years to create the images of four presidents on Mt. Rushmore. He planned the sculptures to extend to the waists but died before they were completed.

Sculptor Korcazk Ziolkowski worked from 1948 until his death in 1982 to fashion an equestrian image of Crazy Horse out of a 600-foot-high mountain near Mt. Rushmore. Being completed by his family, the work will feature an outstretched arm the length of a football field and a horse's head 22 stories high.

South Dakota has its own state jewelry, Black Hills gold. It combines rose, green, and yellow gold in grapes-and-leaves designs.

PLACES TO VISIT, THINGS TO DO

Badlands National Park (Interior). Etched by erosion, the landscape here is filled with thousands of bizarre and beautiful rock formations.

Custer State Park (Custer). One of the world's largest herds of buffalo roams this park in the forested Black Hills, where Needles Highway winds around giant granite pinnacles.

Jewel Cave National Monument (Custer). The jewels within this labyrinthine cavern are calcite crystals that gleam from its walls and ceiling.

Shrine to Music Museum (Vermillion). On view are more than 3,000 instruments, spanning some five millennia.

Walleye fishing The Missouri River and the many glacial lakes in the eastern half of the state teem with this popular fish.

Wind Cave National Park (Hot Springs). Odd formations called boxwork, frostwork, and popcorn adorn the 53-mile maze of passageways in Wind Cave.

Tennessee

Misty mountains, music, and the Mississippi

Road signs at the Tennessee border once welcomed puzzled visitors to the "Three States of Tennessee," and residents, when asked where they hail from, still specify East, Middle, or West Tennessee. Stretching from the craggy Appalachian Mountains to the banks of the Mississippi River, Tennessee does, in fact, encompass three distinctly different regions.

MOUNTAINS AND WALKING HORSES

The first East Tennesseans settled isolated mountain ridges in the mid-1700's. They labored tirelessly to hew beams for their homes, clear the land for crops, and preserve foods for winter — often entertaining themselves with songs and fiddle music whose roots go back to the British Isles.

The natural beauty of Great Smoky Mountains National Park attracts millions of visitors each year. Late in spring, rhododendron and mountain laurel blossoms adorn the mountainsides with a show of red and pink, and in autumn, a fiery brilliance sweeps south along the undulating peaks. Hovering over the landscape year-round is a bluish haze — created by moisture and oils released by trees — that inspired the names of both the Blue Ridge and the Smoky Mountains.

In Middle Tennessee the land rises and falls at a gentler pace. The Cumberland River, which meanders through the center of the state, once served as a highway through the wilderness. It brought the first settlers to the site of present-day Nashville on Christmas Day, 1779.

The golden meadows of Percy Warner Park look decidedly rural but are not far from downtown Nashville.

Atop Chattanooga's Lookout Mountain, a Civil War cannon looms over the Tennessee River.

Cades Cove, in the Great Smoky Mountains, was a thriving farm community in the 1800's.

Today the city of Nashville is a cosmopolitan center where universities and financial institutions mingle with the machinery of state government. The city owes its world renown, however, not to the progress on which it prides itself, but to the earthy sounds of country music. The largest and most venerable of Nashville's music halls is, of course, the Grand Ole Opry.

Just south of Nashville, back roads make their way through rolling bluegrass country, often skirting white-columned, antebellum

mansions. Farther south, near Wartrace and Shelbyville, long, low stables and white-fenced pastures mark what is known as Tennessee walking horse country.

In the late 19th century, farmers in the area, who spent long hours on horseback overseeing their crops, prized those mounts that offered the gentlest ride. With this in mind, they selectively bred animals with smooth gaits. The result was a new breed, the Tennessee walking horse, known for its rhythmic, high-stepping walk.

COTTON AND THE BLUES

From the early 1800's, cotton was the mainstay both of West Tennessee's strong plantation culture and of the emerging city of Memphis, which land speculators laid out on bluffs overlooking the Mississippi.

While most of West Tennessee remains serenely agricultural, Memphis is one of the South's busiest ports and commercial centers. It is also the city where W. C. Handy gave voice to that unique and influential brand of American music known as the blues.

This lush, hazy scene, showing a country pond south of Nashville, typifies midsummer in Middle Tennessee. Nearby are sprawling tobacco farms and the genteel old town of Franklin.

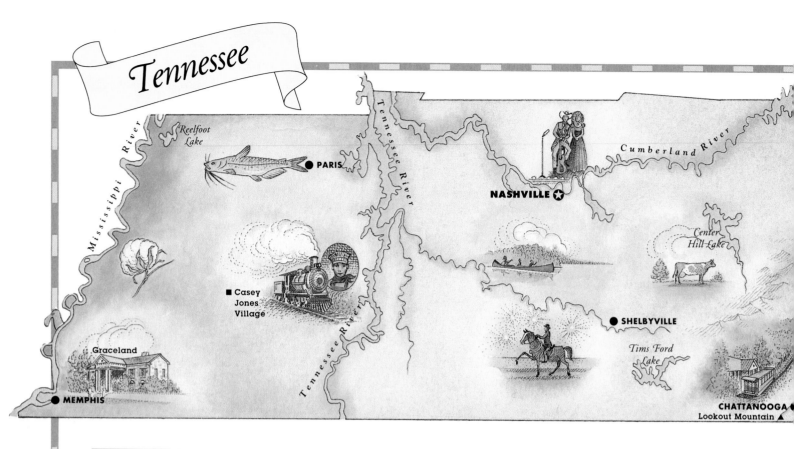

Tennessee

Reelfoot Lake • **PARIS** *Tennessee River* *Cumberland River* **NASHVILLE** ✪ *Center Hill Lake* *Mississippi River* ■ **Casey Jones Village** *Tennessee River* • **SHELBYVILLE** *Tims Ford Lake* **Graceland** • **MEMPHIS** **CHATTANOOGA** *Lookout Mountain* ▲

HISTORICAL HIGHLIGHTS

1540 Hernando de Soto leads Spanish party in raid on Indian villages in Tennessee River valley.

1682 La Salle claims region for king of France.

1763 France cedes land east of Mississippi River to Great Britain.

1772 Settlers form a government, calling it Watauga Association.

1784 East Tennessee settlers establish State of Franklin, which lasted only until 1789.

1796 Tennessee enters Union as 16th state.

1818 U.S. buys West Tennessee from the Chickasaw Indians.

1838 The Cherokees are forced out of Tennessee, taking the Trail of Tears to Oklahoma.

1861 Tennessee secedes from Union, the last state to do so.

1866 Tennessee is first state to be readmitted to Union.

1878 Yellow fever epidemic causes death of more than 5,000 Memphis residents.

1925 The famous Monkey Trial, testing the teaching of evolution in schools, is held in Dayton.

1933 Congress creates Tennessee Valley Authority.

1942 The federal government builds atomic energy research plant at Oak Ridge.

1968 Martin Luther King, Jr., is assassinated in Memphis.

1982 Knoxville World Fair opens on May 1.

1985 Tennessee-Tombigbee Waterway links Tennessee River to Gulf of Mexico.

FAMOUS SONS AND DAUGHTERS

James Agee (1909 – 55). Born in Knoxville, the celebrated writer was best known for his book on southern tenant farmers, *Let Us Now Praise Famous Men,* and for the novel *A Death in the Family.* Published after his death, the novel was awarded the 1957 Pulitzer Prize for fiction.

Eddy Arnold (1918 –). The popular singer known as the Tennessee Plowboy gained a wide audience for country music by performing on radio and television. Over the years he has sold some 85 million records.

Davy Crockett (1786 – 1836).

A legendary frontiersman and Indian fighter, Crockett served three terms in the U.S. House of Representatives. He was killed in Texas, defending the Alamo.

Andrew Jackson (1767 – 1845). The son of poor immigrants, Jackson became a lawyer, landowner, general, and the seventh president of the U.S.

Andrew Johnson (1808 – 75). Johnson became president after Lincoln was assassinated. His treatment of the South, which some thought too lenient, brought about his impeachment, but he was quickly acquitted.

Estes Kefauver (1903 – 63). A Chattanooga lawyer, Kefauver represented Tennessee in both houses of Congress. As a senator he investigated crime, and in 1956 became Adlai Stevenson's presidential running mate.

Grace Moore (1901 – 47). Moore, born in Slabtown, had a beautiful soprano voice that took her from musical comedy to opera to film. She died in a plane crash in Denmark.

James K. Polk (1795 – 1849). Extremely hardworking, the 11th U.S. president accomplished all of his stated goals, including the acquisition of California.

Sequoya (c.1760 – 1843). This highly esteemed Cherokee developed an alphabet and a written language for his tribe. The giant sequoia tree is named for him.

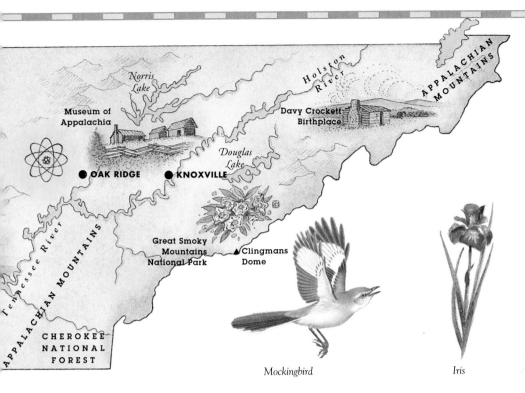

State flag

Mockingbird

Iris

Alvin York (1887 – 1964). "Sergeant York" grew up on a Tennessee farm. A conscientious objector at first, he later became a World War I hero, earning the highest honors for his bravery.

ODDITIES AND SPECIALTIES

The ramp, which grows in the foothills of the Appalachian Mountains, has been called the world's "vilest-smelling, sweetest-tasting" vegetable. The town of Cosby celebrates the onionlike delicacy with an annual festival.

Kenton, in western Tennessee, is home to a rare colony of white squirrels, which are in fact albino gray squirrels.

Paris, Tenn., claims that its annual feast — of over 8,500 pounds of catfish — is the "World's Largest Fish Fry."

Casey Jones, the railroad engineer who inspired the well-known song, was born in Jackson. Seeing that a collision was imminent, Jones remained on his train rather than jump. He saved lives by slowing down the train, which reduced the impact of the crash, though he himself died.

A full-scale replica of the Greek Parthenon can be seen in Nashville, the "Athens of the South." Built in 1897 for the Tennessee Centennial Exhibition, today it houses an art museum.

PLACES TO VISIT, THINGS TO DO

Belle Meade (Nashville). Renowned in the 1800's for the breeding of Thoroughbred horses, this 5,300-acre plantation was one of the Old South's finest.

Cherokee National Forest (headquarters at Cleveland). Some 500 miles of trails, spanning 10 counties, lead hikers through the rugged Appalachians.

Graceland (Memphis). Elvis Presley's estate, open to the public, includes the singer's mansion, memorabilia, and grave.

Grand Ole Opry (Nashville). Begun as a radio show in the 1920's, the Grand Ole Opry became the nation's most venerable showcase for country music. It is now located in Opryland USA.

Great Smoky Mountains National Park (headquarters at Gatlinburg). Evergreen-scented peaks and abundant wildlife attract legions of visitors to this beautiful 520,000-acre park.

Lookout Mountain (Chattanooga). Aptly named, this promontory offers a sweeping view of Moccasin Bend on the Tennessee River. Visitors can take a steep ride to the summit on the Incline Railway.

Museum of Appalachia (Norris). This replica of a pioneer village features some 30 buildings, including a smokehouse, corn mill, church, and loom house.

THE PEOPLE AND THE LAND

Population: 4,877,200

Area: 42,144 sq. mi.

Population per sq. mi.: 116

Capital and largest city: Nashville (pop. 985,100)

Major rivers: Cumberland, Mississippi, Tennessee

Elevation: 182 ft. (Mississippi River) to 6,643 ft. (Clingmans Dome)

Leading industries: Wholesale and retail trade, community and personal services, chemical manufacturing, food products (dairy and produce), machinery

Bird: Mockingbird

Flower: Iris

Tree: Tulip poplar

Motto: Agriculture and Commerce

Song: The state has five official songs, including "The Tennessee Waltz"

Origin of name: From the Cherokee word *tanasi*, referring to a village and a river of the same name

Nicknames: Big Bend State, Mother of Southwestern Statesmen, Volunteer State

INFORMATION

Department of Tourist Development
P.O. Box 23170
Nashville, TN 37202
Telephone: 615-741-2158

Texas

The giant state
that was once a nation

Texas encompasses so many regions that it might as well be a country — and it once was. As a sovereign nation after its separation from Mexico in 1836, Texas was unique among territories admitted to the Union. Also unique was the agreement that it negotiated with the United States: a promise that Texas can, if it chooses, form as many as five new states within its borders.

It is unlikely that the Lone Star State will ever break up into smaller units. But if it were to do so, no one who believes in natural boundaries would be surprised. Beyond the Texas of the popular imagination — endless flat plains peopled with cowboys and oilmen — lie dense forests, craggy hills, white sand beaches, silent deserts, and even the southern tip of the Rocky Mountains.

THE SHEER SIZE OF IT

"Big," the Texan's world-famous brag, is no exaggeration. Texas has two time zones and takes up one-twelfth of the contiguous United States. Its coast on the Gulf of Mexico, lined with resorts like those on Galveston and Padre islands, is the third-longest of any state's, after Florida and California.

The sheer size of Texas explains not only its range of landscapes but also its diversity of plant and animal life. The state supports more than 5,000 species of flowering plants and 100 kinds of cacti. It is also home to mountain lions, ocelots, coyotes, prairie dogs, and two of nature's stranger creatures — the horned toad and the armadillo.

In Big Bend National Park, prickly pears and scrub grass glisten in the wake of a rare frost storm. Rising from the mist are the Chisos Mountains.

The leaves of an agave fall into shadow as the rays of the setting sun strike Lost Mine Peak (left) and Casa Grande (far right) in Big Bend National Park.

The human population is varied as well. Some 26 percent of the state's residents are Hispanic in origin, and many cities are virtually bilingual. This long-standing cultural mix goes by the name of Tex-Mex, and bears fruit in everything from the state's fiery-hot cooking to the Spanish-style architecture of the modern suburbs. But Texans are still Texans: the big event in most small towns remains the annual rodeo or quarter horse show, no matter what language the proceedings are conducted in. And an enduring fondness for cowboy boots, wide-brimmed Stetsons, and pickup trucks seems to cross all ethnic lines.

EAST TEXAS, DEEP SOUTH

White settlement in Texas took hold in the fertile valleys of the Brazos and Colorado rivers, with the influx of Stephen F. Austin's Old Three Hundred — Anglo-Americans allowed in by the Mexican government in 1821. Most were farmers, tilling the rich river bottoms and establishing lucrative cotton plantations.

Cotton is still a mainstay of the Texas economy, blanketing much of the flat black land in the eastern half of the state. Interspersed with fields of alfalfa and sweet potatoes, cotton fields stretch right up to the dense Piney Woods along the Louisiana border, an area where the main industry is logging.

With its forests and farmland, East Texas has more in common with the Deep South than it does with the Southwest. Even bayous and bald cypresses are found within the Piney Woods — particularly at Caddo Lake and farther south, in the Big Thicket.

Until this century, the tangle of trees and underbrush in the swamps of the Big Thicket was virtually impenetrable. Three million acres in size before man began to whittle away at it, the thicket is now considerably smaller. But it remains one of the state's environmental treasures — a biological crossroads where eastern forests intertwine with southeastern swamp plants, southwestern desert flora, and subtropical species from Mexico.

Ushering in the Texas spring, a thick carpet of bluebonnets and Indian paintbrushes blooms on a Hill Country slope.

Deer abound in the Piney Woods of East Texas.

A crop duster flies low over an emerald green rice field on the Gulf Coast. Texas ranks as one of the nation's largest rice producers.

THE WEST'S "BARKING SQUIRRELS"

Prairie dogs — actually members of the squirrel family — were given their fanciful name by early explorers, who thought their barks sounded more canine than rodentlike. Scientists later called them *Cynomys,* or "dog mouse," a term that reflects both their voice and appearance.

Prairie dogs inhabit shortgrass prairies in the western half of the continent, including the flat grasslands of the Texas panhandle and the arid grazing lands farther south. Because the creatures are a favorite prey of coyotes, as well as hawks and other raptors, they dig their burrows in areas where the grass is low and they can more easily see their predators approaching. A small mound constructed at the mouth of each tunnel provides an elevated van-

tage point for the prairie dog's characteristic upright lookout stance.

Prairie dog "towns" throughout the West once held huge populations. The Lewis and Clark expedition in the early 19th century recorded that it had found the animals "in infinite numbers." Like the bison that shared the plains, the prairie dog suffered as the land was fenced and plowed. Cattle ranchers saw them as competing with their livestock for forage, and countless millions of prairie dogs were destroyed.

Still, these little barking squirrels survive today in Texas and points west, especially at preserves like the Muleshoe National Wildlife Refuge, where they remain safe from human interference.

Another distinct region exists in south-central Texas. After the flatness of East Texas, the rough-hewn beauty of this part of the state, called the Hill Country, comes as a surprise. Rocky, juniper-cloaked hills are cut through by clear green rivers. Along the roadsides, deer leap cedar-rail fences and flocks of doves take flight.

Also unexpected is the Hill Country's German character. German immigrants established the town of New Braunfels in 1845 and later moved west to found the hamlets that thrive in the area today. The German heritage of Fredericksburg, Boerne, and other towns is evident in their wurst houses, festivals, and even their buildings. Quaint "Sunday houses" — neat little timber-and-limestone houses built by 19th-century farmers for their weekend visits to town — still stand.

RANCHES AND DESERTS

Beyond the Hill Country, Texas belongs to the arid West. Cedars melt into mesquite, the mesquite into cactus-covered desert. In the north, cotton fields and farms give way to the vast ranches and wheat fields of the panhandle.

Cowboys still work these ranches, some of which are hundreds of thousands of acres in size. Much of the shortgrass prairie is used for grazing cattle or sheep, all the way to the mountains in the far western part of the state.

Southernmost of these mountains are the Chisos, which Spanish explorers considered hopelessly inhospitable. But eventually a few prospectors and other hardy souls moved to what became known as Big Bend Country (after the 80-mile northward bend of the Rio Grande). Today Big Bend National Park encompasses the scenic canyons and deserts of the region.

From this dramatic western landscape to the fertile fields of the east, one common factor has united the huge state — oil. When the first gusher blew in at Spindletop in 1901, the Texas oil boom was born, and today there is not a county without a history of oil exploration.

Oil, cotton, and cattle created Texas and the outsize myths that surround it. Now, with an economy sustained by finance and trade, the state has become more urbanized, more sophisticated. Yet the Texas mystique seems unshakable and still larger than life.

Mariscal Canyon, most isolated of the three major canyons in Big Bend, can be reached on foot only by a 6½-mile hike. Rafting down the Rio Grande makes it more accessible.

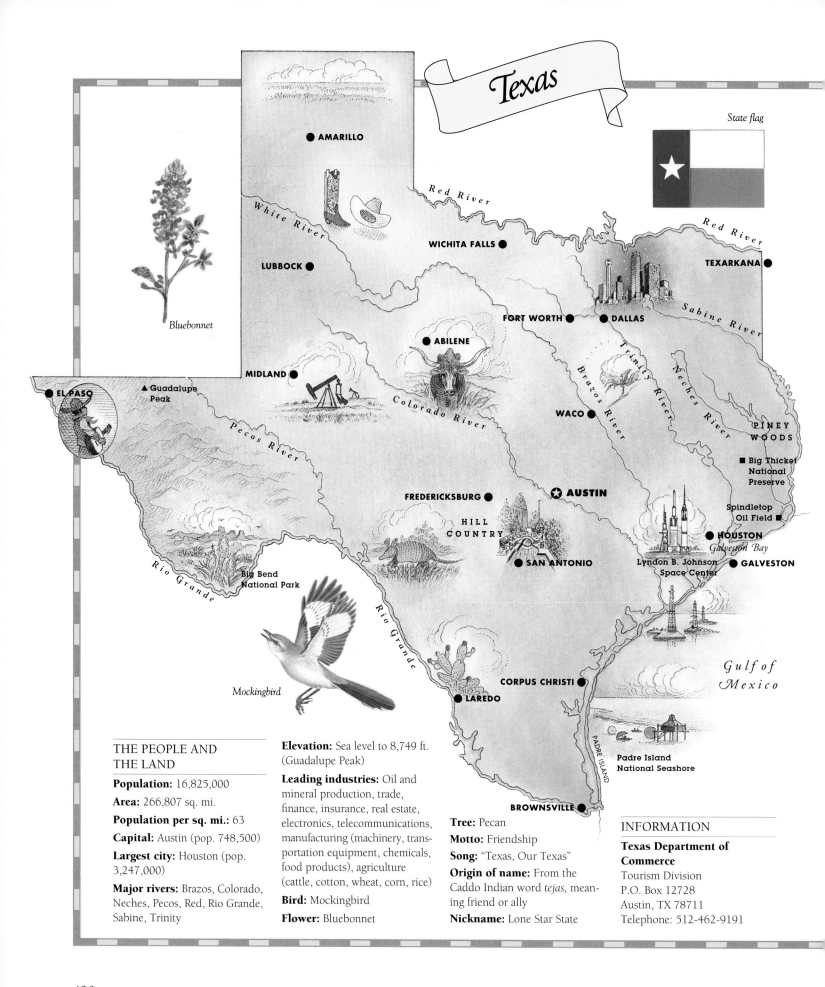

Texas

State flag

AMARILLO

Red River

White River

WICHITA FALLS

TEXARKANA

LUBBOCK

Sabine River

FORT WORTH · **DALLAS**

ABILENE

Trinity River

MIDLAND

Colorado River

Neches River

WACO

Brazos River

PINEY WOODS

Bluebonnet

▲ Guadalupe Peak

● **EL PASO**

Pecos River

■ Big Thicket National Preserve

Spindletop Oil Field ■

FREDERICKSBURG

☆ **AUSTIN**

HILL COUNTRY

● **HOUSTON**
Galveston Bay

Lyndon B. Johnson Space Center

SAN ANTONIO

Big Bend National Park

Rio Grande

● **GALVESTON**

Mockingbird

Rio Grande

CORPUS CHRISTI

Gulf of Mexico

● **LAREDO**

PADRE ISLAND

Padre Island National Seashore

THE PEOPLE AND THE LAND

Population: 16,825,000

Area: 266,807 sq. mi.

Population per sq. mi.: 63

Capital: Austin (pop. 748,500)

Largest city: Houston (pop. 3,247,000)

Major rivers: Brazos, Colorado, Neches, Pecos, Red, Rio Grande, Sabine, Trinity

Elevation: Sea level to 8,749 ft. (Guadalupe Peak)

Leading industries: Oil and mineral production, trade, finance, insurance, real estate, electronics, telecommunications, manufacturing (machinery, transportation equipment, chemicals, food products), agriculture (cattle, cotton, wheat, corn, rice)

Bird: Mockingbird

Flower: Bluebonnet

BROWNSVILLE

Tree: Pecan

Motto: Friendship

Song: "Texas, Our Texas"

Origin of name: From the Caddo Indian word *tejas*, meaning friend or ally

Nickname: Lone Star State

INFORMATION

Texas Department of Commerce
Tourism Division
P.O. Box 12728
Austin, TX 78711
Telephone: 512-462-9191

HISTORICAL HIGHLIGHTS

1519 Spaniard Alonso Alvarez de Piñeda explores and maps Texas coast.

1528 After being shipwrecked, Cabeza de Vaca and party venture into Texas interior.

1541 Coronado and his party travel into West Texas.

1682 Spanish Franciscans build two missions near present-day city of El Paso.

1685 La Salle builds Fort St. Louis on coast.

1718 Spaniards found San Antonio de Valero mission, later called the Alamo, on San Antonio River.

1821 When Mexico gains independence from Spain, Texas becomes part of Republic of Mexico. Mexico allows Stephen F. Austin to bring Anglo-American settlers to Texas.

1835 Anglo-Americans revolt against Mexico.

1836 Americans are defeated at Battle of the Alamo, which pitted 184 Texans against several thousand Mexicans. Six weeks later, Texans win Battle of San Jacinto and form Republic of Texas.

1845 Texas enters the Union as the 28th state.

1861 Texas joins Confederacy.

1900 Hurricane in Galveston takes 6,000 lives.

1901 Spindletop oil field, near Beaumont, begins production, signaling the birth of the modern petroleum industry.

1947 Ship explosion at Texas City refinery dock kills 500 and injures 4,000.

1963 President John F. Kennedy is assassinated in Dallas. Vice President Lyndon B. Johnson, a former Texas senator, is sworn in as president.

1986 Drop in oil prices sends Texas economy into recession.

FAMOUS SONS AND DAUGHTERS

Stephen F. Austin (1793 – 1836). When Moses Austin died soon after being granted a charter to bring 300 Anglo-American families into Texas, his son Stephen stepped in and carried out the mission. Later he played a significant part in Texas's revolt against Mexico.

Sam Houston (1793 – 1863). This former congressman from Tennessee moved to Texas in 1833. As army commander, he liberated Texas from Mexico at the Battle of San Jacinto and later was elected first president of the new republic.

Howard Hughes (1905 – 76). After inheriting his father's Houston oil well supply business, Hughes became a motion picture producer, aviator, and America's best-known recluse. He was also one of the world's richest men.

Lyndon B. Johnson (1908 – 73). Raised on a Hill Country farm, this earthy, skillful politician rose from state politics to Congress to the presidency. He was the architect of the "Great Society" social programs.

Mary Martin (1914 – 90).

A voice and dance teacher from the town of Weatherford, Martin moved to New York City in the 1930's and later became the celebrated star of *Peter Pan* and other musicals.

Babe Didrickson Zaharias (1914 – 56). An extraordinary all-round athlete, Zaharias won two gold medals in track and field at the 1932 Olympics. Later she became a professional golfer, winning every major tournament before she died of cancer at age 42.

ODDITIES AND SPECIALTIES

Every fall, millions of people flock to State Fair Park in Dallas to attend the country's largest state fair. Greeting them is a talking, 52-foot-tall mechanical cowboy named Big Tex.

Chili, known locally as "a bowl o' red," is Texas's culinary gift to the world. It originated in the hills of south-central Texas in the mid-19th century.

Before oil was considered "black gold," workers drilling a city water well in Corsicana in 1894 were chagrined to find that their efforts yielded petroleum instead of water. But they soon found a way to make use of the state's first major oil strike, sprinkling the sticky fluid on city streets to keep the dust down.

A horned toad was found alive after 31 years in a time capsule at the Eastland County courthouse. Old Rip, now embalmed, is today on constant display in the courthouse foyer.

PLACES TO VISIT, THINGS TO DO

The Alamo (San Antonio).

The most famous battle of the Texas Revolution was fought over this old Spanish mission. The building, surrounded by skyscrapers in the heart of downtown, is open daily for tours.

Big Bend National Park (headquarters at Panther Junction). The Rio Grande has cut colorful canyons through the mountainous desert of West Texas. The area also hosts a wide assortment of plant life, including the giant dagger, a rare variety of yucca.

Guadalupe Mountains National Park (headquarters at Salt Flat). These low-slung mountains, remnants of an ancient ocean reef, contain historic Indian ruins, fossils, forests, canyons, desert, and Guadalupe Peak, the state's highest mountain.

Lyndon B. Johnson Space Center (Houston). The headquarters for NASA's spacecraft projects has extensive exhibits that include films and photos taken from space.

Padre Island National Seashore (headquarters at Corpus Christi). This flat, 80-mile-long barrier island draws shell collectors, snorkelers, and scuba divers, as well as sunbathers, to its sandy white shores.

Utah

Where the earth is sculpted into fantastic forms

Francisco Coronado was Spain's most ambitious conquistador, but even he had to admit defeat when it came to exploring Utah. In 1540 he reported to Mexico that the land north of the Grand Canyon was impenetrable desert unsuited to human habitation. For the next three centuries Utah largely remained a mysterious black hole on the North American continent. Not until 1843 did explorer John C. Frémont systematically survey the country "around which," he wrote, "the vague and superstitious accounts of trappers had thrown a delightful obscurity."

Frémont's reports described a severe and forbidding land filled with "rivers and lakes which have no communication with the sea" and "savage tribes which no traveler has seen or described." Thus forewarned, most American pioneers avoided the mountainous badlands. Those who entered, seeking a shortcut to California, soon wished they had not. Their suffering and misadventures became public lore through the lyrics of one of the West's most popular songs, "Sweet Betsy from Pike":

They came to the desert and salt water lakes,
The ground it was teemin' with varmints
*   and snakes,*
Beset by wild Indians, Comanche and Sioux,
'Tis a glorious tale how they ever got through!

THE FERTILE VALLEY

Brigham Young, president of the Church of Jesus Christ of Latter-day Saints — the Mormons — studied Frémont's reports and noted an intriguing fact. Nestled between the Great

The Anasazi pueblos of Utah overlooked a world of rock and sand. This scene, with the ruins of a granary in the foreground, is in Canyonlands National Park.

In Goosenecks State Park, a January snow brings the terraces of the San Juan River canyon into sharp relief. The river flows in symmetrical bends for six miles to cover a point-to-point distance of one mile.

Salt Lake Desert on the west, the towering Wasatch Range on the east, and the barren Colorado Plateau to the southeast was a large valley uninhabited by Indians. Moreover, the valley appeared to be a veritable oasis. Storms moving east dropped most of their moisture on the western slopes of the Wasatch Range, where mountain streams created fertile alluvial deltas that could produce enough food to support a considerable population.

In 1847 Young urged the Mormons to follow him to the Salt Lake Valley. By the end of

THE BEAUTY AND SPLENDOR OF NORTH AMERICA

Brigham Young's imperial vision ended in 1850 when Congress transformed Deseret into the territory of Utah. But the dismantling of the Mormon government did not diminish the church's position of primacy. Mormons still dominate the state's economy and politics.

Salt Lake City, the capital the Mormons built, is among the most orderly of America's metropolises. It seems immune even to traffic jams — Young laid out streets wide enough to turn a span of oxen.

The city takes its name from the Great Salt Lake, a shallow saline sea whose size has fluctuated dramatically over the centuries. During the Ice Age, when the lake was fed by glaciers, it was so large it covered all of northern Utah west of the Wasatch Range. Today, the silvery lake that remains is surrounded by enormous desert salt flats stippled with cactus and a series of terraces scoured into the mountain slopes by the waves of the once-vast inland sea.

FIVE NATIONAL PARKS

South of the Salt Lake Valley lies the rugged Colorado Plateau, thrust upward some 15 million years ago. Over time, rivers and the elements have carved the soft sandstone of the plateau into remarkably intricate forms, creating some of the most extraordinary landscapes

the first year more than 4,000 had answered the call, making the soon-to-be-proclaimed State of Deseret (from a word in the *Book of Mormon* that means honeybee) the first functioning theocracy since the early days of the Massachusetts Bay Colony.

Balanced Rock (left) is among the hundreds of unusual sandstone formations in Arches National Park. The park has the world's largest concentration of natural arches, some of which are seen here in the background.

on earth. Not surprisingly, southern Utah is the site of five national parks.

The first chunk of Utah scenery to be protected, in 1909, was Zion National Park, whose focal point is a canyon with sheer walls plunging 2,000 feet. Within a 330-mile drive to the northeast lie four other national parks: Bryce Canyon, a fantasyland of rose-colored pinnacles; Capitol Reef, some of whose formations reminded early American explorers of an ocean reef and the dome of the capitol in

Washington, D.C.; Canyonlands, a vast badlands of mesas and gorges; and Arches, named for its natural bridges of red sandstone.

Nearby, Monument Valley has scenery as magnificent as that of the parks — a series of huge red sandstone monoliths rising from the desert floor. Ever since John Ford filmed *Stagecoach* in 1938, these flat-topped giants have been used as a backdrop in dozens of western movies. Today they are among the most familiar icons of the American West.

THE MORMON CRICKET

Locusts, grasshoppers, and crickets inhabit every part of the United States. But in few places are they as unpredictable as in the arid regions west of the Rocky Mountains, where the hot weather and lack of food sometimes prompt them to migrate in great swarms. The early Mormons of Utah found that one variety was capable of inflicting a plague of biblical dimensions.

Certainly in the summer of 1848 it seemed that Brigham Young's infant settlement was the object of God's wrath, when millions of voracious crickets began advancing over the horizon. "We were a thousand miles from supplies, our provisions were giving out and what little we had grow-

ing was being eaten up," pioneer Priddy Meeks recalled in his autobiography.

As if in answer to the settlers' prayers, a flock of sea gulls appeared and began devouring the crickets. Each day the birds returned, until all of the insects were consumed. Wrote one diarist: "It seems the hand of the Lord is in our favor."

Though Utah's farmers use insecticides today to control the occasional invasions of the Mormon cricket, as it is now called, they have not forgotten the plague of the summer of 1848. Just east of Salt Lake City's Assembly Hall is a monument to the sea gulls (left), whose timely intervention is still considered a miracle.

A thin layer of galleta grass covers the South Desert in Capitol Reef National Park. Looming behind are the Henry Mountains.

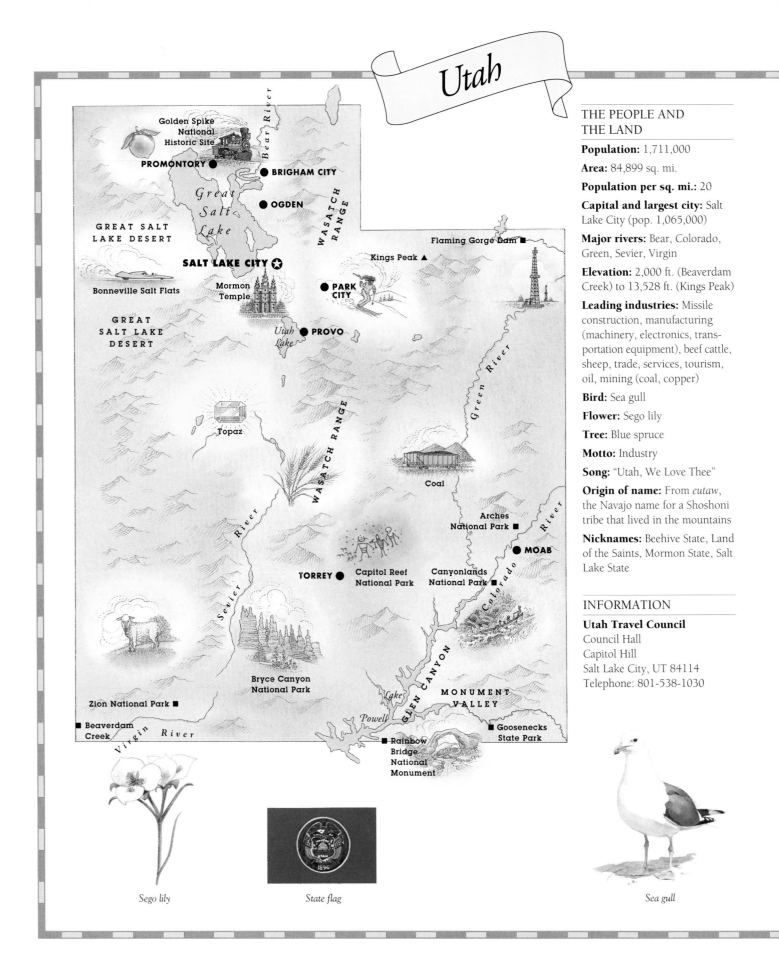

Utah

THE PEOPLE AND THE LAND

Population: 1,711,000

Area: 84,899 sq. mi.

Population per sq. mi.: 20

Capital and largest city: Salt Lake City (pop. 1,065,000)

Major rivers: Bear, Colorado, Green, Sevier, Virgin

Elevation: 2,000 ft. (Beaverdam Creek) to 13,528 ft. (Kings Peak)

Leading industries: Missile construction, manufacturing (machinery, electronics, transportation equipment), beef cattle, sheep, trade, services, tourism, oil, mining (coal, copper)

Bird: Sea gull

Flower: Sego lily

Tree: Blue spruce

Motto: Industry

Song: "Utah, We Love Thee"

Origin of name: From *eutaw*, the Navajo name for a Shoshoni tribe that lived in the mountains

Nicknames: Beehive State, Land of the Saints, Mormon State, Salt Lake State

INFORMATION

Utah Travel Council
Council Hall
Capitol Hill
Salt Lake City, UT 84114
Telephone: 801-538-1030

Map labels

Golden Spike National Historic Site
PROMONTORY
BRIGHAM CITY
OGDEN
Bear River
Great Salt Lake
GREAT SALT LAKE DESERT
SALT LAKE CITY
WASATCH RANGE
Flaming Gorge Dam
Kings Peak
Bonneville Salt Flats
Mormon Temple
PARK CITY
GREAT SALT LAKE DESERT
Utah Lake
PROVO
Green River
Topaz
WASATCH RANGE
Coal
Sevier River
Arches National Park
Colorado River
MOAB
TORREY
Capitol Reef National Park
Canyonlands National Park
Bryce Canyon National Park
Zion National Park
Beaverdam Creek
Virgin River
Lake Powell
GLEN CANYON
Rainbow Bridge National Monument
MONUMENT VALLEY
Goosenecks State Park

Sego lily

State flag

Sea gull

HISTORICAL HIGHLIGHTS

1776 Franciscans Francisco Atanasio Dominguez and Silvestre Velez de Escalante explore region.

1826 Jedediah Smith leads trading party across Utah.

1837 Antoine Robidoux builds Utah's first trading post on Green River.

1847 Brigham Young brings Mormon pioneers to the fertile valley east of the Great Salt Lake.

1849 Mormons establish the State of Deseret.

1850 Congress designates Utah a U.S. territory.

1855 Population grows from 10,000 to 60,000 in five years.

1857 Army troops accompany governor sent to Utah to replace Brigham Young.

1869 First transcontinental railroad is completed at Promontory.

1890 Mormon leaders renounce polygamy.

1896 Utah enters Union as the 45th state.

1911 Strawberry Reservoir diverts Colorado River to provide power and irrigation.

1952 Uranium deposits are discovered near Moab.

1964 Flaming Gorge Dam on Green River begins generating electrical power and spurs industrial growth.

1977 In first U.S. execution in 10 years, Gary Gilmore is killed by firing squad in Provo.

1985 Great Salt Lake floods area.

FAMOUS SONS AND DAUGHTERS

Maude Adams (1872 – 1953). One of the most beloved of American actresses, Adams made her first appearance on stage at the age of nine months. Her most famous role was in *Peter Pan*.

John Moses Browning (1855 – 1926). Son of a Mormon gunsmith, this inventor developed the Browning automatic rifle, which became a standard army shoulder weapon from 1918 until the late 1950's.

Philo T. Farnsworth (1906 – 71). Farnsworth invented an electronic camera tube that became known as the image dissector. The dissector was later combined with other technology to create modern television.

George Romney (1907 –). Romney grew up in Utah and held high positions in the Mormon Church. After serving as president of American Motors, he became governor of Michigan and U.S. secretary of housing and urban development under President Richard M. Nixon.

Brigham Young (1801 – 77).

Young rose to leadership of the Mormon Church after founder Joseph Smith's assassination. He established and headed the community in Salt Lake City.

ODDITIES AND SPECIALTIES

In Zion National Park live canyon frogs, whose bleat is often mistaken for that of a sheep's, and tiny Zion snails, found only here.

The Bonneville Salt Flats provide an ideal surface for racing cars — a 12-mile strip of tightly packed salt that is almost like concrete. World speed records have been set here.

When frontier scout Jim Bridger tasted the water of the Great Salt Lake in 1824, he mistook the lake for an ocean. Actually, it has a higher saline content than either the Atlantic or Pacific oceans.

Communities in agriculturally rich Box Elder County celebrate the harvest every year with such festivals as Peach Days and Wheat and Beet Days.

Utah is a rockhound's dream, an endless source of agate, obsidian, and other stones. The world's largest topaz beds lie just west of the Little Sahara Recreation Area.

PLACES TO VISIT, THINGS TO DO

Arches National Park (headquarters at Moab). More than 2,000 sandstone arches stand alongside balanced rocks, pinnacles, and other formations in this unique landscape.

Bryce Canyon National Park (near Panguitch). The vertical, deeply eroded formations of red sandstone here resemble everything from standing crowds of people to cathedrals.

Canyonlands National Park (headquarters at Moab). The Colorado and Green rivers, along with wind and rain, slowly sculpted these chasms, mesas, and the dramatic range of pinnacles known as The Needles.

Capitol Reef National Park (near Torrey). Embracing a long bulge in the earth's crust called the Waterpocket Fold, this park has monolithic cliffs, some with figure drawings that were made by Fremont Indians more than 700 years ago.

Glen Canyon National Recreation Area (south-central Utah). Lake Powell, the nation's second-largest man-made lake, is surrounded by the red sandstone cliffs of Glen Canyon. Among the attractions is Rainbow Bridge, a massive natural arch.

Golden Spike National Historic Site (32 miles west of Brigham City). Every May 10, local citizens celebrate the completion of the transcontinental railroad in 1869 and reenact the driving of the last spike. Period locomotives and other railroad exhibits are on display from May to September.

Park City Ski Area (Park City). This ski resort, Utah's largest, is one of nine within an hour's drive of Salt Lake City. Also near Park City are the resorts of Park West and Deer Valley.

Temple Square (Salt Lake City). This 10-acre center of the Mormon faith includes such architecturally impressive buildings as the six-spired Mormon Temple, imposing Tabernacle, and picturesque Assembly Hall.

Zion National Park (headquarters at Springdale). Waterfalls and hanging gardens adorn Zion Canyon, a 2,500-foot-deep chasm carved by the Virgin River. Lofty cliffs and templelike formations add to the grandeur.

Vermont

*Green mountains, green valleys —
America's northern Eden*

To find solace from the hectic life of cities and suburbs, Americans often head to places where, it is said, "time seems to have stopped," places where vestiges of a slower era still exist. In Vermont, time not only stopped, it went backward. Hills and valleys that were once stripped bare of trees for agriculture turned green again as forests reclaimed abandoned fields and pastures. Moose, salmon, and the peregrine falcon, which were chased from the region decades ago, have started to come back, though the lordly mountain lion may never be seen here again.

NORMAN ROCKWELL'S AMERICA

In the 1800's, farmers gave up on the thin, stony soil and ventured either west or to the state's industrial centers. Fortunately, the handsome, sturdy buildings of Vermont's small towns survived. White church spires, outlined against a green hillside, continue to preside over peaceful town commons, where these days groups of touring bicyclists pause to rest. Both the places and the people of Vermont provided Norman Rockwell with the subjects for some of his most famous works — paintings that virtually define the popular notion of what it was to be an American in a small town in the days when time passed with sweet slowness.

The poet Robert Frost, who lived for a while in South Shaftsbury in the 1920's, said that Vermont is "a state in a natural state." To outsiders it does seem that Vermont has managed to reclaim some stake on a preindustrial Eden. Native Vermonters, however, can be

An early morning mist hovers over East Corinth, in central Vermont. The quiet charm so evident here is shared by villages all across the Vermont landscape.

In autumn, the trees lining virtually every roadside in Vermont explode with colors as brilliant as those in the showiest flower gardens. This route winds through Jacksonville, in southern Vermont, where a white table wine is made from the juice of locally grown apples.

The Middlebury River, a favorite of swimmers in summer, is clothed in snow and ice as it journeys down the Green Mountains in winter.

and Mount Mansfield one can find holdouts of alpine tundra left over from the Ice Age. Red spruce trees grow in the colder northern areas and at high elevations. As tough as they are, these trees are sensitive to pollution. It was an analysis of dying red spruce trees on Camels Hump that first demonstrated the effects of acid rain on our forests.

Today the sugar maple is the most common hardwood species in Vermont. It is sap from this tree that gives Vermont its maple syrup, the balm that brings a dollop of cheer to mud season. On the other end of the calendar, it will be the sugar maple that puts on the spectacular show of reds and purples for which the state is famous. Botanists who have studied the secret workings of autumnal beauty have discovered that an accumulation of sugar gives these leaves their vibrant colors. It is sweetness itself that blazes across Vermont in the fall.

Pumpkins shine beneath a moody sky at the Ethan Allen homestead in Burlington.

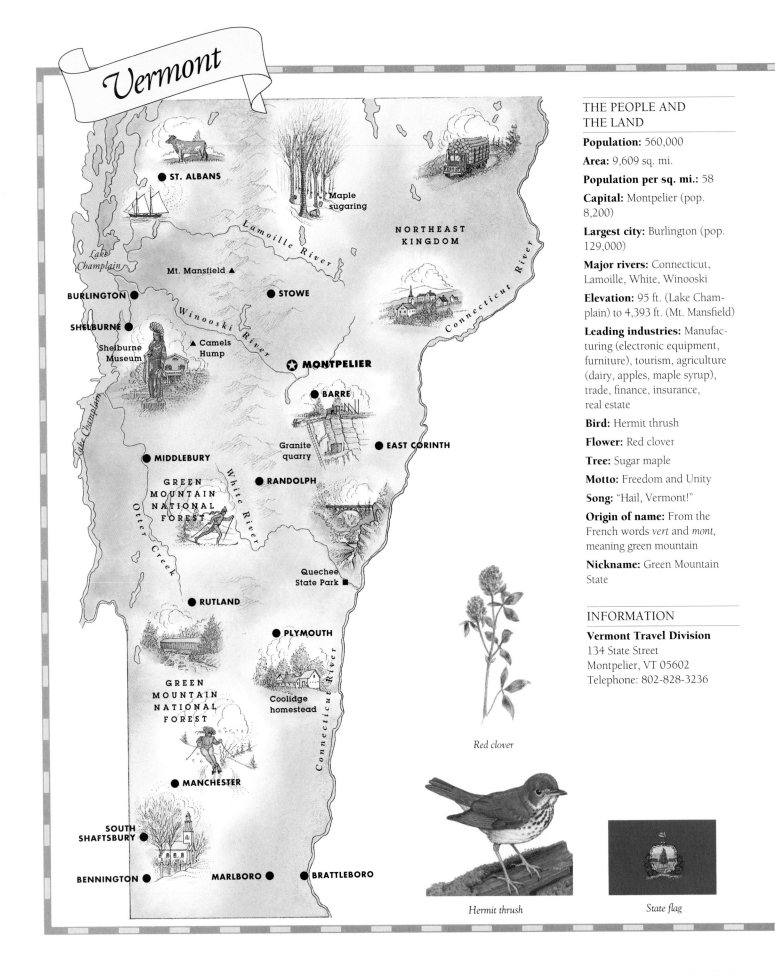

Vermont

ST. ALBANS

Maple sugaring

NORTHEAST KINGDOM

Lamoille River

Lake Champlain

Mt. Mansfield ▲

BURLINGTON

STOWE

Winooski River

Connecticut River

SHELBURNE

Shelburne Museum

▲ Camels Hump

★ **MONTPELIER**

BARRE

Granite quarry

EAST CORINTH

MIDDLEBURY

White River

GREEN MOUNTAIN NATIONAL FOREST

RANDOLPH

Otter Creek

Lake Champlain

Quechee State Park ■

RUTLAND

PLYMOUTH

Connecticut River

GREEN MOUNTAIN NATIONAL FOREST

Coolidge homestead

MANCHESTER

SOUTH SHAFTSBURY

BENNINGTON

MARLBORO

BRATTLEBORO

THE PEOPLE AND THE LAND

Population: 560,000

Area: 9,609 sq. mi.

Population per sq. mi.: 58

Capital: Montpelier (pop. 8,200)

Largest city: Burlington (pop. 129,000)

Major rivers: Connecticut, Lamoille, White, Winooski

Elevation: 95 ft. (Lake Champlain) to 4,393 ft. (Mt. Mansfield)

Leading industries: Manufacturing (electronic equipment, furniture), tourism, agriculture (dairy, apples, maple syrup), trade, finance, insurance, real estate

Bird: Hermit thrush

Flower: Red clover

Tree: Sugar maple

Motto: Freedom and Unity

Song: "Hail, Vermont!"

Origin of name: From the French words *vert* and *mont*, meaning green mountain

Nickname: Green Mountain State

INFORMATION

Vermont Travel Division
134 State Street
Montpelier, VT 05602
Telephone: 802-828-3236

Red clover

Hermit thrush

State flag

HISTORICAL HIGHLIGHTS

1609 Samuel de Champlain claims area for France and discovers Lake Champlain.

1724 First permanent settlement is built at Fort Dummer (present-day Brattleboro).

1764 New York gains jurisdiction over Vermont.

1770 Green Mountain Boys, led by Ethan Allen, drive New York settlers from Vermont.

1775 Green Mountain Boys help capture Fort Ticonderoga from British forces.

1777 Vermont declares independence from Great Britain and prohibits slavery in its constitution.

1791 Vermont joins Union as 14th state.

1823 Opening of Champlain Canal links Vermont to Hudson River and New York City.

1864 Confederate soldiers raid St. Albans.

1923 Calvin Coolidge accedes to presidency.

1934 Nation's first ski tow is built in Woodstock.

1940 First chair lift makes its ascent on Mt. Mansfield.

1970 Environmental Control Act limits major developments.

1984 State elects its first woman governor, Madeleine M. Kunin.

FAMOUS SONS AND DAUGHTERS

Ethan Allen (1738 – 89). As leader of the Green Mountain Boys, organized to keep New York from taking over Vermont land, Allen had a price put on his head by New York's governor. In 1775, Allen was taken by the British and held captive in Canada for nearly three years.

Chester A. Arthur (1830 – 86). Arthur became president when James Garfield was assassinated in 1881. Though a machine politician, he was known for his honesty and efficiency.

Calvin Coolidge (1872 – 1933). The embodiment of Republican conservatism, "Silent Cal" was elected Warren G. Harding's vice president in 1920. When Harding died in 1923 Coolidge succeeded him in office.

George Dewey (1837 – 1917). Dewey's naval maneuvers in the Battle of Manila Bay in 1898, in which he swiftly defeated the Spanish fleet, made him a hero of the Spanish-American War.

John Dewey (1859 – 1952). A philosopher and psychologist, Dewey is best known for his influence on American education. His principles were the basis for the progressive education movement.

Dorothy Canfield Fisher (1879 – 1958). This writer celebrated Vermont life in novels and other books. But neither her outlook nor her life was provincial. She wrote books on the Montessori method of education and, during World War I, moved to France to do war work.

ODDITIES AND SPECIALTIES

Only three Vermont cities — Bennington, Burlington, and Rutland — have more than 15,000 people. Montpelier is the smallest capital city in the nation.

Starting in the 1850's, Vermonters chose only Republican candidates for Congress, governor, and president. This remarkable consistency was broken in 1958 for Congress, 1962 for governor, and 1964 for president.

The world's largest granite quarry, 350 feet deep and covering 20 acres, is in Barre. Vermont also boasts the country's largest marble-production center, at Proctor. The Lincoln Memorial is made of Vermont marble.

Given Vermont's many dairy farms, it's no surprise that the state produces over 100 million pounds of cheese a year, including its famous Cheddar.

George Washington granted the first U.S. patent to Pittsford resident Samuel Hopkins, who made potash out of wood ashes.

The Morgan horse is Vermont's state animal.

PLACES TO VISIT, THINGS TO DO

Camels Hump State Park and Forest (Huntington Center). Trails lead to the summit of Camels Hump and a sweeping view of Lake Champlain.

Green Mountain National Forest (headquarters at Rutland). Encompassing much of the Green Mountains, this 295,000-acre forest has miles of scenic roads and, for hikers, the 261-mile Long Trail that winds through the length of the state.

Lake Champlain (west Vermont). Several choice areas, including Burton Island and Sand Bar state parks, offer many opportunities for water sports.

Marlboro Music Festival World-famous performing artists play chamber music on the Marlboro College campus every July and August.

Mt. Mansfield State Forest (between Stowe and Jefferson). This forest includes the state's highest peak and Smuggler's Notch, a deep, scenic gorge.

Quechee State Park (White River Junction). The beautiful, mile-long Quechee Gorge is lined with hemlock, wild columbine, violets, and asters.

Shelburne Museum (Shelburne). Preserved here is Electra Webb's collection of Americana, including 37 restored buildings, a covered bridge, an old railroad station, and the paddle wheeler S.S. *Ticonderoga*.

Skiing Vermont's 24 alpine and nearly 50 cross-country ski areas, including the popular Stowe, have some of the best slopes in the Northeast.

Sugarhouses From late February into April, watch the process of turning maple sap to syrup and sample the results.

Virginia

The gracious home of America's forefathers

Virginia's many nicknames — Old Dominion, Mother of Presidents, Mother of States — attest to the state's deep roots in American history. It was in Virginia in 1607 that Jamestown, the first permanent English colony in America, was founded. Eight of America's presidents were born in Virginia, and eight other states, in whole or in part, were carved out of Virginia's original territory. Two great wars ended on Virginia soil — the Revolutionary War at Yorktown and the Civil War at Appomattox.

THE PAST PRESERVED

The flavor of Virginia's past is nowhere more evident than in Colonial Williamsburg. When Williamsburg was the state capital, between 1699 and 1780, it was the busiest city in the colonies, but it fell into a decline after 1780. Not until the 1920's was the town brought back to life. Teams of experts followed a 1781 "Frenchman's Map" and copied minute architectural details supplied by a 1740 copperplate engraving of the city. Today, with block after block of restored and reconstructed buildings, the town is a living time capsule showing life as it was in colonial days.

Williamsburg is set amid the low, sandy plain known as the Tidewater. Roads with names like the "Plantation Route" and "Colonial Parkway" lead to former battlefields, historic towns, and stately plantations along the James River. At the Tidewater's southern limits, the James flows by the naval ships at Norfolk and empties into the Chesapeake Bay.

The solitude and simplicity of rural life in old Virginia are evoked by this log cabin built on the densely wooded shores of the Dan River, near Danville.

Dense forests and lush, rolling fields are beautifully intermingled in much of western Virginia's Shenandoah Valley. One of America's first frontiers, the rich valley was called "the breadbasket of the Confederacy," and today is host to some two million visitors a year.

THE BEAUTY AND SPLENDOR OF NORTH AMERICA

Just across the bay lies Virginia's Eastern Shore, a section of the long Delmarva Peninsula that the state shares with Delaware and Maryland. It is occupied by salt marshes, truck farms, fishing villages, and windswept dunes. Parallel to the peninsula are the barrier islands of Chincoteague and Assateague, sanctuaries for herons, ospreys, and other wildlife.

A HERITAGE OF STATELY HOMES

Northern Virginia, though close to the hubbub of greater Washington, D.C., is not without its islands of serenity too. Across the Potomac from the nation's capital, Arlington National Cemetery occupies the land once owned by Robert E. Lee. Nearby are the now-tranquil sites of bloody Civil War battles: Chancellorsville, Fredericksburg, and Manassas (or Bull Run). In autumn, the baying of hounds can be heard in the green valleys of hunt country, where red-coated equestrians have chased foxes since George Washington's day.

South of Washington, D.C., lies Mount Vernon, the plantation home of George Washington for some 45 years. An excellent farmer, Washington was also a tireless host who in 1785 alone entertained well over 400 dinner guests at his beloved estate.

In Virginia's midsection a wide, fertile plateau of farms and forests extends from the Tidewater in the east to the Blue Ridge in the west. Interspersed among vineyards, tobacco fields, and peach orchards are thriving cities like Richmond, the lovely capital overlooking the falls of the James River. A French architect, together with America's most esteemed Renaissance man, Thomas Jefferson, created its distinctive capitol building. Jefferson's architectural legacy continues beyond Richmond. In Charlottesville is his celebrated home, Monticello, which he meticulously built and rebuilt over a period of 40 years.

"DAUGHTER OF THE STARS"

To the west of the Blue Ridge Mountains, the beautiful Shenandoah Valley stretches for more than 200 miles from Winchester in the north to Roanoke in the south. Viewed from Skyline

A lone school bus makes its way over the hills of Highland County in a remote part of western Virginia, where sheep outnumber people. Old-fashioned rail fences like the one along this roadside originated in old Virginia.

Elegant cascades adorn the Upper Doyle River Falls in Shenandoah National Park.

THE FLOWERS OF DARKNESS

South of Front Royal, in the Shenandoah Valley, are caves containing lovely and mysterious underground treasures. Called anthodites by geologists, these mineral formations, found on the ceilings of rooms in Skyline Caverns, are popularly known as cave flowers.

The formations grow in fragile clusters made up of thin needles of snow-white calcite up to four inches long. The slender projections radiate in all directions, defying the law of gravity, and the shapes they take suggest delicate blossoms.

Estimated to grow at a rate of only one inch every 7,000 years, the cave flowers are, to say the least, irreplaceable. To reach them, visitors must pass through a double set of doors, which keep bats from entering the chamber and causing dam-

age. If well cared for, the cave flowers will be on view for some time to come — perhaps even seven millennia from now, when they will be an inch longer.

Drive, the valley (whose Indian name means "daughter of the stars") presents a broad, colorful patchwork of vineyards, apple orchards, emerald pastures, and fields of grain.

The valley was carved by an ancient sea,

which left behind spectacular limestone formations, including the famous Natural Bridge and Luray Caverns. In the early 1800's, Grand Caverns was the scene of candlelit dances held in a ballroom-sized "grand hall," and during the Civil War, Stonewall Jackson's troops camped in the caves. No corner of Virginia — not even its darkest subterranean realms — has remained untouched by the pageant of American history.

Oaks tower over neat rows of young corn in a field near Tazewell, in southwestern Virginia.

HISTORICAL HIGHLIGHTS

1607 Jamestown, first permanent English settlement in America, is founded.

1619 House of Burgesses, America's first representative legislature, convenes. Dutch traders bring Africans to sell as indentured servants.

1693 College of William and Mary, named for the king and queen of England, is founded.

1781 Britain's Lord Cornwallis surrenders at Yorktown, ending Revolutionary War.

1788 Virginia enters Union as 10th state.

1789 George Washington becomes first U.S. president.

1831 Nat Turner's rebellion leads to stricter slavery laws.

1861 Virginia secedes from Union. Richmond becomes Confederate capital.

1863 Northwestern Virginia splits off to join Union, forming West Virginia.

1865 General Lee surrenders at Appomattox, ending Civil War.

1902 A new state constitution disenfranchises blacks by instituting a poll tax and a literacy test.

1918 College of William and Mary admits women.

1959 The first school integration in Virginia history takes place.

1964 Chesapeake Bay Bridge – Tunnel links Norfolk/Virginia Beach to Eastern Shore.

1969 A Republican governor is elected, the first since 1869.

1971 A new, more liberal state constitution goes into effect.

1989 L. Douglas Wilder becomes the first elected black governor in U.S. history.

FAMOUS SONS AND DAUGHTERS

Richard E. Byrd (1888 – 1957). A daring and renowned aviator, Byrd, along with Floyd Bennett, was first to fly over the North Pole. He later led several U.S. expeditions to Antarctica.

Patrick Henry (1736 – 99). A brilliant orator, Henry spoke out for liberty at the time of the American Revolution. He also served as governor of the Commonwealth of Virginia.

Robert E. Lee (1807 – 70). General Lee, who led the Confederate armies during the Civil War, not only was idolized in the South but was also greatly respected in the North.

Cyrus H. McCormick (1809 – 84). McCormick succeeded where his father had failed, in inventing the first mechanical reaper, which revolutionized grain harvesting.

Edgar Allan Poe (1809 – 49). A brilliant critic, poet, and fiction writer, Poe is best known for his macabre short stories.

Walter Reed (1851 – 1902). While working in Havana, this U.S. army surgeon demonstrated that yellow fever was transmitted by a mosquito.

Booker T. Washington (1856 – 1915). The eminent black educator founded Tuskegee Institute in Alabama and wrote many books, including *Up From Slavery*, his autobiography.

ODDITIES AND SPECIALTIES

Virginia Beach has managed to combine trash disposal with public beautification. The city covered a 70-foot-high mound of garbage with soil and landscaped it to create a park, called Mt. Trashmore.

Eight U.S. presidents were born in Virginia: George Washington, Thomas Jefferson, James Madison, James Monroe, William Henry Harrison, John Tyler, Zachary Taylor, and Woodrow Wilson.

Loudoun County is the home of fox-hunting and steeplechasing, equestrian sports whose roots go back further in Virginia than in any other state — all the way to the 17th century.

The smell of hickory smoke pervades the town of Smithfield, where a secret curing process produces the distinctive flavor of Smithfield ham.

Chincoteague Island is known both for its salt oysters and its finely crafted duck decoys.

In the mountains of southwestern Virginia, fiddlers and other musicians play in a traditional style, called Old Time, which is similar to bluegrass and can be traced back to Great Britain.

George Washington carved his initials on it. Thomas Jefferson bought it. The Monocan Indians worshiped it. Today Natural Bridge is called one of the seven natural wonders of the world.

Virginia is dubbed the Mother of States because land from its original territory now makes up, wholly or in part, the states of Illinois, Indiana, Kentucky, Michigan, Minnesota, Ohio, West Virginia, and Wisconsin.

PLACES TO VISIT, THINGS TO DO

Luray Caverns (near Luray). This huge cave abounds in colorful formations reflected in clear pools. Visitors are amazed by an organ whose tone-producing pipes are stalactites.

Plantations along the James River Among the many historic plantations in this area are Berkeley, birthplace of President William Henry Harrison, and Carter's Grove, an elegant Georgian mansion.

Shenandoah National Park (Luray). Stretching for some 105 miles through the Blue Ridge Mountains, the park is an untamed wilderness endowed with waterfalls and wildflowers.

Skyline Drive and Blue Ridge Parkway Splendid vistas are commonplace along this drive through Shenandoah National Park, the George Washington and Jefferson national forests, and the Blue Ridge Mountains.

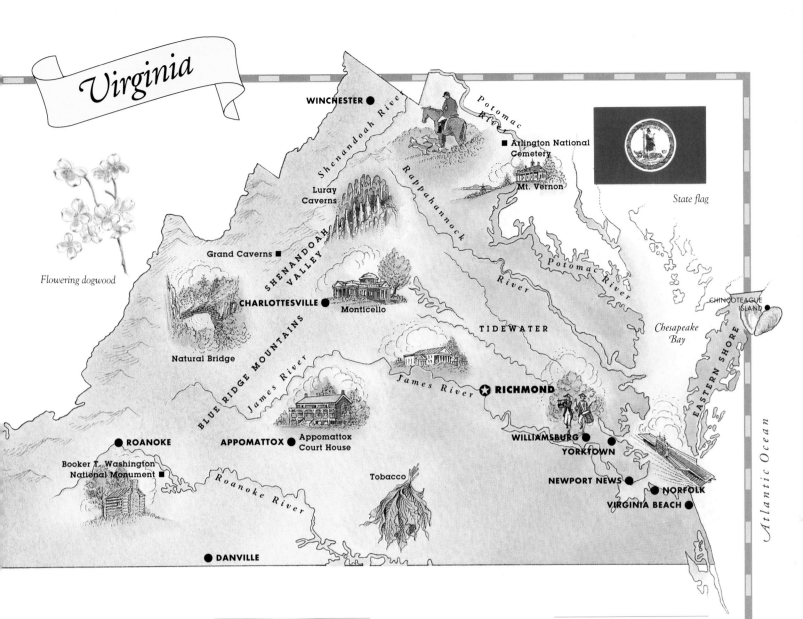

Virginia

WINCHESTER

Shenandoah River

Potomac Rio

Arlington National Cemetery

Mt. Vernon

State flag

Rappahannock River

Luray Caverns

Potomac River

Flowering dogwood

Grand Caverns

CHINCOTEAGUE ISLAND

SHENANDOAH VALLEY

Chesapeake Bay

CHARLOTTESVILLE

Monticello

TIDEWATER

EASTERN SHORE

Natural Bridge

BLUE RIDGE MOUNTAINS

James River

James River

★ RICHMOND

Atlantic Ocean

ROANOKE

APPOMATTOX

Appomattox Court House

WILLIAMSBURG

YORKTOWN

Booker T. Washington National Monument

Tobacco

NEWPORT NEWS

NORFOLK

Roanoke River

VIRGINIA BEACH

DANVILLE

Williamsburg Historic District
The first and finest of America's restored towns, Colonial Williamsburg takes visitors back in time, allowing them to experience everyday life in early America.

THE PEOPLE AND THE LAND

Population: 6,128,000

Area: 40,767 sq. mi.

Population per sq. mi.: 150

Capital: Richmond (pop. 844,300)

Largest city: Norfolk – Virginia Beach – Newport News (pop. 1,380,000)

Major rivers: James, Potomac, Rappahannock, Roanoke, Shenandoah, York

Elevation: Sea level to 5,729 ft. (Mt. Rogers)

Leading industries: Government and community services, trade, manufacturing (textiles, transportation equipment, electronics, food processing, chemicals), agriculture (tobacco), coal mining

Bird: Cardinal

Flower: Flowering dogwood

Tree: Flowering dogwood

Motto: *Sic Semper Tyrannis* (Thus Always to Tyrants)

Song: "Carry Me Back to Old Virginia"

Origin of name: For Queen Elizabeth I, "Virgin Queen" of England, by Sir Walter Raleigh

Nicknames: Cavalier State, Mother of Presidents, Mother of States, Mother of Statesmen, Old Dominion

INFORMATION

Virginia Division of Tourism
1021 East Cary Street
Richmond, VA 23219
Telephone: 804-786-4484

Cardinal

VIRGINIA

445

Washington

The picture-perfect corner of the Northwest

The classic postcard picture of Washington is a photographer's dream — glistening, snow-white mountains looming over a wilderness of evergreens. But that much-reproduced image presents only one side of this state in the Pacific Northwest. Like neighboring Oregon, Washington is divided by a mighty mountain range into two quite different worlds: lush alpine landscapes to the west; semiarid plains and hills to the east.

The Cascade Range forms this great divide, running from north to south in a broad band of tall peaks, glacial lakes, and thickly wooded valleys. No fewer than three national parks, two of them in Washington and one in Oregon, have been marked out in the most spectacular stretches of the range.

In the north, extending down from the Canadian border, is North Cascades National Park, site of some 750 of the 1,100-odd glaciers found in the lower 48 states. Grinding away for millennia, the glaciers have worked the granite mountains into sharp points. Climbers who meet the challenge of Mount Terror, Mount Triumph, and other park summits are rewarded with a stunning sight — the icebound Cascades receding into the distance like the breaking waves of an ocean, for as far as the eye can see.

THE MOUNTAIN

As the great range moves southward it becomes less rugged, though no less spectacular. Crowning the southern Cascades is the glacier-clad volcano that Washingtonians simply call

A hiker threads through boulders and fallen trees to approach the beach at Cape Flattery, the point of land at the extreme northwest corner of the state.

In April, tulips bloom in the commercial flower fields south and east of Puget Sound. These red specimens grow in Skagit Flats, one of the largest bulb-producing areas in the world.

A month-old cougar kitten explores the world in Okanogan National Forest in northeastern Washington.

the Mountain, known to the rest of the world as Mount Rainier. The immense white cone, centerpiece of the state's second national park, dominates the south-central Washington landscape. It is visible on clear days from more than 100 miles away. Seen from Seattle skyscrapers, the distant Rainier seems to float among the clouds.

Two more volcanoes punctuate the southern Cascades. One is Mount Adams, which geologists think may still be active. The other is Mount St. Helens, the restless giant that achieved the notoriety of a Vesuvius in 1980 when it blasted away 1,200 feet of its summit and devastated the surrounding countryside with ash and debris.

A NEW TERRITORY

The world west of the Cascades is moist and green, a place of huge trees and legendary lumberjacks. It was here that pioneers first settled.

Once part of Oregon Territory, this timberland bore its first real wave of white settlement when "Oregon fever" swept the country in the 1840's. Most pioneers made their way

The rain forests of Olympic National Park sustain vegetation that is among the most luxuriant on the continent. Here a bigleaf maple, its gnarled branches lying prone, is enveloped in club moss and huckleberry fern.

West Virginia

High in the mountains, deep forests and a love of home

Take me home, country roads" — so go the lyrics to a song about West Virginia popularized by John Denver. There is something about this state — the most mountainous east of the Mississippi River — that taps the American longing for home, summoning up the taste of hot buttered biscuits, the whine of a lonesome fiddle, and the creak of a rocking chair out on the front porch.

West Virginia is mountain country. The Blue Ridge cuts across the state's eastern neck, while the Allegheny Plateau dominates the interior. Looking west from the tiny hamlets near the Virginia border, you can see ridge after ridge rising toward a line of distant summits silhouetted against the sky.

The first settlers who trickled into the area in the early 1700's from Pennsylvania and the Atlantic coast put down roots in valleys carved out by rampaging rivers. There they cleared pastures for their cows and found hunting grounds in the virgin forests that swathed the surrounding hillsides. After they broke away from Virginia in 1861 at the start of the Civil War, their state became the first and only one to be formed through secession.

NATURE'S PAGEANT

Now, as in the past, nature is the state's main event. Springtime is always awash in ethereal clouds of pink crabapple and white hawthorn. Black-eyed Susans, daisies, and goldenrod dot the roadsides during the halcyon days of summer. A circus pageant of color transforms the mountains with the turning leaves of autumn.

Despite its rugged appearance, 63-foot-high Blackwater Falls near the northern edge of Monongahela National Forest is accessible year-round via an easy path.

And in winter, the highlands fall under the white grip of snow, as much as 100 inches of it annually along the Alleghenies.

Eastern West Virginia is a place so high and wild that in some of its most sequestered corners, like Cranberry Glades and the Dolly Sods Wilderness Area, the heath barrens and waist-deep bogs seem almost subarctic. The mountains are blanketed in awe-inspiring forests — spruce, hemlock, oak, and hickory — where black bears, gray and red foxes, and wildcats lurk in the dense shade. A stand of 300-year-old virgin red spruce at Gaudineer Knob is a stately vestige of the primeval woodlands the pioneers encountered.

To the west, the state is speckled with small farms and quiet hamlets tilting down the western slopes of the Alleghenies toward the Ohio River. The presence of pure silica sand made glassmaking a major industry throughout the northwestern part of the state, while hulking steel mills mushroomed around the northern panhandle city of Wheeling.

South of Charleston is coal country, where miners descend into a dark and chilly subterranean world to hack out more than 40 percent of all the bituminous coal the United States produces. Here also is one of America's wildest waterways, the New River, a playground for white-water rafters. Contrary to its name, the New may be the second-oldest river in the world, dating from the Cenozoic era 65 million years ago, when it began carving a gorge now 700 to 1,300 feet deep.

Periodically in recent decades, West Virginians have seen their progeny move away with fluxes in the coal and lumber markets. But their culture has endured in the whirling colors of handmade quilts, bittersweet folk tunes, the breathless glee of a clog dance, and the graceful curves of an Appalachian basket. Residents view their state with wry good humor. As one old-timer quipped, "It's right spread out, and it's might rough; but it's a damned good state for the shape it's in." Above all, it is a place that speaks to a yearning for peace and independence, dual needs that are perfectly satisfied by the picture of a winding country road leading home in the mountains of West Virginia.

Sunrise is peaceful along the Cranberry River high on the Allegheny Plateau. A favorite haunt of backpackers, the Cranberry wilderness also attracts fishermen, who enjoy its many trout streams.

Shy but playful, a young foal snuggles against its mother, as fresh and full of promise as the surrounding springtime pasture.

THE BEAUTY AND SPLENDOR OF NORTH AMERICA

The restored pioneer farm at Twin Falls State Park recalls the settlers whose commitment reshaped a wilderness into a place they made their home.

Wisconsin

Rolling pastureland and cool north woods

On the map of America the fist of Wisconsin delivers an uppercut to Lake Superior while its thumb pokes out, like a hitchhiker's, into Lake Michigan. That hand is a beautiful appendage, clothed in cool north woods and rolling green pastureland and studded with diamond-blue glacial lakes. The quiet Mississippi, which delineates much of Wisconsin's western border, is edged with dramatic limestone and sandstone bluffs. Other rivers twine through the deep forests, sometimes driven to frothy rage by melting snow.

A MOVE TO CONSERVE

From the beginning, this luxuriant, river-scored land possessed a seemingly inexhaustible inventory of natural abundance — fur-bearing animals, towering white pines, whitefish and lake trout by the millions, and loamy soil for farming. Within a century of white settlement, however, the cornucopia no longer overflowed. By the 1870's wheat farmers had depleted the soil of southern Wisconsin. Ten years later the Milwaukee River had become so defiled with raw sewage that fish could not live in it. And by the turn of the century, most of Wisconsin's virgin white pines had been cut to the ground.

Precisely because its splendid landscapes were being marred by the hand of man, Wisconsin took an early lead in the incipient American conservation movement. The state fostered some of the crusade's most farsighted and charismatic leaders. William Dempster Hoard used his newspaper, *Hoard's Dairyman*, to convince farmers to stop growing wheat

Dairy farms, here awash in October fog, occupy the rolling land near the hamlet of Cassville in the southwest corner of Wisconsin.

Rock-strewn streams are among the sights along the Ice Age National Scenic Trail, which marks the farthest advance of the last glacier that pushed into Wisconsin. The glacier, the Wisconsinan, covered much of the state up until about 10,000 years ago.

and to take up dairying instead. By doing so, they not only rescued the soil but also secured Wisconsin's economic future as the nation's prime producer of milk, butter, and cheese. Another man, a Scottish immigrant named John Muir, spent his boyhood on a farm in the hills of south-central Wisconsin before going on to become an esteemed naturalist and the founder of the Sierra Club.

One of the earliest environmental victories in America was the fight to save the 32,000-acre Horicon Marsh. Horicon and the other wetlands in Wisconsin were first seen only as an impediment to agriculture, and many tracts were drained in an effort to extend farmland. But in the 1920's Wisconsin conservationists banded together to restore the marsh to its natural state and sought federal and state protection for the land. Situated only 50 miles northwest of Milwaukee, Horicon is now one of the largest freshwater cattail marshes in the United States. It teems with wildlife — otters,

herons, migrating Canada geese, and the imperiled redheaded duck.

Beyond the wetlands, the splendor of Wisconsin is apparent on the shores of the Great Lakes. Door Peninsula, Wisconsin's hitchhiking thumb, is strung with rocky coves and fishing villages reminiscent of the New England coastline. Just off the tip of the peninsula is Washington Island, a craggy outpost that offers sweeping views of Lake Michigan from its majestic limestone cliffs.

At the far north of the state, offshore from the little Victorian lakeport of Bayfield, is a cluster of 22 islands called the Apostles. Standing in Lake Superior like sculpted brownstone platforms, these islands support dense forests of white pine, birch, spruce, and cedar. All but one are now protected as Apostle Islands National Lakeshore. On these wild fragments of land a visitor can enjoy the untouched beauty that residents of Wisconsin have fought for so long to preserve.

Cana Island hugs the shoreline of Door Peninsula, the 80-mile-long limestone promontory that juts into Lake Michigan. The quaint towns and Victorian inns of the region lure weekenders from Wisconsin's larger cities.

Cardinals nest in the white pines of Chequamegon National Forest.

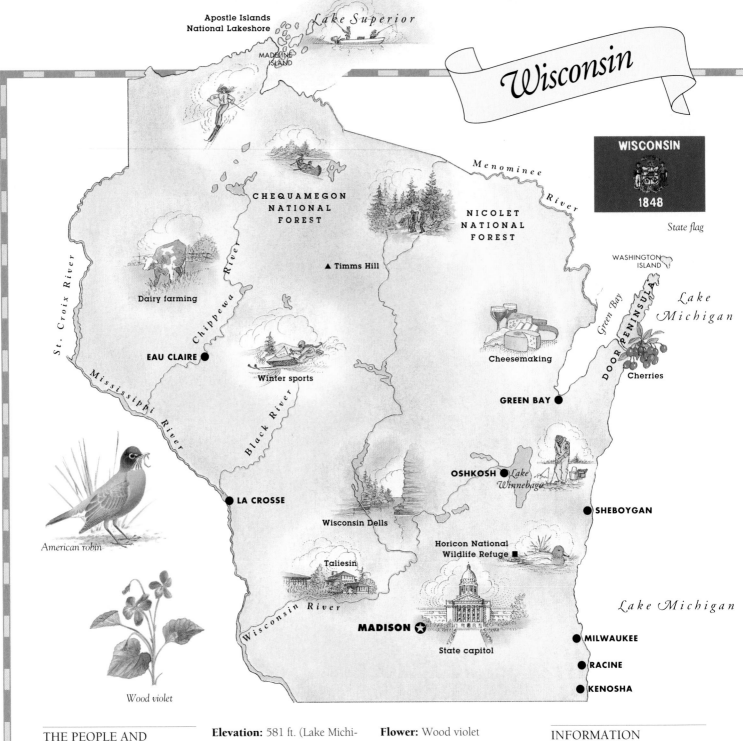

Wisconsin

State flag

WISCONSIN
1848

Apostle Islands National Lakeshore

Lake Superior

MADELINE ISLAND

CHEQUAMEGON NATIONAL FOREST

Menominee River

NICOLET NATIONAL FOREST

▲ Timms Hill

WASHINGTON ISLAND

Green Bay

DOOR PENINSULA

Lake Michigan

Dairy farming

St. Croix River

Chippewa River

EAU CLAIRE ●

Winter sports

Cheesemaking

Cherries

Mississippi River

Black River

GREEN BAY ●

OSHKOSH ● *Lake Winnebago*

SHEBOYGAN ●

American robin

LA CROSSE ●

Wisconsin Dells

Horicon National Wildlife Refuge ■

Lake Michigan

Wood violet

Taliesin

Wisconsin River

MADISON ★

State capitol

MILWAUKEE ●

RACINE ●

KENOSHA ●

THE PEOPLE AND THE LAND

Population: 4,869,600

Area: 56,153 sq. mi.

Population per sq. mi.: 87

Capital: Madison (pop. 352,800)

Largest city: Milwaukee (pop. 1,398,000)

Major rivers: Black, Chippewa, Menominee, Mississippi, St. Croix, Wisconsin

Elevation: 581 ft. (Lake Michigan) to 1,952 ft. (Timms Hill)

Leading industries: Manufacturing (machinery, food products, paper products, fabricated metals), trade, finance, insurance, real estate, transportation, communications, agriculture (dairy, cattle)

Bird: American robin

Flower: Wood violet

Tree: Sugar maple

Motto: Forward

Song: "On, Wisconsin!"

Origin of name: From the Chippewa word, spelled *Ouisconsin* by early explorers, meaning gathering of the waters

Nicknames: America's Dairyland, Badger State

INFORMATION

Wisconsin Department of Development
Division of Tourism
Box 7606
Madison, WI 53702
Telephone: 608-266-2161

HISTORICAL HIGHLIGHTS

1634 French explorer Jean Nicolet lands on Green Bay shore.

c. 1670 Jesuit priests build mission at De Pere.

1673 Louis Jolliet and Fr. Jacques Marquette discover upper Mississippi River.

1701 First permanent settlement is started at Green Bay.

1763 France cedes area to England after French-Indian War.

1783 Wisconsin ceded to U.S. as part of Northwest Territory.

1836 Congress creates Wisconsin Territory.

1848 Wisconsin joins Union as 30th state.

1853 Railway links Milwaukee and Madison.

1854 Republican Party founded in the town of Ripon.

1871 Six-county forest fire kills more than 1,000 people.

1872 William D. Hoard founds state Dairymen's Association.

1901 Progressive era of social reform begins as Robert M. La Follette, Sr., becomes governor.

1911 State legislature sets up teachers' pensions.

1924 La Follette runs unsuccessfully as a Progressive party candidate for U.S. presidency.

1932 Wisconsin passes country's first state unemployment-compensation act.

1959 St. Lawrence Seaway opens, linking Great Lakes with Atlantic Ocean.

1971 State universities are consolidated, forming University of Wisconsin system.

1981 After 133 years, Joseph Schlitz Brewing Company closes its Milwaukee brewery.

1988 When Chrysler Corporation closes Kenosha plant, 5,500 workers lose jobs.

FAMOUS SONS AND DAUGHTERS

Zona Gale (1874 – 1938). This novelist was known for her realistic portrayal of the people of the Midwest. After she adapted her best-known book, *Miss Lulu Bett*, for the stage, she won a Pulitzer Prize for drama.

Harry Houdini (1874 – 1926).

The world's most famous escape artist astounded audiences in America and Europe by escaping from handcuffs, leg-irons, jail cells, and even locked trunks submerged in water. He also worked to expose fraudulent spiritualists.

Robert Marion La Follette (1855 – 1925). As Wisconsin governor (1901 – 06) and U.S. senator (1906 – 25), this progressive Republican was the force behind a number of social reforms, working for what would eventually become the nation's first minimum wage and worker's compensation laws.

Alfred Lunt (1892 – 1977). Lunt and his wife, Lynn Fontanne, were one of the most celebrated acting teams on the American stage, known especially for their performances in sophisticated modern comedies on Broadway.

Spencer Tracy (1900 – 67). This beloved actor starred in more than 60 films, winning Oscars as Best Actor for two of them: *Captains Courageous* (1937) and *Boys' Town* (1938).

Frank Lloyd Wright (1869 – 1959). A towering figure of American architecture, Wright sought to merge his buildings with their settings. A prime example of such organic architecture is Taliesin, Wright's Wisconsin home, which is now an architectural school.

ODDITIES AND SPECIALTIES

Wisconsin, with almost 37,000 dairy farms, banned the sale of margarine until the 1960's.

The nickname of Badger State dates from the 1820's, when miners dug holes in the hillsides to use as winter homes, just as badgers do. Those who fled the severe cold were called suckers, after a fish that migrates south in winter.

When it comes to winter sports, residents of snowy Wisconsin have gone beyond mere skiing. Games played on ice include bowling, volleyball, and broomball, a variation of hockey.

The Belle of Wisconsin was the largest cheese ever made — a 40,060-pound Cheddar. It was said that the yellow monster could top more than a million crackers or provide more than 300,000 grilled cheese sandwiches. After touring the country in its Cheesemobile, the Belle was sliced and sold in 1989.

PLACES TO VISIT, THINGS TO DO

Chequamegon National Forest (headquarters at Park Falls). More than 400 lakes spangle the three separate sections of this vast forest in northern Wisconsin. The rivers are excellent for canoeing, while the Ice Age Trail is popular with hikers.

House on the Rock (near Dodgeville). This unique house, perched atop a column of rock, is the centerpiece of a series of unusual exhibitions, including the world's largest carousel.

Nicolet National Forest (headquarters at Rhinelander). Located in the northern lake district are swamp forests and woodlands, with a deer trail, a natural arch, and plenty of fishing streams.

Summerfest (Milwaukee).

Billed as the World's Greatest Music Festival, this lakefront event is held for 11 days every summer, starting the last Thursday in June. Jazz, blues, country, big band, and rock performers occupy 11 stages.

Wisconsin Dells (south-central Wisconsin). The Wisconsin River carved this beautiful gorge through sandstone, creating cliffs and unusual rock formations.

Wyoming

In the fabled West, a wealth of natural wonders

In the towering mountain ranges and sweeping grazing lands of Wyoming live fewer people than in any other state. Even Cheyenne, the largest city, has only 75,000 inhabitants. One can wander for weeks through the rugged Tetons without seeing a sign of another person — and when ranch houses are found in the wide open spaces, they often are more than 100 miles apart.

THE ISOLATED FRONTIER

If the place names of this sparsely populated state — Bighorn, Yellowstone, Medicine Bow, and Wind River among them — sound as if they belong in a western novel, it may be because the pioneers wanted to make the isolated region seem as romantic as possible. Settlers were desperately needed to populate the territory so that it could apply for statehood. To encourage women to migrate, the territorial legislature in 1869 guaranteed them equal rights to vote and hold office — a radical reform no other democratic government was even willing to consider at the time.

Many of the settlers who did show up kept right on going once they discovered that the euphonious Wind River Range was bounded by wastelands like Red Desert, Alkali Flat, and Bad Lands Hills. Certainly Wyoming did not impress Daniel Webster. All it would bring to the Union, he warned, was "savages, wild beasts, shifting sands, whirlwinds of dust, cactus and prairie dogs."

What Webster did not know was that Wyoming was also the site of natural wonders that one day would bring the world to its doorstep.

Over time, the mineral deposits left by the waters of Mammoth Hot Springs have created eerie terraces.

HUNTING GROUND OF THE WEST

Wyoming Territory teemed with so much game in the 19th century that it became one of the continent's prime hunting grounds. Fur trappers sought out the region's millions of beavers, whose misfortune it was to have barbed fur that pressed easily into felt. Settlers moving west dined heartily on bison, and wild game disappeared for miles on both sides of the Oregon Trail.

Professional hunters, eager for buffalo hides to ship back east, flooded into the territory. The most efficient of them boasted that they could pick off as many as 100 animals on a good day. And gentlemen sportsmen traveled from afar to reap their share: one Sir St. George Gore, visiting from England, massacred an estimated 2,000 buffaloes and

100 bears, plus 1,600 elk and deer on a three-year hunting trip that began in 1854.

Wyoming's animals finally received protection in the 1870s, when the territorial assembly outlawed the sale of wild meat during the spring and summer months, the time when larger mammals give birth. The territory was also the first to establish penalties for hunting game birds out of season.

Today the only real threats to Wyoming's wildlife come from competition for grazing land and encroaching development. But federal game preserves and judicious range management ensure that the wilderness areas essential for the survival of elk, moose, buffalo, deer, beaver, and other species will remain as they are.

Steam wafts from geyser vents along the Firehole River in Yellowstone National Park.

THE GLORIES OF YELLOWSTONE

Chief among those wonders is the Yellowstone River region, a surreal quadrant of steam-vented land in the northwest corner of the state. John Colter, a private on leave from the Lewis and Clark expedition, was the first white man to see it, in 1807. Yellowstone's mysterious geysers, hot springs, petrified forests, and waterfalls stirred the imagination of all who heard of them. Before long, tale-spinning trappers like Jim Bridger were describing a sulfurous land where a man could catch a fish in a stream, then toss it over his shoulder to cook in a boiling pool.

Preserved for posterity in 1872 as the world's first national park, Yellowstone has lost none of its supernatural aura. Because hot molten rock, or magma, which is usually 10 to 30 miles below the surface, is only one to three miles below the earth's crust here, the region has more geysers, hot springs, mud pots, and volcanic steam vents than are found in all the rest of the world. Attractions such as Old Faithful draw more than 2.5 million visitors to the park each year.

For wildlife lovers, to enter Yellowstone National Park is to step back in time 200 years, to an era when moose and mule deer, bighorn sheep, and bison were kept in rough equilibrium by the dispassionate forces of nature. Some people consider the entire state of Wyoming to be a giant game preserve of sorts.

His world changed to ice by a February storm, an elk forages for food in the Lamar Valley south of Yellowstone.

Elderberries are plentiful in Medicine Bow National Forest.

Nearly half of the state's land, in fact, is controlled in some manner by the federal government. Wyoming's two national parks, along with vast forests and wilderness areas, make it one of the few remaining states that still have plenty of room for threatened species such as the majestic grizzly bear, the peregrine falcon, the trumpeter swan, and the black-footed ferret.

Bordering Yellowstone on the south is Wyoming's second national park, Grand Teton, where the Teton Range rises abruptly from a green valley named Jackson Hole. Seven lakes shimmer at the foot of the peaks. Jackson Lake, by far the largest, is an established recreation area. But perhaps the most beautiful is Lake Solitude, which mirrors Grand Teton, the tallest mountain in the range. Its name notwithstanding, Lake Solitude attracts so many hikers that the Park Service has banned camping there since the 1970's.

THE CATTLEMAN'S COMMONWEALTH

Although the outside world thinks of Wyoming in terms of Yellowstone and the Tetons, the majority of the state's population lives on the High Plains. This arid grazing country extends from the Colorado border up to the pine-clad Bighorn Mountains, whose tallest peaks soar to 13,000 feet.

By the time Wyoming entered the Union it had come to be called the Cattleman's Commonwealth, dominated by ranchers who grazed their huge herds on public lands. But this affluent domain had its problems. Cattlemen resented the encroachment of homesteaders, who sometimes acquired herds of their own by appropriating the mavericks (unbranded calves) of the larger ranches. When the ranchers accused the newcomers of rustling, anger erupted on both sides. It boiled over in 1892, when a vigilante group of ranch-

ON THE TIMBERLINE

At elevations above 10,000 feet, Wyoming's mountains become desolate, icy realms of wind-scoured rock debris and boulders. Only lichens and sedges grow there, clinging precariously to rocky crevices and ledges.

But on the timberline just below, where the climate can barely support trees, the topmost firs, pines, and spruces have adapted to the inhospitable environment. Windblown ice particles inhibit the growth of their needles and branches on the windward side, so that the trees take on the look of wizened, asymmetrical topiary. Some appear normal at the base of the trunk, which is protected during the winter by drifting snow, but branches higher up are invariably twisted and worn smooth by abrasive arctic blasts.

The trees that are able to tolerate this severe climate grow very slowly. The whitebark pine, for example, takes from 250 to 300 years to reach maturity. Often the winter snows are so heavy that the pine's weighted branches touch the ground and gradually take root. These crooked trees become part of Wyoming's glorious scenery for a few weeks each summer, when the eagles soar above them and the tiny flowers of white phlox and delicate blue forget-me-nots burst into bloom on the slopes.

ers invaded suspected rustler territory and killed two men — an incident known as the Johnson County War.

Today ranching continues to be one of Wyoming's leading industries. Cattlemen no longer contend with rustlers, but blizzards, hail, and winds that reach a velocity of 60 miles per hour remain problems.

West of the plains the forested slopes of the Rocky Mountains begin. Five national forests, including Shoshone and Bridger-Teton, lie entirely inside Wyoming, and five others are par-

tially within its borders. Lodgepole pines cover a large part of the woodlands, but spruces, Douglas firs, and aspens also are common.

This green and wildly beautiful part of the state holds on to its aura of seclusion, despite the campers that flock here to Yellow-stone and the tourists that stroll the board-walks of pioneer towns in the shadow of the towering Tetons. In the splendid isolation of Wyoming one can sense the real West, the fabled West that remains an everlasting part of the American dream.

The Wind River Range forms an imposing backdrop for the trees and shallow rivers of Shoshone National Forest. Seen here is the group of peaks known as the Cirque of the Towers.

Index

478

CREDITS

The following abbreviation has been used:

FL FIRST LIGHT ASSOCIATED PHOTOGRAPHERS (TORONTO, ONT.)

1 Gene Ahrens. **2-3** © 1984 Bill Weems. **4-5** Willard Clay. **6-7** © David Nunuk/FL. **8-9** John Marshall. **12-13** Darwin Wiggett/FL. **14** Steve Short/FL. **15-21** Darwin Wiggett/FL. **23** *bottom left* Ted Grant; *middle left* Aaron Chang/LGI/PonoPresse; *middle right* Jerry Kobalenko/FL; *right top & bottom* Larry MacDougal/FL. **24-25** Ron Watts/FL. **26** *top* Darwin Wiggett /FL; *bottom* David Nunuk/FL. **27** *top* Thomas Kitchin/FL; *bottom* David Nunuk/FL. **28** Jerry Kobalenko /FL. **29** David Nunuk/FL. **30-31** Darwin Wiggett/FL. **32** Ron Watts/FL. **33** Darwin Wiggett/FL. **34** *top* B.C. Archive & Record Service (C-5229); *middle* courtesy Canada Post Corp.; *right* Darwin Wiggett/FL. **36-39** Darwin Wiggett/FL. **40** *top* left Wayne Wegner/FL; *bottom* Darwin Wiggett. **41** Paul von Baich/FL. **43** left Glenbow Foundation; *middle* Darwin Wiggett /FL; *right* Brian Milne/FL. **44-45** Mary Ellen McQuay/FL. **46** John Sylvester/ FL. **47** *top* John Sylvester/ FL; *bottom* Graham Vivian Sutherland, sketch of Lord Beaverbrook, 1950 oil on canvas 50.8 x 40.6 cm (20 x 16 in.) The Beaverbrook Foundation, The Beaverbrook Art Gallery, Fredericton, N.B., Canada. **48** *top* Wayne Wegner/ FL; *bottom* John Sylvester/FL. **49** John Sylvester/FL. **50** *left* John Sylvester/ FL; *right* P. Roussel/Publiphoto. **51** *top right* Wayne Wegner/FL. **52-56** John Sylvester/FL. **57** *top* Jerry Kobalenko/ FL; *bottom* John Sylvester/FL. **58** *left* National Archives of Canada (C22876); *top* Greg Locke/FL; Industry, Science and Technology Canada Photo. **60-61** Robert Semeniuk/FL. **62** Brian Vikander, WL/FL. **63** *top* Jerry Kobalenko/ FL; Brian Milne/FL. **65** *top left* René Fumoleau; *top right* Tim Atherton; *middle* Robert Semeniuk/ FL; *bottom left* Brian Milne/FL. **66-67** John Sylvester/FL. **68** *top* John Sylvester/FL; *bottom* Alex Wilson/ Nova Scotia Museum of Natural History. **69** Ken Straiton/FL. **70-73** John Sylvester/FL. **74** Parks Canada. **75** *top* National Archives of Canada (C6087); *bottom* Irwin Barrett, Earthscapes/FL. **76-77** Grant Black/FL. **78** Alan Marsh/FL. **79** *top* Alan Marsh/FL; *bottom* D.A.Wilkes/Point Pelee National Park. **80** Alan Marsh/FL. **81** Ron Watts/FL. **82** Irwin Barrett/FL. **83** *top* Mark Burnham/FL; *bottom* Thomas Kitchin/FL. **84** Brian Milne/ FL. **85** Stephen Homer/FL. **86** *top left* ©Yousuf Karsh/Comstock; *top right* Mark Burnham/FL; *bottom* Alan Marsh/FL. **87** "The Harvester" c.1921, L.L. FitzGerald, oil on canvas, 66.8 x 59.5 cm, The McMichael Canadian Art Collection, gift from the Douglas M. Duncan Collection. **88-90** John Sylvester/FL. **91** *top* Lorraine C. Parrow/FL; *bottom* John Sylvester/FL. **93** *left* National Archives of Canada (C66950); *middle* John Sylvester/P.E.I. Tourism; *bottom* Brian Milne/FL. **94-95** Ron Watts/FL. **96-97** Thomas Kitchin/FL. **97** *right* Stephen Homer/ FL. **98** Mark Burnham/FL. **99-101** Alan Marsh/FL. **101** *right* Thomas Kitchin/FL. **102** *top* Thomas Kitchin/ FL; Industry, Science and Technology Canada Photo. **103** Thomas Kitchin/ FL. **105** *left* National Archives of Canada (C88566); *top* Allen McInnis/FL; *bottom* Ken Straiton/FL. **106-108** Darwin Eiggett/FL. **108-109** *middle* Thomas Kitchin/FL. **110** *top* McCord Museum, Montreal; Darwin Wiggett/FL. **111** Darwin Wiggett/FL. **113** *top* Canada Wide; *bottom left* Parks Canada; *bottom middle* Canada Wide; *right* Ron Watts/FL. **114-115** Pat Morrow/FL. **116-117 & 119** Richard Hartmier/FL. **122-123** David Muench. **124 & 125** Ed Malles. **127** *left* Photograph courtesy of the Country Music Foundation, Inc.; *right* Helen Kittinger/Photo Options. **128-129** Tom Bean. **130** Ed Cooper. **131** Tom Bean. **132** *left* The Bettmann Archive; *right* Lael Morgan. **134-135** John Gerlach/DRK Photo. **136-137** Tom Bean. **137** *top* Jeff Gnass; *bottom* Tom Bean/DRK Photo. **139** *top* David Muench; *bottom* Matt Bradley. **138** *top* Kenneth W. Fink/Bruce Coleman Inc.; *bottom* David Muench. **140** *right* Jen & Des Bartlett/Bruce Coleman Inc. **141** *left* Library of Congress; *right* Bob Clemenz. **142-143** Matt Bradley. **144 & 145** Matt Bradley. **146** Garry D. McMichael/Photo Researchers, Inc. **147** J.H. Robinson/Photo Researchers, Inc. **149** *left* Breck Kent/Earth Scenes; *middle* UPI/Betmann; *right* Chuck O'Rear/West Light. **150-151** Larry Ulrich. **152** *top* Pat O'Hara; *bottom* Carr Clifton. **153** *top* Larry Ulrich; *bottom* Carr Clifton. **154** Harald Sund/The Image Bank. **155** *top* Reproduced by permission of The Huntington Library, San Marino, California; *bottom* David Muench. **156** Tim Thompson. **157** *top left* Ralph Clevenger/West Light; *top right* Larry Ulrich; *bottom* Tim Thompson. **159** *left* The Bettmann Archive; *right* Suzanne J. Engelmann/SuperStock International. **160-161** David Muench. **162** *top* Carr Clifton; *bottom* David Muench. **163** *top* David Muench; *bottom* Carr Clifton. **164** *top* David Muench; *bottom* Steve Mulligan. **165** Tom Till. **167** *left* Culver Pictures; upper *right* Thomas Kitchin/ Tom Stack & Associates; *bottom right* SuperStock International. **168-169** Ira Block/The Image Bank. **170** William Hubbell. **171** Steve Dunwell/The Image Bank. **172** *top* Ken Laffal/Mark MacLaren Inc.; *bottom* New York State Office of Parks, Recreation and Historic Preservation/Olana State Historic Site. **172-173** Steve Dunwell. **175** *top* Culver Pictures; *bottom left* Jessica Anne Ehlers/Bruce Coleman Inc.; *bottom right* Paul Rocheleau. **176-177** Mike Biggs. **178** David Muench. **179** *top* Mike Biggs; *bottom* Kevin Fleming. **180** *right* Delaware Art Museum. **181** *left* Courtesy of the Historical Society of Delaware; *right* Everett C. Johnson. **182-183** C.C. Lockwood. **184** *top* David Muench; *bottom* Bruce Hands/Comstock. **185** James Valentine. **186** *top* James Valentine; *bottom* John Netherton. **187** *left* Steven C. Kaufman; *right* Matt Bradley. **188** *center* Historical Pictures Service, Chicago; *bottom left* Photri; *bottom right* John Netherton. **190-191** James Valentine. **192-193** David Muench. **193** *top right* James Valentine; *bottom right* Pat Canova; *bottom* Jack Alterman. **195** *left* Flip Schulke/Black Star; *middle* Paul G. Beswick/Courtesy Callaway Gardens; *right* Ed Cooper. **196-197** Douglas Peebles. **198** *top* Douglas Peebles; *bottom* Camerique/H. Armstrong Roberts. **199** Larry Ulrich. **200** *top* Larry Ulrich; *bottom* Jeff Gnass. **200-201** Jeff Gnass. **202** *left* Historical Pictures Service, Chicago; *bottom* FPG International. **203** *bottom left* Darrell Jones/The Stock Market. **204-205** John Marshall. **206** John Marshall. **207** *top* John Marshall; *bottom* David Boehlke. **208** *left* George Wuerthner. **208-209** David R. Stoecklein. **211** *top left* Reproduced by permission of the Huntington Library, San Marino, California; *top right* Ed Cooper; *bottom* Fritz Prenzel/Animals Animals. **212-213** Gary Irving. **214-215** Gene Ahrens. **215** *top right* Terry Donnelly: TSW-Click/Chicago; *bottom right* Gary Irving. **216** *top* Hedrich Blessing; *bottom* Appel Color Photography. **217** Willard Clay. **219** *left* Historical Pictures Service, Chicago; *top* The Bettmann Archive; *right* Photograph © 1990, The Art Institute of Chicago. All Rights Reserved. **220-221** Tom Till. **222 & 223** Darryl Jones. **224** Darryl Jones. **225** *top left* Michael Medford; *top right* Darryl Jones; *bottom* Lee Casebere/Indiana Division of Nature Preserves. **227** *left* The Bettmann Archive; *middle* Photri; *right* Spring Mill State Park. **228-229** Robert Frerck/Odyssey Productions, Chicago. **230** *top left* Grant Heilman/Grant Heilman Photography, Inc.; *bottom left* David Cavagnaro. **230-231** David Cavagnaro. **232** *top* Appel Color Photography; *bottom* M. Dunlap/Living History Farms. **233** Tom Till. **235** *left* Thomas Hovland/Grant Heilman Photography, Inc.; *middle* Culver Pictures; *right* Charles Schneider/FPG International. **236-237** Daniel Dancer. **238-239** Cotton Coulson/Woodfin Camp & Associates. **239** *top right* Daniel Dancer; *bottom right* Jim Brandenburg. **241** *left* New York Public Library, Picture Collection; *middle* UPI/Bettmann; *right* Stephen J. Krasemann/ DRK Photo. **242-243** William Strode/ Woodfin Camp & Associates. **244** James Archambeault. **245** David Muench. **246** *top* Fred Kaplan/Focus On Sports Inc.; *lower left* Culver Pictures; *bottom right* Lewis Portnoy/ Spectra-Action, Inc. 248-249 C.C. Lockwood. **250** *top left* David Muench; *bottom left* D. Donne Bryant Stock Photography Agency. **250-251** David Muench. **253** *left* The Bettmann Archive; *right* Philip Gould; *bottom* D. Donne Bryant Stock Photography Agency. **254-255** Gene Ahrens. **256** Glenn Van Nimwegen. **257** *top* J.L. Stage/The Image Bank; *bottom* Carr Clifton. **258** Don Gray: f/Stop Pictures Inc. **259** *top* John Eastcott/Yva Momatiuk/DRK Photo; *bottom* Linda Bartlett/Photo Researchers, Inc. **261** *left* National Gallery of Art, Washington, D.C.; *top right* Stan Tess/The Stock Market; *bottom right* S.D. Halperin/Earth Scenes. **262-263** Middleton Evans. **264-265** Kevin Fleming. **265** *top* David Muench; *bottom* Middleton Evans. **266** *left* Maryland Historical Society; *right* Middleton Evans; *bottom* AP/Wide World Photos. **268-269** Dan McCoy/Rainbow. **270** David Muench. **271** *top* Tom Leigh/ Rainbow; *bottom* The Granger Collection, New York. **272** Paul Rocheleau. **273** *top* David Binder/Stock Boston; *bottom* Michael Melford/The Image Bank. **274** *left* Plimoth Plantation; *middle* Culver Pictures; *right* Frank Siteman/The Marilyn Gartman Agency. **276-277** Ed Cooper. **278** Ken Dequaine. **279** *top* David Muench; *bottom* Rod Planck/Photo Researchers, Inc. **280** Ken Dequaine. **281** *top* John & Ann Mahan; *bottom* Daniel J. Cox. **283** *left* Culver Pictures; *top* Traverse City Record-Eagle; *right* Veldheer Tulip Gardens, Inc. **284-285** Craig Blacklock/Blacklock Nature Photography. **286** Daniel J. Cox. **287** *left* Steve Schneider; *right* Daniel J. Cox. **289** *left* The Bettmann Archive; *middle* Peabody Museum/Harvard University, Photography by Hillel Burger; *right* Mitch Kezar. **290-291** Gene Ahrens. **292** *top left* Ken Murphy; *bottom left* Connie Toops. **292-293** Balthazar Korab Ltd. **295** *left* The Bettmann Archive; *bottom right* SuperStock International. **296-297** Grant Heilman/ Grant Heilman Photography, Inc. **298** Charles Gurche. **299** *top* Culver Pictures; *bottom* Charles Gurche. **301** *left* The Bettmann Archive; *middle* Missouri Historical Society; *right* © Rick Warner/Journalism Services. **302-303** Alan & Sandy Carey. **304** David Muench. **305** *left* Amon Carter Museum; *right* Jeff Gnass. **306-307** Larry Ulrich. **307** *top right* Larry Burton; *bottom right* Carr Clifton. **309** *left* Photofest; *middle* The Bettmann Archive; *right* Elaine Swanson. **310-311** © 1991 R. Bruhn. **312-313** Tom Bean. **313** *top right* Terry Evans; *bottom right* David Muench. **314** *left* Culver Pictures; *right* Father Flanagan's Boys Home. **316-317** Tom Till. **318-319** William Carr/Mountain Stock. **319** *right* David Muench. **321** *left* Culver Pictures; *middle* Stephen Green-Armytage/The Stock Market; *right* Mark E. Gibson/The Stock Market. **322-323** Clyde H. Smith: f/Stop Pictures Inc. **324-325** Craig Blouin. **325** *top right* David Brownell; *bottom right* David Muench. **327** *left* Library of Congress; *middle* John M Burnley/ Bruce Coleman Inc.; *right* Fred Sieb. **328-329** Scott Barrow, Inc. **330** Scott Barrow, Inc. **331** *top* Gene Ahrens; *bottom* Len Rue Jr. **333** *left* The Bettmann Archive; *right* UPI/ Bettmann; *bottom* Culver Pictures. **334-335** Jim Bones. **336** Michael Nichols/Magnum. **337** *top* Ed Cooper; *bottom* Mark E. Gibson. **338** *top* Eduardo Fuss Photography; *bottom* Willard Clay. **339** *top* Tom Bean; *bottom* Jim Bones. **341** *left* Malcolm Varon; *middle* Tom Bean; *right* Ray Garduno. **342-343** Carr Clifton. **344** Carr Clifton. **345** *left* Susan Desser; *right* Carr Clifton. **346** *top* Scott Barrow, Inc.; *bottom* Tom Brakefield. **347** Henryk T. Kaiser. **348** *left* The Bettmann Archive; *middle* SEF/Art Resource, N.Y.; *right* Thomas Zimmerman/FPG International. **350-351** David Muench. **352** William Bake/Picturesque. **353** David Muench. **354** both Culver Pictures. **356-357** Grant Heilman/Grant Heilman Photography, Inc. **358** Glenn Van Nimwegan. **359** David Muench. **361** *left* Culver Pictures; *middle* Erwin and Peggy Bauer/Bruce Coleman Inc.; *right* Sheldon Green. **362-363** Ian J. Adams. **364** Ian J. Adams/Dembinsky Photo Associates. **365** *left* Richard A. Cooke III; *right* Ian J. Adams. **367** *left & top* The Bettmann Archive; *right* Roscoe Village Foundation. **368-369** David Fitzgerald. **370** *left* David Muench. **370-371** David Fitzgerald. **372** *left* The Bettmann Archive; *middle* Culver Pictures; *right* Fred W. Marvel/Oklahoma Tourism Photo. **374-375** Bob & Suzanne Clemenz. **376** Larry Ulrich. **377** Ray Atkeson/American Landscapes. **378** Bureau of Land Management. **379** *top* Willard Clay; *bottom* J. Carmichael, Jr./The Image Bank. **381** *left* Hope Harris Collection/Photography by James McInnis; *top* Oregon Historical Society; *right* F. Stuart Westmoreland. **382-383** Stephen Simpson/View Finder Stock Photography. **384** Ian J. Adams. **385** Larry Lefever/Grant Heilman Photography, Inc. **386** Blair Seitz. **387** *left* Lefever/Grushow/Grant Heilman Photography, Inc.; *right* Jeff Gnass. **388** *right* Giraudon/Art Resource, N.Y. **389** *left* The Bettmann Archive; *right* Culver Pictures. **390-391** Anthony Botelho. **392** David Witbeck. **393** *top* David Witbeck; *bottom* Robert D. Hagan. **395** *left* Rhode Island Tourism Division; *top* Nicholas De Vore/Photographers Aspen; *right* Courtesy of the Rhode Island Historical Society/ Photography by John Miller Documents. **396-397** George Schwartz/Ric Ergenbright Photography. **398** Tom Blagden, Jr. **399** David Muench. **401** *left* The National Portrait Gallery, Smithsonian Institution; *middle* Rick Sebak; *right* Tom Blagden, Jr. **402-403** Alex S. MacLean/Landslides. **405** *top* Glenn Van Nimwegan; *bottom* John Gerlach/Dembinsky Photo Associates. **404** Laurance B. Aiuppy/Aiuppy Photographs. **407** *left* The Bettmann Archive; *middle* Al Michaud/FPG International; *right* The Shrine to Music Museum, University of South Dakota at Vermillion. **408-409** Bob Schatz. **410** *top left* David Muench; *bottom left* Willard Clay. **410-411** John Netherton. **412** Culver Pictures. **413** John Netherton. **414-415** David Muench. **416** Jeff Gnass. **417** *top* David Muench; *bottom* Wyman Meinzer. **418** *top* Walter Frerck/ Odyssey Productions, Chicago; *bottom* Tom Brakefield. **419** Walter Frerck/ Odyssey Productions, Chicago. **421** *left* NBC/Globe Photos; *middle* State Fair of Texas; *right* Richard & Mary Magruder/The Image Bank. **422-423** Tom Till. **424-425** Tom Till. **425** Ric Ergenbright Photography; **426** David Muench. **427** *top* Lee Foster/Bruce Coleman Inc.; *bottom left* Jeff Gnass. **429** *left* The Granger Collection, New York; *middle* Brown Brothers; *right* George Lepp/Comstock. **430-431** Gary Irving. **432-433** Fred M. Dole: f/Stop Pictures Inc. **433** *top right* David Brownell; *bottom* Courtesy of Vermont Historical Society/Photography by Lizzari Photographic. **434** Gene Ahrens. **435** *top* Gene Ahrens; *bottom* Kindra Clineff/The Picture Cube. **437** *left* Mt. Mansfield Company, Inc.; *top* The Bettmann Archive; *right* Clemens Kalischer/Image Photos. **438-439** Steve Solum. **440** Rudi Von Briel. **441** Everett C. Johnson. **442** *top left* Ian J. Adams; *bottom left* Skyline Cavern. **442-443** Charles Gurche. **444** Art Resource, N.Y. **445** Virginia Division of Tourism. **446-447** David Muench/The Image Bank. **448** *top left* Charles Gurche; *bottom left* Thomas Kitchin/Tom Stack & Associates. **448-449** Ray Atkeson/American Landscapes. **450** David Cavagnaro/Peter Arnold, Inc. **451** *top* Gene Ahrens; *bottom* Jeff Foott/Bruce Coleman Inc. **453** *top left* Roger Werth/Woodfin Camp & Associates; *bottom left* Culver Pictures; *right* Tom Algire. **454-455** Carr Clifton. **456** *top* David Muench; *bottom* Marc Rosenthal. **457** Arnout Hyde, Jr. **459** *left* UPI/Bettmann; *middle* Peggy Powell/West Virginia Division of Tourism and Parks; *right* Larry Belcher. **460-461** Richard Hamilton Smith. **462** Tom Algire/Tom Stack & Associates. **463** both Richard Hamilton Smith. **465** *left* UPI/Bettmann; *bottom* Wisconsin Milk Marketing Board; *right* Summerfest—"The Big Gig" Milwaukee, Wisconsin/Photography by James McInnis. **466-467** Steve Mulligan. **469** *top* Bob & Clara Calhoun/Bruce Coleman Inc.; *bottom* Irwin & Peggy Bauer/Bruce Coleman Inc. **470** *left* W.H. Hodge/Peter Arnold, Inc. **422-423** Carr Clifton. **468** *top* Photoworld/FPG International; *bottom* Carr Clifton. **473** *top left* The Bettmann Archive; *bottom left* © 1991 Pollock-Krasner Foundation/ ARS, N.Y.; *right* Jeff Gnass.